A Greek Roman Empire

The publisher gratefully acknowledges
the generous contribution to this book provided by
The Jane K. Sather Professorship
in Classical Literature Fund.

SATHER CLASSICAL LECTURES

Volume Sixty-Four

A Greek Roman Empire

A Greek Roman Empire

Power and Belief under Theodosius II (408–450)

FERGUS MILLAR

University of California Press

BERKELEY   LOS ANGELES   LONDON

University of California Press, one of the most distinguished university presses in the United States, enriches lives around the world by advancing scholarship in the humanities, social sciences, and natural sciences. Its activities are supported by the UC Press Foundation and by philanthropic contributions from individuals and institutions. For more information, visit www.ucpress.edu.

University of California Press
Berkeley and Los Angeles, California

University of California Press, Ltd.
London, England

Library of Congress Cataloging-in-Publication Data

Millar, Fergus.
    A Greek Roman Empire : power and belief under Theodosius II (408/450) / Fergus Millar.
        p.   cm.—(Sather classical lectures ; v. 64)
    Includes bibliographical references and index.
    ISBN 0-520-24703-5 (cloth : alk. paper)
        1. Byzantine Empire—History—Theodosius II, 408–450.
    I. Title: Power and belief under Theodosius II (408/450).   II. Title.
    III. Series.

DF562.M55   2006
949.5'013—dc22   2006003042

Manufactured in the United States of America
15   14   13   12   11   10   09   08   07   06
10 9 8 7 6 5 4 3 2 1

This book is printed on Natures Book, containing 50% post-consumer waste and meets the minimum requirements of ANSI/NISO Z39.48-1992 (R 1997) (Permanence of Paper).

To Susanna

Contents

Preface

The extremely welcome invitation to give the Sather Lectures at Berkeley arrived when my tenure of the Camden Chair of Ancient History at Oxford had only a few years to run, and in the event it proved possible, thanks to the courtesy and consideration of the Sather Committee, to hold the professorship in the first year of my retirement, 2002/3. The invitation also served, however, to focus and bring together a number of half-formed, and mutually related, objectives. The first was to immerse myself more fully than ever before in the history, functioning, and culture of the Later Roman Empire. That in itself was intended as a step towards a larger and longer-term second objective, which may or may not be capable of fulfillment, namely a social and religious history of the Roman Near East in the fourth to sixth centuries.

The third objective, for which, as it turned out, there was incomparably richer material than I had realized in advance, was to attempt, as an Ancient Historian, to live up to the challenge posed by the formal title of the post, "The Sather Professorship of Classical Literature," and to try to demonstrate both the wealth of literature which survives from the Late Empire, and the way in which the public documents of the period can be seen as representing in themselves a branch of a literature of persuasion and self-justification.

This notion took its origins from the legal texts, in the *Codex Theodosianus*, the *Novellae* of Theodosius, and the *Codex Justinianus*. This material is of course inevitable as the starting point of all enquiries into the nature of the Late Roman system (even if only A. H. M. Jones ever possessed the sheer analytical power required actually to read these often extremely difficult and allusive texts, and to understand what they are saying). But, as will be clear on almost every page of this book, the great revelation to me was the enormous wealth of material contained in the Acts of the great Church Councils—

the *Acta Conciliorum Oecumenicorum,* in the matchless edition by Eduard Schwartz. Though other sources are of course used, it would not be inaccurate to describe this book as balanced between the legal documents on the one hand and the *Acta* on the other. Its aim, in essence, is to treat all this material, whether addressed to the Emperor or issued by him or his officials, as examples of the rhetoric of persuasion and self-justification.

Put in other words, its purpose could be described as forming a bridge between the governmental and administrative history practiced by A. H. M. Jones and the style of cultural history exemplified by Peter Brown and Averil Cameron. If Peter Brown had not already published his book *Power and Persuasion in Late Antiquity,* and if Averil Cameron had not entitled her distinguished Sather Lectures *Christianity and the Rhetoric of Empire,* either title might have served quite well for what follows. Readers of *Power and Persuasion* in particular will quickly see how much this book owes to it. Similarly, many of the themes of this book will be found expressed independently, and in very stimulating terms, in the review article by Mark Vessey, "Sacred letters of the law: The emperor's hand in late Roman (literary) history," in *Antiquité Tardive* for 2003.

At any rate, given the need to stay within the framework of a series of six lectures on the one hand and the opportunity offered by the conjunction, and at times the actual overlap, between material in the legal *Codices* and that in the *Acta,* it seemed best to explore my chosen themes within the framework of a single long reign, that of Theodosius II between 408 and 450. In finding my way in this period, I also owe an enormous debt to two other books: to the late A.-J. Festugière's truly heroic feat, in *Éphèse et Chalcédoine,* of translating nearly the whole of the *Acta* of the fifth-century councils (those of Ephesus I of 431, of Ephesus II of 449, as quoted very extensively in those of Chalcedon, and those of Chalcedon in 451). Without this great work, I can hardly imagine that I would ever have found my way through the material. In a very different way, my conviction that the history of the period really can be understood in terms of the beliefs of participants, both at Court and far beyond it, was stimulated by Kenneth Holum's exceptionally fine study, *Theodosian Empresses.*

Added to these there comes Susan Wessel's *Cyril of Alexandria and the Nestorian Controversy,* published by Oxford University Press in 2004, which I had the privilege of seeing both at an earlier stage and in proof. This book offers both a masterly treatment of the complex interchanges that characterized the conflicts which came to a head at Ephesus I, and a fine analysis of the rhetoric of persuasion as deployed in a Christian context. Further, I should note that the Nouvelle Clio volume edited by Cécile Morrisson, *Le monde byzantin* I: *L'empire romain d'Orient (330–641)*, published in 2004, reached me, as a gift from Denis Feissel, when it was too late to undertake the systematic revision which would have been desirable. That it too, in effect, marks out as its theme the "Greek Roman Empire" is very welcome. Whether the two books will be understood in the future as having initiated a trend remains to be seen. It is certainly true, in this area, that, in the words of my former teacher, Ronald Syme, "there is work to be done." One example of just that is the volume *La pétition à Byzance*, edited by Denis Feissel and Jean Gascou, also published in 2004.

It should be made clear that the aim of this book, apart from a missionary impulse on my part to deploy at least some selected items from the enormously rich body of primary material from this relatively neglected period, is to concentrate heavily on arguments and narratives produced by contemporaries, as incorporated in surviving documents, and as designed to express their point of view in what were often (and not merely in the sphere of theology) situations of profound debate and disagreement.

Consequently, contemporary expressions of opinion as to who wielded power and influence, and in what manner, are extremely relevant. But reports about political events on this reign found in later narrative works, such as the *Ecclesiastical History* of Evagrius, John Malalas, the *Chronicon Paschale*, Marcellinus Comes, or Theophanes, play a much lesser part. I am not attempting to reconstruct from all the sources what the "real" political history of the reign was. Equally, I have not set out to do more than explain enough about the structure of the Imperial system for the particular episodes which I highlight to be intelligible; and similar considerations apply both to the narrative of conflicts with Sasanid Persia or with the Huns, and to the sequence of exchanges, documented in immense detail, before, during, and after the two Councils of Ephesus.

Behind the book as presented there lurks all too substantial a ghost. That is to say the long Appendix which had been intended to register all the public documents of the reign, namely all the pronouncements by the Emperor or by holders of public office, on the one hand, and on the other all communications addressed *to* the Emperor, or to holders of public office, or (as is a very notable feature of the period) to one or more of the women of the Imperial household; the Emperor's influential elder sister, Pulcheria, his two younger sisters, and his wife, Aelia Eudocia. The list also includes communications from the Western Imperial family and from bishops in the West, and, as we will see, the only example from the whole of Antiquity of a letter on a matter of public policy addressed by one woman to another.

This intended Appendix, which exists in an advanced draft, would have served in a very concrete way to exhibit the sheer scale of the material bearing on the operations of government in this reign (out of all proportion to that available for any earlier period), and also to illuminate one of the principal themes of the book, namely the complex functional balance between Greek and Latin which marked the "Greek Roman Empire." However, occupying over seventy printed pages, and with well over four hundred fifty entries, it would have materially disbalanced the book, and I have decided to omit it. Its contents, nonetheless, inform nearly every page, and I remain extremely grateful for the sterling work done on it by Dr. David Lambert, now of St Andrews University. It may perhaps even be possible to find a context in which to publish it separately. But as a result the book reflects quite closely, with the addition of two slighter Appendixes, and in an expanded version, the six lectures given in Berkeley in February and March 2003.

Our stay in Berkeley provided much to look back on with pleasure: our house on Sunset Lane, perched on the very summit of the Berkeley Hills, and looking out over the Bay, the Golden Gate Bridge, and the city of San Francisco; the wonderful walks in Wildcat Canyon and Tilden Park, or across the Bay in Mt. Tamalpais State Park, above the Pacific Ocean; the beauty of the campus itself, with its unique atmosphere of intellectual energy; and the company and hospitality of Erich and Joan Gruen, Robert and Caroline Knapp, Tony and Monique Long, and Ron and Connie Stroud. We look back with love and sorrow on the companionship of Joan Gruen, and her unique warmth and vitality. It remains impossible to come to terms with the illness which struck her only a few months after we left, and with her death in October of 2004.

In the happier setting of the early months of 2003, my graduate class on the Late Roman Near East was a real pleasure, and my two excellent assistants, Meg Foster and Antonia Young, did splendid work in maintaining communications with my office in Oxford, preparing handouts for the lectures, assembling books, and limiting the acute stresses imposed on students of the Ancient World by the Library of Congress system.

The fact that, after retiring in 2002, I still had an office in Oxford was due first to the award of an Emeritus Fellowship for 2002/4 by the Leverhulme Trust, for which I owe the most profound thanks. Secondly, it was due to my becoming a member of the Teaching and Research Unit in Hebrew and Jewish Studies, a constituent element of the Faculty of Oriental Studies, a step made possible by the Oxford Centre for Hebrew and Jewish Studies. As a result, I have enjoyed the priceless privilege of working space in the Oriental Institute, that perfect model of what an academic institution should be, with ample opportunities for serious and not-so-serious exchanges in an open, casual, and unhierarchical framework. These two great benefits have also allowed the production of this book still to be the responsibility of my secretary since 1989, Priscilla Lange, whose friendship, supportiveness, and good humor seem unaffected by my increasing inability to regard any stretch of text as actually finished. For help of various kinds with the figures, I am also much indebted to Bert Smith, David Taylor, Charles Crowther, and Ian Cartwright. Work on the text has continued until now, greatly helped by the perceptive and constructive comments on the draft submitted in September 2004 which have been received from Mark Griffith as Chairman of the Sather Committee. The Committee's support and understanding have been vital throughout, from the initial invitation, to the period of the delivery of the lectures themselves and to the stage of final revision. I hope that this book, whose subject matter falls at the margin of "classical literature" as normally conceived, will seem worthy of their confidence, and of the series.

At the most profound level I owe everything, including still being in shape to write a book at all, to Susanna. It is a gift of fortune that, after forty-five years of marriage, three children, five grandchildren, too many books (by both), and innumerable visits to universities round the world, our partnership of equals is still going strong. The dedication will have to act as a symbol of all that should be said.

Fergus Millar
Oxford, March 2005

Abbreviations

AB	*Analecta Bollandiana*
ACO	*Acta Conciliorum Oecumenicorum,* ed. E. Schwartz, I.1–5; II.1–6 (see in more detail App. A)
ACW	*Ancient Christian Writers*
AGWG	J. P. G. Flemming, *Akten der ephesinischen Synode vom Jahre 449 (Abh. der Königl. Ges. der Wiss. zu Göttingen,* Phil.-hist. Kl., N. F. 15, 1917)
AT	*Antiquité Tardive*
BGU	*Aegyptische Urkunden aus den Königlichen* (later *Staatlichen) Museen zu Berlin, Griechische Urkunden*
CCL	*Corpus Christianorum, Series Latina*
CJ	*Codex Justinianus*
Coleman-Norton	P. R. Coleman-Norton, *Roman State and Christian Church* II
CPL	*Corpus Papyrorum Latinarum*
CPR	*Corpus Papyrorum Raineri*
CSCO	*Corpus Scriptorum Christianorum Orientalium (Scriptores Syri; Scriptores Coptici)*
CSEL	*Corpus Scriptorum Ecclesiasticorum Latinorum*
CSHB	*Corpus Scriptorum Historiae Byzantinae*
CTh	*Codex Theodosianus*
DOP	*Dumbarton Oaks Papers*
DTC	*Dictionnaire de Théologie Catholique*

FC	*Fathers of the Church*
Festugière	A.-J. Festugière, *Éphèse et Chalcédoine: actes des conciles* (1982)
GCS	*Die Griechischen Christlichen Schriftsteller*
HE	*Historia Ecclesiastica*
I.K.	*Inschriften Griechischer Städte aus Kleinasien*
JAOS	*Journal of the American Oriental Society*
JEH	*Journal of Ecclesiastical History*
JJS	*Journal of Jewish Studies*
Jones	A.H.M. Jones, *The Later Roman Empire* I–III (1964)
JRA	*Journal of Roman Archaeology*
JRS	*Journal of Roman Studies*
JThSt	*Journal of Theological Studies*
Linder	A. Linder (ed.), *The Jews in Roman Imperial Legislation* (1987)
Med. Ant.	*Mediterraneo Antico*
Nov. Th.	*Novellae* of Theodosius II
Nov. Val.	*Novellae* of Valentinian III
NPNF	*Nicene and Post-Nicene Fathers*
PBSR	*Papers of the British School at Rome*
Perry	S. G. F. Perry, *The Second Synod of Ephesus* (1881)
PG	J.-P. Migne, *Patrologia Graeca*
Pharr	C. Pharr, *The Theodosian Code and Novels and the Sirmondian Constitutions* (1952)
PL	J.-P. Migne, *Patrologia Latina*
PLRE II	J. Martindale (ed.), *Prosopography of the Later Roman Empire* II
P. Mich.	*Papyri in the University of Michigan Collection*
P. Oxy.	*The Oxyrhynchus Papyri*
P. Vindob.	*Einige Wiener Papyri*
SB	*Sammelbuch Griechischer Urkunden aus Aegypten*
SBAW	*Sitzungsberichte der Bayerischen Akademie der Wissenschaften*
SC	*Sources Chrétiennes*
SCI	*Scripta Classica Israelica*

SEG	*Supplementum Epigraphicum Graecum*
Stud. Pal.	*Studien zur Palaeographie und Papyruskunde,* ed. C. Wessely
Tanner, *Decrees*	N. P. Tanner, *Decrees of the Ecumenical Councils* I *(Nicaea I-Lateran V)* (1990)
TM	*Travaux et Mémoires, Centre de recherche d'histoire et civilisation byzantine*
TTH	*Translated Texts for Historians*
TU	*Texte und Untersuchungen*
YCS	*Yale Classical Studies*
ZPE	*Zeitschrift für Papyrologie und Epigraphik*

Ancient Sources:
Texts, Editions, and Translations

Alexander Akoimetos, Life of. Ed. and Latin tr. by E. de Stoop, *Vie d'Alexandre l'Acémète, PO* VI (1911), pp. 643–701. Eng. tr. by D. Caner, *Wandering, Begging Monks* (2002), pp. 249–80.

Auxentius, Life of. PG CXIV, cols. 1377–1436; cf. L. Clugnet, "Vie de Saint Auxence, texte grec," *Rev. de l'Orient Chr.* 8 (1903), 1.

Barsaumas, Syriac Life of. Ed. and French tr., in part, by F. Nau, *Rev. de l'Orient Chr.* 18 (1913), 272; 379; 19 (1914), 113; 278; *Rev. Ét. Juives* 83 (1927), 184.

Besa. *Life of Shenoute of Atripe.* Coptic text and Latin trans. by J. Leipoldt and W. Crum, *CSCO* XLI, *Scr. Copt.* I (1906). Eng. tr. and introd. by D. N. Bell, *Besa, the Life of Shenoute* (1983).

Bonifatius, bishop of Rome. *Epp. PL* XX, cols. 749–92.

Caelestinus (Coelestinus, Celestine), bishop of Rome. *Epp. PL* L, cols. 417–558; cf. *ACO* I.2, paras. i–x; xvi; xxii (pp. 5–101), letters to or from Caelestinus.

Callinicus. *Life of Hypatius.* Ed. and French tr. by G. J. M. Bartelink, *Callinicos, Vie d'Hypatios, SC* CLXXVII (1971).

Chronicle of Edessa. Syriac text and German tr. by L. Hallier, *Untersuchungen über die Edessenische Chronik, TU* IX (1892).

Chronicon Paschale. Ed. by L. Dindorf, 2 vols., *CSHB* IV, 1–2 (1832). Eng. tr., introd., and com. by M. and M. Whitby, *TTH* VII (1989).

Codex Justinianus. Ed. by P. Krueger, *Corpus Iuris Civilis* II: *Codex Iustinianus* (1877, repr. 1963). No modern translation.

Codex Theodosianus. Ed. by Th. Mommsen and P. M. Meyer, *Theodosiani Libri XVI* I.2 (1905, repr. 1962). Eng. tr. by Pharr, pp. 11–476.

Cyril of Alexandria. *Epp. PG* LXXVII, cols. 9–390. Partial Eng. tr. by L. R. Wickham, *Cyril of Alexandria: Select Letters* (1983). Eng. tr. by J. I. McEnerney, *St Cyril of Alexandria, letters,* 2 vols., *FC* LXXVI–VII (1987).

Cyril of Scythopolis. *Lives.* Ed. by E. Schwartz, *TU* XLIX.2 (1939). Eng. tr. by R. M. Price, *Cyril of Scythopolis, Lives of the Monks of Palestine* (1989).

Daniel Stylites, Life of. Ed. by H. Delehaye, *AB* 32 (1913), 121; idem, *Les Saints*

Stylites, Subsidia Hagiographica XIV (1923), ch. 2. Eng. tr. by E. Dawes and N. H. Baynes, *Three Byzantine Saints* (1948), 1–84.

Evagrius. *Historia Ecclesiastica.* Ed. by J. Bidez and L. Parmentier (1898). Eng. tr., introd. and com. M. Whitby, *The Ecclesiastical History of Evagrius Scholasticus, TTH* XXXII (2000).

Fontes Historiae Nubiorum III. Ed. by T. Eide, T. Hägg, R. H. Pierce, and L. Török (1998).

Gesta Senatus. Ed. by Th. Mommsen and P. M. Meyer, *Theodosiani Libri XVI* I.2 (1905, repr. 1962), 1–4. Eng. tr. Pharr, 3–7.

Innocentius, bishop of Rome. *Epp. PL* XX, cols. 463–612.

Inscriptions grecques chrétiennes d'Asie Mineure. Ed. by H.Grégoire (1922).

Irenaeus. *Tragoedia.* Ed. by E. Schwartz, *ACO* I.4, pp. 25–225 (the abbreviated Latin version provided by Rusticus, *Synodicum*).

Isidore of Pelusium. *Epp.* I–V. *PG* LXXVIII, cols. 177–1646; new ed. and French tr. in progress, by P. Evieux, *Isidore de Péluse, Lettres* I– (1997–).

Jerome (Hieronymus). *Epp.* Ed. by I. Hilberg, *CSEL* LIV–VI (1996). Ed., French tr., and com. by J. Labourt, *Saint Jérôme, Lettres* I–V (Budé, 1949–55). Eng. tr. of *Letters* 1–22, C. C. Mierow, *Letters of St Jerome, ACW* XXXIII (1963).

John Malalas. *Chronicle.* Ed. by L. Dindorf, *CSHB* XXVII (1831). Ed. by H. Thurn, *Corpus Fontium Historiae Byzantinae,* Series Berolinensis, XXXV (2000). Eng. tr. by E. Jeffreys and R. Scott, *The Chronicle of John Malalas* (1986).

John Rufus (John of Maiuma). *Plerophoriae.* Syr. text and French tr. by F. Nau, *Jean Rufus, évêque de Maiouma, Plérophories* (1899, repr. 1971), and in *PO* VIII.I (1912), pp. 5–161.

Leo, bishop of Rome. *Epp. PL* LIV, cols. 593–1213. Conciliar letters, ed. by E. Schwartz, *ACO* II.4, pp. 3–169. Partial Eng. tr. by C. L. Feltoe, *Letters and Sermons of Leo the Great, NPNF,* 2nd ser., XII (1895).

Liberatus. *Breviarium Causae Nestorianorum et Eutychianorum.* Ed. by E. Schwartz, *ACO* II.5, pp. 98–141.

Marcellus, Life of. Ed. by G. Dagron, "La vie ancienne de St Marcel l'Acémite," *AB* 86 (1968), 271.

Marcus Diaconus. *Life of Porphyry.* Ed. and French tr. by H. Grégoire and M.-A. Kugener, *Marc le Diacre, Vie de Porphyre, Évêque de Gaza* (1930).

Marinus. *Life of Proclus.* Ed. and French tr. by H. D. Saffrey and A.-P. Segonds, *Marinus, Proclus ou sur la bonheur* (2002). Eng. tr. by M. Edwards, *Neoplatonic Saints: The Lives of Plotinus and Proclus by their Students, TTH* XXXV (2000).

Marius Mercator. *Commonitorium . . . adversum haeresim Pelagii et Caelestii vel etiam scripta Iuliani.* Ed. by E. Schwartz, *ACO* I.5.1, pp. 5–215.

Melania, Life of. Ed. and French tr. by D. Gorce, *Vie de Ste Mélanie, SC* XC (1962). Eng. tr. by E. A. Clark, *The Life of Melania the Younger* (1983).

Nestorius. *Book* (or *Bazaar*) *of Heraclides.* Syr. text. ed. by P. Bedjan, *Le livre d'Héraclide de Damas* (1910). French tr. by F. Nau, *Le livre d'Héraclide de Damas* (1910). Eng. tr. by G. R. Driver and L. Hodgson, *Nestorius, the Bazaar of Heraclides* (1925).

————. *Fragments*. Ed. by F. Loofs, *Nestoriana: Die Fragmente des Nestorius* (1905).

Notitia Dignitatum. Ed. by O. Seeck (1905).

Notitia Urbis Constantinopolitanae. Ed. by O. Seeck (1905), pp. 229–43.

Novellae of Theodosius. Ed. by Th. Mommsen and P. M. Meyer, *Theodosiani Libri XVI* II (1905, repr. 1962), pp. 1–68. Eng. tr. by Pharr, pp. 487–514.

Novellae of Valentinian III. Ed. by Th. Mommsen and P. M. Meyer 1905 (repr. 1962). Eng. tr. by Pharr, pp. 515–50.

Olympiodorus. *History*. Ed. and Eng. tr. by R. C. Blockley, *The Fragmentary Classicising Historians of the Later Roman Empire* II (1983), pp. 152–220.

Palladius. *Dialogue on the Life of John Chrysostom*. Ed. and French tr. by A.-M. Malingrey and Ph. Leclercq, *Palladios, Dialogue sur la vie de Jean Chrysostome*, SC CCCXLI–II (1988). Eng. tr. by H. Moore, *The Dialogue of Palladius Concerning the Life of Chrysostom* (1921).

————. *Historia Lausiaca*. Ed. by E. C. Butler, *The Lausiac History of Palladius*, 2 vols. (1898–1904). Eng. tr. by R. T. Meyer, *Palladius, the Lausiac History*, *ACW* XXXIV (1965).

Peter the Iberian, Life of. Ed. and German tr. by R. Raabe, *Petrus der Iberer. Ein Charakterbild zur Kirchen- und Sittengeschichte des fünften Jahrhunderts. Syrische Übersetzung einer um das Jahr 500 verfassten griechischen Biographie* (1895).

Philostorgius. *Historia Ecclesiastica*. Ed. by J. Bidez and F. Winkelmann, *GCS* XXI (1981).

Priscus. *History*. Ed. and Eng. tr. by R. C. Blockley, *Fragmentary Classicising Historians* II (1983), pp. 221–400.

Proclus, bishop of Constantinople. *Epp. PG* LXV, cols. 851–86.

Rabbula, Syriac Life of. Ed. by J. Overbeck, *S. Ephraimi Syri, Rabulae Episcopi Edesseni, Balaei aliorumque Opera Selecta* (1865), pp. 159–209; P. Bedjan, *Acta Martyrum et Sanctorum* IV (1894), pp. 396–450. Extracts with French tr. and discussion by F. Nau, "Les 'belles actions' de Mar Rabboula évêque d'Edesse de 412 au 7me août 435 (ou 436)," *Rev. de l'Hist. des Rel.* 103 (1931), pp. 92–135.

Sixtus (Xystus), bishop of Rome. *Epp. PL* L, cols. 581–618.

Socrates. *Historia Ecclesiastica*. Ed. by G. C. Hansen, *GCS* IV. F. 1 (1995). Eng. tr. by A. C. Zenos, *NPNF*, 2nd ser., II (1891, repr. 1976), pp. 1–178.

Sozomenus. *Historia Ecclesiastica*. Ed. by J. Bidez and G. C. Hansen, *GCS*, N. F. IV (1995). Books I–II ed. and French tr. by A.-J. Festugière, B. Grillet, and G. Sabah, *Sozomène, Histoire Ecclésiastique*, SC CCCVI (1983). I–V ed. and German tr. by G. C. Hansen (2004). Eng. tr. by C. D. Hartranft, *NPNF*, 2nd ser. (1891, repr. 1976).

Symeon (or Simeon) *Stylites, Syriac Life of*. Syriac text ed. by P. Bedjan, *Acta Martyrum et Sanctorum* IV (1894), pp. 507–644. German tr. by H. Hilgenfeld, *TU* XXXII.3 (1908), pp. 79–188. Eng. tr. by F. Lent, *JAOS* 35 (1915–17), 103 ff.; R. Doran, *The Lives of Simeon Stylites* (1992), pp. 101–98.

Synesius. *Epp*. Ed. and French tr. by A. Garzya, *Synesios de Cyrène, Correspon-*

dance, 2 vols. (2000). Eng. tr. by A. Fitzgerald, *The Letters of Synesius of Cyrene* (1926).

———. *Katastaseis.* Ed. by N. Terzaghi, *Synesii Cyrenensis Opuscula* II (1944), pp. 282–93.

Thekla, Life and Miracles of. Ed. and French tr. by G. Dagron, *Vie et Miracles de Sainte Thècle, Subsidia Hagiographica* LXII (1978).

Theodoret. *Epp. PG* LXXXIII, cols. 1171–1494. Ed. and French tr. by Y. Azéma, *Théodoret de Cyr, Correspondance,* 4 vols., *SC* XL, LXXXXVIII, CXI, CCCCXXIX (1964–98). Note that in the *SC* edition vol. I contains letters numbered I–XLV; vol. II, letters numbered 1–95, vol. III, letters numbered 96–147; and vol. IV, the conciliar letters from *ACO,* numbered Ia–35. Eng. tr. by B. Jackson, *NPNF,* 2nd ser., II (1892, repr. 1975), pp. 230–348.

———. *Eranistes.* Ed. by G. H. Ettlinger (1975). Eng. tr. by G. H. Ettlinger, *Theodoret, Eranistes, FC* CVI (2003).

———. *Haereticarum Fabularum Compendium. PG* LXXXIII, cols. 336–556.

———. *Historia Ecclesiastica.* Ed. by L. Parmentier and G. C. Hansen, *GCS,* N. F. V (1998). Eng. tr. by B. Jackson, *NPNF,* 2nd ser., III (1892, repr. 1975), pp. 33–159.

———. *Historia Philotheos.* Ed. by E. Schwartz (1939). Ed. and French tr. by P. Canivet and A. Leroy-Molinghen, *Théodoret de Cyr, Histoire des Moines de Syrie: Histoire Philothée,* 2 vols., *SC* CCXXXIV, CCLVII (1977–79). Eng. tr. by R. M. Price, *Theodoret of Cyrrhus, A History of the Monks of Syria* (1985).

———. *Therapeutic for Hellenic Maladies. PG* LXXXIII, cols. 783–1152. Ed. and French tr. by P. Canivet, *Théodoret, Thérapeutique des maladies helléniques,* 2 vols., *SC* LVII (1958, rev. ed. 2000).

Zosimus. *Historia Nova.* Ed. by L. Mendelsson (1887). Ed. and French tr. and com. by F. Paschoud, *Zosime, Histoire Nouvelle* I–III (1971–89); I² (2000).

Zosimus, bishop of Rome. *Epp. PL* XX, cols. 639–704.

I Roman and Greek

State and Subject

1. INTRODUCTION: ROMAN AND GREEK

We may begin with an apology, addressed by Theodosius II, writing from Constantinople, to his younger co-Emperor, Valentinian III, ruling in Italy. The year was 447; a decade had passed since the first-ever official collection of Roman laws, the *Codex Theodosianus*, had been completed in Constantinople, and nine years since it had been formally presented to the Senate in Rome.[1] By its very nature, beginning with the legislation of the first Christian Emperor, Constantine, and incorporating laws issued in both East and West, all of them in Latin, the *Codex* had been intended to symbolize and embody the unity of the Christian Roman empire. Practice, however, had fallen far behind theory. In principle, all legislation, whether generated in East or West, should be communicated to the other half of the Empire, and promulgated there. In reality, it seems clear, Theodosius had sent nothing, and he apologizes profusely:[2]

> Because, therefore, various causes have emerged and the necessity
> of circumstances that has arisen has persuaded Us to issue, during
> the interval of time that has elapsed, other laws which We have not
> been able to bring to the knowledge of Your Majesty, since We have
> been engrossed in the continuous duties of the State, We consider it
> necessary that now at least all the laws should be transmitted to Your
> Serenity, with the subscription of Our Majesty. Thus they may become

---

1. See the *Gesta Senatus Urbis Romae*, in *Theodosiani Libri XVI* I.2 , ed. Th. Mommsen and P. M. Meyer, 1–4 (1905); trans. Pharr, pp. 3–7. See esp. J. F. Matthews, *Laying down the Law: A Study of the Theodosian Code* (2000), ch. 3.

2. *Nov. Th.* 2, trans. Pharr.

formally known to Your subjects, provinces, and peoples, and their
tenor may begin to be observed in the western part of the Empire also.

This letter is one sign among many demonstrating that, for all the real,
and very significant, commitment to the unity of the Roman Empire, the
reality was that, not of two separate Empires, but of twin Empires, in one
of which, that which Theodosius ruled from Constantinople, the normal language of the vast majority of the population was Greek. It is this "Greek
Roman Empire" which is the subject of this book. There were indeed many
senses in which it was still unambiguously Roman; but there were more,
and more fundamental, senses in which it was Greek—in its culture and literature, in the language spoken in the street, in the language in which individuals and groups addressed the State and its agents, and above all in the
language of its Church. These latter two aspects come together in the major controversies over the nature, or natures, of Christ which led to the two
Councils of Ephesus in 431 and 449, and to that of Chalcedon, held a year
after Theodosius's death in 450.

How had a "Greek Roman Empire" come about? In one sense there had
been such a thing for centuries. The wider Greek world, created first by the
colonizing activity of the Archaic period, and then by the conquests of
Alexander in the second half of the fourth century B.C.E., had come under
Roman rule between the second century B.C.E. and the second century C.E.
Roman rule never extended to some more distant areas conquered by
Alexander, namely Babylonia, Iran, Bactria, and northern India, all of which
had been affected in varying degrees by Greek culture and language. But it
did incorporate the whole Greek-speaking area from the Balkans to Asia Mi-
nor, Syria, Palestine, Egypt, and Cyrenaica (Libya). In the late second century, in a move of immense significance, it had extended across the middle
Euphrates to the Tigris, only to lose the eastern half of Mesopotamia in 363.

In all this vast area, where St. Paul had preached, entirely in Greek, and
the Christian Church had developed, Latin never took root as a language of
everyday speech. So, in one sense, the pattern analyzed in this book—a
Greek world ruled by an Imperial administration which used Latin—was
not novel at all. The correspondence of Pliny the Younger with the Emperor
Trajan, in 109–11, about the affairs of the Greek-speaking double province
of Pontus and Bithynia, is only one example.[3] In another sense, in looking
at the eastern Roman Empire of the fifth century, we are in an entirely new

---

3. Pliny, *Epp.* X; see A. N. Sherwin-White, *The Letters of Pliny: A Historical and
Social Commentary* (1966), 525–26.

world. Two fundamental features of this world were the work of Constantine, ruling between 306 and 337: his conversion to Christianity, followed by all subsequent Emperors except Julian (361–63); and his foundation of Constantinople as a "new Rome."

The crucial next step, the division into twin Empires, had come about, as it seems, almost by accident. Theodosius I (379–95) had ruled a unified Empire, with his two sons, Arcadius and Honorius, sharing the Imperial name "Augustus" with him. But on his death, the elder, Arcadius, ruled from Constantinople until his death in 408; while the younger, Honorius, ruled from Italy until his death in 423.

No one seems to have intended a permanent division, and certainly no one could have anticipated at the time how important this parting of the ways was to be: in the fifth century the Greek words "orthodox" and "catholic" were both used of the same Church—but the roots of conflict over precedence between Rome and Constantinople were already visible.[4] So also, and indeed much more clearly, was the complete linguistic divide between the Latin-speaking Church of the West and the Greek-speaking Church in the East.

In the short term, it cannot be shown that it was more than a practical arrangement for the division of rule between two brothers which led to the establishment of Arcadius in Constantinople in 395. But it was that which meant that his son Theodosius was born there on April 10, 401. Granted the name "Augustus" before his first birthday, he was left as sole Emperor in the East when his father died early, still aged only about thirty-one, on May 1, 408. It is of great relevance that Theodosius was the first Roman Emperor both to be born in Constantinople and to rule from there for the whole of his long reign, and that his was to be, formally speaking, the longest reign enjoyed by any Emperor: forty-eight years with the name "Augustus," forty-two as (at least) the nominal source of the legislation issued from Constantinople. Even then, it was only a riding accident which led to his death on July 28, 450.

Before we return to the complex nature of the "Greek Roman Empire" and its relations with its western twin, it is worth underlining the distinctive character of the particular phase, lasting about a century and a half, represented by a Greek empire. This phase itself divides into two halves: from 395 until the disappearance of the last western Emperor in 476; and then from 476 to the reconquest by Justinian of Roman North Africa, a large part of

---

4. See now H. Chadwick, *East and West: The Making of a Rift in the Church from Apostolic Times until the Council of Florence* (2003), esp. ch. 7.

Italy, and part of Spain, thus recreating something like a unified Roman Empire, then to be drastically truncated a century later by the Islamic conquests.

It is perfectly legitimate to write histories of "the Later Roman Empire," and that is indeed the title of the greatest intellectual achievement of twentieth-century ancient history, A. H. M. Jones's monumental three-volume study of 1964. But in fact the successive phases of that empire were so drastically different, in structure and in geographical shape, that they can and should also be studied separately from each other: the unified Empire of 324 to 395; the Roman or Italian Empire of 395 to 476, marked by almost total territorial losses outside Italy, and by a conjunction of Emperor, Pope, and Senate;[5] the Greek Empire of 395 to the 530s; and the united Empire of the following century. In this connection, it is perhaps worth noting that, if Theodosius had not fallen off his horse in July 450, and had lived as long as either Anastasius (Emperor in 491–518) or Justinian (Emperor in 527–65), he would have outlived the entire phase of the twin empires.

It is a matter of pure choice, convention, or convenience to what periods we apply the terms "Late Empire," "Byzantium," or "Late Antiquity." We can, for instance, quite reasonably choose to use "Byzantine" only for the period after the loss of Syria, Egypt, and Libya to Islam. But we could also choose to see the long and stable reign of Theodosius II as the beginning of "Byzantium:" the first extended reign by an Emperor born in Constantinople; the first regime conducted from there (allowing for occasional minor excursions) continuously for four decades; the reign most emphatically marked by Christian piety; and the one for which our evidence allows us to see, far more fully and clearly than any other, the intimate relations between the Emperor and the Greek-speaking Church.

But in what sense was this "Roman" empire, now ruled by an Emperor established in Constantinople, really Greek? On the surface, such a claim seems entirely misleading. The coinage issued by the Imperial state was stamped with legends in Latin.[6] The "laws" which Emperors issued, from West or East, were written in Latin, and dated by the consuls of the year, and by the Roman calendar. As was noted above, the *Codex Theodosianus*, completed in 437 in Constantinople, was designed to collect in a single volume the relevant laws issued since 313, and to arrange them in a long se-

5. The foundation for the history of this truly "Roman" empire, and especially of its last quarter century, after the Emperors had made Rome once again their normal residence, is laid in the important paper by A. Gillett, "Rome, Ravenna and the last western emperors," *PBSR* 69 (2001), 131 ff.

6. See J. P. C. Kent, ed., *The Roman Imperial Coinage* X: *The Divided Empire and the Fall of the Western Parts* (1994).

ries of chapters, divided between sixteen books, within each section of which those laws which were incorporated were to be set out in a single chronological sequence. The entire massive volume, produced in a Greek city, is in Latin. As we will see more clearly when we look at the political context in which it was planned and produced, it had in fact been specifically designed as an expression of the unity of the Empire, East and West, and of the unity and consistency of the legal and administrative principles by which it was governed.[7]

What is more, every "law" contained in it had been issued in the names of both, or all, of the current Emperors, in order of seniority, without regard to whether they had currently been located in the same place, or had in fact had the opportunity to consult on its content. If we take as an example the laws issued between 408 and 437, until the death of Honorius in 423 all laws were in the name of Honorius and Theodosius, in that order. Then we find a period when Theodosius rules alone, after which his name is followed by that of Valentinian III, first as "Caesar," then as an equal "Augustus." So it continues up to and beyond 437, when the *Novellae* of Theodosius (those laws issued after 437) are invariably in the names of both Theodosius and Valentinian.

As indicated, we will come back later to the political, and military, background to these formal changes, and to the ways in which there were indeed still profound links, both governmental and ecclesiastical, between East and West. What is unmistakable in the ideology of Imperial legislation is the determination to assert the continuing formal unity of the Roman Empire.

This determination has achieved remarkable success, not least in convincing modern historians that there was at all periods a single "Late Roman Empire." In the fourth century there had been, and after Justinian's reconquests in the sixth there would be again. But in the time of Theodosius II there was not; there were twin Empires, closely linked, but distinct in administrative and military structure, in their central decision-making procedures, and, in every sphere except one, in language.

This division is absolutely explicit in that remarkable summary, written in Latin, of the structure of Late Roman government, the *Notitia Dignitatum*, which itself is divided between "Oriens" and "Occidens," and whose first, eastern, half, seems to date to 401, only a few years after the division

---

7. For the composition of the *Codex* see above all J. F. Matthews, *Laying down the Law* (n. 1), and for its purpose see also T. Honoré, *Law in the Crisis of Empire 379–455 AD: The Theodosian Dynasty and its Quaestors* (1998), ch. 5–6, and J. Harries, *Law and Empire in Late Antiquity* (1999), ch. 1.

of 395.[8] The briefest sketch of what the eastern half, ruled from Constantinople, consisted of is required to make sense of what follows. The map on figure I is of primary importance. As will become clear, it is vital to understand both the geographical extent of the eastern Empire, and the hierarchy of posts within it. For, to look ahead to themes explored more fully later, we need both to understand its nature as a Greek-speaking world and to conceive the function within it of what we call "laws," in terms of their role in communication between the Emperor and the administrative hierarchy.

The evolution of Imperial government in the fourth century had produced four major regional officials at the apex of the hierarchy, immediately below the Emperor, or (normally) Emperors: the (now entirely civilian) Praetorian Prefects. The division of 395 left two of these "in partibus Orientis," as the *Notitia Dignitatum* puts it. It will save confusion if it is realized that contemporary usage deployed the word "Oriens" in three different senses: the whole eastern Empire; the Praetorian Prefecture of "Oriens" which covered most, but not all, of it; and the (secular) diocese of Oriens which was part of the Prefecture. Of the two Prefectures in "Oriens" (in the widest sense), the first was that of Illyricum, covering Greece and the islands and the western Balkans, divided into two "dioceses" under Vicarii (or delegates of the Praetorian Prefect): Dacia in the north, comprising five provinces, each under its own governor; and "Macedonia" in the south, with seven.

All the rest of the eastern Empire came under the Praetorian Prefect of Oriens, whose territory stretched in a circle round from the lower Danube and eastern Balkans to the whole of Asia Minor, Syria and Mesopotamia, Palestine, Arabia, Egypt, and Libya. Here there were five vicariates, each subdivided into provinces: "Thraciae" in the eastern Balkans; "Asiana," roughly western Asia Minor; "Pontica" (eastern Asia Minor); "Oriens" (in the third sense), whose holder had the title "Comes Orientis," and which covered from Cyprus and Cilicia round to Palestine; and "Aegyptus," covering both Egypt and Libya, whose holder had the title "Praefectus Augustalis."

These dry administrative details (paralleled by separate military and financial hierarchies, which we can ignore for the moment) are of immense importance: for the scale and extent of the Greek-speaking world; for the hierarchy of the Church, which—if erratically and imperfectly—mirrored that of the State; and for what we mean by "government" and the issuing of "laws" in this period.

It is time to confront the central paradox. On the one hand, as we have

---

8. For the latest discussion of the date see C. Zuckerman, "Comtes et ducs en Égypte autour de l'an 400 et la date de la *Notitia Dignitatum Orientis*," *AT* 6 (1998): 137 ff.

seen, Imperial legislation, all issued in Latin, embodied the principle of the collegiality of the Emperors, and of the unity of the "Roman" Empire. On the other hand, the entire administrative structure described by the *Notitia Dignitatum* is divided into two halves; and what it calls "Oriens" (in the broadest sense) is a coherent, and very extensive, Greek-speaking world. So what justifies the claim made earlier, that in the first half of the fifth century the unity of the Empire, though very significant conceptually, was in practical terms an illusion? In reality, the claim made here is, there was a separate "Greek Roman Empire," twinned with its western, Latin-speaking, counterpart—but separate all the same.

2. IMPERIAL LEGISLATION

The answer to the paradox comes in the form of two very simple propositions. Firstly, the Imperial pronouncements which we normally (and contemporaries sometimes) refer to as "laws" *(leges)* were in form, with only the rarest of exceptions, *letters,* almost always addressed to officials, occasionally to the Senate.[9] This is true of both western and eastern legislation; but its significance in the eastern context is far greater. For what it means is that the entire body of "legal" material, on which in all essentials the history of the Late Roman State has been based, consists of internal communications within the administration. All of them were issued in the name of the current Emperors, western and eastern, and virtually all of them were addressed to high officials, predominantly one or other Praetorian Prefect. We are not speaking, in this context, of "laws" published as such to the public. Such a process of publication is in fact very well attested, as we will see; but, as they stand, the Imperial pronouncements *(constitutiones),* addressed in the form of letters to individual holders of office, are not examples of it.

Secondly, in spite of the principle of unity which informed both the au-

---

9. Of the eastern "laws" from Theodosius's reign (as defined by the criteria set out on pp. 8–13 below), found in the *Codex,* the *Novellae,* and the *Codex Justinianus,* all are in form letters addressed to office-holders, with only the following exceptions: *CTh* III.1.9 (*CJ* II.19.12), of Feb. 17, 415, addressed *Ad populum; CJ* VI.23.20, of March 9, 416, addressed *Ad populum urbis Constantinopolitanae et ad omnes provinciales; CTh* IV.4.5 (*CJ* VI.23.20), of March 13, 416, same address; *CTh* I.1.5, of March 26, 429, addressed *Ad Senatum* (on the plan for *CTh*); presumably also I.1.6, of Dec. 20, 435 (second plan); *Nov. Th.* 15.1, of Sept. 12, 439, addressed *Ad Senatum urbis Constantinopolitanae; CJ* I.14.8, of Oct. 17, 446, addressed *Ad Senatum* (eastern or western?). See chapter 6.

thorship attributed to the *constitutiones* themselves and the compilation of the *Codex Theodosianus*, there are a set of perfectly clear and unambiguous criteria which allow an almost complete separation of western and eastern "laws." In summary, the criteria are: (1) the place of issue; (2) the post held by the official addressed; (3) the regions or cities referred to in the text; (4) the mode of reference to other Emperors, whether deceased or still alive.[10] All these criteria might still be of limited significance, as indicating purely formal characteristics of pronouncements whose content nonetheless reflected the decision making and priorities of a unified Empire, but for the fact that so many of them are responses to memoranda (*suggestiones* in Latin, *anaphorai* in Greek) from officials, detailing circumstances which had arisen in particular contexts and localities. Even where this origin for a particular law is not explicitly attested, it is evident that the vast majority do not constitute contributions to the principles of Roman law itself, but are in essence administrative measures, of greater or lesser degrees of generality, often laying down penalties for nonobservance. Even from the Imperial "laws" themselves we can divine perfectly clearly that a large proportion were responses to issues arising at particular moments in particular localities. But we are not dependent simply on reading between the lines of the Imperial "laws." For we also have a mass of evidence for communications addressed to the holders of office by bishops and other clerics and by private individuals. We shall even see later the letter of a bishop, Synesius of Ptolemais in Libya, addressed to a local military official, and providing him with the content of the two *anaphorai* which he is asked to write and send to the Emperor. The first thing that makes the eastern Roman Empire of Theodosius into a "Greek Roman Empire" is that every single one of these communications addressed to holders of office, from the Emperor down, is in Greek.

We will take the criteria in the order indicated above:

a. Place of Issue

It is quite clear that the complete original text of any letter written by Theodosius (or any other Emperor) included at the end a statement of the place of issue, the date (given by the Roman calendar), and the year, using the names of the consuls. The entries in the *Codex Theodosianus* are characteristically (and probably invariably) extracts, not complete texts (and those in *Codex Justinianus* are often even more incomplete). But nonetheless the

---

10. A separation on this basis can be seen, as regards the period from 408 to 450, set out on facing pages in O. Seeck's magnificent *Regesten der Kaiser und Päpste für die Jahre 311 bis 476 n. Chr.* (1919), pp. 312–87.

place of issue is indicated very frequently, even in the texts as we have them, and "Constantinopolis" is recorded in a high proportion of cases.

That fact reflects another major historical change that came about with the division of 395. Theodosius I had led his own forces in the field, not least on two expeditions to the West, in the 380s and early 390s, thus following the tradition of Emperors since the second century. But his sons did not lead armies in person, and ruled from a civilian context. Theodosius followed this pattern, and in essence his work as Emperor was carried out from the Imperial residence in Constantinople; the places of issue indicated in his "laws" amply confirm this.

But that was not quite the whole story, and the list of his "laws," along with some other evidence, does make clear that the Imperial court was not wholly immobile, but moved around on occasion along the Thracian coast and into the nearer provinces of Asia Minor.[11] The records of places of issue show, for instance, that in August 416 the Imperial court was at Eudoxiopolis (ancient Selymbria) along the coast, evidently renamed after the Emperor's mother, and on September 9 was at Heraclea. As it happens, the sixth-century *Paschal Chronicle* records that on September 30 in this same year the Emperor returned from Heraclea, and was ceremonially offered a gold crown by the Prefect of the City and the Senate, in the Forum of Theodosius.[12] In 423, as the places of issue of "laws" show, the court was again at Eudoxiopolis during August.[13] Far from the Emperor's having been perpetually invisible behind the walls of the palace, the evidence will show repeated examples of appearances before large crowds in the city, and also demonstrates that Imperial "expeditions," within the relatively modest geographical range indicated above, were in fact a recurrent feature, referred to in enactments of 439/41 and 445.[14] Without going into all the examples, we may note that Sozomenus refers to a journey by Theodosius to another Heraclea (Heraclea Pontica),[15] while Theodosius himself, in a *Novella* of 443, written from Aphrodisias in Caria, to which he had gone to fulfill a vow, reports an appeal made to him en route by the people of yet another place called Heraclea (which must be Heraclea ad Latmum) about the repair of

---

11. For the movements of the court see G. Dagron, *Naissance d'une capitale: Constantinople et ses institutions de 330 à 451* (1974), 85–86.

12. "Laws" issued from Eudoxiopolis in 416: *CTh* XVI.5.61, Aug. 8; *CTh* XII.3.2 (*CJ* X.34.1), Aug. 9; *CTh* XII.1.182, Aug. 26; *CJ* I.46.2, Aug. 27; *CTh* IX.40.23, Aug. 30. From Heraclea: *CTh* XI.28.11, Sept. 9; *Chron. Pasch.* 574.

13. *CTh* XVI.5.61, Aug. 8; *CTh* XII.3.2 (*CJ* X.34.1), Aug. 9.

14. *CJ* XII.50.21, 439/41; *CJ* I.2.11 + X.49.2, Feb. 17, 445.

15. Sozomenus, *HE, Praef.* 13.

public buildings. In this year, too, the *Paschal Chronicle* duly records the Emperor's return from his expedition to Asia.[16]

In other words, both the mass of pronouncements issued from Constantinople itself, and those which reflect, in quite consistent ways, the "expeditions" which the Emperor made to the neighboring provinces (though never to Syria, Egypt, or the Danube), are a real reflection of the working of a "Roman" regime in a world of Greek cities.

b. Posts Held by the Officials Addressed in Imperial "Laws"

As was stressed above, and will need to be reemphasized repeatedly, in effect the entire mass of the extensive evidence for the government of the Late Empire, derived from the *Codex Theodosianus,* the *Novellae,* or the *Codex Justinianus,* consists of documents which in form and function were letters, addressed to individual holders of office. Our evidence divides between cases where the geographical area for which the official addressed was responsible is explicitly mentioned in his title, and many others where, if only a function but not a specific area is given, we know from other evidence which the area concerned was. It will perhaps be sufficient, given all the material which will be discussed later, to give examples where, as is quite rare, the geographical area for which the official concerned was responsible is explicit in his title as preserved: for instance a letter of January 28, 412, to Constantius, Magister Militum per Thracias;[17] of October 24, 417, to Vitalianus, Dux Libyae;[18] or of September 7, 439, to Thalassius, Praefectus Praetorio per Illyricum.[19]

c. References to Regions and Places in the Greek East

Again, the "laws" of Theodosius's reign show a large number of examples of reflections of the geography of the Greek East, from a whole series of measures concerning Constantinople itself,[20] to others embracing whole regions,

---

16. *Nov.* 23, May 22, 443; *Chron. Pasch.* 583–84. See C. M. Roueché, "Theodosius II, the Cities and the Date of the 'Church History' of Sozomen," *JThSt* 37 (1986): 130 ff. Note also *CTh* XI.1.37 + 5.4 (*CJ* X.17.2), written from Apamea on Aug. 28, 436 (see p. 11 below); *CTh* VI.10.4 + 22.8, written from "Topisus" (Topeiros, Rhodope) on Sept. 22, 425; *ACO* II.1.1, para. 48 and 47 (p. 71), written on May 14 and 15, 449, from two unidentified places, "Alexandrianae" and "Therallum;" and the report in Malalas, *Chron.* XIV.366, that shortly before his accidental death Theodosius had returned from a visit to Ephesus.

17. *CTh* VII.17.1.

18. *CTh* VIII.1.16 (*CJ* I.51.6).

19. *CJ* II.7.7.

20. For example *CTh* XV.1.47 (*CJ* VIII.11.17), Feb. 21, 409; *CTh* XIV.16.1, Apr. 26, 409; *CTh* XV.1.51 (*CJ* VIII.11.18), Apr. 4, 413 (walls of Constantinople); *CTh*

such as the letter of May 5, 420, to the Praetorian Prefect of Oriens, which reflects the Persian war of 420/1, and permits the fortification of rural properties in the provinces of Mesopotamia, Osrhoena, Euphratensis, Syria Secunda, Phoenice Libanensis, the two Armenias and two Cappadocias and so forth.[21] Then there are others which reflect circumstances in particular places—for instance the letter sent in 417 to the same Praetorian Prefect of Oriens in response to a complaint from the *officium* of the governor of Euphratensis, that people transporting wild beasts (for shows in Constantinople) to the court, had stopped for several months in Hierapolis.[22] As always in the history of the Empire, the regions along the Danube, whether those further east, in the Prefecture of Oriens, or those in that of Illyricum, claimed less of the attention of the Imperial government. So when a letter goes to the Praetorian Prefect of Illyricum, it is more likely to concern an ancient Greek city like Delphi, which was also in this Prefecture.[23] But a letter does, for instance, go to the Praetorian Prefect of Illyricum in 413, adjusting curial obligations in the light of the recent devastation of the region by barbarian raids.[24]

Another example is provided by a letter written from Apamea in 436 to the Praetorian Prefect of Oriens. Which of the various cities called Apamea is meant is not quite clear; but since the letter deals with taxation, and allows a special exemption for Cyrus, the bishop of Aphrodisias, the exemption very probably reflects a personal appeal, in which case the Apamea concerned may well be Apamea-Celaenae, further inland. It is worthy of note that Aphrodisias, the metropolis of Caria, and archaeologically one of the best-known late antique cities, makes two significant appearances in the *Codex*.[25]

Again, there is no need to multiply examples, since the Imperial "laws" or letters issued by Theodosius provide a vast scatter of glimpses of the Greek world as it was in the fifth century. One further example, a letter of 419, to which we will return in another context, concerns an appeal by Asclepiades, the bishop of a place which we would not otherwise have been sure came within the Empire at all, namely Chersonesus on the southwest corner of the Crimea.[26]

XIV.6.5, Oct. 4, 419; *CTh* XV.1.52 (*CJ* VIII.11.19), Jan. 9, 424; *CTh* XIV.9.3 (*CJ* I.19.1) + XV.1.53, Feb. 1, 425, and *CTh* VI.21.1 (*CJ* XII.15.1), Feb. 27, 425 (both on higher education in Constantinople), and so forth.

21. *CJ* VIII.10.10.
22. *CTh* XV.11.2 (*CJ* XI.45.1), Sept. 27, 417. See p. 72 below.
23. *CTh* XV.5.4, Apr. 22, 424.
24. *CTh* XII.1.177, Apr. 16, 413.
25. *CTh* XI.1.37 + 5.4 (*CJ* X.17.2), Aug. 28, 436. See p. 9 above.
26. *CTh* IX.40.24 (*CJ* IX.47.25). See further p. 77 in chapter 2.

d. References to Other Emperors, Contemporary or Deceased

The "laws," or letters, noted under the other categories, are reflections of the way in which it is possible to discern, without any significant ambiguity, the activity of a "Roman" government responding to the concerns of its Greek subjects. The final category demonstrates the individuality of the Emperor, Theodosius, whose "voice" speaks in these letters (including those which are too early actually to have been his own work), an individuality which contrasts sharply, and indeed illogically, with the fact that all "his" letters, except for a brief period in 423/4, when there was a usurper in the West whom he did not recognize, were issued in the name of both himself and his western colleague. Equally, as we will see repeatedly, letters and petitions to him, written in Greek, were formally addressed to both Emperors. But in the case of both incoming and outgoing communications that was indeed a pure formality.

This aspect of the documentation is quite important, and needs to be spelled out. It concerns both allusions to the current western co-Emperor, and references to relationships to deceased Emperors which are true of Theodosius, and not of his current co-Emperor. All the letters, it should be repeated, carry the names of both Emperors as their "authors." The relevant cases are: in 410, references to a law "of the divine father of my Clemency" and to "my uncle Honorius;" in 416, "the deified grandfather of my Piety"—Theodosius I; in 418, "Augusta Pulcheria, our sister;" in 423, measures of "the sainted grandfather and father of our Clemency;" and also of "our grandfather;" in 424, "my father and uncle [Honorius] of sainted memory;" in 425, "our grandfather;" in 430, "my father Arcadius of sainted memory."[27] These examples will be enough to show that Theodosius spoke in his own person to his officials, and that the attachment of the name either of Honorius, or subsequently of Valentinian, was a pure formality.

The same message is conveyed by the nature of the decisions or statements of policy contained in the letters, which often relate to very particular circumstances in regions or cities or branches of the administration. There is nothing whatsoever to suggest that there was consultation with the West (or vice versa) before such "laws" were issued, or indeed that there was automatic and regular transmission of the texts of laws once they had been

27. *CTh* XVI.5.49, Mar. 1, 410; *CTh* VII.16.2, Apr. 24, 410; *CTh* XIV.16.2 (*CJ* XI.24.1), Jul. 23, 416; *CTh* XIII.1.21, Aug. 21, 418; *CTh* XVI.5.60 + 8.27 + 10.23–24 (*CJ* I.11.6), Jun. 8, 423; *CTh* XII.3.2 (*CJ* X.34.1), Aug. 9, 423; *CTh* XI.20.5, May 13, 425; *CTh* 10.4 + 22.8, Sept. 22, 425; *CTh* XI.20.6, Dec. 31, 430.

issued. Indeed, Theodosius's apology to Valentinian, with which we began, indicates that there had been no such transmission over the whole previous decade.

That is not to say that no transmission ever took place. The compilers of the *Codex Theodosianus*, working in Constantinople, could use the texts of western laws issued up to 432, but not after.[28] When Valentinian received Theodosius's apology, dated October 1, 447, and accompanied by the texts of the missing laws, he did indeed see to their diffusion—but only on June 3, 448.[29] Quite apart from the common legal and administrative heritage and common ideology which the twin Empires shared, we need not doubt that the principles expressed, even in constitutions essentially arising from particular local circumstances, did, or might often, become known in the other half of the Empire, and might influence attitudes and legislation there. The tracing of such delayed, or secondary, influences would be an important task, not addressed in this study.

What is asserted categorically, as the basis of this study, is that day-to-day administration, decision making, and legislation, as conducted by the Imperial court in Constantinople, did not depend at all on immediate consultation with Rome or Ravenna, but should be seen instead as reflecting a constant dialogue with the Greek world which it ruled. We do, however, have to allow for communications addressed to the Emperor by his co-Emperor in Italy, and towards the end of the reign also by the female members of the Imperial family in Rome, and—very significantly—by the bishops of Rome, above all Leo the Great (440–61). We shall see below many instances of the way in which events in the West, and views held in Italy, had a significant impact on policy in Constantinople, in the sphere of religion at least.

But, with that said, the eastern Empire was in its day-to-day functioning a separate regime, functioning internally in Latin, but interacting with its subjects in Greek. Before we look a little more closely at the nature of that interaction, we need to remind ourselves of just how extensive and substantial an empire this "Greek Roman Empire" really was.

3. THEODOSIUS'S GREEK EMPIRE

We are talking of a coherent block, or half-circle, of territory surrounding the eastern Mediterranean, with roughly some two thousand kilometers

---

28. The latest "western" law included in the *Codex* is *CTh* VI.23.3, of Mar. 24, 432.
29. *Nov. Val.* 26.

separating Viminacium on the middle Danube, in its northwest corner, from
Aela on the Red Sea, and approximately the same distance separating the
northern coasts of the Black Sea from Libya (as we will see, Synesius was
very well aware that this was a remote and neglected corner of the system).
If we measure east–west, it was again some two thousand kilometers from
the Roman-Persian border in Mesopotamia to the Ionian Sea west of Greece.
It is worth underlining the significance of these facts, obvious as it may seem.
Modern estimates tend to put the population of the Roman Empire at some
fifty million, and may well be too low. What we are concerned with is, in
broad terms, half of the Empire, but very probably represents what was always the more populous half. What is more, in those areas where we have
relevant archaeological evidence—all of them, admittedly, in the secular diocese of Oriens—the indications are unmistakably of both an extension and
an intensification of settlement: that is, in the Limestone Massif of northern Syria, in the neighboring north-Syrian steppe, along the frontier in Syria
(the military road known as the Strata Diocletiana), along the frontier in
present-day Jordan, and in the Negev.[30] Far from this having been a period
of "decline," we may hazard the guess, which can be no more than that, that
this was a period of increased population. An estimate of thirty million for
the population ruled from Constantinople in the reign of Theodosius II
would probably be an underestimate.

This population supported a tax-gathering and administrative service of
many thousands, whose management, grading, rights, privileges, and status
on discharge formed one of the dominant themes of the Imperial communications collected in the *Codex Theodosianus*. It also supported an army of
perhaps three hundred thousand,[31] which, as we will see, faced innumerable
small, or local, problems of security along thousands of kilometers of frontier; which fought occasional significant, but brief, wars against Sasanid Persia; and which confronted really major threats only along the Danube. Even
here, after invasions by the Huns under Attila in the 440s, no territory had
actually been lost when Theodosius died unexpectedly in 450.

The sheer scale, and the geographical, administrative, and military coherence, of this half of what was in principle still a single Roman Empire,
and in practical reality was one of a pair of twin Empires, are significant

30. The evidence on the extension and intensification of rural settlement is now
conveniently collected and assessed by R. Duncan-Jones, "Economic Change and
the Transition to Late Antiquity", in *Approaching Late Antiquity*, ed. S. Swain and
M. Edwards (2004), 21 ff., on pp. 38–39.

31. See p. 45 below in chapter 2.

enough. But what is more significant still is its cultural, linguistic, and religious coherence. We will look more closely at these issues in later chapters, but the first thing to stress is that, as a historical phenomenon, this "Greek Roman Empire" represented the fulfillment of over a thousand years of the progressive extension of Greek culture, from the Greek colonization of the Archaic period to Alexander's conquests, to the role of the Roman Empire itself in protecting Greek urban culture, and actually founding new Greek cities, or renaming existing cities. This process still continued: we have already encountered "Eudoxiopolis," and there was also an "Arcadiopolis" and two different places called "Theodosiopolis." At the Council of Chalcedon in 451, the bishops were to provide explicitly for the consequences for the Church hierarchy if the Emperor founded a new city.[32] Broadly speaking, what needs to be emphasized is that this very large, functionally coherent zone was not only an area of Greek culture but, in effect, represented or incorporated the whole heritage of Greek culture and Greek expansion. There are qualifications to be entered as regards bilingualism, or biculturalism, in certain areas: a developed Christian literary culture in Syriac, dramatically represented by the earliest known codex in Syriac, written in Edessa in 411 (see figure II); the bi- or even tri-lingual religious culture (in Hebrew, Aramaic, and Greek) of Jews and Samaritans in Palestine; and a Christian community in Egypt within which both Greek and Coptic were current. We should certainly allow also for a continuing role for Latin, probably among the communities stretching along the Danube,[33] and certainly as regards at least a few cities on the Adriatic coast.

Equally, it would be rash to deny the survival of Greek in Sicily, which belonged to the western Empire,[34] or in the Sasanid half of Mesopotamia, or in Babylonia. But these are marginal exceptions. In broad terms Theodosius's empire was not only *a* Greek-speaking world, it was *the* Greek-speaking world.

By far our most important evidence for this fact is represented by the mass of material contained in the *Acta* of the three fifth-century Oecumen-

---

32. *ACO* II.1.2, p. 161 [357], Canon 17. Note also *CJ* I.3.35, from the reign of Zeno.

33. For a proposed Latin-Greek "frontier" in Moesia, running in its eastern section south of the Danube and parallel to it, see the excellent paper by B. Gerov, "Die lateinisch-griechische Sprachgrenze auf der Balkanhalbinsel," in *Die Sprachen im römischen Reich*, ed. G. Neumann and J. Untermann (1980), 147 ff., on p. 149. However, as we will see below (p. 17), the evidence of the languages spoken at the Church Councils by bishops from cities along the lower Danube does not wholly support Gerov's conclusions.

34. For the survival of Greek in Sicily see now J. Irigoin, "Viri divites et eruditi omni doctrina, graeca quoque et latina," *Kokalos* 43/4 (1997/8): 139 ff.

ical Councils of the Church: Theodosius called the first at Ephesus in 431, and the second, again at Ephesus, in 449. The *Acta* of the latter, so far as preserved in Greek, owe their survival to the fact that they were extensively quoted in the *Acta* of the Council of Chalcedon, called by the Emperor Marcian in 451, a year after Theodosius's death, and containing also a vast range of other material from his reign.

Various aspects of this material, which the truly great edition by Eduard Schwartz still leaves as an extremely difficult task for the historian to use, are explored in detail in the two appendixes to this study, and documents drawn from this collection will be discussed throughout the following chapters. But certain fundamental historical conclusions, which derive from this material and provide the framework within which the Imperial pronouncements in the *Codex Theodosianus* have to be understood, need to be presented starkly.

The three great Church Councils of the fifth century drew bishops from all parts of the Theodosian Empire except the northwestern corner of the Prefecture of Illyricum. The language of all three Councils was Greek. That is no doubt no more than would be expected—but it is essential to stress just how specific and how extensive is the evidence which these records provide for the currency of the Greek language. In broad terms, the *Acta* provide (1) a narrative, written in Greek; (2) quotation in Greek of documents or texts laid before the relevant session; (3) verbatim quotation of the spoken interventions made by individual bishops; (4) a record of the written "subscriptions" (in essence statements of individual assent to the collective decisions reached) by the bishops (and sometimes lower clergy) attending.

Between them, therefore, the record of hundreds, perhaps in total thousands, of spoken interventions and of the long lists of subscriptions written—on the original text—in the hand of the individual (with an explanation if he could not) represents both in quality and in volume some of the best evidence—and for spoken Greek by far the best evidence—for the Greek language that survives from Antiquity.[35] Of course what is accessible to us is not the original autographs, but medieval manuscripts; and, as regards the texts of spoken interventions, we have to allow for the vagaries of recording procedures, and perhaps for subsequent correction of errors.[36] But, if we think of the history of language, this apparently unexplored evidence is without parallel.

---

35. As a nonexpert in linguistic history, I am amazed to discover that there is no allusion to this material in the otherwise masterly work of G. Horrocks, *Greek: A History of the Language and Its Speakers* (1997).

36. See more fully appendix B.

A philologist would need to analyze these texts to see if there were any traces of systematic variation between the spoken Greek of bishops from (say) Moesia or from Arabia. On the surface there is not the slightest indication that there was any difficulty in mutual understanding. Greek appears in the record as representing a wholly problem-free and variation-free common language, allowing mutual communication between bishops whose sees could lie up to two thousand kilometers apart.

As we will see more fully in chapter 3, other languages do appear, but through the medium of the Greek record: Syriac, in quite a significant way, though perhaps less so than might have been expected, given the contemporary flowering of Syriac culture and literature; Coptic—but only once; and Persian, also only once. But the major historical conclusion that arises, and which needs to be stressed at this point, is the relation of the Greek-speaking Church to Latin.

The conclusion is clear and unambiguous. If we take the several hundred bishops from (almost) all over the Theodosian Empire who attended the three Councils as a reasonably representative sample of (to very varying degrees) educated men, they did not understand spoken Latin, and had to have all written material in Latin translated for them.

This evidence needs to be spelled out in more detail, since it is the basis for all the propositions which follow concerning the role of Greek and Latin in the Theodosian Empire. Firstly, in the complex written exchanges between the Emperor or his officials and the bishops attending the Councils, the issue of Latin does not arise: both Emperor and officials communicated with the Church in Greek.

Secondly, as regards the participation of bishops from within Theodosius's domains, not a single bishop is recorded as either making a spoken intervention in Latin or writing his subscription in Latin, except for two from places on the Adriatic coast; we shall look at the evidence in a moment. As hinted above, we might have expected a similar pattern on the part of bishops from cities lying along the Danube or in the province which was now called Scythia (see the map in figure X)—that is, to the north of the Latin-Greek border as proposed in the excellent work of B. Gerov. But in fact we find that the bishops of, for instance, Novae and Durostorum in Moesia Secunda on the lower Danube both seem to have used Greek when attending a Council or hearing.[37] What we lack is evidence from the cities lying further upstream, such as Ratiaria and Aquae in Dacia Ripensis, or Viminacium

---

37. For bishops from Durostorum and Novae apparently using Greek see, e.g., *ACO* I.1.5, para. 16^{34} (Durostorum, 431); II.1, para. 555^{25} (Novae, Apr. 13, 449).

or Margus in Moesia Prima, very close to the (somewhat arbitrary) border with the western Empire. No bishops from these places attended any of the Councils; if they had, they might well have used Latin.

Nonetheless, the prevalence of Greek as (at least) the chosen vehicle for self-expression at a Greek-speaking council on the part of bishops from the lower Danube, and also from Scythia (Tomoi and Histria) is noteworthy. So far as the evidence from the *Acta* of the Councils goes, the only reflection of the existence of Latin-speaking Christian communities within Theodosius's domains is provided by the two places on the Adriatic coast, mentioned above, which we might well have assumed to have been Greek-speaking: Apollonia and Byllis (a single bishopric) in Epirus Nova, and Scodra in the northern-most Theodosian province on the Adriatic, now called Praevalitana. At the first Council of Ephesus in 431, Senecio, the bishop of Scodra, spoke in Latin, with his intervention being recorded in the *Acta* in Greek,[38] and both he and Felix, bishop of Apollonia, subscribed in Latin. In our manuscripts, with one exception, these "subscriptions" too appear in Greek translation. But one manuscript, which will play a significant part in this study, happens to pre-serve in Latin elements which were originally in Latin.[39] So here we find, again of course in a medieval copy, the reflection of their two original auto-graph *subscriptiones* in Latin: "Senecion episcopus Scodrinae civitatis sub-scribsi," and "Felix episcopus civitatum Apolloniensium subscribsi."[40]

The same manuscript carries a similar reflection of the presence at Ephesus of three emissaries from the bishop of Rome, and of Bessulas, a presbyter from Carthage. Their subscriptions too are recorded here in Latin.[41] In all other versions of the *Acta*, and in all the various relevant contexts, mate-rial in Latin, whether written or spoken, is both translated for the benefit of the immediate readers or hearers, and is then recorded only in its Greek version. This also applies to correspondence between bishops in West and East, for instance between Caelestinus of Rome and Nestorius in Constan-tinople and Cyril in Alexandria—and here the letters themselves contain occasional references to the process of translation.[42] It equally applies to the

38. *ACO* I.1.2, para. 33.85 (p. 25). It is possible, as asserted by Schwartz, *ACO* II.1.3, p. xxiii, that the original official *Acta* incorporated the Latin texts, as well as the Greek translations, of interventions in Latin. But practice may have varied, and my remarks relate to the MSS as we have them.

39. See appendix A, and F. Millar, "Repentant Heretics in Fifth-century Lydia: Identity and Literacy," *SCI* 23 (2004): 111 ff.; for the Athens codex, pp. 117–18.

40. *ACO* I.1.7, para. 79[49,172] (pp. 113, 116).

41. *ACO* I.1.7, para. 79[2,4,5,191] (pp. 111–12, 117).

42. See, e.g., *ACO* I.1.1, para. 10, pp. 77–83 (Caelestinus to Nestorius); para. 17, pp. 99–100 (Acacius to Cyril); I.1.5, para. 144.5, p. 12 (Cyril to Caelestinus). Note

very moving letter from Capreolus, bishop of Carthage, which was read before the first session of Ephesus I, on June 22, 431. He was unable to attend, he wrote, or even to summon a regional synod in Africa to discuss the heretical doctrines of Nestorius, because of the Vandal invasion. What was more, Augustine, bishop of Hippo, whom Theodosius had specially invited to the Council, had, unknown to the Emperor, died in the previous year. In this case the record makes clear that the letter was read aloud twice, once in the original Latin, and once in Greek. But it was the Greek text which was recorded in the *Acta*.[43]

As mentioned above, three emissaries were sent by Caelestinus of Rome to participate in the Council, joining it for the first time at a session held on July 10. Their statements of support for the Cyrillian, or "one-nature," position were all delivered in Latin, and recorded in Greek; a letter from Caelestinus was, again, read in both Latin and Greek, and recorded in Greek. After a further session on the following day, the emissaries from Rome gave their autograph subscriptions to the doctrines espoused by the Council, and the deposition of Nestorius. A Greek translation *(hermēneia)* of these subscriptions appears in the record. It is at this session that the Roman emissaries explicitly state that "there are many of our saintly brother-bishops who do not know Latin."[44]

It is not necessary to set out in comparable detail the similar record (quoted at vast length in the *Acta* of Chalcedon) of the participation of Roman emissaries at Ephesus II, except to note that one of them was reduced, by indignation at the scandalous proceedings leading to the deposition of Flavianus of Constantinople, to shout out "Contradicitur!" ("It is objected!"), which was duly recorded in Greek transliteration, with an explanation of what the term meant.[45]

As already mentioned, the implications for the history of language, and specifically for the currency of Latin among educated men in the Greek East, are unambiguous. Latin was not current. An assembly of bishops from the various regions of the Greek Empire could not be expected to understand either spoken or written Latin. Everything had to be translated. In the en-

---

ACO II.1, Epistularum Collectio M, nos. 1–9, texts (explicitly described as Greek translations) of Western letters, of Leo and the Imperial family, to Theodosius.

43. *ACO* I.1.2, para. 61 (pp. 52–54).

44. *ACO* I.1.3, para. 106 (pp. 53–63). The phrase quoted is from *ACO* I.1.3, para. 106.9 (p. 55): πολλοί εἰσι τῶν ἁγίων ἀδελφῶν καὶ ἐπισκόπων ἡμῶν, οἵτινες Ῥωμαιστὶ ἀγνοοῦσι.

45. *ACO* II.1, para. 964 (p. 191).

tire, and enormously extensive, record of the two Councils of Ephesus (see appendix B on verbatim reports of proceedings from Theodosius's reign), as of that of Chalcedon, precisely one bishop emerges, namely Florentius of Sardis, who is capable of impromptu translation of spoken Latin for the benefit of his fellow bishops.[46]

The full details of the way in which, firstly, written or spoken material in Latin was presented to the successive Councils, and second, of how the process of presentation and translation was recorded in the *Acta*, could and should be analyzed more fully. But, as already stated, the overall conclusion is beyond question. In this half of the "Roman" Empire, Latin was not familiar.

4. LATIN AND GREEK

The first question which arises is obvious: if even bishops did not understand Latin, let alone the mass of the population, what was the function of the flood of detailed "laws," or letters, issued by the Emperor in Latin, and often dealing, as we have seen, with issues arising in particular areas or regions of the Greek world? Part of the answer has already been given: these so-called "laws" were, almost without exception, letters addressed to individual holders of office. In its internal workings, this Empire was still Latin-speaking. But three documents allow us to spell out the boundaries between Latin and Greek, and their functional relations, much more precisely than that. The first comes from the same eccentric manuscript of the *Acta* of Ephesus I which we have already encountered, and which incorporates some elements still in their original Latin.[47] At one of the later sessions of the Council, a report was made on what was alleged to be scandalous interference by the State in the affairs of the church of Cyprus. Cyprus, though part of the

46. *ACO* II.1, paras. 82–83 (pp. 82–83); 117 (p. 86); 218 (p. 99); 952, 958 (p. 190). Of course I am not the first to notice this striking exception. See, e.g., the illuminating paper, viewing the linguistic divide from the western viewpoint, of C. Rapp, "Hagiography and Monastic Literature between Greek East and Latin West in Late Antiquity," *Settimane di Studio* LI. *Cristianità d'Occidente e Cristianità d'Oriente (secoli VI–XI)* (2004), 1221 ff., on p. 1240. I am grateful to the author for letting me read this in advance of publication. Note also the stimulating observations by Alan Cameron, "Vergil illustrated between Pagans and Christians," *JRA* 17 (2004): 502 ff., which would imply a more flourishing Latin literary culture in Constantinople than is suggested here.

47. *ACO* I.7, para. 81 (pp. 118–20) with the text provided by the Codex Atheniensis. See also pp. 138–39 below, where the Latin text is printed and translated, and appendix A.

secular diocese of Oriens, and hence (on the normal presumption) within the sphere of the bishop, or Patriarch, of Antioch, claimed to have an ancestral right to independence. But in the run-up to the Council the bishop of Constantia, the metropolis of Cyprus, had died, and (so it was alleged) the clergy of Antioch had persuaded Flavius Dionysius, the Magister Militum in Oriens, stationed at Antioch, to intervene. Why it was the military commander of the region who was approached, and not the civilian Comes Orientis, is not explained. At any rate Flavius Dionysius had assented, and had written two letters giving what seem on the surface to be harmless and neutral instructions on the procedure to be followed in electing a new bishop. One was written from Antioch on May 21, 431, and addressed to the governor (Consularis) of Cyprus. The other, with essentially the same content, and presumably sent on the same day, was addressed to the clergy of Cyprus. The first was written in Latin, and is quoted in Latin in the *Acta*, followed by a Greek translation *(hermēneia)*. It thus represents one of the closest and fullest contemporary parallels to the language and style of the pronouncements in the *Codex Theodosianus*. The other was written in Greek. In short, as soon as the administration stepped outside the bounds of its internal communications (which is what the documents in the *Codex* were), and addressed its subjects, it shifted automatically into Greek.

As it happens, two other contemporary documents, one from an inscription and the other on papyrus, perfectly illustrate other aspects of the way in which Greek and Latin functioned in communications between the State, in these cases the Emperor himself, and the population. The first is an inscription, or a group of inscriptions, from Mylasa in Caria, probably dating to 427.[48] What we come to first is the partially preserved Latin text of an Imperial letter (with the names of the authors omitted), which we know to have been addressed to Flavius Eudoxius, the Comes Sacrarum Largitionum. As was absolutely characteristic, and as we shall see more fully in chapter 6, what the Emperors (in reality Theodosius) wrote was in response to a memorandum *(suggestio)* from Eudoxius. As always, the official is addressed politely in the second person singular—"the *suggestio* of your Sublimity"—and the Greek translation which follows incorporates an address in the vocative, "brother Eudoxius." The fact that a Greek translation *(hermēneia)* does follow is very significant. The letter from the Emperor(s) to Eudoxius had to be written, as always, in Latin. But if its content needed to be made known to the public, then a Greek version had to be produced,

48. H. Grégoire, *Inscriptions grecques chrétiennes d'Asie Mineure* (1922), no. 242 = *I.K. Mylasa*, no. 612.

in this case transliterating the Latin term *suggestio.* Like so many of the documents preserved in the *Codex* and *Novellae,* these exchanges concerned a very localized issue indeed, namely the harbor-tax payable in one village in the territory of Mylasa. In this case neither of the two incomplete versions of the Imperial letter reveals the expression of any general principle, which is perhaps why it was not incorporated in the *Codex,* as two other letters addressed to Eudoxius were.[49] But there was evidently more to it than that, as is revealed by the third document, again a Greek translation *(hermēneia)* of a letter originally written in Latin, from Flavius Eudoxius to Flavius Baralach, the Praeses (governor) of Caria. For this refers to a case heard before Eudoxius between an Imperial Cubicularius, Domninus, and the leading citizens *(politeuomenoi)* of Mylasa. As we will see in chapter 6, five years later Domninus was influential enough to be one of the beneficiaries of the lavish expenditure of bribes by Cyril of Alexandria.

In the immediate context, the importance of the document is that Eudoxius wrote to Baralach in Latin, but that, for an inscribed version to have any function, it had to be in Greek. But Greek was not only the language in which, indirectly, the word of the Emperor was made known to his subjects: it was also, and without exception, the language in which they addressed him. We see this in the most remarkable and striking of all the documents which, in one way or another, survive from Theodosius's reign, the papyrus containing the petition addressed in Greek to Theodosius (and notionally Valentinian) by Appion, bishop of Syene in the province of the Thebais in remote southern Egypt.[50] We will come later (chapter 2) to the content of the petition, which describes itself as a *deēsis* and *hikesia,* and is written in a fine rhetorical style, closely parallel to that found in many petitions preserved in the *Acta* of the Councils. What matters in this context is that the petition was brought to Constantinople, where it was copied under the Latin heading "Exemplum precum," and that the Emperor did communicate with the military commander of the frontier in the Thebaid,

---

49. The other letters are *CJ* XI.78.2 and XII.23.13, both addressed to Eudoxius, Comes Sacrarum Largitionum (427?); the Eudoxius addressed in *CJ* I.18.1, and described there as P(raefectus) P(raetorio), may be the same man (*PLRE* II, Eudoxius 5).

50. *P. Leiden* Z; *SB* XX, no. 14606; reedited by D. Feissel and K. A. Worp, "La requête d'Appion, évêque de Syene, à Théodose II," *Oudheidkundige Mededelingen* 68 (1988): 97 ff., whence the text, with English translation, in *Fontes Historiae Nubiorum* III, ed. T. Eide, T. Hägg, R. H. Pierce and L. Török (1998), no. 314. Note D. Feissel, "Pétitions aux Empereurs et formes du rescrit dans les sources documentaires du IVe au VIe siècle," in *La pétition à Byzance,* ed. D. Feissel and J. Gascou (2004), 33 ff.

as Appion had requested. We know this both because the papyrus was found in Egypt, and because there appears, at the end of what is evidently the (illegible) Latin text, a standard example of the sort of personal greeting attached as a courtesy on concluding the message: "Bene valere te cupimus" ("We hope that you are in good health"). The thought is routine and banal, but the text is truly remarkable nonetheless—for it is the only surviving autograph of a Roman Emperor (figure III). Again, though the matter concerned public security, this document in itself was an internal communication to an official, and the issue of publication (and hence translation) did not arise.

Once again, however, we see that such an internal communication in Latin arose out of local circumstances in a Greek-speaking context, circumstances which were brought to the attention of the authorities in Greek, either via an official or directly to the Emperor himself. In short, the Theodosian documents in Latin, as collected in the *Codex* along with others from the West, or from the united Empire of the fourth century, should be seen as having been, almost without exception, responses to circumstances arising in a Greek environment. But they were not literally "responses," in the sense of answers or decisions announced to the public at large, but internal documents laying down lines of policy or legal definition, or practical decisions. As will be seen throughout this study, it is the much fuller texts preserved in the *Novellae* of 438 onwards which reveal how high a proportion of Imperial "laws" were in fact responses to *suggestiones* from officials; and, even more important, which show that it was a matter of routine that replies to officials should embody instructions for the incorporation of their contents in *edicta*, and for the posting-up of these for public information. But it is the overlap, and complementarity, between the texts derived from legal collections and those found in the *Acta* of the Councils which show how the secondary diffusion of the Imperial word through the posting-up of *edicta* for public information necessarily took place in Greek (chapters 4 and 5).

The "Roman" Empire of Theodosius, therefore, functioned in constant dialogue, conducted in Greek, with its Greek-speaking subjects, who—if we may take their bishops as a (quite extensive) sample—had no secure or reliable understanding of Latin, written or spoken. At the lower levels of the administration, as illustrated by papyri from Egypt, it is quite clear that written exchanges with persons holding official posts took place in Greek,[51]

51. See, e.g., *P. Mich.*, no. 613 (Aug. 19, 415); *P. Vindol.* G. 25933 (see F. A. J. Hoogendijk, *ZPE* 107 [1995]: 105 ff. (May 5, 419); *BGU* III, no. 936 = Wilcken, *Chrestomathie* I.2, no. 123 (Apr., 426); *P. Oxy.* XVI, nos. 1880–81 (Feb. 25 and Mar.

as did verbal ones, for example proceedings in court.[52] At the highest level, we will see that when the Nestorian controversy arose, the Emperor himself engaged in heated verbal exchanges in Greek with the conflicting parties (chapters 5–6).

It was stressed earlier that the Greek world with which the Empire was in constant dialogue represented very nearly the whole area where Greek was spoken, and that there are indications, at least from some areas in the Near East (or, in different terms, within the secular diocese of Oriens, governed from Antioch), that rural settlement was both expanding and intensifying. Hence it is possible, if entirely unprovable, that the population was actually larger than at earlier periods of antiquity. Beyond that, it needs also to be stressed that in those same areas there are clear indications of an expanding process of the establishment, construction, and elaboration of churches. One illustration of that process is provided by the still-standing church at Dar Qita on the Jebel Barisha, one of the low ranges of hills which make up the Limestone Massif of northern Syria. The church, as an inscription records, was built in 418, and the hostel attached to it in 431, while the baptistery came a century later (figure IV).[53] Given that the Church by its nature carried with it a message preached (almost everywhere) in Greek, and based on a sacred text, the Bible, which was known in Greek translation, it would not be rash to assert that this was the period when Greek, either in the form of the sacred text itself, or in the form of the reading-aloud of parts of the text, or of preaching based on it, reached more people than ever before. Theodoret, bishop of Cyrrhus in northern Syria (the province of Euphratesia), who will be one of the central figures in this study, was perhaps guilty of rhetorical exaggeration when he claimed that his bishopric included eight hundred villages.[54] But it is for certain that there will have been hundreds of such villages, mostly now equipped with a church which was normally (it seems) under a *presbuteros*. Some of these congregations subscribed to varieties of Christianity which their bishop considered heretical, and he mounted what were in effect missions, or expeditions, to rid them of heresy.[55] As we will see, Theodoret himself labored

---

14, 427); *BGU* III, no. 936 (Apr. 30, 428); *P. Oxy.* XVI, no. 1879 (434); *Stud. Pal.* XX, no. 143 (c. 435); *P. Oxy.* L, no. 3583 (Nov. 13, 444).

52. See appendix B, nos. 10–11.

53. For the inscriptions see *IGLS* II, nos. 535–37. See G. Tchalenko and E. Baccache, *Églises de village de la Syrie du Nord* (1979–80): I, figs. 299–312; II, pp. 60–64 and fig. IV below, from I. Peña, *The Christian Art of Byzantine Syria* (1996), 87 ff.

54. Theodoret, *Epp.* III. 113.

55. Theodoret, *Epp.* II. 81.

for most of his episcopacy under suspicion of heresy, as a follower of Nestorius. But if anything these incessant conflicts and debates will have lent extra force to the delivery to the people of doctrines derived from a sacred text in Greek. The sheer spatial diffusion of the social and physical structures designed for the delivery of these messages is a factor of crucial importance in understanding the period. To take only one further example, we have the inscriptions from the mosaic floor of the church at Khirbet Mouqa, some thirty kilometers northeast of Apamea in Syria. The main part of the mosaic floor was laid in 394/5, and a subsequent section under Alexander, bishop of Apamea (who, like Theodoret, attended the first Council of Ephesus in 431); the inscription also mentions the local *presbuteros,* a *diakonos* and a *hupodiakonos.*[56]

Even so relatively remote a church was thus within the territory of the nearest city, and therefore under its bishop. In the Greek world of the fifth century cities were, if anything, even more central than they had always been in Greek culture. This is true whether we look out, or down, from the city to the villages of its territory, or laterally to the network of city-based bishoprics covering the whole Empire, or upwards to the governing structures of the Empire. Indeed, as is well known, the structure of the Church mirrored very closely, if (as we will see in more detail in chapter 4) imperfectly, and with many anomalies, the structure of civil government. There was (in principle at least) a clear hierarchy going from ordinary cities to the *mētropolis* of each province, whose bishop was the *mētropolitēs,* and then to the chief city of each secular diocese, governed by a deputy, Vicarius, of the Praetorian Prefect; the relevant bishop might still be called just *episkopos,* but might be termed *archiepiskopos* or *patriarches.* Cities were thus essential to the structure of both State and Church.

5. THE GREEK CITY, AND GREEK LITERARY CULTURE

This study cannot claim the role of an overall social, economic, and cultural study of the Greek Empire (which still awaits its Rostovtzeff). But it is legitimate to stress that the most detailed of modern studies of the late Roman city, and one arguing specifically for the reality of decline, and against the prevalent, and more optimistic, notion of a painless cultural transition to "Late Antiquity," cannot show any systematic evidence for decline or dis-

---

56. P. Donceel-Voûte, *Les pavements des églises byzantines de Syrie et du Liban* (1988), 159–60.

ruption in Greek cities of the first half of the fifth century.[57] But one enormous structural change in the nature of the Greek city had, it seems clear, already occurred, namely, the disappearance from the center of city life of functioning temples, and of communal—and publicly financed—sacrifices, rituals, and processions. In some cities, temples had also been destroyed, and on occasion replaced by churches. The most vivid and dramatic of all accounts of this process remains Mark the Deacon's *Life* of Porphyry, describing events in Gaza about the time of the birth of Theodosius in 401; in spite of problems in the text, it still seems probable that this powerful Greek narrative is, as it claims, the work of a contemporary, and was written not long after the death of bishop Porphyry in 420.[58] As will be seen in chapter 3, pagans and paganism were still ever-present in the minds of both bishops and Emperors, and prominent individuals were still known as pagans, and even celebrated as such. The *Life* of the great Neoplatonist philosopher Proclus by Marinus is the best testimony to the surviving ideals of pagan piety. What is more, Theodoret's extraordinary work of learning, the *Therapeutic of Hellenic Maladies*, certainly also written in the 420s, in spite of its hostile and critical purpose, is the most complete and wide-ranging surviving survey of the intellectual heritage of the Classical pagan world. There is no evidence that its author had ever spent any extended period outside the Syrian region.

The ancient pagan rituals and sacrifices, nonetheless, seem by now to have disappeared from the communal life of the Greek city, and the major city temples were either closed or destroyed. But, with that very major proviso, along with one other, it can be asserted that the now Christianized Greek city, as the context for an urban community, as a physical structure, as a self-governing organization and as a channel for contacts with, and communications to and from, the Imperial power, played as essential a role as it had since the earliest stages of Roman rule. Indeed, with the building of churches

---

57. See J. H. W. G. Liebeschuetz, *The Decline and Fall of the Roman City* (2001).

58. H. Grégoire and M. A. Kugener, eds., *Marc le Diacre, Vie de Porphyre, évêque de Gaza* (1930). Strong arguments for authenticity are advanced by F. R. Trombley, *Hellenic Religion and Christianisation c. 370–529*[2] I (1995), 246–47. With regret, I have to regard the case for an original version in Syriac, as proposed by Z. Rubin, "Porphyrius of Gaza and the Conflict between Christianity and Paganism in Southern Palestine," in *Sharing the Sacred*, ed. A. Kofsky and G. G. Stroumsa (1998), 31 ff., as completely at variance with the wider cultural patterns of the period. As will be seen in chapter 3, Christian literary composition in Syriac is hardly attested west of the Euphrates in the first half of the fifth century, and there is no other evidence for such composition at this period in Palestine. In any case the author (chapter 5) represents himself as a Greek immigrant to the Holy Land from Asia.

and the central role of the bishop of each city, both within the community and outside it, in attending regional and oecumenical Church Councils, and in making representations to the authorities, it might be argued that the city was even more central to the functioning of the Empire than before.

The other proviso, which does have to be mentioned, is the question of whether in the first half of the fifth century the city council *(curia* or *boulē)* still functioned as a deliberative body, as opposed to being merely a status which imposed certain burdens on its individual members. Individuals with the traditional title *bouleutēs* (city councilor) are certainly attested,[59] but the evidence for collective deliberations is undeniably slight. Nonetheless, in the Imperial "laws," or letters, of the period, we can find clear evidence of meetings and collective decision making by councils; for instance in a letter of Theodosius in 413 to the Praetorian Prefect of Illyricum; or that of 416 to Monaxius, Praetorian Prefect of Oriens, laying down that embassies from Alexandria must be selected by the whole council there; or, it seems, in 424, when Theodosius writes to the Praetorian Prefect of Illyricum about a drain on the resources of the *curia* of Delphi.[60] If we may believe the *Paschal Chronicle,* the Empress Eudocia, whom Theodosius had married in 421, when on her way to Jerusalem in 444, made a speech in the council-chamber *(bouleutērion)* in Antioch, was acclaimed by the citizens, and was rewarded with a gilded statue there, and a bronze one in the city's Mouseion.[61]

In nearly all of those cities in the Greek East whose condition in late antiquity has been analyzed on the basis of the archaeological and epigraphic record, the picture is of a still-functioning monumental center, with a marked impact from the construction of churches; this would be true, for instance, of Gerasa, of Scythopolis, of Caesarea in Palestine, of Ephesus, and of Athens,[62] and is perhaps illustrated most strikingly of all at Aphrodisias in Caria. Late antique Aphrodisias, with a strongly marked presence of Ju-

---

59. For example Mark the Deacon, *Life* of Porphyry, 95, "the remaining [members] of the *bouleutērion;*" Syriac *Life* of Symeon Stylites, 60, question of service on city council; *Vie et miracles de Ste. Thècle,* Mir. 35; Theodoret, *Hist. Rel.* V.1; XIV. 4. Note also Isidorus, *Epp.* I. 226, to the *bouleutērion* of Pelusium. For the *boulē* of Ephesus honoring a Proconsul and Vicarius, see *I.K. Eph.* VII.2, no. 5115; see D. Feissel, *AT* 6 (1998): 98–102.

60. *CTh* XII.1.177, Apr. 16, 413; *CTh* XII.12.15 (*CJ* X.65.6), Oct. 5, 416; *CTh* XV.5.4, Apr. 22, 424.

61. *Chron. Pasch.* 585. Note however that Evagrius, *HE* I.20, speaks only of her addressing the people there.

62. C. H. Kraeling, ed., *Gerasa, City of the Decapolis* (1938); Y. Tsafrir and G. Foerster, "Urbanism at Scythopolis—Bet Shean in the Fourth to Seventh Centuries," *DOP* 51 (1997): 85 ff.; K. G. Holum et al., *King Herod's Dream: Caesarea*

daism and paganism as well as of Christianity, provides the fullest epigraphic record.[63] But a recent discovery there gives it a special status in any attempt to envisage the complex relations between Greek city and "Roman" Empire. For, as is very rare, it has been possible both to reunite a statue-base, with its Greek inscription, and the relevant statue (with its head reattached), representing a governor named Oecumenius, and also to establish its original position—in the monumental street running past the front of the *bouleutērion* (see figures V and VI).[64]

This location is highly relevant, for the inscribed Greek verses honoring Oecumenius are offered by the *boulē* of the city, and combine in elegant style allusions to his Greek culture, to his moral qualities, and to his training in Roman law:

> You who are expert in the laws, who have blended the Italian muse
> with the sweet-voiced honey of the Attic, Oecumenius, the famous
> governor, the friendly council *(boulē)* of the Aphrodisians has set up
> your statue here; for what greater reward than that of being remem-
> bered can that man find who is pure in mind and deed?

The statue represents Oecumenius as a serious, grave, and intellectual person, dressed in a long cloak *(chlamys)* and holding a scroll in his right hand. The date is uncertain, but perhaps not far from the time of Theodosius's birth in 401. At any rate, nothing could more perfectly symbolize the polite and formal relations between city and governor, or the expectations which marked their view of him, and will have informed their relations with Oecumenius and other governors.

It is one of the central themes of the modern study of the late antique city that, however great the continuities in physical and social structure were, it is undeniable that bishops came to play a role, both internally and externally, which did come to represent a substitution for long-standing elements in local self-government. One well-known example is the letter of Theo-

---

on the Sea (1988), ch. 5 (much new work on late antique Caesarea awaits publication); C. Foss, *Ephesus after Antiquity* (1979); A. Frantz, *The Athenian Agora* XXIV: *Late antiquity, AD 267–700* (1988); P. Castrén, ed., *Post-Herulian Athens: Aspects of Life and Culture in Athens, AD 267–529* (1994).

63. See esp. C. M. Roueché, *Performers and Partisans at Aphrodisias in the Roman and Late Roman Periods* (1993); and note esp. A. Chaniotis, "Zwischen Konfrontation und Interaktion: Christen, Juden und Heiden im spätantiken Aphrodisias," in *Patchwork: Dimensionen multikulturellen Gesellschaften*, ed. A. Ackerman and K. E. Müller (2002), 83 ff.

64. R. R. R. Smith, "The Statue Monument of Oecumenius: A New Portrait of a Late Antique Governor from Aphrodisias," *JRS* 92 (2002): 134 ff. Translation, with some adjustments, from p. 144; figures V and VI are taken from plate XVI and fig. 1.

doret, defending his achievements in twenty-five years as bishop of Cyrrhus: among other things, two public stoas constructed out of church funds, two bridges, and the repair of the public baths and the aqueduct.[65] No less than sixty surviving letters of Theodoret are addressed to holders of Imperial office, and seven of these concern efforts to reduce the level of taxation in the area of Cyrrhus.[66] There is no doubt about the validity of the general proposition associated with the name of Peter Brown, that bishops had come to exercise, both internally and externally, many functions formerly performed by the city authorities.[67]

That, however, indicates a significant shift in the nature of the city as a communal institution, not a decline in the perceived, or actual, importance of the city itself. Moreover, of all the literature of the Imperial period, there is no work which expresses the values of the city more vividly than the *Life and Miracles of St. Thekla,* written in the mid-fifth century, and speaking of Seleucia, the metropolis of Isauria:[68]

> This is a city which lies at the threshold of the region of Oriens, enjoying the first rank and precedence over all other cities of Isauria, situated beside the sea, and neighbor to a river. The name of the river is Calycadnus, springing from higher regions in the most remote area of the Kêtis, watering many territories and cities, and in its course towards us gathering in other rivers flowing in from the districts and places on either side. . . . An admirable and most delightful city, on a scale such that it does not lack the charm conferred by proportion. She is also brilliant and graceful as to outdo most others, to equal some, and to rival fair Tarsus as regards its territory and situation, the temperance of its climate, the abundance of its crops, the variety of goods on sale, the profusion of its waters, the beauty of its baths—as well as the distinction of its magistrates, the refinement of its culture, the brilliance of its people, the eloquence of its orators and the fame of those (of its citizens) in Imperial service.

As a literary work, the *Life and Miracles,* devoted to the legend of St. Thekla and to the wonders performed at her famous shrine outside Seleucia, is perhaps unique among the products of this period in its evocation of a locality and a provincial society, and its links with the wider Empire. In being a profoundly Christian work, however, it is entirely typical. It is not

---

65. Theodoret, *Epp.* II. 81. See pp. 146–47 below.
66. Theodoret, *Epp.* XVIII = XXI (434?); XVII; II. 42–45 (all 446/7); II. 23 (447/8?).
67. See esp. P. Brown, "Religious Coercion in Late Antiquity: The Case of North Africa," in *Religion and Society in the Age of Saint Augustine* (1972), 301 ff.
68. See G. Dagron, *Vie et miracles de Sainte Thècle* (1978), *Vita* 27.

that there was no explicitly pagan writing in this period, or that a form of censorship operated as regards literature. For instance the final version of the (largely lost) pagan *History* of Eunapius of Sardis, covering the period 270 to 404, was completed about 414,[69] while that of Olympiodorus of Thebes, also a pagan, in Greek but providing a detailed account of events in the West, concluded with the establishment of Valentinian III in 425.[70] Equally, the famous Praetorian and Urban Prefect Cyrus ("Flavius Taurus Seleucus Cyrus Hierax") from Panopolis in Egypt, known as a poet, and for a time one of the most powerful men in the Empire, was supposed by some to be a pagan.[71]

But, firstly, as we will see (chapter 3), explicit argument in favor of the truth of pagan belief or in the cause of the protection of temples or priests, played very little part in the vociferous public discourse of the Greek Empire. Secondly, the few examples of explicitly pagan writing are wholly outweighed by the mass of surviving Christian writing in Greek. Such writing might be *about* pagan culture and beliefs, like Theodoret's *Therapeutic of Hellenic Maladies*, mentioned earlier, or might represent a deliberate adaptation of a long-established Classical literary genre, like his pseudo-Platonic dialogue exploring rival Christologies, the *Eranistes*, written in the 440s. But without this being the occasion for a catalogue, the major Christian works of the period offered a wide range of different genres: Biblical commentaries, for instance by Theodoret and by Cyril of Alexandria; polemical works, such as Cyril's multivolume attack on the Emperor Julian's *Against the Galileans*; four *Church Histories*, by Philostorgius, Socrates, Sozomenus, and Theodoret, all starting from Constantine, and concluding at various points in Theodosius's reign.[72] Of these, only Socrates faced up to the challenge of describing the "heresy" of Nestorius, as bishop of Con-

69. For Eunapius see now W. Liebeschuetz, "Pagan Historiography and the Decline of the Empire," in *Greek and Roman Historiography in Late Antiquity*, ed. G. Marasco (2003), 177 ff.

70. On Olympiodorus see J. F. Matthews, "Olympiodorus of Thebes and the History of the West (AD 407–425)," *JRS* 60 (1970): 79 ff.; A. Gillett, "The Date and Circumstances of Olympiodorus of Thebes," *Traditio* 48 (1993): 1 ff.; and Liebeschuetz, "Pagan Historiography and the Decline of the Empire," (n. 69).

71. See A. Cameron, "The Emperor and the Poet: Paganism and Politics at the Court of Theodosius II," *YCS* 27 (1982): 217 ff., for the best evocation of the literary culture of the period.

72. On the Church Historians see F. Young, *From Nicaea to Chalcedon* (1983) 23–24; G. F. Chesnut, *The First Christian Histories* (1977); also T. Urbainczyk, *Socrates of Constantinople: Historian of Church and State* (1997); H. Leppin, "The Church Historians (I): Socrates, Sozomenus and Theodoretus," in Marasco, *Greek and Roman Historiography in Late Antiquity* (n. 69), 219 ff. Note also E. I. Argov,

stantinople in 428–31, as well as the first Council of Ephesus, in 431, and its aftermath.

The *Church Histories*, embracing quite substantial areas of the secular political and military history of the previous century since Constantine, must count as one of the characteristic genres of the period. Much in these *Histories* inevitably revolved round the role of individuals, their piety (whether seen as heretical or not), and the fortunes of the Church in the face of wavering Imperial attitudes. That aspect of "Church history" naturally leads on to the second of the most prominent and characteristic genres, the Saint's Life. Typically, these explorations of the life histories, and the spiritual qualities and powers, of their subjects did not relate to ordained clergy, even bishops. Palladius's *Dialogue on the Life of John Chrysostom*, written soon after John's death in exile in 407, and hence in the early years of Theodosius's sole rule, is untypical, even though its subject had lived as a hermit in an earlier phase of his life. It owes its existence to the still extremely controversial circumstances of John's deposition from the bishopric of Constantinople, and his subsequent exile and death. Reconciliation was only to be achieved when Proclus, as bishop (434–46), brought his remains back for reburial in Constantinople in 438.[73]

Normally, the Christian biographical portrait was focused not on any member of the ordained clergy, but on the holy men (and some women) who spontaneously chose the path of asceticism, whether living as solitaries *(monachoi)*, or founding or joining loosely organized groups *(laurae)*, or living in tightly organized communities. It is difficult not to see the holy man as offering the dominant image of the true Christian life in this period, not only for the (relatively) few who took up the ascetic life themselves, but for all believing Christians, not excluding the Emperor himself.[74] The life actually lived by any such person both was, and in a sense, if it were to achieve its full purpose, had to be in the strict sense exemplary, that is to say on show for others. As is very fully attested, visitors and pilgrims came in large numbers to contemplate the holy men to be seen in Egypt or Syria. But actual seeing was systematically supplemented by the writing and diffusion of lit-

---

"Giving the Heretic a Voice: Philostorgius of Borissus and Greek Ecclesiastical Historiography," *Athenaeum* 89 (2001): 497 ff.

73. Socrates, *HE* VII.45.

74. Note Socrates, *HE* VII.22, comparing the Imperial court under Theodosius to a monastery; cf. J. Harries, "*Pius Princeps:* Theodosius II and Fifth-century Constantinople," in *New Constantines*, ed. P. Magdalino (1994), 35 ff., and G. Zecchini, "L'imagine di Teodosio II nella storiografia ecclesiastica," *Med. Ant.* 5 (2002): 529 ff.

erary accounts.[75] These might take various forms. One example is the record by the same Palladius, bishop of Helenopolis, addressed in about 420 to Lausus, Praepositus Sacri Cubiculi of Theodosius, mainly devoted to the holy men whom he had visited in Egypt in the later years of the fourth century.[76] Or there is Theodoret's *Historia Philotheos*, written in the 440s, on the successive generations of holy men in Syria and Osrhoene from Constantine's reign to his own time; or a succession of saints' *Lives* either written under Theodosius or looking back from the following decades, or from the sixth century. A prime example is the *Life* of Alexander Akoimetos (the "nonsleeper"). But there are also the *Life* of Auxentius; Callinicus's *Life* of Hypatius, the head of the monastery of Rufinianae in Constantinople; the *Life* of Marcellus; Gerontius's *Life* of the younger Melania; or, from the second half of the century but looking back to Theodosius's reign, the *Life* of Daniel the Stylite, or later that of Peter the Iberian.[77]

To list these Greek works as examples is to omit the fifth-century *Life* of Shenute, head of the great monastery at Atripe in Egypt, and written in Coptic; or the Syriac *Life* of Symeon Stylites, which cannot have been written long after the saint's death in 459, for the earliest manuscript dates to 473. It would also be to omit the most systematic presentation of the issues facing Palestinian monasticism in the period, the *Life* of Euthymius in the sixth-century *History of the Monks of Palestine* by Cyril of Scythopolis. The relevance of both the actual lives lived, and of the literary representations of them, however, is not merely as a key to the nature of fifth-century Christian piety, but lies in the very important, sometimes even dominant, role played in the impassioned religious conflicts of the period by holy men who might happen to be ordained, and might eventually become bishops, but did not have to do either.[78] It was their self-chosen role as models, not any process of approval or ordination by the Church, which, as we will see in later chapters (4–5) gave them their prominence, and their voices in the affairs of State and Church.

75. See now W. Harmless, *Desert Christians: An Introduction to the Literature of Early Monasticism* (2004), essentially devoted to Egyptian ascetics.

76. See C. Rapp, "Palladius, Lausus and the *Historia Lausiaca*," in *Novum Millennium: Studies on Byzantine History and Culture dedicated to Paul Speck*, ed. C. Sode and S. Takács (2001), 279 ff.

77. Details of editions, commentaries, and translations are provided after Abbreviations, on pp. xxiii–xxvi.

78. See now A. Sterk, *Renouncing the World yet Leading the Church:The Monk-bishop in Late Antiquity* (2004).

"Voice" might mean, in their case, actual speaking before Church Councils (at Ephesus in 449 on the personal invitation of the Emperor) or before the Emperor in person. They might also write to the Emperor to persuade him to persevere in one course, or drop another. But writing to the Emperor, or to high officials or—very significantly—to his powerful sister, Pulcheria, or to his wife, Eudocia, was normally the preserve of bishops. With that, with the Christian letter as the vehicle for the exposition of doctrine, for the correction of doctrinal error, for persuasion or protest, we come to the last of the characteristic literary forms of the period. Again, we may briefly recall some of the major examples of episcopal correspondence from the reign, from Cyril of Alexandria, Nestorius, Proclus, Firmus of Caesarea in Cappadocia, Isidorus, a presbyter at Pelusium with over two thousand letters to his name, and above all (once again) Theodoret, bishop of Cyrrhus in Euphratesia from 423 onwards.

The surviving letters of bishops from Theodosius's domains, addressed to the Emperor himself, or his wife or sister (or in one case sisters), or to Imperial officials, are a very distinctive feature of the political culture of the time. To stress these particular letters is, to be sure, potentially misleading. For by definition it is to fail to set these letters in their wider context, namely the letters, in enormous numbers, which were addressed by bishops to each other. These will have been, without exception, in Greek, and so also will every single one of those addressed to representatives of the State; equally, as we have seen, when holders of office wrote to bishops or clergy, they too wrote in Greek.

Letters should be seen as the most significant literary form in which the "rhetoric of empire" was expressed, and the most important vehicle of influence at a distance, in an Empire where the exercise of power was conducted, in both the secular and the religious sphere (which cannot always be separated anyway), against a barrage of persuasion fired off by interested parties, convinced that they had either rights or privileges on the one hand, or the key to correct belief on the other. In the context of the Church, another essential vehicle of persuasion was the homily, or sermon—in the first instance, of course, as delivered orally to a congregation. As mentioned earlier, in connection with the diffusion of churches, especially into rural contexts, the spoken Christian homily must have been one of the fundamental vehicles of persuasion and information (and of the spread of educated Greek discourse, based on a sacred text in Greek). But, as the *Acta* of the Councils abundantly show, written texts of homilies, when incorporated in dossiers bearing on disputed theological issues, contributed important material for persuasion, and could be laid before secular holders of power as well as before meetings of bishops.[79]

6. LETTERS AND THE RHETORIC OF PERSUASION

Homilies should thus be seen, like letters, as key elements in the literary culture of the fifth-century Greek world, as examples of rhetoric, as expressions of belief, and as forms of reasoning which could be directed to the holders of power. Nonetheless, it was the letter, written in Greek, which was the essential vehicle of persuasion, along with the closely allied form of the petition setting out wrongs and demanding their correction. The evidence provides many examples of petitions, both as deployed within the context of the Church, and as directed to secular authorities or the Emperor. Paradoxically, it was those which were deployed within the Church for which the transliterated Latin term *libellus* tended to be used.[80] A petition addressed to the Emperor (or rather, notionally, to both Emperors) was a *deēsis* and *hikesia*, like that of bishop Appion of Syene, referred to earlier (p. 22), or the petition addressed to Theodosius (and Valentinian) by a group of monks in Constantinople against oppression by Nestorius,[81] or from another group of clergy in Constantinople in 431.[82] In Latin such a petition was referred to as *preces,* as in the papyrus with Appion's petition, and as in the Imperial letter of 419 to the Praetorian Prefect, referring to the petition of bishop Asclepiades of Chersonesus.[83] Alternatively, a written submission to the Emperor by one or more bishops could be called an *anaphora,* and (as we have seen with the inscriptions from Mylasa, pp. 21–22 above) the same word was used in Greek to describe a *suggestio* sent by an official to the Emperor. In one of the most striking of the letters of Synesius, to which we will return in chapter 2, he supplies the local military commander with the content of two *anaphorai* which he is asked to send to the Emperor. Duly translated into Latin, as used in internal official communications, these would be *suggestiones.*

79. A corpus of contemporary homilies, collected from *ACO* would be of great value.

80. For examples found in the *Acta* of petitions deployed within the Church, and described as *libelloi,* see: *ACO* I.1.3, para. 88 (pp. 16–17); *ACO* I.1.4, para. 122 (pp. 6–7); *ACO* I.1.7, para. 81 (pp. 118–19); I.1.7, para. 82 (pp. 122–23); I.1.7, paras. 93–94 (pp. 139–40); *ACO* II.1.1, para. 225 (pp. 100–101); II.1.2, para. 47 (pp. 15–16 [211–12]); para. 51 (pp. 17–19 [213–15]). Again, there are other examples, and the genre would deserve study in its own right.

81. *ACO* I.1.5, para. 143 (pp. 7–10). See pp. 155–57 below.

82. *ACO* I.1.3, para. 103 (pp. 49–50).

83. P. 11 above and pp. 77–78 below.

Thus, to repeat, the Imperial "laws" written in Latin, which can be found in the *Codex Theodosianus* and other collections, have to be read as letters to individual office-holders, very often as replies to specific *suggestiones,* and more generally as responses to problems arising in particular local contexts in the Greek empire, problems which will in every case have been brought to the attention of the relevant official in Greek. Our evidence is biased to Christian, or ecclesiastical, material, not least in the form of the enormous volume of evidence for the period from 428 onwards supplied by the *Acta* of the Councils. All the same, the role of the Church, and of individual bishops, in generating persuasion addressed to officials and the Emperor is beyond question; and, as we have noted, and will see in more detail later, an extra force was lent to Christian persuasion by the prestige enjoyed by monks.

Two other features of the complex interactions between subject and State need to be mentioned now, to be explored more fully later. Firstly, repeated reference has been made to the way in which material generated by either the lay population or the Church was expressed first in Greek, and needed then to be converted into Latin if it were to form the content of official letters; and correspondingly, that Imperial "laws" were expressed, almost without exception, in Latin, but needed either to be translated as they stood or to be converted into edicts *(diatagmata)* in Greek if they were to become known to the people; as we will see below (pp. 176–78) a Greek text of an Imperial letter might be posted up and accompanied by an edict in Greek from the Praetorian Prefect. The evidence from the Councils shows beyond doubt that the training received by the ordinary educated person did not produce an assured comprehension of either spoken or written Latin. So, for all the different ranks of Imperial officialdom, drawn from all quarters of the Empire, the acquisition of Latin must have been a necessary extra qualification, a requirement for the holding of public office. The official documentation of the period, written in Latin, was the work of men whose native language was Greek. We will look later at the officials who conducted the government of the Empire. But to take only one example, Flavius Dionysius, Magister Ultriusque Militiae in 431, was from Thrace. When he wrote in Greek to the clergy of Cyprus, he was using his native language; when he wrote at the same time to the Consularis of Cyprus, he had to switch into a second, learned language, Latin.[84]

The second distinctive feature of the public communications of the period is that both the preeminent prestige attached to personal piety and

84. *PLRE* II Dionysius 13; see p. 21 above.

the reputation for piety enjoyed by the Imperial household gave a unique prominence to the women of the household: above all to Pulcheria, Theodosius's powerful elder sister, born two years before him. It accrued to a lesser degree to his younger sisters, Arcadia and Marina, and later to his wife, Aelia Eudocia, whom he married in 421. Various studies have covered the role of women at court under Theodosius, and especially a major work by Kenneth Holum;[85] but none, to my knowledge, has stressed the significance of the fact that persons seeking to influence Imperial decisions might write formal letters to these ladies.[86] Again, we shall return to this theme in the context of the wide range of people at court, or in high office, whom contemporaries perceived as being relevant to the formation of public policy (chapter 6). The writing of letters, which would subsequently form part of dossiers that were in general circulation, is something much more significant than the reports of behind-the-scenes influence characteristic of earlier periods. It implies that the Imperial women in question, Pulcheria in particular, had a recognized role in the formation of decisions.

In contrast with this slight, but highly significant, scatter of approaches, all in Greek, from within the Theodosian Empire, we have the letters to female members of Theodosius's family from the Latin West. They too represent merely an aspect of a wider correspondence, naturally all in Latin, which Theodosius received either from his co-Emperor of the time (Honorius, and then Valentinian III) or from successive bishops of Rome, above all Leo the Great (440–61). We may note also a passing allusion to the fact that the bishop of Milan, Martin, sent Theodosius a copy of the *On the Incarnation* of his great predecessor, Ambrose.[87] We will look later at the intense (and, until the Emperor's sudden death, unavailing) pressure which Leo of Rome, acting partly through members of the Western Imperial family, exercised on Theo-

---

85. *Theodosian Empresses: Women and Imperial Dominion in Late Antiquity* (1982), in my view the best introduction not only to the history of the Theodosian dynasty and to the politics of the reign, but to the religious issues in which the court was involved. See also L. James, *Empresses and Power in Early Byzantium* (2001).

86. Note (1) *ACO* I.1.5, para. 149 (pp. 26–61), Cyril of Alexandria, *Logos Prosphōnētikos* addressed to the "Empresses" (Pulcheria and Eudocia), c. Mar. 430; (2) ACO I.1.5, para. 150 (pp. 62–118), Cyril, *Logos Prosphōnētikos* to "the most pious mistresses" (Arcadia and Marina), c. Mar. 430 (note *ACO* I.1.1, para. 8, [pp. 73–74], Theodosius complaining to Cyril about his having written to Pulcheria and Eudocia, autumn 430?); (3) *ACO* I.1.5, para. 160 (pp. 131–32), "Easterners" at Ephesus to "Empresses," Jun./Jul. 431; (4) *ACO* I.4, no. 223 (pp. 162–63) bishops of Euphratensis to Augustae, 434? (Latin translation of Greek original); (5) Theodoret, *Epp.* II. 43 to Pulcheria Augusta, 446/7.

87. *ACO* I.1.3, para. 97 (pp. 41–42).

dosius in 449–50, before and after the Second Council of Ephesus (chapter 6). This is another reminder that what we are speaking of is one of a pair of Empires, or twin Empires, not two separate powers—and that, as regards the Emperor, who was certainly bilingual,[88] any interested party in the West could express himself in Latin. But one item from the correspondence of this period deserves a special emphasis in advance, since, more than any other, it serves to underline the distinctiveness of this phase in the history of the Imperial government. For it is, to the best of the author's knowledge, the only example from the whole of antiquity of a letter dealing with a major matter of policy, which was written by one woman and addressed to another.

The context, as we will see in more detail later, was the pressure applied by Pope Leo for Theodosius to convene a Council in Italy which would undo the scandalous results of the Second Council of Ephesus. To this end, Leo himself wrote to both Theodosius and to Pulcheria.[89] But he also petitioned the Roman branch of the Imperial family in Italy to write to their opposite numbers in Constantinople. It was thus that early in 450 Galla Placidia, the half-sister of Arcadius, Theodosius's father, and the mother of Valentinian III, sent a strongly worded letter to Pulcheria.[90] Galla Placidia was now about sixty-two, and Pulcheria fifty. Given the importance which Theodosius, as the senior Emperor, attached to the defense of Ephesus II, and given the already growing tension between Rome and Constantinople over authority in the Church, whose long-term significance hardly needs to be stressed, the content of the letter represents no marginal matter of intercession or personal benefit, but the most serious possible aspect of Imperial policy. The letter, preserved in the correspondence of Leo, seems never to have been translated into English.[91] After recalling the approach made to her and other members of the western Imperial family by Leo on their return to Rome (in February 450), Placidia speaks of the improper deposition of the bishop of Constantinople (Flavianus), and of the scandalousness of the proceedings at the Council. She then concludes in uncompromising terms:

88. Note however that it is in fact Theodosius's sister Pulcheria to whom Sozomenus (*HE* IX.1) attributes the ability to speak and write both Greek and Latin with complete accuracy.

89. Leo to Theodosius: *Epp.* 44 = *ACO* II.4, para. 18 (pp. 19–21); *Epp.* 45 = *ACO* II.4, para. 23 (pp. 23–25); *Epp.* 54 = *ACO* II.4, para. 9 (p. 118). Leo to Pulcheria: *Epp.* 60 = *ACO* II.4, para. 28 (p. 29). See pp. 230–31 below.

90. Leo, *Epp.* 58 = *ACO* II.3.1, para. 18 (p. 13): Galla Placidia Augusta to Aelia Pulcheria Augusta.

91. It is not translated even in the illuminating study by S. I. Oost, *Galla Placidia Augusta: A Biographical Essay* (1968).

So it is appropriate, most holy and venerable daughter Augusta, that piety should prevail. Therefore, may your clemency, in accordance with the Catholic faith, once again, as it always has along with us, now in the same way share our objectives, so that whatever was done at that disorderly and most wretched council should by every effort be subverted, and with all the issues remaining in suspense, that the case of the episcopal see [of Constantinople] should be referred to the Apostolic see, in which the blessed Peter, the first of the Apostles, who also held the keys of the heavenly kingdoms, was the prince of bishops. For we ought in all things, in our immortal conduct, to yield the primacy to that city which filled the whole world with the domination of its own *virtus,* and committed the globe to being governed and preserved by our empire.

As we will see later, Pulcheria evidently agreed on the need for a new Council, but could not act until her brother's accidental death at the end of July. At that, she brought Marcian to the throne, and married him, and by October 451 the new Council was in session, and duly reversed the measures taken at Ephesus II. But it was not held in the West, but at Chalcedon, so that the new Emperor could easily attend, and where the proceedings would be in Greek. It also widened the breach between Rome and Constantinople, and, in its immensely detailed proceedings, rehearsed word for word many of the most intense debates and conflicts which had marked not only Ephesus II itself but a whole series of other confrontations that had characterized the interaction of Church and State in the latter years of the "Greek Roman Empire" under Theodosius II.

II   Security and Insecurity

1. INTRODUCTION

In April 428 the newly elected bishop of Constantinople, in his first sermon, apparently preached in the presence of the Emperor himself, uttered words whose arrogance and presumption caused outrage, and began the series of conflicts which led to his deposition only three years later: "Give me, King, the earth purged of heretics, and I will give you heaven in return. Aid me in destroying heretics, and I will assist you in vanquishing the Persians."[1] How the empire of Theodosius functioned in relation to groups within its borders—heretics, pagans, Jews, Samaritans—who were perceived as dissenting from the truth ordained by God, we will examine later (chapter 3). But Nestorius's scandalous utterance was a true, if rhetorically exaggerated, reflection of fundamental features of the Greek Roman Empire of his time: the integral relation between Church and State; the absorption into the Church, or into Imperial service, of men from all corners of the Greek-speaking world (Nestorius came from the very modest city of Germanicia in Euphratensis); the centrality of military success in the ideology of the Empire; and the constant pressure of persuasion which assailed the Emperor in every sphere, from the maintenance of correct belief and appropriate practice in the Church to the provision of security along the frontiers.

Nestorius's words are indicative and characteristic also in implying, or indeed directly stating, an organic connection between correct belief and military success, and this is a theme which reappears constantly in contemporary narrative accounts of the reign, whether it is the contrast with the great

---

1. Socrates, *HE* VII.29.5.

military disasters which marked the history of the twin Empire in the West, or conflicts with the Huns or with the Persians themselves. On occasion, indeed, clerical groups seeking to influence the emperor could deploy an assumption that he had an active mission, or responsibility, for the protection of Christians in the Persian Empire. Thus we find that Nestorius's supporters at the Council of Ephesus in 431, in writing one of innumerable missives to Theodosius, both compare the followers of his great opponent, Cyril of Alexandria, to barbarians taking part in a raid, and argue from the Emperor's role as protector of the churches in Persia and elsewhere to his duty to protect those inside the Empire:[2]

> We therefore implore and beseech your Majesty to bring speedy help to afflicted orthodoxy and to inflict prompt correction on their madness and tyranny, which like a violent cloudburst sweeps the most audacious into heretical perfidy. It is right that your Piety, which has assured the protection of the churches in Persia and among the barbarians, should not neglect the battered churches in the Roman Empire.

We will see that the Emperor did indeed on occasion show concern for Christians in the Sasanid Empire. But any notion that his unquestionable sense of Christian mission was accompanied by an active imperialism, seeking either to extend the bounds of the Empire or to use force to reunite its two halves, would be quite misleading. There would be no trace of any ambition to imitate the disastrous campaign of the Emperor Julian in 363 into the heart of the Sasanid empire, namely Babylonia (Iraq)—a story told in at least one pagan history completed early in Theodosius's reign, that of Eunapius, and in no fewer than four ecclesiastical histories from the later years, those of Philostorgius, Socrates, Sozomenus, and Theodoret.[3] Nor did the Emperor seek to take advantage of the death of his uncle Honorius in 423, and the regime in the West of a usurper, Ioannes, in 423–25, to reintegrate the two halves of the Empire. As will become clear later, the installation of the young Valentinian as Emperor in the West, achieved by a military expedition in 425, was a major event in Theodosius's reign, and must also be seen as the essential background to his project for a codification, or at least collection, of late Roman law (or rather "laws").[4] But, however much the *Codex Theodosianus*, projected in 429 and completed in 437, was intended as both a symbol and a functional expression of Imperial unity, the reality

---

2. *ACO* I.1.5, para. 158 (pp. 129–31).
3. Eunapius (ed. Blockley), F. 27–29; Philostorgius, *HE* V–VII (fragments only); Socrates, *HE* III; Sozomenus, *HE* V–VI.2; Theodoret, *HE* III.
4. See pp. 54–57 below.

fell far short of that. In practice there were still two Imperial courts, two separate administrative and tax-gathering structures, and two armies.

That is not to say that the fortunes, and the generally disastrous military history, of the western Empire were not of due concern throughout Theodosius's reign, and all the more so after the Vandal settlement in Africa, and their capture of Carthage in 439. Looking back on the very first year of Theodosius, Sozomenus could still contrast the catastrophes which struck the West with the stability which marked the East. Apparently minimizing the disruption currently being caused by the Huns in Thrace and Moesia (see pp. 80–83), Sozomenus writes:[5]

> Thus was the Eastern Empire preserved from the evils of war, and governed with high order, contrary to all expectations, for its ruler was still young. In the meantime, the Western Empire fell a prey to disorders, because many tyrants arose.

By "tyrants" he means "usurpers," and we will see also how closely their fortunes, and the eventual fall of each, were followed in Constantinople. Overall, both the internal stability of Theodosius's reign, which did not witness even any attempted usurpations, and its external success were indeed remarkable. But in the 440s, when Sozomenus was writing, a major threat had arisen in the form of the Huns under Attila, and a very powerful sense of danger pervades both contemporary writing and later accounts of these years. The most important and detailed of these is that of Priscus, writing in the second half of the century, after participating personally in key episodes on the Danubian frontier in the 440s. His impression of how the strategic situation had looked in 447, in the face of demands by Attila, deserves quotation:[6]

> For the barbarian, mindful of the Romans' liberality, which they showed out of caution lest the treaty be broken, sent to them those of his retinue whom he wished to benefit, inventing new reasons and discovering new pretexts. The Romans heeded his every bidding and obeyed whatever order their master issued. They were not only wary of starting a war with Attila, but they were afraid also of the Parthians [Persians], who were preparing for hostilities, the Vandals who were harrying the coastal regions, the Isaurians whose banditry was reviving, the Saracens who were ravaging the eastern parts of their dominions, and the Ethiopian tribes who were in the process of uniting. Therefore, having been humbled by Attila, they paid him court while

---

5. Sozomenus, *HE* IX.6.1, trans. Hartranft.
6. Priscus (ed. and trans. Blockley), F. 10.

they tried to organize themselves to face the other peoples by collecting their forces and appointing generals.

We shall come back later to the context of the threat of the Huns in the 440s, but for the moment it will be enough to repeat that, in contemporary conceptions, the military success which would be the reward of Imperial piety and of the imposition of correct belief would be a defensive one, the protection of the Empire against outside enemies from all sides (and one from inside, namely the Isaurians of southern Asia Minor). The sense of menace is reflected also in works written far from the center, for instance in the long chapter of Theodoret's *History of the Monks of Syria* about Symeon Stylites:[7]

> He once had a vision of two rods borne from the heavens, one falling to the ground on the east and one on the west. The holy man interpreted these as the rising of the Persian and the Scythian nations against the Roman Empire. He explained the vision to those present and by abundant tears and ceaseless prayers he arrested the blows aimed at the (Roman) world . . .

Even more vivid is the description provided by Callinicus in his *Life* of Hypatius, the head of the monastery of Rufinianae in Constantinople, who died in 446. After his death, natural and man-made disasters had coincided:[8]

> For within five months there took place the great earthquakes, which continued for some time, and the barbarian race of the Huns which was in Thrace became so great that more than a hundred cities were taken, Constantinople was all but in danger and most fled from her. It got to the point that the monks wanted to flee to Jerusalem, for fear that they (the Huns) had approached and would sack Constantinople.

In the face of such circumstances, it was natural to conclude that piety and correct belief had not been successfully pursued, and that it was this failing which had led to disaster. The ever-polemical Nestorius, still in exile for his beliefs far away in the Oasis in Egypt, was hardly going to miss this opportunity. In his combative, semiautobiographical work, *The Bazaar* (or *Book*) *of Heraclides,* he took the new-found unity of the Huns and their successes against the Empire as a sign of God's wrath, caused by the heretical "one-nature" theology under which it was impossible to separate God the Word from the human who suffered on the Cross.[9]

It was not, however, merely at the level of theology or of historical ex-

7. Theodoret, *HR* XXVI.19, trans. Price.
8. Callinicus, *V. Hypatii* 52.
9. See the trans. by F. Nau, pp. 317–19; by Driver and Hodgson, pp. 363–68. On Nestorius and his polemical writing, see more fully chapter 5.

planation that a link was perceived between religious belief and military success or failure. It was also that arguments, disputes, and claims about rights and obligations which are directly parallel to those which marked the relations of the Church to the Emperor also lie behind a large proportion of the "laws" issued by the Emperor in the form of letters to his high officials; in a few cases, indeed, we can find what is actually the same document— whether in its Greek or its Latin form—incorporated both in the *Acta* of one or other of the three fifth-century Councils and in the *Codex Theodosianus* or *Codex Justinianus*.[10]

Those specific cases apart, we will also shortly see three episodes in which propositions or requests relating either to military dispositions or to relations with barbarians, and addressed, directly or indirectly, to the Emperor, emanate from bishops representing the interests of their sees or of individuals in their congregations. As such, these requests merely parallel the much larger number of letters from bishops—Theodoret above all—and other clergy raising issues of civil government, justice, or taxation.

Neither the Emperor nor his subjects would have needed reminding of the contemporary doctrine of "frontier studies:" that a frontier cannot be seen just as a line on the map, possibly garrisoned, or marked by a chain of military posts, but has to be studied as a complex zone of human, commercial, juridical, and cultural interactions, both with the "enemy" and between the army, and individual soldiers, and the population among whom they were stationed.[11] Our evidence reveals a flow of information, requests, and complaints from the most remote frontiers to the political center, and a return flow of orders, general and particular, often marked, like Imperial pronouncements of all kinds, by the rhetoric of self-justification.[12] Issues of these types play a large part in the *Codex Theodosianus* and the *Novellae:* for instance, civilians should not occupy *castella* intended for soldiers;[13] in reply to an

---

10. The three cases, each extremely important for the nature of the documentation available for the reign, are: (1) *CTh* IX.45.4 + *CJ* I.12.3 + *ACO* I.1.4, para. 137 (pp. 61–65), law on asylum in church, 431; see further chapter 4, pp. 142–45; (2) *CTh* XVI.5.66 +*CJ* I.5.6 + *ACO* I.1.3, para. 111 (p. 68) + I.4, para. 280 (p.204), banning of Nestorian teaching, 435; (3) *CJ* I.1.3 + *ACO* I.1.4, paras. 138–39 (pp. 66–67), 448, also against Nestorian doctrines. For (2) and (3) see chapter 5, pp. 176–78 and 184–89.

11. See, for example, C. R. Whittaker, *Frontiers of the Roman Empire: A Social and Economic Study* (1994).

12. For this theme see F. Millar, "De la frontière au centre: la monarchie centralisée de Théodose II (408–450 ap. J.-C.)," in *La mobilité des personnes en Méditerranée, de l'Antiquité à l'époque moderne. Procédures de contrôle et documents d'identification*, ed. C. Moatti (2004), 567 ff.

13. *CTh* VII.15.2 (*CJ* XI.60.2), Mar. 7, 423.

adsertio from the Magister Militum, frontier troops *(limitanei)* should not be summoned to Court to answer petitions from civilians;[14] in reply to a *suggestio* from the Praetorian Prefect, individuals should not seek military rank to qualify themselves as lessees.[15]

As is clear, in these and innumerable other cases, such rulings, or "laws," very often arose from particular circumstances. Sweeping general laws, laying down a new system, are much less common. One example, however, comes from 443, nearly at the height of the military crisis created by Attila, when a very extensive, and quite novel, supervisory role was conferred on one of the most influential figures at Court, Nomus, the Magister Officiorum.[16] The law is typical of the much fuller and more extensive (and verbose and rhetorical) texts which derive from the *Novellae* and not from the truncated versions quoted in the *Codex*, and is untypical of these only in not deriving from a *suggestio* from a particular official. The overall purpose is propriety and the eradication of corruption, in the appointment of *duces* (commanders of frontier troops), and in their handling of provisions intended for barbarian allies, and of extortion from soldiers by their supreme commanders, the Magistri Militum. The agricultural lands *(prata)* reserved for the frontier troops should also be protected.

The extensive text of the law, written as always in the form of a personal letter, ends with unprecedented arrangements for annual reports from the different frontiers, which may serve to give an impression both of the geographical scale of these frontiers—which stretched for some five thousand kilometers in all, in a discontinuous half circle from the middle Danube to Libya—and of the ideas that information could be transmitted back effectively to the Emperor in Constantinople, and that the system could and should be made known to all:

> Moreover, We believe that this must be enjoined as a perpetual responsibility upon Your Excellency, namely, that annually in the month of January in the sacred imperial consistory, you shall take care to indicate to Us by your own report, how the number of soldiers is faring and how the care of the camps and of the river patrol boats of the borders of Thrace as well as of Illyricum, and also of the Orient and of Pontus, and in addition, those of Egyptian Thebes and Libya, is proceeding. Thus when the industry as well as the indolence of each person is made known to Our ears, the diligent may obtain worthy rewards, and suitable indig-

---

14. *Nov. Th.* 4, Feb. 25, 438. More fully on p. 75 below.
15. *Nov. Th.* 7.1 (*CJ* III.25.1), Jan. 20, 439.
16. *Nov. Th.* 24 (*CJ* I.31.4 + I.46.4 + XI.60.3), Sept. 12, 443, trans. Pharr. For Nomus see *PLRE* II, Nomus 1, and chapter 6, pp. 192–94, below.

nation may be visited upon the pretenders. For We believe that if military affairs should be observed in the manner in which We have decreed, in whatever lands the enemy should attempt to move himself against us, a victory which is propitious to Us, according to the will of God, will be announced even before the battle, O Nomus, most beloved Brother.

Therefore Your Illustrious Authority, whose inviolate loyalty Our Eternity has proved by actual events, shall command this general and most salutary sanction of Our Clemency to be delivered to perpetual enforcement and execution, and by posting edicts everywhere you shall cause it to come to the knowledge of all.

Given on the day before the ides of September at Constantinople in the year of the second consulship of the Most Noble Maximus and the consulship of the most Noble Paterius. —September 12, 443.

2. THE MILITARY STRUCTURE

A vivid, concrete, but also extraordinarily incomplete, picture of what we mean by the army of the "Greek Roman Empire" is provided by the *Notitia Dignitatum*, whose eastern half was composed in Latin apparently in about 401.[17] The army which it (erratically) lists has been estimated by Warren Treadgold at some three hundred thousand men, a reasonable estimate from which there is no reason to depart.[18] What the *Notitia* does, in the case of its military sections, is to structure the information by the major officials, then listing the various units which served under each.[19] The strength of the document is its very clear specification of the upper ranks of the military hierarchy, and its detailed listing of all the units of different types. Its fatal weakness, if we wish to understand the nature of the presence of the army within the Empire and along its frontiers, is that it is only in the case of frontier troops, or to be more precise of those under the command of middle-ranking officers—Comites and Duces—that the location of each unit is indicated.

In terms of status, therefore, we begin with two "Masters of the Soldiers" (Magistri Militum) "in the (Imperial) presence," each with a list of units under their command (*Not. Dig.* ch. V–VI). We have to presume, but do not

17. See pp. 5–6 above.

18. See W. Treadgold, *Byzantium and Its Army, 284–1081* (1995), ch. 2, with the schematic map on p. 48, from which figure VII is copied.

19. For the fullest treatment, see D. Hoffmann, *Das spätrömische Bewegungsheer und die Notitia Dignitatum,* 2 vols. (1969–70), from which the two maps of military dispositions on the Danube frontier (figure VIII), and in Oriens (figure IX) are derived.

strictly know, that these were stationed either in Constantinople or near it. Then we find that the Empire divides, for military purposes, into three zones under regional Magistri Militum, contrasting with the two civilian Praetorian Prefectures: the three regions are Oriens (ch. VII), Thraciae (VIII), and Illyricum (IX). In other words, the Thracian (east Balkan) area, which in the civil hierarchy fell rather anomalously under the Praetorian Prefect of Oriens, constituted a separate zone within the military structure.

These dry details are necessary because of some anomalous and unexpected features in the structure of our evidence (whether these features really mirror the actual working of the Empire is a more difficult question). As we saw in chapter 1, the vast majority of the "laws" issued by the Emperor were letters addressed to one or other Praetorian Prefect, and much more often to the Prefect of Oriens than to that of Illyricum. It was normally the role of the Prefect to disseminate the Imperial command to lower officials. Occasionally, as we will see later, elaborate instructions are given as to which other officials are to be informed. For the moment all that we need note is that the seven civil officials in charge of regions ("dioceses"), the Vicarii of Macedonia and Dacia, under the Prefect of Illyricum, and the Vicarii of Thraciae, Asiana, and Pontica, along with the Comes Orientis and Praefectus Augustalis (of Egypt), all under the Prefect of Oriens, play a very modest part in the Imperial legislation, either as receiving Imperial letters, or even as being referred to in those addressed to Prefects, while the civilian governors of the individual provinces play even less.

We will return to the working structure of the state in chapter 4, "State and Church," but the reason for recalling both the bare facts and the relative invisibility of the civil hierarchy is that the Magistri Militum play a larger role than might be expected, and one which seems very clearly to extend into what we would have presumed to be the civilian sphere. We have already seen one striking example, namely the fact that it was the Magister Militum in Oriens, Flavius Dionysius, stationed at Antioch, who in 431 chose, or (as was alleged) was persuaded by power-hungry Antiochene clergy, to issue procedural guidelines for the election of a bishop in Cyprus.[20]

Magistri Militum have a number of "laws" addressed to them directly by the Emperor, several, it is true, relating to the perennial topic of the statuses, rights, and obligations of those serving under them.[21] But two per-

---

20. *ACO* I.1.7, para. 81 (pp. 119–21). See chapter 1, pp. 20–22, and chapter 4, pp. 137–39.

21. For example, *CTh* XII.1.175, May 12, 412; *CTh* I.7.4 (*CJ* I.29.2), Dec. 13, 414; *CTh* VIII.1.15, Mar. 16, 415; *CTh* I.8.1, Oct. 15, 415, following a report from the

haps deserve mention as illustrating the way in which communication, persuasion, and decision functioned, on the military side of the Imperial structure as well as the civilian. The first is a letter of 441 from Theodosius to Ariobindus, Magister Militum, in reply to a *suggestio* from Ariobindus on the question of whether members of his staff *(apparitores)* could enjoy the privilege granted to soldiers, of being able to have cases heard before a special court *(praescriptio fori)*. The decision is that up to three hundred of them may do so, and that *edicta* should be posted to announce this. A copy is also sent to another Magister Militum, Aspar, apparently in Oriens, and also to Cyrus, Praetorian Prefect of Oriens.[22] Though the topic will not be pursued in detail in this study, such a letter is a reminder that, in rewarding its own officials while preserving differentials of status, the late Roman State faced complexities no less insistent than those raised by issues of doctrine, practice, and hierarchy within the Church.[23] In both cases competitive persuasion played a significant part. Secondly, a closely comparable issue—the rights of retired *numerarii* of a Magister Militum—arises in a letter of the mid-440s addressed to a Magister Militum Praesentalis and to the then Magister Militum per Orientem, Anatolius. The fact that this is the only appearance of the term "Praesentalis" in the legal documents from Theodosius's reign illustrates how erratic our evidence is. Anatolius, however, as we will see later, plays a large part in relations with Church and society in Oriens, in ways which seem in no way to be distinctively "military."[24]

The second of the two general "laws" mentioned above belongs much earlier in the reign, and illustrates the complexity of the issues with which the Emperor, or those determining matters in his name, had to deal, and also the way in which military and civilian matters overlapped (just as soldiers and civilians did in ordinary life). On September 5, 415, Theodosius wrote to the Praetorian Prefect of Oriens, Aurelianus, limiting the tax obligations of landowners, and saying that soldiers must not take possession of any fields *(prata)* not covered by a specific Imperial act of largesse *(largitas)*. On the same day he wrote what was evidently a circular letter to the "Comites"

Quaestor (Sacri) Palatii, and with copies to another Magister Militum, to the Magister Officiorum, and to the Quaestor himself; *CJ* III.21.2, May 31, 423.

22. *Nov. Th.* 7.4, Mar. 6, 441. See *PLRE* II, Ariobindus 2; Fl. Ardabur Aspar; Fl. Taurus Seleucus Cyrus 7.

23. For issues relating to Imperial officials, see now C. Kelly, *Governing the Later Roman Empire* (2004).

24. *CJ* XII.54.4 (443/6). For Anatolius see *PLRE* II, Anatolius 10, and pp. 96 and 198, below.

(which ones, is not indicated in the surviving address) and the Magistri Militum (presumably all five) to notify them of the "law" *(lex)* on *prata* which had been promulgated. As always, the copy which we have is a letter addressed to a single individual ("your Magnificence"); between them, the paired documents illustrate perfectly the principle that what was a letter in form was conceived of as a "law" in content.[25]

As we noted earlier, the forces under the five Magistri Militum are listed in the *Notitia* of about 401; but nothing is said about where they were stationed, or how they were distributed over the different provinces of the Empire. So, as regards this vital aspect of the functioning of the State and the nature of its interactions with its subjects, we are almost entirely in the dark. Figure VII gives a schematic presentation, taken from the work of Warren Treadgold, of the forces of the Empire.

That situation changes when we come to the forces under officers of the next two levels, Comites and Duces, namely the frontier troops who are presumably the ones referred to in legal sources as *limitanei*. So we find in Illyricum a Dux of Moesia I (*Notitia*, ch. XLI) with twenty-seven units and two fleets under his command. The station of each unit is indicated. Three of these units are legions, and the map in Fig. VIII indicates for Moesia I, as for the other provinces along the Danube, the locations of the legions, as a sample of the full pattern of distribution of units of all types. The location of each of the three legions is shown—from west to east, Singidunum, Viminacium, and Cuppae, all directly on the Danube. In other words we are in the extreme northwest corner of what would soon be Theodosius's empire, and in an area of which (as at all periods) our literary sources reveal little, and to which we will return only with the remarkably detailed narrative of Priscus on operations against Attila (pp. 80–82 below).

Also in Illyricum comes the province of Dacia Ripensis (*Notitia*, ch. XLII), whose forces, again under a Dux, consisted of thirty units and two fleets. In this central section of the frontier there were nine legions, which will have been of the reduced size typical of the late Empire, and of which the positions of seven can be identified. West to East along the Danube, they run: Transdrobeta (apparently on the northern bank), Egeta, Ratiaria, Cebrus, Variana, and Oescus, with Sucidava across the bridge on the northern bank.

In the military command of Thraciae, there were again two provinces along the Danube, each under a Dux. First comes Moesia II (*Notitia*, ch. XL) with twenty-two units (and one fleet), of which six are listed as "legiones

25. *CTh* VII.7.4–5 (*CJ* XI.61.3).

riparienses"— riverbank legions: west to east, they were stationed at Novae (two legions), Sexaginta Prista, Transmarisca (two legions), and Durostorum. It may be noted that this lower-Danube area was less remote from the
concerns of the central Greek-speaking area of the Empire, and bishops functioning in Greek come to one or other of the Church Councils from both
Novae and Durostorum (p. 17 above).

Finally, we come to what was now known as "Scythia," the zone between
the Black Sea and the substantial stretch of the Danube where it runs north
before turning to the sea. The province contained ancient Greek cities such
as Histria and Tomoi, but may well also have contained a Latin-speaking
population. The forces under its Dux are listed in *Notitia* XXXIX: twenty-
three units, of which seven were legions. Four different stations can be
identified: Axiopolis, Troesmis, Noviodunum (two legions), and Aegissus.

A sketch of this remote frontier is necessary, both as an important element in what the Empire of Theodosius consisted of and because, for all the
relatively low profile it can claim in the abundant literature of the reign (including Imperial "laws"), it was the successful maintenance of this line which
made possible the survival of the Empire.

The Magister Militum of Oriens commanded a much more extensive and
more varied series of frontier areas. It will not be necessary to follow the
disposition of forces in the same detail (for a map indicating the positions
of these legions, see figure IX), but rather to indicate some key features, and
some significant anomalies. All along the eastern frontier there were forces
grouped under Duces: in Armenia and Pontus (*Notitia* XXXVIII), Mesopotamia (XXXVI), Osrhoena (XXXV), Euphratensis and Syria (XXXIII),
Phoenice Libanensis (XXXII), Arabia (XXXVII) and Palaestina (XXXIV)—
meaning Palaestina Tertia or Salutaris, now embracing the Negev and southern Transjordan, including Petra, and stretching down to the Red Sea. Along
this line the northern half clearly owed its structure to the potential threat
from the still-pagan Sasanid Persia; but both there and, predominantly, in
the southern half, the map itself demonstrates that the primary military mission was policing the border between cultivated land and the steppe, and between cultivators and nomads.

Egypt was a separate military zone, with an officer of superior rank, the
"Comes of the Egyptian Limes" (forces listed in *Notitia* XXVIII), and two
Duces, of the Thebaid (XXXI) and the two Libyas (XXX). Given the very
significant information which Synesius provides for the military situation
in Libya (pp. 59–62 below), it is unfortunate that the list of units for this
area is missing in the manuscript of the *Notitia*. But the great anomaly in
the military structure of Oriens is the second "Comes" who served there,

the "Comes per Isauriam," whose forces are listed in ch. XXIX—with two legions, whose stations are not indicated.

In short, this mountainous zone, under a very senior officer, was an internal frontier, whose unsubdued population posed a major threat. It was not merely that they were unsubdued, but that they carried out raids down to the sea and across into Syria and Palestine. As with other aspects of fifth-century life, the most vivid accounts of living in the shadow of the Isaurian threat are provided by the *Life and Miracles of S. Thekla*, describing the situation of Seleucia on the Calycadnus.[26] But Jerome, writing from his monastery in Bethlehem, and others, also provide vivid accounts of Isaurian raids reaching Syria and Palestine in the early fifth century.[27] The exceptional status of the Isaurians is, conversely, reflected with great clarity in one of the earliest "laws" issued under Theodosius. Addressed to the Praetorian Prefect of Oriens on April 27, 408, it instructs him to inform provincial governors that the examination under torture of Isaurian brigands should not be subject to the normal suspension out of respect for Christian festivals.[28] Under Theodosius, we do not in fact hear of further major raids by the Isaurians, but both the "internal frontier" and the fear of their brigandage remained, as is shown in the report by Priscus on the strategic anxieties felt in the later 440s (p. 41 above).

Such, in the very broadest terms, was the massive military structure which was in the end to maintain successfully the integrity of Theodosius's Empire. One purpose in sketching it is simply as a reminder of the scale and geographical shape of that Empire, and of the very varied regions which it encompassed. Another is for it to serve as a background to the following survey of the Empire's engagement with different regions outside its own borders, starting with its twin Empire in the Latin West, and proceeding counterclockwise from Libya to Egypt, Oriens, and then the Danubian frontier (Thrace and Illyricum). What follows will be the merest sketch of the narrative of events in each theater; the purpose is not to write military history, but first, to examine the communications between center and periphery, and also, more important, to explore the conceptual, social, and religious issues to which each zone gave rise, and the nature of the Imperial response to them.

26. See p. 29 above.

27. See Jerome, *Epp.* 114; Sozomenus, *HE* VIII.25; Philostorgius, *HE* XI.8. See J. N. D. Kelly, *Jerome: His Life, Writings and Controversies* (1975), 287.

28. *CTh* IX.35.7.

3. CONSTANTINOPLE AND THE WEST

When Theodosius found himself, at the age of seven, the sole possessor of the Imperial name "Augustus" in the Eastern Empire, it was only thirteen years since his grandfather Theodosius had died in Constantinople, not long after reasserting, by victory in a civil war, his control of the West. On the one hand, therefore, it can hardly have been assumed without question by contemporaries that the division of East and West between Arcadius and Honorius had been set to endure. On the other hand, as we have seen in outline, and will see in even more detail in what follows, a "Greek Roman Empire" is shown by the evidence to have been in existence already in the earliest years of Theodosius: millions of Greek speakers, the vast majority members of a Greek-speaking Church, found themselves in an organic relationship with a bilingual Imperial administration in Constantinople, a relationship not just of "government," but of persuasion, protest, and the assertion of rights on the one hand, and of admonition, self-justification, and the threat of force or legal penalties on the other. To repeat, in day-to-day decision making and in military structure, the Eastern Empire was a separate, self-contained organization. As we have seen (pp. 12–13 above), even if all of the Emperor's pronouncements bore the name of whoever was then his colleague in the West, within those communications he spoke of other Emperors of the dynasty in terms of their relationship to him personally. Furthermore, as will be seen in a moment, from the beginning he (or whoever wrote for him) spoke of the Western Empire as something separate.

At the same time, the heritage of the united Empire created by and from Rome remained of fundamental importance. Both concern for its fate and the aspiration to give expression to the principle of unity were essential features of Theodosian policy.[29] In any case, in the first few years of the reign there could have been no certainty that the East would, as it unquestionably did, survive barbarian attack essentially unscathed, while the West suffered disaster. One major factor which swung the balance was that it had been only in 407/8 that the Goths under Alaric had finally moved west from the Balkans to Noricum.[30] During Theodosius's reign there was to be no internal "Gothic problem" in his Empire. But from 405 onwards there had

29. This theme is best treated by W. Kaegi, *Byzantium and the Decline of Rome* (1968), to which the following pages are heavily indebted.

30. See P. Heather, *Goths and Romans 332–489* (1991), 208 ff.

been both invasions by the Huns across the Danube and major Isaurian raids. Sozomenus, writing in the last decade of Theodosius's reign, reports that on hearing of his brother Arcadius's death in 408, Honorius had at first thought of going to Constantinople to prop up the regime of his very young nephew, but was dissuaded by the Magister Militum, Stilicho, who planned to go himself at the head of four legions. But then he was killed in August 408, on suspicion of treachery.[31] Subsequent events turned in a very different direction. Alaric, with his Gothic forces, threatened Rome repeatedly, and proclaimed a rival Emperor to Honorius, Attalus. At some point in 409/10, so it is reported, four thousand soldiers sent from the East arrived in Ravenna to support Honorius.[32] More significant for conceptions of the West as seen from the East at this moment is the remarkable letter sent in the name of Theodosius to Anthemius, the Praetorian Prefect of Oriens, from Constantinople, on April 24, 410, and clearly reflecting anxieties as to which Emperor or usurper ("tyrant") was ruling in the West, and whether the consequent divisions might communicate themselves to the East. We may leave aside until chapter 6 the question of who, with an Emperor aged nine, was currently determining policy. What is clear is that a notion of the (separate) "regions of our Empire" has already emerged, and that a document which is formally in the name of Honorius and Theodosius can speak of "my Lord and uncle, Honorius" in the third person:[33]

> The same Augustuses to Anthemius, Praetorian Prefect.
>
> All naval bases, harbors, shores, and all points of departure from the provinces, even remote places and islands, shall be encircled and guarded by the skillful regulation of Your Magnificence, so that no person may be able to infiltrate into the regions of Our Empire *(nostri . . . imperii regiones)* either by violence or by stealth, either openly or secretly, who shall not either be prevented by the barriers which have been interposed, or who when he approaches, shall not be held immediately unless he should show in a very clear manner that he bears sacred imperial letters *(apices)* from my uncle, Lord Honorius, to Me. It must be observed with the same diligence that if the intruder should say that he has messages from the aforesaid Emperor to any other person than Me, the bearer shall be detained, and the sacred imperial letter, with all the documents, shall be sealed and transmitted to My Clemency. For an occasion of tyrannical madness and barbarous savagery persuades Us to this measure, which has been agreed upon

31. Zosimus, IX.4.
32. Socrates, *HE* VII.10.6; Sozomenus *HE* IX.8.6.
33. *CTh* VII.16.2, trans. Pharr.

between Me and My Lord and uncle, Honorius, in memoranda that we have exchanged with each other.

In the course of 410 Attalus was deposed by Alaric, Rome was taken and sacked before the Goths withdrew, and Alaric died. Honorius's rule was saved, at the cost of vast losses of territory in Gaul, Spain, and the upper Danube region, and later in Africa also. Given the scale of these losses, and the very truncated nature of the Empire now ruled, normally, from Ravenna,[34] it is, if anything, remarkable that the notion of balanced, twin, Empires proved so tenacious, and that four decades later the primacy of Rome could be asserted as vigorously as it was by Galla Placidia (p. 53 above). For that matter, even in the immediate aftermath of these great disasters, the bishop of Rome, Innocentius, was writing in 412 to the bishop of Thessalonica, to assert the claim that the latter was his *vicarius*, and represented the channel for his authority over all the churches of Illyricum.[35] We shall see below that this anomaly was to lead to sharp exchanges between the Imperial uncle and nephew.

Even though, as we will see, Theodosius's Empire also suffered a serious barbarian threat in Illyricum in these years, the contrast in the fortunes of the twin Empires was still very clearly marked, and is the theme of a substantial series of chapters in Sozomenus's *Ecclesiastical History*, exploring in striking detail the usurpations and barbarian invasions which had ravaged the West (IX.5–16).

Thereafter, with what remained of the Western Empire now in a state of relative stability, for more than a decade no very profound issues concerning it presented themselves to the regime in Constantinople. Nonetheless, crucial events there were noted. Public celebrations were held at Constantinople on the news of the death in 415 of the Visigothic king, Athaulf, and of the defeat of Attalus, after a second usurpation, in 416.[36] In this period there was a discordance between the relative seniority of the two Emperors on the one hand, and the real disparity in strength and stability between the twin Empires on the other. Communications between the two Emper-

34. For the residences of fifth-century Western Emperors see Gillett, "Rome, Ravenna and the last western emperors" (chapter 1, n. 5).

35. Innocentius, *Epp.* 13. For the vicariate of the bishop of Rome over the churches of Illyricum, established in a period of fluctuating control of Illyricum at the end of the fourth century, see S. L. Greenslade, "The Illyrian Churches and the Vicariate of Thessalonica, 378–95," *JThSt* 46 (1945): 17 ff.; C. Pietri, "La géographie de l'Illyricum ecclésiastique et ses relations avec l'Eglise de Rome," in *Villes et peuplement dans l'Illyricum protobyzantin* (1984), 21 ff.

36. *Chron. Pasch.*, 572–73; See M. MacCormick, *Eternal Victory: Triumphal Rulership in Late Antiquity, Byzantium, and the Early Medieval West* (1986), 56–58.

ors were presumably normal, and may even have been common. But we do not know. As with so much else, it is only in the last two decades of Theodosius's reign, in the era of both the formation of the *Codex Theodosianus*, and then of the *Novellae*, and also of the controversies surrounding the two Councils of Ephesus, that we can illustrate such exchanges in any detail. But one exchange in the summer of 421, when Theodosius was twenty and Honorius thirty-six, deserves attention.

On July 21, 421, Theodosius wrote to Philippus, the Praetorian Prefect of Illyricum, to assert the right to have a say in the affairs of the Church in Illyricum on the part of the bishop of Constantinople "which enjoys the prerogative of Old Rome." When the *Codex Theodosianus* was being compiled in the 430s, this letter was duly incorporated, and it was later to be reincorporated in the *Codex* of Justinian. In fact, however, letters preserved in the correspondence of Bonifatius, bishop of Rome, show that a delegation from Illyricum made its way to Honorius to complain, and that he, with scrupulous politeness but unmistakable firmness, wrote to Theodosius to insist that the status quo should be maintained:

> Whence, after our Piety's address has been reviewed, your Majesty, mindful of Christianity, which celestial compassion instills in our breasts, should ordain that the ancient arrangement should be maintained, after there have been removed all things which are said to be procured by the plottings of hostile bishops throughout Illyricum, lest under Christian sovereigns the Roman Church may lose that which is has not lost under other emperors.

Theodosius promptly caved in, and replied to Honorius that he had written to the Praetorian Prefect of Illyricum to say that the existing arrangement should be observed. This letter was not incorporated in the *Codex*.[37]

Within a few years, everything had changed. Honorius died on August 15, 423, and an Imperial official, Ioannes, seized power. Theodosius responded first by nonrecognition, and then by mounting an expedition to establish an Emperor in the West, namely the very young Valentinian, the son of his widowed aunt (the half-sister of Arcadius and Honorius), Galla Placidia. We need not follow the details, except to note that it is reported to have been Theodosius's intention to accompany the troops to Italy himself. In fact, he went as far as Thessalonica, was kept there by illness, and returned to Constantinople.[38] When news of the defeat of Ioannes arrived,

---

37. *CTh* XVI.2.45 (*CJ* I.2.6 + XI.21.1); Bonifatius, *Epp.* 9–11. The dossier of three documents on this issue is translated in Coleman-Norton, no. 375.

38. Socrates, *HE* VII.24.

the Emperor led public celebrations in a manner designed to demonstrate the piety of his rule:[39]

> This event afforded that most devout emperor an opportunity of giving a fresh demonstration of his piety towards God. For the news of the usurper's being destroyed having arrived while he was engaged at the exhibition of the sports of the Hippodrome, he immediately said to the people: "Come now, if you please, let us leave these diversions, and proceed to the church to offer thanksgivings to God, whose hand has overthrown the usurper." Thus did he address them; and the spectacles were immediately forsaken and neglected, the people all passing out of the circus singing praises together with him, as with one heart and one voice. And arriving at the church, the whole city again became one congregation; and once in the church they passed the remainder of the day in these devotional exercises.

Whether the crowd really preferred a thanksgiving service to the traditional shows in the hippodrome is not recorded.

Secondly, as the "laws" of this period show clearly, if with some errors in recording, we can trace in Imperial communications of 423–25, once reassembled in chronological order, the reflection of Theodosius's period as sole "Augustus;" then the award of the Imperial name "Caesar" to the five-year-old Valentinian (at Thessalonica on October 23, 424); and then that of "Augustus" (at Rome on October 25, 425).[40] Thereafter, as the texts show without exception, Theodosius appears as the senior Augustus and Valentinian as the junior.

As we noted earlier, there is no sign that Theodosius ever thought of restoring the unified Empire of his grandfather, or still less of moving his base back to Italy. Instead, a separate court was reestablished in Italy, ruling mainly from Ravenna. As the evidence collected by Andrew Gillett demonstrates for the first time, the Western court did eventually move back to Rome—and in fact the letters from members of the Western Imperial family denouncing the "Robber Council of Ephesus" which were instigated by Leo, bishop of Rome, and were sent in early 450, happen to mark the precise moment when a truly "Roman" empire was reestablished, if with only a quarter century of life before it.[41]

What did *not* happen in 424–25 is therefore extremely significant, namely

---

39. Socrates, *HE* VII.23, trans. Hartranft.

40. For the details see *PLRE* II, Placidus Valentinianus 4.

41. Gillett, "Rome, Ravenna and the last western emperors" (chapter 1, n. 5). on p. 144. For Galla Placidia's letter to Pulcheria, see p. 37 above. See also pp. 230–31 below, in chapter 6.

a decision to abandon the "Greek Roman Empire" for a united one ruled from Italy. That did not mean that the principle of organic unity was not going to be asserted. On the contrary, as both Andrew Gillett and Tony Honoré have argued,[42] the legal measures taken in the next few years should be interpreted as an assertion of exactly that principle. It is of some significance that the project for the first-ever Imperial collection of Roman "laws" should have been initiated in Constantinople and carried out by a committee—or two successive committees—of high officials from the Greek Empire, all of whom will have had Greek as their first language.[43]

Before this major project was formally inaugurated in 429, however, the laws issued by the now seven-year-old Valentinian from Ravenna in November 426 should surely be seen as a product of the codifying impulse emanating from Constantinople, and the commitment of the Court there to the principle of the unity and consistency of the law as currently enforced throughout the Empire. These laws attempted to delineate the criteria for determining which Imperial pronouncements should count as general laws, and also set out the celebrated "law of citations," defining the relative authority to be attributed to the major jurists of the Classical period. The view that this step must have been instigated in Constantinople, and can hardly have been the initiative of the Court of Valentinian, one year after his proclamation—announced by the Eastern Magister Officiorum, Helion, as Theodosius's agent—could not be formally proved.[44] But it is very probable, and it is also entirely reasonable to see it as a step towards the project for codification announced in a letter to the Senate in Constantinople dispatched on March 26, 429. Since the genesis of the Codex Theodosianus has been discussed in great detail in recent years, we need pick out only the key features which are relevant to the relations of East and West, and the principle of Imperial unity. Firstly, as indicated, the plan was designed and announced in Constantinople. Secondly, it was to be carried out by a commission of eight high Imperial officials, or ex-officials and one scholasticus (jurist), all from Theodosius's Empire (and all with Greek names); there was no "representation" on it from the West. Thirdly, that part of the original project which was eventually carried out, the Codex Theodosianus, involved the collection of relevant items of Imperial legislation since Constantine,

---

42. See A. Gillett, "The Date and Circumstances of Olympiodorus of Thebes," Traditio 48 (1993): 1 ff., on pp. 19–20; T. Honoré, Law in the Crisis of Empire 379–455 AD: The Theodosian Dynasty and its Quaestors (1998), 116–17.

43. Honoré, Law in the Crisis of Empire (n. 42), ch. 6; J. F. Matthews, Laying down the Law: A Study of the Theodosian Code (2000), 71–72.

44. Honoré, Law in the Crisis of Empire (n. 42), 248–49.

arranged under headings, and under each heading in chronological order. Implicitly, but not explicitly, no distinction was to be made as to where laws had been issued, and the *Codex* as published therefore groups "western" and "eastern" laws together.[45] Fourthly, it is made explicit at the end of the letter to the Senate of 429 that subsequently there should be mutual transmission of laws between East and West:[46]

> Furthermore, if in the future it should be Our pleasure to promulgate any law in one part of this very closely united *(coniunctissimi)* Empire, it shall be valid in the other part on condition that it does not rest upon doubtful trustworthiness or upon a private assertion; but from that part of the Empire, in which it will be established, it shall be transmitted with the sacred imperial letters, it shall be received in the bureaus of the other part of the Empire also, and it shall be published with the due formality of edicts *(cum edictorum sollemnitate vulgandum)*. For a law that has been sent must be accepted and must undoubtedly be valid, and the power to emend and to revoke shall be reserved to Our Clemency. Moreover, the laws must be mutually announced, and they must not be admitted otherwise.

We need not pursue the details of the generation of the *Codex*, or the restart ordered by Theodosius in 435.[47] Rather we may note than this was a period of stable relations, with Theodosius occupying the senior position. The letter of November 430, summoning the Council of Ephesus, sent from Constantinople, was of course issued in the name of both Emperors,[48] and a copy must also have gone to the current bishop of Rome, Caelestinus, who subsequently sent several letters to Theodosius.[49] We may note also that a *magistrianus* was sent from Constantinople to Africa with a personal invitation to Augustine to attend the Council, only to discover that he had died in the previous year.[50] As we saw earlier (pp. 18–19), a presbyter from Carthage and delegates from Caelestinus participated in the Council, and for the next few years there was repeated correspondence between East and West. Nonetheless the Council was in essence a Greek affair, and

45. For the criteria by which we can identify "eastern" laws, see chapter 1, pp. 8–13.

46. *CTh* I.1.5 (repeated in *Gesta Senatus* 4). Trans. Pharr.

47. *CTh* I.1.6.

48. *ACO* I.1.1, para. 25 (pp. 114–16).

49. E.g., *ACO* I.2, para. 9 (pp. 25–26), May 8, 431; Caelestinus, *Epp.* 19. It is remarkable that no modern edition, commentary, and translation is available for the letters of the fifth-century popes.

50. *ACO* II.5, para. IV/17 (p. 103), from Liberatus's *Breviarium Causae Nestorianorum et Eutychianorum*.

all the measures following it were taken by Theodosius and his officials (chapters 4 and 5).

The military dominance of Constantinople was symbolized above all by the fact that a major naval and military expedition was sent to Africa to confront the Vandal invasion, and stayed there for some three years, without however dislodging them.[51] Its political dominance was reflected by the arrival of Valentinian there in 437, to marry Theodosius's daughter, Licinia Eudoxia. It was then that a copy of the completed *Codex Theodosianus* was formally handed over to the aristocratic representative of the Roman Senate, Anicius Acilius Glabrio Faustus. The balance of power between the two Emperors, the confidence as regards external threats, and the ambitious self-image of Theodosius himself are nowhere better reflected than in the speech which Anicius delivered to the Senate back in Rome, when he presented the volume before it in 438:[52]

> The felicity which emanates from our immortal Emperors proceeds
> in its increase to the point that it arrays with the ornaments of peace
> those whom it defends in the fortunes of war. Last year when I attended,
> as a mark of devotion, the most felicitous union of all the sacred cere-
> monies, after the nuptials had been felicitously solemnized, the most
> sacred Emperor, Our Lord Theodosius, desired to add the following
> high honor also to His world, namely, that He should order to be es-
> tablished the regulations that must be observed throughout the world,
> in accordance with the precepts of the laws which had been gathered
> together in a compendium of sixteen books, and these books he had
> desired to be consecrated by His most sacred name. The immortal
> Emperor, Our Lord Valentinian, with the loyalty of a colleague and
> the affection of a son, approved this undertaking.

As we have seen earlier, the principle that all legislation should be communicated between East and West, and thus become effective universally, was not adhered to in practice, and it was a whole decade before Theodosius actually sent a set of laws (pp. 1–2). Nor did peace remain undisturbed. In 439 the Vandals, already settled in Africa, took the crucial step of capturing Carthage, and, as we saw earlier, their raids were one of the fears which haunted the government in Constantinople in the 440s (p. 41 above). It is no accident that it was in 439 that the seawalls of Constantinople were built.[53]

Both the devastation of Africa and the threat of Vandal raiding in the

---

51. See R. C. Blockley, *East Roman Foreign Policy: Formation and Conduct from Diocletian to Anastasius* (1992), 60.

52. *Gesta Senatus* 2, trans. Pharr.

53. *Chron. Pasch.*, 583.

Mediterranean made a deep impact. Far away in a city of modest rank, Cyrrhus, in a province of no great prominence, Euphratensis, Theodoret repeatedly refers in his letters to the sufferings of refugees from Africa.[54] Another major expedition was mounted, and sailed to Sicily to help the Western Empire against the Vandals, but had to be recalled because of the invasion of Illyricum and Thrace by the Huns. Valentinian and the Vandal king, Gaiseric, made peace (for a time), on what terms is not known. According to the ninth-century *Chronicle* of Theophanes, perhaps using the major contemporary historian, Priscus, this was precisely the moment when Attila made himself sole ruler of the Huns (p. 80 below). The next few years were to be by far the most difficult, in military terms, of Theodosius's reign, and it is perhaps not surprising that it was not until 447 that he found a moment to fulfill the ideal of the Empire in which the twin regimes, East and West, operated a common system of legislation. The ideal of unity was real and important; but the defense and administration of the Greek Empire, and the maintenance there of whatever was felt to be Christian orthodoxy, came first.

4. BORDER WARS IN LIBYA AND EGYPT

By comparison with the major threats present in the central Mediterranean and on the Danube, the raiding by barbarian peoples which proved a serious threat to the stability and prosperity of Libya and southern Egypt (as a province, the Thebaid) was a minor local affair. But both spheres happen to produce documents of exceptional importance, which illuminate almost more vividly than any others how demands and communications directed to the distant Emperor were generated in local environments, and then made their way—or were intended to—into the Latin-using world of officialdom.

We may start with the two provinces of Libya, whose life as a Greek-speaking area had begun over a millennium earlier with the Greek colonization of Cyrene. By accident, as we saw earlier, the information on the units under the Dux Libyarum is missing from the *Notitia*, and in the documents preserved in the *Codex* for Theodosius's reign the area hardly registers. A single letter to the Dux in 417 about conditions of service will not help us much.[55]

Where our view of this provincial backwater, and its relation to the cen-

---

54. Theodoret, *Epp.* II. 22–23; 29–36; 52; 70. This group of letters would deserve study in its own right.

55. *CTh* VIII.1.16 (*CJ* I.51.6), Oct. 24, 417.

ter and the Emperor, is vividly illuminated, if only for a couple of years early in the reign, is in the correspondence of Synesius, a highly educated local landowner who could trace his ancestry back to the original settlers,[56] and who reluctantly became bishop of Ptolemais in 410. In an earlier letter he makes elaborate play with the remoteness of Libya and the idea that its inhabitants hardly know who the current Emperor is. In fact however, as we will see in chapter 6, Synesius shared with people in other relatively remote provinces (such as Theodoret, or the people of Edessa in Osrhoene) a quite clear set of convictions as to who the individuals at Court were who really exercised influence.

In the military context, we need only note that the cities of Libya, defended by a combination of *limitanei* and central forces as well as some barbarian units recruited from allied peoples outside the Empire, fought a prolonged low-level war over the years 405–13 (and perhaps longer, but Synesius's evidence ceases at this point) against two nomadic tribes, the Maketai and the Ausuriani. An interesting and vivid picture emerges of a local society with complex relations between the cities, the civil governor (Praeses), the Dux, and the Church (all under the ultimate supervision of higher authorities in Alexandria) on the one hand, and their tribal enemies on the other. But we may select the truly remarkable letter of, it seems, 410/11 addressed to the Dux Libyarum, Anysius. It concerns the services in the current frontier wars performed by a small unit of only forty mounted soldiers called Unnigardae, and apparently drawn from an allied Hunnish people on the Danube. In effect nothing is known of them except their name, and there is no information on how or when they had come to be stationed in Libya. Synesius's letter to Anysius, written of course in Greek, is concerned both to pay tribute to their military services and to follow up a letter sent by them to him, as bishop of Ptolemais. Their fear was that they might lose their special status, whatever that was, and be categorized with the ordinary local troops, presumably ranked as *limitanei*. Their letter also must presumably have been written, by one of them, or by someone for them, in Greek. Synesius therefore asks the Dux to send a submission *(anaphora)* to the Emperor, to which is to be attached a request for a further one hundred and sixty Unnigardae to be sent. But it is time to see precisely what Synesius says in the key passage of his letter:[57]

56. Synesius on his ancestry: *Epp.* 41. For the background, and Synesius's life, see D. Roques, *Synésius de Cyrène et la Cyrénaïque du Bas-Empire* (1987).

57. Synesius, *Epp.* 78, trans. Fitzgerald.

Assisted by God and led by you (Anysius), they have gained the greatest and most glorious victories. The barbarians had scarcely shown themselves when some were killed on the spot and others put to flight. They still patrol the heights, ever on the watch to drive back attacks of the enemy, like whelps springing out from the courtyard, that no wild beast may attack the flock. But we blush when we see these brave fellows weeping in the very midst of their strenuous service in our cause. It is not without sadness that I have read a letter which they sent me, and I think that you also ought not to remain unmoved at their prayer *(hikesia)*. They make a request *(deēsis)* of you through me, and of the Emperor through you, which it were only fair that we ourselves should have made, even had they been silent, to wit, that their men should not be enrolled amongst the native units. They would be useless both to themselves and to us if they were deprived of the Emperor's largesse, and if, moreover, they were deprived of their relays of horses and of their equipment, and of the pay which is due to troops on active service. I beg of you who were the bravest amongst these, not to allow your comrades-in-arms to enter an inferior rank, but to let them remain without loss of their honours, in the security of their former position.

This might well be, if our most kind Emperor should learn through your representation *(anaphora)*, how useful they have been to Pentapolis. Make of the Emperor another request on my behalf in your letter, namely, to add one hundred and sixty of these soldiers to the forty that we have already; for who would not admit that two hundred Unnigardae, with the aid of God, like unto these in heart and hand, and no less docile than brave, would suffice, when commanded by you, to bring the Ausurian war to an end for the Emperor?

We should not fail to take note of how extraordinary (in one sense) this procedure is. These barbarian soldiers can approach the bishop, and he can ask the Dux to send a submission to the distant Emperor. No heed is paid to the fact that the latter was currently aged about ten. The word used for the prospective submission to the Emperor is the technical term *anaphora*, which appears repeatedly in the *Acta* of the first Council of Ephesus.[58] If that submission were in fact written and sent, it would of course have been in Latin, and would have been a *suggestio*. The primary subject matter was to be the status, equipment, and pay of a mere forty barbarian soldiers, engaged in a very minor war on a strategically insignificant frontier, with tacked onto it

58. See, e.g., *ACO* I.1.3, para. 81 (pp. 3–5); para. 84 (pp. 10–13); para. 92 (pp. 28–30); para. 107 (pp. 63–64); I.1.5, paras. 158–60 (pp. 129–32); I.1.7, para. 68 (pp. 78–79).

a request for an increase of the force to two hundred in all (a minute proportion of the army of some three hundred thousand which protected Theodosius's empire). But, precisely such issues of the statuses and rights of different grades of staff form the subject matter of many Imperial "laws" issued in the form of letters addressed to officials, both military (pp. 46–47 above) and civilian. One precise example is Theodosius's letter of 417 to the Dux of Libya (p. 59). So Synesius's presumption that it would be feasible for the current Dux to send such an *anaphora*, or *suggestio*, direct to the Emperor was not necessarily misplaced. As will be discussed later, in connection with central decision making (chapter 6), the much fuller texts of "laws" preserved in the post-437 *Novellae* of Theodosius, show that, of thirty-five texts, twenty-three refer explicitly to the *suggestiones* from officials which had prompted them. What is most valuable about Synesius's letter is that it illustrates how a prominent local figure, writing in Greek, could feel able to demand that the nearest military commander should compose such a *suggestio* and send it to the Emperor.

In military and strategic terms, Egypt must have been much more important to the Theodosian Empire than the two Libyas, and the threat posed by the "Ethiopians" on its southern frontier duly appears among the multiple anxieties that Priscus attributes to the 440s (p. 41 above). As the *Notitia Dignitatum* records, there was a substantial garrison, under the command of the "Comes of the Limes of Aegyptus," consisting of thirty different units at various points on the lower Nile, the Delta, and the small Oasis to the west (*Notitia* XXVIII); and in Upper Egypt, under the "Dux of Thebais," there were no fewer than forty-five units, including two at Syene, at the First Cataract of the Nile, with the "Cohors Prima Felix Theodosiana" close by at Elephantine (XXXI). Both lay some eight hundred kilometers from the Mediterranean coast. With so extended and narrow a territory, with desert to the west and south, and desert and mountain to the east between the Nile and the Red Sea, as well as isolated Oases, the Small and the Great, to the west, both garrisoned, Egypt was by its nature heavily exposed to raiding, but well protected against all but the most major invasions, necessarily from the Near East. As will be seen, the Persian Empire, though of recurrent concern, did not at this period pose anything resembling a threat which might affect Egypt (as it was to two centuries later). So the insecurities to which Egypt was exposed, though very serious for those directly concerned, were no strategic problem to the Empire. Nonetheless, the multiple anxieties to which Priscus alludes did include the fear that the Ethiopian tribes were uniting.

Fifth-century Egypt, from which there are in any case relatively few published papyri, still awaits the very high-level analysis provided in Bagnall's *Egypt in Late Antiquity*, directed essentially to the fourth century.[59] So we may again pick out just a couple of salient items of evidence, some collected, translated, and annotated in the invaluable *Fontes Historiae Nubiorum*. First comes the report by the historian Olympiodorus (p. 30 above) of a visit to Syene in the early 420s, when the tribal chiefs *(phularchoi)* and *prophētai* of the Blemmyes met him and took him further south, to explore territory around Talmis and Prima (Qasr Ibrim) which had once been under Roman control.[60] However, the most important document from this frontier, and in many ways the most significant item in the entire evidence on the reign of Theodosius, is the papyrus containing the petition of bishop Appion of Syene, written at some point in the joint reign of Theodosius and Valentinian, so 425/50. We have already noted its significance for the coexistence, and mutual functions, of Greek and Latin. To summarize, the text is written in Greek, and is addressed notionally to both Emperors; what we have is a bureaucratic copy made at Court, and supplied with a Latin heading, "Copy of the Petition" *(exemplum precum)*. The undecipherable text of part of a letter in Latin is then followed by the autograph subscription of the Emperor, also in Latin, addressed to a single individual (figure III). Since the papyrus was found in Egypt, it is beyond question that this petition did reach Constantinople, some nineteen hundred kilometers as the crow flies from its starting point, and was attended to there, and that the copy and the response were brought back. The importance of the text is such that it needs to be quoted in full:[61]

> To the masters of land and sea and of every nation and race of men, Flavius Theodosius and Flavius Valentinianus, Eternal Augusti: Entreaty *(deēsis)* and supplication *(hikesia)* from Appion, bishop of the region of Syene and Contra Syene and Elephantine, in Your province *(eparchia)* of Upper Thebais.
>
> Your Benevolence is wont to extend your right hand to all who bring their requests, wherefore I too, being fully aware of this, have had recourse to these entreaties, the situation being as follows:
>
> Since I find myself with my churches in the midst of those merciless barbarians, between the Blemmyes and the Annoubades, we suffer many attacks from them, coming upon us as if from nowhere, with no soldier to protect our places. As the churches in my care for this reason are humiliated and unable to defend even those who are fleeing for refuge

59. R. Bagnall, *Egypt in Late Antiquity* (1993).
60. Olympiodorus (ed. Blockley), F. 35.2 = *Fontes Historiae Nubiorum* III, ed. T. Eide, T. Hägg, R. H. Pierce, and L. Török (1998), no. 309.
61. Trans. from *Fontes* III, no. 314. See chapter 1, pp. 22–23.

to them I prostrate myself and grovel at your divine and unsullied foot-
prints so that you may deign to ordain that the holy churches [under
my care?] be defended by troops (stationed) near us and that they obey
me and be placed under my orders in all matters just as the troops stationed in the garrison of Philae, as it called, in Your Upper Thebaid serve
God's holy churches on Philae. For in that way we shall be able to live
without fear and pursue [. . .] once the strictest legislation is laid down
against those who have transgressed [. . .] what You have divinely
ordained, all plundering by our adversaries, present or future is checked,
and a special and divine [. . .] grace *(charis)* on Your part in this matter
goes to the Magnificent and Notable Count and Duke of the Thebaid
Frontier.

If I obtain this, I shall (be able to) send my customary prayers to God
for Your eternal power uninterruptedly.

Philae lies very close to Syene, so the background cannot be that the effective frontier had been withdrawn northwards, but that some local dispute
had arisen over the responsibilities of the military units in the neighbor-
hood. A Greek inscription put up by contemporary king "of the Noubades
and all the Aithiopes" at Talmus shows that he defined the Blemmyes as
enemies against whom he had fought a victorious campaign.[62] However,
what is important in the broader context is not the precise circumstances
which we may be able to discern between the lines, but the fact of the composition of this very formally composed and rhetorical petition, its awareness of who the rulers of the twin Empires were, and their respective seniority, the confidence shown in demanding military redispositions, however
minor, on this very distant frontier, and the reliance on the supposition that
protection of the Church was an Imperial duty—and one which needed to
be carried out as a condition of continued prayer for the safety of both Emperors. We shall see an identical mode of designation of the document, and
the same concluding implications about the conditionality of continued
prayer, when we come to the petition in Greek addressed to Theodosius (and
Valentinian) against the violence of Nestorius (pp. 155–57 below).

This was therefore a different route, not via the military commander of
this frontier (the Dux, evidently honored also with the superior title
"Comes"), but directly to the Emperor himself. We do not know whether
his reply was positive or negative, and it is certain that he will not have written it himself. But he will have indicated the essence of what its contents
should be, and he did add a greeting in Latin, presumably addressed to the
"Comes and Dux," in his own hand.

---

62. *Fontes* III, no. 317.

Appion was not, however, the only strong-minded and assertive bishop, or ex-bishop, to be found in Egypt in these years. As we will see in much more detail later (chapter 5), Nestorius was deposed by the Council of Ephesus in 431, and in 436 (it seems) was ordered to be exiled to Petra. In the following years, and indeed until his death early in Marcian's reign, he continued in exile; not however, at Petra in Palaestina Tertia, but in the Great Oasis in Egypt. Protesting at the brutal conditions under which he suffered, he wrote, at some date after 436, two letters to the "governor" *(hēgoumenos)* of the Thebaid—which for various reasons probably means, once again, the military commander, the "Comes and Dux." We owe our knowledge of these letters to the quotation of extracts from them in the *Ecclesiastical History* of Evagrius.[63]

The first letter records that, following an Imperial command *(thespisma)*, Nestorius had as his assigned place of residence "Oasis, which is also Ibis"—in other words the Great Oasis, some two hundred and fifty kilometers west of the Nile valley, and over three hundred kilometers northwest of Syene. The Oasis, he says, had been overrun by barbarians, who also claimed that other barbarians, the Mazici, were about to follow them. So (as it seems) Nestorius and other exiles had fled northeast to the Nile valley at Panopolis, and were anxious to prove that they had not escaped deliberately.

In the second letter, he complains that he and the other exiles had been taken under escort from Panopolis to Syene (a distance of some three hundred and fifty to four hundred kilometers, following the Nile valley), and were then ordered back to Panopolis, and instructed to reside somewhere in its territory. He concludes by referring to what seem to be separate consultations of the Emperors both by his addressee and himself ("what was reported by your magnificence and by us, through whom it was right that it be reported to our gloriously victorious Emperors"), and asks that their decision be awaited.

Again we see the disturbed conditions which marked this frontier zone, the awareness that, formally speaking, there were two Emperors, not one, and the presumption that questions relating to this remote area could be brought to "their" attention, in other words to Theodosius in Constantinople. It will therefore not seem surprising that the Emperor's attention was repeatedly drawn to the complex social, economic, administrative, and military issues which arose on the much more important frontier that divided the Empire from Sasanid territory, and also marked the boundary be-

---

63. Evagrius, *HE* I.7, trans. and commentary by M. Whitby.

tween the area of settled habitation and that of the unsettled peoples of the steppe.

5. THE EASTERN FRONTIER: SASANIDS AND SARACENS

As we saw earlier, the *Notitia* alone would enable us to map out a continuous line of military posts spread out along a line stretching some fifteen hundred kilometers from Trapezus on the Black Sea through the two provinces of Armenia to that of Mesopotamia, reaching east to the Tigris at Amida, and then back to the Euphrates at Circesium, and its confluence with the Chabur, and then southwest through Palmyra to near Damascus, and south to the Red Sea at Aela (p. 49 above and figure IX). The geographical facts show beyond question that the army we can map on the ground was a frontier army. The great anomaly of Isauria apart (p. 50 above), no legions are found to be stationed anywhere except along the frontier. But of course we have no locations for the units under the direct command of the Magister Militum of Oriens, whose normal base seems to have been Antioch.

Archaeology and aerial photography also provide ample evidence of stone-built late Roman forts, at least as regards the "desert frontier" stretching from the Euphrates to the Red Sea.[64] Diplomatic, commercial, social, and religious relations lent this frontier a significance, both for contemporaries and for historians, which far outweighs that of the other frontiers. The Sasanid Empire might at any time pose a major threat, though it was in fact only rarely that war broke out. Relations were complicated by the fact that Persia was still pagan (it remains to be shown that there is ancient evidence to justify the description "Zoroastrian"[65]), but contained communities of Syriac-speaking Christians, who might sporadically be subject to persecution, and whom the Emperor was expected to protect.[66] Equally complex, and in the long run of enormous significance, were relations with the unsettled peoples of the steppe area, who might be found inside as well as

---

64. See the evocative and invaluable book of D. Kennedy and D. Riley, *Rome's Desert Frontier from the Air* (1990), and for details of the numerous surviving forts S. Gregory, *Roman Military Architecture on the Eastern Frontier from AD 200–600*, 3 vols. (1997). See also K. Butcher, *Roman Syria and the Near East* (2003), 411–12.

65. For skeptical observations on this point see F. Millar "Looking East from the Classical World: Colonialism, Culture and Trade from Alexander the Great to Shapur I," *International History Review* 20 (1998): 507 ff., on pp. 523–27.

66. See S. Brock, "Christians in the Sasanian Empire: A Case of Divided Loyalties," in *Religion and National Identity*, ed. S. Mews, *Studies in Church History* 18 (1982): 1 ff.

beyond the frontier, and whom Graeco-Roman contemporaries normally called "Saracens;" they might ally with either Rome or Persia, and might be exposed to Christian (or Jewish) preaching.[67] Not surprisingly, the two forms of attachment, religious and military, might go together. In this area in particular, another factor came into play, the influence of Christian holy men, or hermits, establishing themselves out in the steppe and offering, to local villagers or to passing strangers or to "Saracen" groups, a powerful model of a new ideal of life and piety. The interconnection between the influence of hermits, conversion to Christianity, and making war on the Persians is made quite explicit by Sozomenus, writing in the 440s:[68]

> Some of the Saracens were converted to Christianity not long before the present reign. They shared in the faith of Christ by intercourse with the priests and monks who dwelt near them, and practiced philosophy in the neighboring deserts, and who were distinguished by the excellence of their life, and by their miraculous works. It is said that a whole tribe, and Zocomus, their chief, were converted to Christianity and baptized about this period, under the following circumstances: Zocomus was childless, and went to a certain monk of great celebrity to complain to him of this calamity; for among the Saracens, and I believe other barbarian nations, it was accounted of great importance to have children. The monk desired Zocomus to be of good cheer, engaged in prayer on his behalf, and sent him away with the promise that if he would believe in Christ, he would have a son. When this promise was confirmed by God, and when a son was born to him, Zocomus was initiated, and all his subjects with him. From that period this tribe was peculiarly fortunate, and became strong in point of number, and formidable to the Persians as well as to other Saracens.

This observation precisely catches the key features of the complex relations involved: the influence of the Christian holy men whom nomadic groups encountered in the steppe; endemic conflict between these groups; and the implication that, once Christian, this particular group would be liable to fight against Persian forces, rather than Roman ones.

It is likely therefore that this group was normally found somewhere in the area of the middle Euphrates and Osrhoene, where the two Empires confronted each other. Conflict could, however, take place also farther north, in the area of the two provinces which the Romans designated as "Armenia"

---

67. See chapter 3, pp. 105–7 below, for Saracens as an element in the Church, and, for more detail, F. Millar, "The Theodosian Empire (408–450) and the Arabs: Saracens or Ishmaelites?" in *Cultural Borrowings and Ethnic Appropriations in Antiquity*, ed. E. Gruen (2005), 297ff.

68. Sozomenus, *HE* VI.38, trans. Hartranft.

and of the Armenian territory to the east of the upper Euphrates, which in theory was divided into a smaller area of Roman influence and a larger one of Persian. The very complex and obscure question of what we really know of Armenian culture and society in this period will be touched on briefly later.

Looking south again, the map (figure IX) would suggest, as do the narratives of the two relatively brief wars which broke out in Theodosius's time, that direct Roman-Persian conflicts will mainly have been confined to Osrhoene and the middle Euphrates. The long line of forts stretching from the Euphrates to the Red Sea should, in the first instance anyway, have been relevant only to relations with the nomads of the steppe. But such a view might underestimate the mobility of the Saracens, and hence the possibility that Roman-Saracen relations in the Damascus area, or even along the frontier of the province called "Arabia," may have been affected by their fluctuating relations with the two Empires.

The purpose of the following section, as of the others in this chapter, is not to retell, or attempt to analyze, the narratives of Roman-Persian relations and conflicts, which has already been done very well in recent times by others,[69] but to assess the place of Persia, the Saracens, and the eastern-frontier zone in the public ideology of the Theodosian Empire. A minimal narrative thread will be needed, but pride of place will to go explicit decisions, or formulations of policy, by the Emperor or his officials, and to the conceptions offered by contemporary, or near-contemporary, observers, such as Sozomenus.

The narratives of the episodic major conflicts have in any case to be seen in the context of other information, from a variety of perspectives, whether that of local observers in Oriens, or that of the Emperor himself, in responding to the many complex issues of social and economic relations, or of tensions between soldiers and civilians, or of status as between the holders of different ranks in the Imperial service.

Low-level insecurity, occasionally rising to the level of serious raids, but not affecting the strategic integrity of the Empire, was a feature of this area also. We can see this, for instance, in letters of the one major contemporary Latin writer from within the borders of Theodosius's Empire, Jerome, established in his monastery near Bethlehem from the mid-380s to his death

---

69. Apart from R. C. Blockley, *East Roman Foreign Policy* (1992), already mentioned, the primary modern work, and the best presentation of the sources, on this topic is now G. Greatrex and S. N. C. Lieu, *The Roman Eastern Frontier and the Persian Wars* II, AD *363–630: A Narrative Sourcebook* (2002). The modesty of the title belies the high level of scholarship shown.

in 420. In 414 he describes how "Arabes and Agareni whom they now call Saraceni" could be found near Jerusalem, with a desert full of fierce barbarians beginning just beyond Bethlehem.[70] To Jerome, in many ways the source of the most vivid and concrete, if partial, observations on Oriens as it was in the half century up to 420, these Saracens were by nature robbers, who threatened the borders of Palestine, and might attack travelers on the road down from Jerusalem to Jericho.[71]

Jerome's importance as a contemporary observer is exceeded only by that of Theodoret, born in Antioch in the 390s, and bishop of Cyrrhus from 423 onwards. To take only his *Historia Religiosa*, on the monks of Syria, he records an Isaurian raid in the area of Mt. Amanus, and gives vivid descriptions of rival tribes of Saracens coming to venerate Symeon Stylites on his pillar set up in the Limestone Massif between Beroea (Aleppo) and Antioch. One group had come from near the fortress of Callinicum on the middle Euphrates.[72] In southern Palestine and in the steppe in northern Syria, there were also zones occupied by Saracens that were not far from representing internal frontiers in themselves. But the most powerful impressions of internal insecurity are provided, as mentioned briefly earlier (p. 29 above), by the anecdotes contained in the *Miracles* of St. Thekla, written in the middle of the fifth century, and providing a perspective on Theodosius's Empire as seen from the city of Seleucia in Isauria. Thus, looking outwards to the frontier, the reader encounters a former military commander (Comes), Vitianus, who looks back with pride on his part in the victory over Persia in 421/2.[73] As for the unsubdued and menacing Isaurians of the interior, we meet an Isaurian lady called Bassiane who is a hostage in Seleucia (19); brigands at one stage capture the extra-urban sanctuary of Thekla, and are then driven off by Imperial forces (28); bishop Dexianus, in fear of further raids, has the treasures from the sanctuary transferred into the city (32); and two local city councilors *(bouleutai)* contribute the costs of the rations for soldiers, evidently stationed in the city (35). The text gives a powerful sense both of the values still attached to city life, and of the city's exposure to constant threats from the nearby internal "frontier." As so often also in our sources of this period, we encounter the presence of "soldiers," without being able to identify the name or nature of their unit, still less

70. Jerome, *Epp.* 129.20–23.
71. See now more fully F. Millar, "The Theodosian Empire (408–450) and the Arabs" (n. 67).
72. Theodoret, *HR* X.5 (Isaurians); XXVI.11–16, 21 (Symeon Stylites).
73. *Vie et Miracles, Mir.* 20; *PLRE* II, Vitianus.

form any idea of whether they occupied a camp or fort, or were quartered in the city.

When we turn to the external frontier with Persia, and to the wider zone on both sides of it, the focus will be on the types of problem which arose, the ways in which they came to the Emperor's attention, and the nature of the conceptions and principles which were expressed in his "laws." Most of the time there was no active warfare between the two Empires (the fifth century contrasts markedly with both the fourth on the one hand and the sixth and early seventh on the other). In brief, there were major conflicts only in 420/2 and in 441/2—introducing the period of insecurity of which Priscus gives a vivid reflection (p. 41 above). But Nestorius's first sermon, and the petition by his followers to Theodosius in 431, both give a hint that Persia was at all stages envisaged as a potential threat, and that Theodosius's role as the protector of Christians beyond the frontier was significant.[74]

The story told by sixth-century and later sources, that the Persian king Yazdegerd exercised a sort of guardianship over the infant Theodosius may well be true, but finds no explicit reflection in contemporary documents.[75] Equally, the view which we can derive from Imperial pronouncements, or "laws," themselves is not, by its nature, going to express broad issues of strategy, still less fill in sections of narrative; instead, the "laws" tackle questions which are in fact of greater historical interest, namely the complex relations which arose in frontier zones. Thus, for instance, what seems to be the earliest "law" from the reign is addressed to the famous Anthemius, Praetorian Prefect of Oriens, refers in passing to an existing treaty with Persia, and lays down, first, that there shall be three cities where commercial exchanges with Persia are to be conducted: Callinicum (as we have seen, the site of a Roman fortress on the Euphrates), and Nisibis and Artaxata in Sasanid territory. Complex rules are also laid down to permit the mutual movement of embassies, but not to allow them to discover too much. As the text comes from the *Codex Justinianus* (and hence the peripheral elements of the original have been edited out), we hear nothing of the context which gave rise to it.[76]

A closer insight into military-civilian relations is provided by the two parts of what seems to be a single letter, of March 23, 409, again addressed to Anthemius. Firstly, provincials who acquire booty from the "barbarians"

74. See pp. 39 and 40 above.
75. See G. Greatrex and J. Bardill, "Antiochus the Praepositus: A Persian Eunuch at the Court of Theodosius II," *DOP* 50 (1996): 171 ff.
76. *CJ* IV.63.4, dating to 408/9.

may retain it—unless it consists of free persons or slaves previously seized by the barbarians. Secondly, a dispute has arisen in Palaestina over the exaction of taxes in kind for the support of the frontier troops, and their commutation for cash. The text is notable as being the earliest evidence for the division of Palaestina into three *provinciae*, and also as clearly arising from a complaint relating to the troops of two specific forts, named as "Versaminum" and "Moenocnum;" both appear, under variant names, in the *Notitia*, and can be identified on the ground.[77] The law repeats the relevant rule, adds severe penalties payable by the Dux if there is further contravention, and concludes, "The penalty for sacrilege shall be added, which clearly pursues violators of the divine imperial decrees." This pronouncement is as good an example as any of the way in which the Imperial court maintained, or attempted to maintain, general principles (which one could call "laws" in the normal sense of the word), while also issuing detailed adjustments and corrections, often in response to submissions or complaints, embodied in letters which might refer to themselves as "laws" *(leges)*, but which could more properly be seen as administrative orders, often backed by threats. These, or very similar, patterns of government at a distance, can be seen in the military sphere, but equally in the civilian one and in the Emperor's relations to the life of the Church.

Similar local disputes can easily be perceived as lying behind the letter of July 28, 417, sent to Maximus, Praetorian Prefect of Oriens:[78]

> Although a law was formerly issued which denied to the Tribuni and to Comites of lower rank all license to exact baths from the provincials, We learn that the Duces of the Limes Eufratensis have exacted a tremis per day in respect of wood and baths. We command therefore that the Duces of the aforesaid Limes, since they have evidently taken such money illegally for the past three years, shall restore it twofold, and in future such license for extortion shall be checked by fear of the same penalty.

The Emperor does not reveal by what route this information on a very minor local malpractice has reached him in Constantinople; his reply is also an example of how, in the Imperial system, the spheres of military and civilian jurisdiction continually overlapped, and might do so in either direction.

---

77. *CTh* V.6.2 + ?VII.4.30. (*CJ* XII.37.13). See *Not. Dig.*, Oriens XXXIV.22 ("Birsana") and 19 ("Menochiae"). See Y. Tsafrir, L. Di Segni and J. Green, *Tabula Imperii Romanii: Iudaea/Palaestina. Maps and Gazetteer* (1994), s.v. "Birsana," "Menois, Maon II."

78. *CTh* VII.11.2 (*CJ* I.47.10), trans. Pharr, with adjustments.

A perfect example of just that is provided by another letter to Monaxius, written just two months later. Once again we see an area of conflict between the civilian and military structures, and also gain an unexpected glimpse of a side of the Imperial system which does not at first sight seem to fit with the remorseless piety of the Theodosian regime—the supply of wild animals from distant frontiers, transported to Constantinople for use in shows. But we have of course already encountered Theodosius breaking off public shows in the hippodrome to lead the crowd to church to give thanksgiving (p. 55). Once again a complaint has reached the Emperor, this time from the staff of the civilian governor of Euphratensis:[79]

> Through the lamentation *(deploratio)* of the office staff of the Governor *(praesidiale officium)* of Euphratensis, We learn that those persons who by the ducal office staff are assigned to the task of transporting wild beasts remain, instead of seven or eight days, three or four months in the City of Hierapolis, contrary to the general rule of delegations, and in addition to the expenses for such a long period they also demand cages, which no custom permits to be furnished. We therefore direct that if any beasts are sent by any Dux of the border to the imperial court *(comitatus)*, they shall not be retained longer than seven days within any municipality *(civitas)*. The Duces and their office staffs shall know that if anything contrary hereto is done, they must pay five pounds of gold each to the account of the fisc.

A variety of issues concerning the administration and social life of a distant frontier zone could thus be presented for the attention of the Emperor, even in times of peace (and we should recall that it was nearly a thousand kilometers from Hierapolis to Constantinople, a significant distance even for a messenger crossing Anatolia, let alone for soldiers escorting animals in cages). But, naturally enough, on the two occasions when serious conflict with Persia broke out, more significant issues arose. Few "laws" preserved in either *Codex* are as widespread in their effects as that contained in another letter, noted earlier, sent to Monaxius as Praetorian Prefect of Oriens on May 3, 420, and allowing the fortification of private properties throughout a roll call of provinces which perfectly covers all those which might be in the path of a Persian invasion: Mesopotamia, Osrhoene, Euphratensis, Syria Secunda, Phoenice Libanensis, Cilicia Secunda, both Armenias, Cappadocia, Pontus Polemoniacus, and Helenopontus.[80] As a glance at the map of the eastern frontier will show (figure IX), the areas concerned lie, first,

79. *CTh* XV.11.2 (*CJ* XI.45.1), Sept. 27, 417, trans. Pharr, with adjustments.
80. *CJ* VIII.10.10.

in the northern Syrian region and, second, in eastern Asia Minor. Those in western Asia Minor are not listed, and nor are those on the Mediterranean coast, or Palestine or Arabia. The latter could be drawn, indirectly, into a Persian-Roman conflict, but only through the fluctuating and unreliable loyalties of the Saracen allies of either side. The desert frontier in Palaestina Tertia and Arabia was not a frontier with Persia. Even as regards Phoenice Libanensis, no Persian army ever marched across the steppe from the Euphrates to Palmyra, or could have. The strategic battleground was Osrhoene and Mesopotamia, with the frontier lying west of Nisibis, which had been lost to the Persians in 363.

This measure of 420 must reflect fears of war, which duly broke out in 421/2, after persecution of Christians began, as it seems, in Persia towards the end of the reign of Yazdegerd, who died in autumn 420, and was succeeded by Vahram. According to the detailed contemporary account in Socrates' *Ecclesiastical History*, appeals from the Christians in Persia reached Theodosius, and Roman forces took the initiative in Armenia. The theater of war moved to Mesopotamia, and the Saracen ally of Persia, Alamundarus (al-Mundhir), promised that Antioch would be taken. But the Persians were defeated, a peace treaty was concluded, and the status quo was restored.[81]

Only two aspects of this conflict need to be stressed here. One is the story told in the next century by Cyril of Scythopolis, of how another Saracen ally of the Persians, Aspabetus, entrusted with preventing the escape of Christians to Roman territory, took pity on them, was accused before Yazdegerd, and himself sought Roman protection. Anatolius, Magister Militum in Oriens, made his followers allies, and appointed Aspabetus as Phylarchus of the Saracens in Arabia.[82] It seems to follow that he must have moved, or been transferred, south from his previous area of operations. Later he converted to Christianity, was ordained, and under his new name, Peter, took part in the first Council of Ephesus as the "bishop of the Camps." As we will see (pp. 105-7 below), with that a new element, of immense importance for the future, had entered the structure of the Greek-speaking Church.

The second aspect was a more traditional one, the celebrations held in Constantinople in 422 to mark the victory, in which a leading role was played by the Emperor's new wife, Eudocia, who came from a highly cultivated pagan family in Athens. It is very likely that shows were laid on for the populace (like the chariot races and theatrical shows provided in the previous

---

81. Socrates, *HE* VII.18.1–21.6.
82. Cyril of Scythopolis, *Life of Euthymius* 10.

year to celebrate the wedding).[83] But what is described for us by Socrates is an elegant synthesis of inherited literary forms and Christian piety:[84]

> So signal a victory having through Divine favor been achieved by the Romans, many who were illustrious for their eloquence, wrote panegyrics in honor of the emperor, and recited them in public. The empress herself also composed a poem in heroic verse: for she had excellent literary taste; being the daughter of Leontius the Athenian sophist, she had been instructed in every kind of learning by her father; Atticus the bishop had baptized her a little while previous to her marriage with the emperor, and had then given her the Christian name of Eudocia, instead of her pagan one of Athenaïs. Many, as I have said, produced eulogies on this occasion. Some, indeed, were stimulated by the desire of being noticed by the emperor; while others were anxious to display their talents to the masses, being unwilling that the attainments they had made by dint of great exertion should lie buried in obscurity.

This was in effect the end of serious conflict with Persia during Theodosius's reign. We may note only the brief account in Theodoret's *Ecclesiastical History* of an abortive Persian attack which may perhaps date to 440, as later sources suggest, or may belong a few years earlier. More significant are the two underlying messages in Theodoret's text: that it was the Emperor's Christian piety, as in an attack by some Huns under Roua or Rhoilas, which protected the Empire, and that protection, not conquest, was the aim. The context in Theodoret is a section in Book V in which he looks forward beyond the date (429) at which his main narrative formally concludes (having not in reality covered the succession of events under Theodosius at all). Instead, he stresses the benefits conferred by the piety of the Emperor, mentioning his restoration of the remains of John Chrysostom (which belongs in 438) and his order for the destruction of pagan temples, which should be the measure of 435.[85] It may well be that the passage was written before a major threat from the Huns under Attila had arisen (p. 80 below). At any rate the interpretation, as regards both fronts, is the same:[86]

> In accordance with the same principles he ordered a complete destruction of the remains of the idolatrous shrines, that our posterity might be saved from the sight of even a trace of the ancient error, this being

---

83. *Chron. Pasch.*, 578.
84. Socrates, *HE* VII.21.7–10, trans. Zenos.
85. *CTh* XVI.10.25, Nov. 14, 435. See p. 122 below.
86. Theodoret, *HE* V.37.3–6, trans. Jackson. This must surely be the same episode as the abortive invasion under "Rougas" recorded by Socrates, *HE* VII.43, whose failure is also attributed to divine intervention. It dates to the bishopric of Proclus in Constantinople, so 434 onwards.

the motive which he expressed in the edict published on the subject. Of this good seed sown he is ever reaping the fruits, for he has the Lord of all on his side. So when Rhoïlas, Prince of the Scythian Nomads, had crossed the Danube with a vast host and was ravaging and plundering Thrace, and was threatening to besiege the imperial city, and summarily seize it and deliver it to destruction, God smote him from on high with thunderbolt and storm, burning up the invader and destroying all his host. A similar providence was shewn, too, in the Persian war. The Persians received information that the Romans were occupied elsewhere, and so in violation of the treaty of Peace, marched against their neighbours, who found none to aid them under the attack, because, in reliance on the Peace, the emperor had despatched his generals and his men to other wars. Then the further march of the Persians was stayed by a very violent storm of rain and hail; their horses refused to advance; in twenty days they had not succeeded in advancing as many furlongs. Meanwhile the generals returned and mustered their troops.

The fact that in the last decade of the reign the major problem was presented by the brief unity of the Huns under Attila did not mean that issues concerning the eastern frontier ceased to come before the Emperor. Thus, for instance, we find that in 438 Theodosius received a report (here called an *adsertio*) from Anatolius, the Magister Militum in Oriens, complaining that soldiers there were being taken away from their duties to answer litigation brought against them by civilians. So, in typical style, trying to balance irreconcilable objectives, the Emperor decrees that under no circumstances may a border soldier *(limitaneus miles)* be required to come for judgment to the Imperial Court (in Constantinople); on the other hand cases may be brought against them before military judges. This again is a clear example of the tensions between soldiers and civilians, and between the Imperial officials responsible for each, and the letter is in fact addressed to Florentius, the Praetorian Prefect of Oriens. This letter, which could be read as a highly rhetorical prose poem in celebration of the hard lot of soldiers on distant frontiers, and their services to the State, ends in fine style with a typical example of the personalized address which marks what is in form a letter to an individual official. The "law" embodied in it was to reach the public in the secondary form of *edicta* put up for public information:[87]

> We must hope, that it will not please the audacious to employ litigation, and thus Our soldiers may be allowed to be at ease, although calumny finds them in obscurity in the farthest parts of the Roman

---

87. *Nov. Th.* 4, Feb. 25, 438; trans. Pharr.

Empire where they have been assigned by the regulations of their
military oaths of service.

Wherefore, O Florentius, dearest and most beloved Father, since
Your Illustrious and Magnificent Authority always consummates the
statutes of Our August Majesty with watchful care and with a suitable
execution, you shall now also by posting edicts cause them to come
to the knowledge of all.

Finally, to illustrate the ways in which issues relating to the frontiers
reached the Emperor, and the forms in which he expressed his responses to
them, we may take Theodosius's letter of June 26, 441, addressed to Cyrus,
the Praetorian Prefect of Oriens.[88] Once again, the relevant information has
come "through the most well-considered report of Your Sublimity *(per con-
sultatissimam tuae sublimitatis suggestionem).*" The problem revealed was
that Imperial properties on the Armenian frontier, in the area exposed to
Persian attacks, and close to the cities of Theodosiopolis and Satala (see figure
IX), had earlier been acquired as private property by petitions to the Emperor, and were not contributing the necessary supplies in kind for the army.
The new owners may retain the property, the Emperor rules, but only if
they fulfill all the relevant requisitions, including post-horses and wagons.
The letter lifts a window on a remote and complex frontier society in which,
as ever, the interests of the military and of civilians conflicted, and we are
far from understanding the wider social context. But it may serve as a reminder that, in keeping his extensive empire together, the Emperor had to
pay heed to innumerable messages from distant frontiers, involving issues
which in their own way were just as complex as the theological disputes
which demanded his attention (and are often even more difficult for us to
grasp).

6. THE DANUBE FRONTIER AND THE HUNS

The facts of geography, and the lessons to be learned from the Gothic invasion of the later 370s, from the defeat and death of the Emperor Valens
at Adrianople in 378, and from the presence of Gothic forces in the Balkans
and Greece until about the time of his father's death, 407/8 (when they had
providentially moved westward), all indicated that if the Empire of Theodosius was to be under serious threat, it would come from barbarians crossing the Danube. From that fear there derived the military structure which

88. *Nov. Th.* 5.3.

we saw earlier: two separate Magistri Militum of Illyricum and Thrace, each with an extensive field army; and four Duces with forces spread all along the Danube, in the provinces of Moesia Prima, Dacia Ripensis, Moesia Secunda, and Scythia. That was to be the key frontier, and in spite of serious threats it emerged intact in the reign of Marcian. It might have been otherwise, and if it had there would have been no "Byzantine" history to follow.

There is just one hint, however, that the memory of a different type of barbarian invasion, in the mid-third century, had not faded. Indeed it cannot have faded altogether, since the anti-Christian *History* of Eunapius, in a somewhat toned-down second edition, appeared in the early years of Theodosius, and referred in detail to the *History* written by the Athenian historian Dexippus and covering the traumatic events of the middle of the third century, including a barbarian attack on Athens itself.[89] His material was to be used, some half a century after Theodosius's death, by another pagan historian, Zosimus.

At that time, in the middle of the third century, barbarians whom our Greek sources call "Scythians" had taken ship from the north coast of the Black Sea, and carried out major invasions of Asia Minor and Greece. Might such a thing happen again? We have no clear picture of the ethnic, political, or military situation on the north coast of the Black Sea in the fifth century, but there were still Greek cities there, and (as always) there were unsubdued barbarians beyond them.[90] Whether the Empire maintained any military presence at all in this area is wholly obscure. But at least one Greek city, Chersonesus, on the southwest tip of the Crimea, evidently regarded itself as within the purview of the Empire, as we learn from a remarkable letter of Theodosius to the Praetorian Prefect of Oriens in 419:[91]

> Those persons who have betrayed to the barbarians the art of building ships, that was hitherto unknown to them, shall be freed from imminent punishment and imprisonment because of the petition *(petitio)*

89. For Dexippus and the Herulian attack on Athens see F. Millar, "P. Herennius Dexippus: The Greek World and the Third-Century Invasions," *JRS* 59 (1969): 12 ff. For Eunapius and Zosimus, see W. Liebeschuetz, "Pagan Historiography and the Decline of the Empire," in *Greek and Roman Historiography in Late Antiquity*, ed. G. Marasco (2003), 177 ff.

90. For the north coast of the Black Sea in Late Antiquity see, e.g., V. M. Zubar', *Chersones taurícheskii v Rimskaya Imperya* (1994), ch. 3. See now the vivid evocation of the history of the city of Chersonesus, and the extraordinarily extensive remains of its urban center and its territory, including a number of late Roman churches, in G. R. Mack and J. C. Carter, eds., *Crimean Chersonese: City, Chora, Museum and Environs* (2003).

91. *CTh* IX.40.24 (*CJ* IX.47.25), Sept. 24, 419; trans. Pharr.

of the Most Reverend Asclepiades, Bishop of the City of Chersonesus, but We decree that capital punishment shall be inflicted both upon these men and upon any others if they should perpetrate anything similar in the future.

Capitale supplicium as used here must surely mean death, a punishment specified in this period only for major crimes,[92] so the offence was being taken with the utmost seriousness. This provision must reflect the fear of another barbarian fleet setting sail to ravage the ungarrisoned coasts of the Black Sea, or even beyond. Thus we find once again, as with Synesius in Ptolemais in Libya or Appion in Syene (and on many occasions Theodoret in Cyrrhus), that it is the local bishop who steps forward to intervene, in one sense or another, with the authorities. In the case of all the other three we know, and in the case of Asclepiades can presume without question, that his *petitio (hikesia* or *deēsis)* will have been in Greek.

At any rate the fears implied here were not fulfilled, and it was to be by land, over the Danube, and not by sea, that a serious invasion would come. In its most threatening form, it materialized only in the last decade of the reign. Moreover, as we have seen (p. 53 above), Sozomenus's extensive account of the disasters in the West in the first couple of years of Theodosius's reign was at least partly designed to underline the contrast with the East, due (as ever) to the piety of the regime. Sozomenus describes with satisfaction how a confederation of Huns under Uldis had invaded, had captured the city of Castra Martis, and had then broken up, with some of Uldis's allies praising the Roman system and joining the Roman forces, while an entire tribe of Sciri were either killed or brought as prisoners to Constantinople. Some were sold as slaves, while others were settled in Bithynia, where they could still be seen, peacefully tilling the soil. This is the same people about whom a letter was sent in the name of Theodosius to Anthemius, the Praetorian Prefect of Oriens, on April 12, 409, settling questions of their legal status.[93]

It is very possible that in stressing the theme of the (quite genuine) greater good fortune and security of the Eastern Empire in these early years, Sozomenus downplayed how serious the devastation of Illyricum had been. As so often, we can see local circumstances reflected, rather than actually described, in Imperial pronouncements. Occasionally also, we find "laws" which are not reactions to immediate problems or conflicts of interest, but regulations of a systematic kind: one example is the letter sent on January

---

92. See J. Harries, *Law and Empire in Late Antiquity* (1999), ch. 6.
93. Sozomenus, *HE* IX.5.4–7; *CTh* V.6.3.

28, 412, to Constans, the Magister Militum in Thrace, laying down detailed provisions for the construction and maintenance of river patrol boats *(lusoriae)* along the two military districts on the Lower Danube, Moesia (Secunda) and Scythia. Typically, the regulation lays down that in case of neglect financial penalties will be imposed both on the relevant Dux and on his staff.[94] By implication, whatever incursions had taken place in previous years, the frontier along the Lower Danube was now fully restored. That did not mean, however, that there were no longer-term consequences of the barbarian raids. Thus on August 17, 413, a letter was sent to Leontius, Praetorian Prefect of Illyricum, laying down an exception to the normal rule that if someone assumed voluntarily the obligations of a town councilor, he was to be regarded subsequently as bound to those obligations. The exception was designed to encourage public volunteering as regards specific functions or contributions, by suspending, for Illyricum alone, the normal rule. The reason is stated explicitly: "taking thought for devastated Illyricum *(vastato Illyrico consulentes)*." What is also striking in this letter is the clear assumption that there were regular city functions *(munera)*, whether involving expenditure or not, which were performed by individuals; that the town council *(ordo)* of each city would meet to confirm the relevant exemption; and that public functions would be greeted by the "applause of the people" *(populi plausus)*.[95] As we have seen earlier, the secular diocese of "Illyricum" included Greece with its ancient cities. But the area affected by devastation will surely have been at least mainly further north, in a zone where we would not necessarily be confident that the institutions of the Classical city had ever taken firm root, or, if they had, that they still survived. But, as was noted earlier, and will be explored in more detail later,[96] the implications offered by the appearances at the fifth-century Church Councils of Greek-speaking bishops from at least a number of cities in northern Illyricum are comparable: in short, there are hints that the Christianized Greek city was more prevalent in this area than we might have supposed. Of course the Imperial letter, written as always in Latin, uses the standard Latin terminology to allude to the relevant city institutions, and it may well be that in the northwest quarter of Illyricum or along the Adriatic coast there were also Latin-using *civitates*. The assumption made at Court, at any rate, is that there were cities, but that measures were needed to encourage individual contributions to their public life. A similar assumption, starting from an is-

94. *CTh* VII.17.1.
95. *CTh* XII.1.177.
96. Pp. 17–18 above and pp. 87–88 and 93–94 in chapter 3.

sue relating to Delphi, but leading to a rule applicable to all the cities of Illyricum, appears in Theodosius's letter to the Praetorian Prefect in 424.[97]

Even granted that this assumption was present, it is characteristic of the entire context within which the "Greek Roman Empire" functioned that the ancient Greek cities bordering on the Mediterranean world (like Delphi) would be in a position to make more insistent claims on the Emperor's attention. So, when a ruling on taxation was issued, also in 424, in response to a report from the Praetorian Prefect, the Achaeans were allowed to pay at a lower rate, and the church of Thessalonica (evidently having made a special submission) escaped altogether.[98]

But even allowing for the lower profile achieved by communities in the central or northern Balkans, it is striking that the Imperial "laws" of the rest of the reign, so far as preserved, shed no further light on the course of hostilities in the areas under the Magistri Militum of Illyricum or Thrace, or on the social consequences of the second phase of violent disruption caused by the Huns. There is no equivalent in Theodosius's *Novellae* to the succession of "laws," or letters, of his co-Emperor, Valentinian, which reflect so vividly the devastating effects of the Vandal invasions in Sicily and Italy from 440 onward.[99] As we have seen (p. 75 above) there was one raid by the Huns, which perhaps belongs in the 430s, and which came providentially to an abortive conclusion. But then we enter a quite new phase from the early 440s onwards, with the achievement of domination over the Huns first by Attila and his brother, and then by Attila alone.[100] Apart from various passing allusions to the invasions in contemporary sources, our only detailed fifth-century narrative is that of Priscus, who participated personally at certain key moments; even his text survives only in long fragments. Consequently, we need only summarize the essentials, and attempt to bring out the significance of these events for the Theodosian Empire, so far as they can be discerned in the surviving fragments of the narrative of a close contemporary observer, writing perhaps in the 470s.

Priscus's narrative as preserved reveals significant intrusions into Roman territory (see the map in figure VIII), with the capture of Noviodunum

97. *CTh* XV.5.4, Apr. 22, 424. Cf p. 11 above.

98. *CTh* XI.1.33 (*CJ* I.2.8 + X.16.12), Oct. 10, 424.

99. See, e.g., *Nov. Val.* 1.2 (440/1), remission of taxation in Sicily; 6.1 (Mar. 20, 440), recruits and deserters; 9 (June 9, 440), Gaiseric's invasion, right to bear arms (note the conclusion: "et manu divina 'Proponetur amantissimo nostro populo Romano'"); 2.3 (Aug. 17, 443), refugees from Africa, and so forth.

100. For the history of these events the most detailed modern treatment is that of J. O. Maenchen-Haelfen, *The World of the Huns* (1973), 89 ff.

on the Danube (F.5), as well as Viminacium, far to the northwest in Moesia Prima (6.1), and then Naissus, a hundred kilometers south of the river (6.2). To Attila, Priscus's narrative attributes an attack on Ratiaria, another place on the Danube (9.1), and massive demands for tribute and the return of fugitives, as well as an unsuccessful attack on Asemus, whose inhabitants resisted vigorously (9.3). The ninth-century *Chronicle* of Theophanes, perhaps based on Priscus, reports sweeping gains by Attila, with the capture of Ratiaria, Naissus, Philippolis, Arcadiopolis, Constantia, and other cities—all the cities of the region indeed, except Adrianople and Perinthus/Heraclea, thus bringing Hunnish forces almost to Constantinople itself, and leading to further promises of tribute.[101] It is at this point in the narrative of Priscus, as reconstructed, that we come to the expression of anxiety on all fronts, relating to the year 447, which we saw earlier.[102] There follows the passage which offers the most precise view of what might have been the long-term consequences for the Empire of Theodosius and his successors, if the regime of Attila had lasted:[103]

> Edeco, a Scythian who had performed outstanding deeds in war, came again as ambassador together with Orestes, a Roman by origin who lived in the part of Pannonia close to the river Save which became subject to the barbarian by the treaty made with Aetius, the general of the western Romans. This Edeco came to the court and handed over the letters from Attila, in which he blamed the Romans in respect of the fugitives. In retaliation he threatened to resort to arms if the Romans did not surrender them and if they did not cease cultivating the land which he had won in the war. This, he asserted, was a strip five days' journey wide and extending along the Danube from Pannonia to Novae in Thrace. Furthermore, he said that the market in Illyria was not (now) on the bank of the Danube, as it had been before, but at Naissus, which he had laid waste and established as the border point between the Scythian and the Roman territory, it being five days' journey from the Danube for an unladen man. He ordered that ambassadors come to him and not just ordinary men but the highest ranking of the consulars; if the Romans were wary of sending them, he would cross to Serdica to receive them.

Many significant points arise from this account. Attila himself is still to be found north of the Danube, and (as a glance at the map on figure VIII

101. Priscus (ed. Blockley), F. 9.[4]; Theophanes, *Chron.* A. M. 5942; see C. Mango and R. Scott, *The Chronicle of Theophanes Confessor* (1996), ad loc.
102. P. 41 above.
103. Priscus, F.11.1, trans. Blockley.

will show) the advanced frontier which he proposes does indeed lie some hundred kilometers or so ("five days' journey") south of the Danube. Here too we find the "western Romans" identified as a separate power; where the twin Empires meet, near Viminacium on the middle Danube, their diplomatic dealings with Attila also intersect. Finally, the indication at the end that Attila expects to deal only with individuals who belonged to the inner circle of power at Constantinople is borne out with remarkable clarity in the surviving sections of narrative which follow. As we will see later (chapter 6), the account confirms to a remarkable degree the evidence of other sources as to who the holders of power in the last years of Theodosius were.

We need not follow further details, except to note that Priscus's famous account of the embassy to Attila in which he himself participated (11.2) shows that a Magister Militum, Agintheus, was still operating near Naissus, that Attila's court was still located north of the river, and that he was negotiating at the same time with representatives of the "western Romans." A later embassy, conducted by two very prominent office-holders, Anatolius and Nomus (see chapter 6), is described as having persuaded Attila to moderate his demands, and even to withdraw from the Roman territory along the Danube (15.4). The precise dates of each phase are not clear, but at any rate the narrative brings us close to the time of Theodosius's unexpected death in July 450. In the first year of Marcian's reign the threat from Attila was still present. But in 451 he marched west, to meet, first, defeat in Gaul in the same year, and then his own sudden death in 453. The Danube frontier remained intact.

This is not to say that the 440s had not been a profound shock for the Empire, expressed for instance by Theodoret, far away in Cyrrhus, in a letter which seems to date to 447, and which speaks of how, as a punishment for sin, God "has shaken the earth against us, and set the tribes of barbarians on us from all directions."[104]

The disasters of these years were also to provide ample material for Nestorius, who was equally well informed about them in his exile in the Great Oasis in Egypt, where he died early in Marcian's reign, just as the new Emperor was taking steps to release him. As we will see later (chapter 5), to his polemical and combative mind it was not difficult to interpret all these troubles as a sign of God's wrath, and that wrath itself as a punishment for the Empire's support for heretical doctrines.

Overall, however, in spite of military pressures, whether major or of mi-

---

104. Theodoret, *Epp.* II.41.

nor local significance, the Empire exhibited both a remarkable sensitivity to problems and conflicts in its border regions, and in the end maintained all of its frontiers intact. As a governmental and military system, it showed great coherence. It remains to ask whether, internally, it was marked by a similar level of coherence, or by diversity and conflict.

III Integration and Diversity

1. LATIN IN GOVERNMENT

Looked at from a distance, in broad terms, Theodosius's Empire was firstly, and in a very profound sense, Roman. Its administrative structure was inherited from the unified Roman Empire of the first four centuries of the Christian era, as was its army. It also generated the first Code of Roman Law to be compiled on the instructions of an Emperor and to be explicitly named after him, the *Codex Theodosianus*, itself deliberately intended as an expression of the principle of the unity of East and West. All the Imperial "laws" contained in it, including those from the reign of Theodosius himself, were in Latin. That they could be so, however, was a simple product of the fact that in form and function they were all, with minimal exceptions, letters from the Emperor to office-holders.[1] In the nature of the case no one formed a plan to generate a *Codex* of letters produced in the middle reaches of the administration, from officials to the Emperor, or from one official to another of whatever rank. So the evidence available at this level is much less complete. But the indications are unambiguous: all correspondence written within the administration was also written in Latin.[2]

---

1. It is in this specific sense that it is wholly correct to describe Latin as the "langue d'état" of Theodosius's empire. See the classic treatment by G. Dagron, "Aux Origines de la civilization byzantine: langue de culture et langue d'État," *Rev. Hist.* 241 (1969): 23 ff. = *La romanité chrétienne en Orient: Héritages et mutations* (1984), no. I. Note also the suggestive survey by V. Poggi, "Situazione linguistica dell'Oriente bizantino nel secolo V," in *Autori classici in lingue del Vicino e Medio Oriente,* ed. G. Fiaccadori (1990), 105 ff.

2. For examples of intermediate-level official correspondence which is either preserved in its original Latin or which we know to have been in Latin, see chapter 1, pp. 20–22 (Magister Militum in Oriens to Consularis of Cyprus; Comes Sacrarum Largitionum to Praeses of Caria). As we will see in more detail in chapter 5, the *Tra-*

That is the first sense in which the Theodosian Empire was an example of integration: the internal business of government, over the whole area of some two thousand kilometers corner to corner, was conducted in Latin, as an expression of its character as a "Roman" Empire. But the continued use of Latin as a *langue d'état* deserves more emphasis. We have already encountered the general proposition that all communications addressed by cities, Church Councils, individual bishops, other members of the clergy, or private individuals to holders of office, from the Emperor down, were written in Greek, and received replies written in Greek. Equally, as we will see in relation to the Church (in chapter 4), and (in chapter 5) to the repression of Nestorianism, the *edicta* which officials were supposed to put up in public for the people were also in Greek, and would be read out, in ecclesiastical contexts at least, in Greek. In its communications with its subjects, this was unambiguously a Greek Empire.

Two very important aspects of this systematic bilingualism, or perhaps better dual-lingualism,[3] need to be explored further. Firstly, it was not an expression of a widespread individual bilingualism prevalent in society at large. If we may take the hundreds of Greek-speaking bishops attending the two Councils of Ephesus and the Council of Chalcedon as a reasonably representative sample of (very variously) educated men, then the overall picture is again unambiguous: it cannot be assumed, and is not assumed, that they can understand either written or spoken Latin. In the entire corpus of verbatim records of meetings of these Councils, only one bishop, Florentius of Sardis, is recorded, at Ephesus II, as being able to provide an extempore translation of interventions in Latin by representatives of the bishop of Rome.[4] (At Ephesus I, translations of written or spoken material in Latin are supplied, and entered in the *Acta*, but there is no clear indication of who does this).[5]

---

goedia of Irenaus contained numerous examples of such letters, translated into Greek (and known to us as retranslated into Latin by Liberatus): *ACO* I.4, para. 230 (pp. 108–109), Magister Militiae to Comes et Vicarius; para. 268 (p. 198), Magister Militum to Iudex (governor) of Cilicia II; para. 272 (p. 200), Magister Militum to Praeses; para. 273 (pp. 200–201), Praeses to Vicarius(?); para. 274 (p. 201), Iudex to Comes Orientis; para. 278 (p. 203), Praetorian Prefect to unidentified subordinate.

3. I owe to my colleague Professor Anna Morpurgo Davies the (perhaps surprising) information that there is no established technical term for a system in which two languages are current, but individual monolingualism is the norm.

4. See pp. 17–20 above.

5. As for Ephesus I, see p. 19 above for the reading of a letter from Capreolus of Carthage at the first session, on June 22, first in Latin and then in Greek translation. Similarly, at the session on July 10, when delegates from the Roman see first join

It therefore seems to follow that the Imperial service, both civilian and military, in continuing to function internally in Latin, must have performed an actively integrative function, by making the learning of Latin a necessary qualification, applicable equally to everybody who entered, from whatever part of the "Greek Roman Empire" they came. Of course we must allow for cases where such a process was not necessary. Firstly, we have to remember that when Theodosius became sole Augustus in the East, the de facto division between East and West had taken place only thirteen years earlier—and was never seen in principle as a formal division. So it would be hard to argue that there were no cases of individuals born in the Latin-speaking West who were already in service in 395 in the East, and continued to pursue a career there. A *praeses* aged thirty in 395 might have risen to the Praetorian Prefecture at sixty in 425, and by then have been able to function in both languages.

But, while the fifth century overall provides evidence on a scale which the earlier Empire cannot remotely match, the evidence is more limited in one crucial respect, namely the absence of the genre of the career inscription, often (in earlier centuries) set up in the individual's home town, and detailing all the posts held by him up to the present, or up to death.[6] Honorific inscriptions for officials in the Greek East in the Late Roman period tend, as the great Louis Robert noted, to expound the personal virtues and qualities of the man honored, but not to record the stages of his "career."[7] We have already seen a precise example of this, from the base of the statue at Aphrodisias in honor of Oecumenius.[8] The effect of this is in fact that, on both the civilian and the military side, we have no clear idea of what a normal career will have been like, of how (for example) a future Praetorian Prefect started in Imperial service, or at what age, and how many posts he will have gone through before reaching the top. As regards the question of regional, and hence linguistic, origins we depend on incidental evidence from literary sources for the information that (for example) Flavius Dionysius,

---

the Cyrillian side, oral addresses in Latin are then translated, and recorded in the *Acta* in Greek. Petros, a presbyter of Alexandria and *primikerios notariōn*, conducts the proceedings, but there is no precise indication of who supplies the translations (*ACO* I.1.3, para. 106, pp. 53–65).

6. For a discussion of the importance of this genre of inscription see W. Eck, "The Prosopographia Imperii Romani and Prosopographical Method," in *Fifty Years of Prosopography: The Later Roman Empire, Byzantium and Beyond*, ed. A. M. Cameron (2003), 11 ff.

7. See L. Robert, "Epigrammes du Bas-Empire," *Hellenica* 4 (1948): 1 ff.

8. P. 28 above.

Magister Militum in Oriens in 431, came from Thrace,[9] or Cyrus, the famous Praetorian and Urban Prefect, from Panopolis in Upper Egypt (the Thebaid).[10] It may be that the letter in Latin which Dionysius sent to the Consularis of Cyprus was composed for him.[11] But when Marcian, a former soldier from Thrace, called the Council of Chalcedon in 451, after being unexpectedly summoned to the role of Emperor in the previous year, he attended the sixth session of the Council in person, and made the same speech to the assembled bishops twice, once in Greek and once in Latin.[12] All three will have been native speakers of Greek, but Marcian at least was already functionally bilingual.

We will need to return shortly to some very important aspects of the recruitment process and its social background. But, to pursue its linguistic aspect, it does not seem possible to provide a single illustrative example of an actual case of the hypothetical pattern sketched above, namely a "westerner" with Latin as his first language, who remained in service in the East under Theodosius. There surely were such, however, and their invisibility must be a function of the nature of our evidence.

The second possibility is that there were areas, on the Adriatic coast or along the Danube, where colonization, settlement, or the influence of the dominant Roman culture over the previous centuries had created an established Latin-speaking population. Again, the possibility cannot be denied, and it would be very hard to believe that at Viminacium, in the extreme northwest corner of the Theodosian Empire, Greek was normally spoken in the street. Priscus records meeting a Greek-speaking prisoner from there at the court of Attila—but the man was a Greek immigrant who had gone there as a trader and stayed on until the city was captured (11.2). But neither the lay society nor the church of these middle-Danubian cities plays a role in our evidence. Further down the river, where we could well have expected a Latin-speaking community, we find in fact, as already noted, that bishops from Novae and Durostorum who appear at the Councils speak Greek.[13] John Cassian, described by Gennadius as "by origin a Scythian" *(natione Scytha)*, was a major ecclesiastical writer in Latin, in the fifth century, and had earlier been a monk in Constantinople. That might be a hint of a Latin-speaking population in the province of Scythia, but it is a frail basis for any such con-

9. *PLRE* II, Dionysius 13.

10. *PLRE* II, Cyrus 7.

11. See p. 21 above and, for the text, p. 138 below.

12. *ACO* II.2, para. 1.2–8 (pp. 138–41 [334–37]). Only the Greek translation is recorded in the *Acta*.

13. P. 17 above.

clusion.[14] As we have seen earlier, it is only, and unexpectedly, from two places on the Adriatic coast, Scodra and Apollonia, both of which we would have assumed to be Greek-speaking, that bishops appear at Ephesus I speaking and subscribing in Latin.[15]

In short, it is a matter of speculation as to whether there were substantial communities of native speakers of Latin within Theodosius's Empire, and if so where. Insofar as there were, we should be open to the possibility that they provided a significant number of recruits for the Latin-using administration and the army. The predominant pattern which our evidence suggests is, however, a quite different one, namely recruitment (civilian and military) from the wider population of native Greek speakers, and from literally anywhere in the Empire, without distinction. Thus, for instance, the future monk Alexander Akoimetos (the "non-sleeper") had been born in what was evidently a respectable family in one of the Aegean islands, went to Constantinople to study *grammatikē*, and then enrolled as what his *Life* calls an *eparchikos*, someone on the staff of either a Praetorian or an Urban Prefect *(Eparchos)*, before giving away his property and going to Syria as a monk.[16] Auxentius, by contrast, came from Syria, and travelled to Constantinople to find an uncle who was the *optio* of a *numerus (noumeros)* in the army, failed to locate him, and signed up in the fourth *schola* of the Scholarii.[17]

Neither *Life* identifies any stage where the individual learned Latin, whether as a normal part of education or as a special qualification. The wonderful *Life* by Marinus of the great pagan Neoplatonist Proclus, by contrast, does, or seems to. Proclus was born in 410/12 in a rich Lycian family, studied with a *grammatikos* there, went to Alexandria, where his studies included *Rōmaika*, an expression which surely includes Latin, and then worked as an advocate in Constantinople. But at that point he too turned away from public life, but in the opposite direction, to Plato and Aristotle.[18]

For those who did aim for a career in the public service or, it seems, as an advocate, Latin will at some stage have been an essential element in their education. Exactly this is expressed in what is now thought to be a text of the first half of the fifth century, the work of Symeon of Mesopotamia. The

14. Gennadius, *De viris illustribus*, 61. On a longer view, incorporating the earlier centuries of the Empire, the inscriptions from Scythia show that both Greek and Latin were in use; see D. M. Pippidi and A. Avram, *Inscriptiile din Scythia Minor Grecesti si Latine*, 3 vols. (1983–99).

15. P. 18 above.

16. See the *Vita* of Alexander, 5–6.

17. *Vita* of Auxentius, 1–2.

18. Marinus, *Vita Prochi*, 1–13.

fact that he is using a picture of a typical secular education as a model for the progression of the soul towards grace makes the image all the more significant:[19]

> Just as he who wishes to learn to read goes off and learns the letters, and when he has reached the top of that class he goes to the school of Roman law, and there he is the lowest beginner, and then when he becomes a *scholasticus,* he is the lowest beginner among the advocates, and then, when he has become first there, then he becomes governor, and when he is in office, he takes his assessor to help him.

Latin was clearly essential for anyone, of any rank, performing a public function, even though all exchanges and communications with the public, whether groups or individuals, took place in Greek. We can see this exemplified in the two papyri of 434 recording proceedings in court before the *praeses* of the Egyptian province of Arcadia.[20] A *libellus* written in Greek has been presented to the governor, and the governor himself speaks in Greek. But the official who recorded the proceedings did so in Latin. The chances of this member of the governor's *officium* having been an immigrant from the Latin West must be minimal. So we can take this as an official language learned for the purpose by a native speaker of Greek. Even if we think only of the civilian, administrative structure, ignoring financial officials and their staffs, we are concerned with two Praetorian Prefectures, seven positions at the rank of Vicarius and sixty-one provincial governorships under various titles. Peter Heather's estimate of some three thousand positions, for officials and their staffs, must be of the right order.[21] But in any case it was dwarfed by an army which was perhaps a hundred times larger.[22] Again the internal use of Latin is surely to be presumed, even if direct documentation for this period seems to be entirely lacking. But the rather slight papyrus documentation available for this period suggests that both in exchanges with civilians, and in private business (sales or contracts) between each other, soldiers reverted to Greek.[23]

We can be certain, therefore, that as a general rule the first language of

---

19. I owe my knowledge of this text, and the translation, to C. M. Roueché, "The Functions of the Governor in Late Antiquity: Some Observations," *AT* 6 (1998): 321 ff., on p. 34.

20. Appendix B, nos. 10–11.

21. P. Heather, "New Men for New Constantines? Creating an Imperial Elite in the Eastern Mediterranean," in *New Constantines,* ed. P. Magdalino (1994), 11 ff.

22. See p. 45 above for an estimate of three hundred thousand for the army.

23. See, e.g., *P. Mich.,* no. 613, Aug. 19, 415; *SB,* no. 9598, c. 435, see H. Hunger, *Jahrb. d. Öst. Byz. Ges.* 9 (1968): 21 ff.; *Stud. Pal.* XX, no. 143 (c. 435).

those who entered the civil administration of the Empire or the army was Greek. But the ability to function in Latin was essential. "Laws" from the Emperor and instructions from higher officials came down to the lower ranks in Latin, and might need to be translated into Greek to form *edicta* posted for public information. All representations from individuals or groups among the civil population were written in Greek, and any consequential reports or positive submissions *(suggestiones)* had to be put into Latin for transmission upwards. We shall see this intermediate level of official internal communications in Latin most clearly when we look at the enforcement of the Imperial will in Syria and Cilicia in 431–36, after the first Council of Ephesus.[24] As for its functioning at the highest level, as between Praetorian Prefects or Magistri Militum and the Emperor (the only level systematically represented in the *Codex Theodosianus* and the *Novellae* of Theodosius), we have already seen many examples, and will encounter many more.

It is not impossible, in principle, that officials who were native speakers of Greek relied on specialist staff members to read and compose communications in Latin. But it seems improbable that such a system of, so to speak, secondary deployment of Latin could have been the norm. We must therefore conclude that those who entered the public service, whether civilian or military, must either have learned Latin as part of their normal education—even though bishops and other clergy, as a rule, did not do so—or must have sought a special training in Latin.

Our evidence for the process of learning Latin—at what age, in what institutions, through what procedures?—is remarkably poor. We have no autobiographical account from this period to rival the description provided by Gregory (the later "Thaumaturgus") from Neocaesarea of the steps by which in the first half of the third century, he approached his intended career as a Roman lawyer.[25] Even passing allusions to teachers of Latin are rare. One such reference is Socrates' mention of Paul, who became bishop of the Novatians in Constantinople in 419; he had earlier been a teacher of Latin before giving it up to be an ascetic.[26]

Since there is no evidence for how, in innumerable local communities,

24. Pp. 163–64 and 178–81 below.

25. See F. Millar, "The Greek East and Roman Law: The Dossier of M. Cn. Licinius Rufinus," *JRS* 89 (1999): 90 ff., on pp. 106–108.

26. Socrates, *HE* VII.17.2. I have not found any detailed treatment of access to instruction in Latin in the Greek East in the earlier fifth century. For the wider background, H.-I. Marrou, *Histoire de l'éducation dans l'Antiquité*, 6th ed. (1965), 374–75. Note also B. Rochette, *Le Latin dans le monde grec* (1997), 165 ff., "Le latin dans l'enseignement des provinces orientales."

people gained access to instruction in Latin, all that we can do is to under-line the fact that, however this was achieved, the result was a massively im-portant, indeed determinative, factor in the making of the Empire. Out of an overall population of perhaps some thirty million, at least several thousand adult males were necessarily in some degree of contact with Latin for the performance of their duties. That leaves out of account what is a potentially much larger group which was presumably exposed to Latin, the soldiers. But our knowledge of the internal functioning of the army is very poor.

On any construction, Latin was an important feature of the "Roman" superstructure of the "Greek Roman Empire," and one whose continuing currency required a learning process from a significant minority of adult males. However there is very little to show that, even among educated per-sons who had learned Latin, the inherited corpus of pagan Latin literature, or of Christian theological writing in Latin, normally entered an individ-ual's culture. In the context of the Greek Church, as the *Acta* of the Coun-cils show, the one Christian Latin writer who functions prominently as a point of reference for orthodox doctrine is Ambrose of Milan.[27]

At the level of the technical vocabulary of office-holding, military ranks and names of units, as well as the terminology of taxation and government, innumerable Latin words became naturalized in Greek,[28] and we will see later an extract from a report of official proceedings from 449, preserved in Greek, where almost the entire vocabulary is Latin.[29]

But beyond the adoption into Greek of transliterated individual words, the composition of official documents in Latin required a grasp of grammar, and in certain cases a real acquaintance with the concepts of Classical Ro-man law. It should be said, however, that only a very small minority of the "laws" of Theodosius's reign actually address the issues of civil law—prop-erty, family, inheritance, or personal status—which represent the primary concerns of "Roman Law" as preserved in the juristic writings of the Clas-sical period, two to three centuries earlier.[30] The majority of the content of

27. For Ambrose as cited in the *Acta* see, e.g., *ACO* I.1.3, para. 97 (p. 41); I.1.5, para. 143 (p. 7); I.1.7, para. 63 (p. 75). A Greek translation of two brief extracts from Ambrose *De fide, ACO* I.1.2, para. 54 (pp. 42–43).

28. For the vocabulary of office-holding, the invaluable monograph of P. Koch, *Die byzantinischen Beamtentitel von 400 bis 700* (1903), has not been superseded.

29. See pp. 166–67 below.

30. For (relatively rare) examples of Theodosian "laws" that address issues which belong to the sphere of Classical Roman Law, as defined in the juristic writ-ings excerpted in the *Digest* (itself of course a sixth-century compilation produced in Constantinople), see *CTh* VIII.17.2–3 (*CJ* VIII.57.2 + 58.1) + *CJ* I.19.6, Sept. 4, 410, on the Lex Papia Poppaea; *CTh* VIII.12.8 (*CJ* VIII.53.27), Mar. 23, 415, on *donationes;*

the *Theodosian Code* concerns not "law" in this technical sense at all, but administration and government.

In conclusion, the "Roman" governmental structure of the eastern Empire functioned internally in Latin, and required the acquisition of at least some knowledge of Latin from those of its Greek-speaking subjects who joined the Imperial service. At the level of personal recruitment, therefore, by not only maintaining a large army and a quite extensive civilian administration, but requiring of individuals the use of a learned, or second, "language of state," it did provide a very significant integrative structure within which the millions of its Greek-speaking subjects lived.

It was not, however, just that they lived within this internally Latin-using structure, but that the "laws" issued by the Emperor in Latin (virtually all, to repeat, letters to office-holders) themselves show that the government operated in constant dialogue with both its own employees and its subjects. We saw in chapter 2 a whole series of examples of responses (or hoped-for responses) to issues arising from the long frontiers of the Empire. It may be useful to note a few further examples of Imperial laws, or rulings, which visibly respond to issues arising in different provinces: the improper influence of an embassy from Achaea; properties in Osrhoena; exemption from taxation of the Church of Thessalonica; Imperial properties in the Thebaid; the cutting down of trees at Daphne near Antioch.[31]

Two examples perhaps deserve rather fuller quotation, to illustrate the reflection in these Latin "laws" of very particular local circumstances in Greek cities. It is no accident that both come from the fuller texts preserved in the *Novellae*. The first is Theodosius's own report, written from Aphrodisias in 443 (p. 9 above), of the requests recently addressed to him by the people of Heraclea:[32]

> Wherefore, when for the sake of a vow *(voti causa)*, We were making a passage through the municipality of Heraclea *(per Heracleotanam civitatem)*, We were moved to great compassion by the petitions of the citizens of the aforesaid *civitas*, who requested that care should be given by Our provisions to their walls as well as their aqueduct, and also their

---

CTh IV.4.5 (CJ VI.23.20), Mar. 13, 416, *Edictum ad populum* on wills; CTh VIII.12.9 (CJ VIII.53.28), Mar. 14, 417, on *donationes*; CJ I.50.2, Oct. 14, 427, legal powers of governors. See also *Nov. Th.* 11, 12, 14, all of 439, on issues of private law.

31. CTh XI.7.18, Sept. 27, 409 (Achaea); CTh XII.3.2 (CJ X.34.1), Aug. 9, 423 (Osrhoena); CTh XI.1.38 (CJ I.2.8 + X.16.12), Oct. 10, 424 (Thessalonica); CTh V.16.34 (CJ XI.68.6), Dec. 13, 425 (Thebaid); CJ XI.78.2, 427? (Antioch).

32. *Nov. Th.* 23, May 22, 443; trans. Pharr, with adjustments.

other public works, on the ground that they had been neglected for a long time.

The requests mentioned lead on to general measures which the addressee, the Praetorian Prefect of Oriens, is to promulgate in *edicta*.

The second is a remarkable disturbance which had arisen in Emesa in the province of Phoenice Libanensis in 444:[33]

> Therefore, in so far as the report *(suggestio)* of Your Magnitude has revealed, Valerianus, a decurion of the *Emesena civitas*, a transgressor of the public law and the statutes, assumed for himself unjustly and surreptitiously the cincture of office of an Illustrious honor, in order that he might rely on the insignia of such high rank and might be able to fulfill his insolent design. For accompanied by a great horde of barbarians, he rushed into the private council chamber *(secretarium)* of the governor of the province, he dared to vindicate a prior place for himself, he seated himself on the right of the man to whom We have committed the laws, to whom We considered that the fate of the provincials should be entrusted, and thus when he had put to flight all the office staff of the governor, he left everything devastated and deserted . . .

This letter too is addressed to the current Praetorian Prefect of Oriens, and it too enumerates general rules, which are to be embodied in *edicta*.

Enough has been said to illustrate the constant dialogue, crossing and recrossing the boundary between Greek and Latin, which marked the government of Theodosius's Empire. But was Greek the only language in use among the population and, if it was not, what was the significance of linguistic diversity, and how did the role and function of other languages relate to that of Greek? Were there recognised non-Greek ethnic elements within the Empire, who were seen as representing an exception to the general pattern of identity as (Christian) Greeks which now characterised the Theodosian world?

2. GREEK AS THE LINGUA FRANCA

As regards the relation of Greek to Latin, we have seen its vertical relation to the Latin used internally in the administration of the Empire, and have touched on its lateral interchange with Latin in the life of the Church: firstly in the long-distance exchange of letters and doctrinal texts between bish-

---

33. *Nov. Th.* 15.2, July 20, 444; trans. Pharr, with adjustments.

ops in the East and West, involving a process of translation at either end;[34] and secondly in the appearance at both Councils of Ephesus, in 431 and 449, of representatives of the Roman see, whose spoken interventions also needed to be translated.[35] In parallel with that, both Caelestinus of Rome at the time of Ephesus I, and far more forcefully (though in the short run ineffectively) Leo of Rome, before and after Ephesus II, engaged in direct correspondence with Theodosius in Latin, which did not require translation.[36]

A comparable process of translation must have been involved also in the quite frequent letters sent by the bishops of Rome to the Church in Illyricum to remind it of the status of the bishops of Thessalonica as their Vicarii, and hence of the preeminent authority claimed by Rome there.[37] It does not seem that any correspondence from Illyricum to Rome is preserved. Equally, there will surely have been areas of linguistic interchange in Illyricum itself, and along the Danube, but the evidence from these areas is too inadequate. The nearest that we come to the conception of a Latin-speaking Church on the Lower Danube is the letter to the Emperor Leo, sent in 458 by the bishops of Abrittus, Appiaria, Durostorum, Nicopolis, Novae, and Odessa, and written in Latin.[38] In all these cities, the likelihood is that both languages were in use.

Latin is of course, for many reasons, a special case, given its role both in secular government and in the life of the Church. Even more complex issues arise over the role of other languages, and their relation to Greek. It should be said at once that the range of languages involved is small, and the areas concerned relatively limited: in crude summary, we should reckon (in principle) with Armenian, though there is no contemporary documentary evidence; with Syriac, in various dialects, between them spoken in most parts of Oriens, but still written, as a language of culture, only in a quite limited area; in Palestine, with Hebrew and Jewish Aramaic, used by both Jews and Samaritans, and perhaps also with a local Christian version of Aramaic; on the fringes of Oriens with Arabic; and in Egypt with Egyptian (Coptic), no

---

34. Pp. 18–19 above.

35. P. 18 above.

36. Caelestinus and Theodosius: *Epp.* 19 = *ACO* I.2, para. 9 (pp. 25–26); *Epp.* 23 (Greek trans. in *ACO* I.1.7, para. 86, pp. 129–30). Leo and Theodosius: *Epp.* 24 = *ACO* II.4, para. 2 (pp. 3–4); 29 = II.4, para. 7 (pp. 9–10); 37 = II.4, para. 15 (pp. 17–18); 44 = II.4, para. 18 (pp. 19–21); 54 = II.4, para. 9 (p. 11); 69 = II.4, para. 30 (pp. 30–31).

37. For examples of letters from the bishops of Rome to Illyricum, note Innocentius (407–17): *Epp.* 13, 16–18; Bonifatius (418–22): *Epp.* 4–5, 13–15; Caelestinus (422–32): *Epp.* 3; Sixtus/Xystus (432–40): *Epp.* 7–10; Leo (440–61)—letters of 440–50: *Epp.* 13–14.

38. *ACO* II.5, para. 18 (p. 32).

longer used for monumental inscriptions, but extensively spoken, and used for Christian literary works.[39] One papyrus from Antinoopolis in Egypt also shows Jewish Aramaic being used for a legal document in 417.[40] As will be obvious, a study such as this will be able to do no more than sketch what is known, or seems to be known, of these complex social, religious, and linguistic contexts. In any case our concern is with public communications, debate, and persuasion. So it should be said, first, that there is no evidence that any holder of a secular post ever received or sent any communication in any language other than Latin or Greek. Second, over large areas of the Theodosian Empire, namely the whole of Illyricum and Thrace, the ancient Greek zone of Achaea and the islands, all of Asia Minor, and Libya, there is no documentary evidence from this period for the currency of any local language, and no trace of the existence of any non-Greek literature, and still less any literature forming the material for debate, persuasion, or the assertion of rights. Passing references in literary sources remind us to be cautious about negative generalizations[41]—but the concern here is with the public forums represented by government on the one hand and the life of the Church on the other. In that specific context the only non-Classical language which is accorded a special place, in the life of the Church, but not in the secular context, is Syriac.

For large areas of the Empire, therefore, the only language (other than Latin) for whose currency we have documentary evidence is Greek. Furthermore, it has to be emphasized that Greek was provably current, as attested by either inscriptions or perishable documents or both, in all of the areas where non-Classical languages were also spoken, including Egypt on the one hand, and Osrhoene, the heartland of Syriac culture, on the other, as well as Palaestina I and II, where Greek coexisted with Hebrew and Aramaic even in the inscriptions incorporated in the mosaic floors of synagogues.[42]

More important to the central theme of this study, honorific inscriptions, all in Greek, from many parts of the Empire, testify to the loyalism for which

39. For a recent survey of literary output in Coptic from this period see M. Smith, "Coptic Literature, 337–425," in *The Cambridge Ancient History* XIII: *The Later Empire, AD 337–425*, ed. A. Cameron and P. Garnsey (1998), 720 ff.

40. See C. Sirat et al., *La Ketouba de Cologne: Un contrat de mariage juif à Antinoopolis* (1986).

41. See P. Charanis, "Ethnic Changes in the Byzantine Empire in the Seventh Century," *DOP* 13 (1959): 23 ff.

42. For the best available survey see A. Ovadiah, *Hellenistic, Roman and Early Byzantine Mosaic Pavements in Israel* (1987).

local communities sought public expression, and to the honor accorded to individual Imperial office-holders. There is no need to multiply examples, but one very prominent case is Anatolius, Magister Utriusque Militiae in Oriens in 433–c. 446, honored on inscriptions at Heliopolis in Phoenice, and at Gerasa and Bostra in Arabia for building work carried out in 440; literary evidence adds the presentation of a reliquary to the church of Edessa and the construction of a basilica at Antioch.[43] A high profile of this sort is highly relevant to the workings of government, for we shall see later that his influence was well known to Theodoret, to the crowd on the streets of Edessa in 449, and to the historian Priscus (chapter 6). Equally, Herculius, who is well attested as Praetorian Prefect of Illyricum in 408–10, is named on several inscriptions from Athens, which will have been placed on the bases of statues of him erected in his honor. One was found near the Library of Hadrian in the Agora, and another was placed on the Acropolis beside the statue of Athena Promachos: as the inscription explicitly says, "for Herculius was the champion *(promachos)* of the laws."[44]

The highly stylized and rhetorical texts of the honorific inscriptions of this period, for instance from Ephesus as well as Athens, represent a branch of rhetoric in themselves, as Louis Robert revealed. In only one case, however, the statue of Oecumenius at Aphrodisias, can statue and inscription and the precise original location all be recovered.[45] But a recently published Greek inscription from Amisus, on the Black Sea coast, in the relatively remote and little-known province now called "Helenopontus," will serve to remind us that a flowery and elaborate rhetoric of praise, combining traditional and Christian elements, could be practiced here too. The honorand, Erythrius, is not known otherwise, and the title "Comes," which could be used in the civil administration, financial posts, or in a military context, gives no clue as to his function or career. It is clear at least that he was a rich native of Amisus, who had risen to Imperial honors. The date, 435, is derived from the era of the city:[46]

WITH GOOD FORTUNE

Epigrams in your honour would require golden *stelai* and oracles from the Pythian Priestess, most magnificent *comes* Erythrius, and even then we would fall far behind in the thanks which we offer in exchange,

43. *PLRE* II, Anatolius 10.
44. *PLRE* II Herculius 2. The inscription quoted is *IG* II², no. 4225 = L. Robert, *Hellenica* 4 (1948): p. 41.
45. Chapter 1, p. 28 above.
46. See C. Marek, "Dank der Stadt an einen Comes in Amisos unter Theodosius II," *Chiron* 30 (2000): 367 ff.

compared with the worth of your benefits. Receive then, pre-eminent and famous man, what is possible as eternal thanks from your fellow-citizens. It is not just we, the town and the people, who say this, but every visiting stranger and all the surrounding area is in awe at your benefactions. For who ever, in food shortages, did so much to feed the people, or was so generous at banquets, or who provided, when water was short, such rich sources of clear streams for use in the baths, for possession by private people and for the enjoyment of the city? Therefore, we all offer a common prayer, all-powerful God: preserve our *euergetēs* with his wife and children, blessing him with your divine light. [date]

Greek was thus by far the most common language of ordinary life, as well as being the language in which Church and people addressed the representatives of the State, and in which they in their turn diffused the content of Imperial laws, as well as being the language used for communications to the Church in the West (which were then translated). Above all, given the massive and unprecedented evidence available from this period represented by the surviving proceedings of the Church Councils, it was the standard language in which bishops, from all parts of the Theodosian Empire, both spoke and gave their written subscriptions. We can deploy a minute fraction of this massive bulk of evidence by way of illustration, while also exploring how Greek, as used at the Councils, functioned in relation to other languages as a lingua franca into which anything in any other language would be translated; in other words, to use the expression of Riccardo Contini, it was a "lingua veicolare"—a "vehicular language," to which any other languages must relate.[47] Even if in fact the public role even of Syriac itself was modest, and if other languages (Persian, Egyptian) are very rarely found in use, that still makes a significant difference between Church and State. No holder of public office is ever addressed in, or himself deploys, any language other than Latin or Greek.

3. GREEK AND OTHER LANGUAGES AT THE CHURCH COUNCILS

The proceedings of the Church Councils, mainly preserved on medieval manuscripts,[48] represent in various ways uniquely important evidence for social

47. See R. Contini, "Il Hauran preislamico: ipotesi di una storia linguistica," *Felix Ravenna* 1/2 (1987): 24 ff.
48. For a guide to this material, as edited by E. Schwartz, see appendix A.

and religious history (not to speak of the history of personal names and of place names), but above all for linguistic history. The detailed ways in which the available texts illustrate the complex relations of Greek and Latin in the fifth century have been touched on already at various points (and could be set out in much greater detail), so they will not be discussed further here. Nor will the complex process of contemporary, or subsequent, translation of the records from their original Greek into Latin—where the resultant texts make up roughly half of the *Acta Conciliorum* as published by Eduard Schwartz—or into Syriac or Coptic.[49] The Syriac translation of the proceedings of the Second Council of Ephesus in 449 is of exceptional interest for Late Antique cultural and linguistic history, since the manuscript is far earlier than that of any of the Greek or Latin texts, having been written in 535 under Justinian. The translation had therefore been made within less than a century of the event, and the surviving copy was made at a time when the relevant issues were being vigorously debated, and when a separate Church, which moderns have labeled "Monophysite," was coming into being.[50]

Our concern here will not be with the *Acta* as examples of the extremely important process by which religious texts, once written, made their way across a number of linguistic boundaries, but with the significance of the original Greek texts. To summarize details set out more fully in appendixes A and B, the *Acta* are significant for the theme of integration and diversity, firstly in the simple fact, which we should not take for granted, that it was possible to assemble bishops from almost every part of Theodosius's Empire to debate issues of theology and Church discipline. Secondly, it is not a trivial fact that nearly every one of these several hundred bishops assembling on each occasion (three occasions, if we include Chalcedon in 451), from places as mutually distant as the Lower Danube, Armenia, the middle Euphrates and Upper Egypt, spoke and wrote the same language, Greek.

The "presence" of these hundreds of bishops in the surviving texts of the *Acta* makes itself felt in three ways. Firstly, there is the list of bishops attending with which the text of each session's proceedings opens, giving the bishop's name, that of his see (almost always a city, though not absolutely always, as we will note later) and sometimes the name of the province. Such a Council was an Imperial affair, and a Greek one. There is no regular representation from the West, except for delegates from the see of Rome, and

---

49. For Coptic versions of the *Acta* of Ephesus I see appendix A.

50. For details, see appendix A. For the religious background in the sixth century see W. H. C. Frend, *The Rise of the Monophysite Movement* (1972), a work to which this book is enormously indebted.

none at all from outside the Empire, for instance in the Sasanid empire. The effect is therefore to produce a sort of gazetteer of a large selection of the cities and provinces which made up Theodosius's Empire.

Secondly, the *Acta* incorporate what are represented as verbatim transcriptions of the spoken interventions by individual bishops: not of course that all participants spoke, but at the extremes the numbers of bishops who speak at a particular session can reach into three figures. As appendix B shows in detail, we are less well informed about recording processes at these Greek Councils than for instance at the Council of Carthage in 411. We cannot be certain that, even in the case of interventions which were not subsequently the subject of controversy, there had been no silent process of correction of vocabulary or grammar. In any case, as appendix B illustrates, there was vigorous dispute at Chalcedon as to whether the record of Ephesus II had been falsified as regards matters of substance.

All the same, none of these considerations should be allowed to minimize the huge significance of these records. Firstly, the overwhelming mass of bishops, from widely separated locations, could debate in the same language, and without any overt indications of mutual difficulty with dialect or pronunciation (a moment's reflection on what would be required for a conference of delegates from the same region now might be instructive). Secondly, however imperfect the original recording process may have been, and however far the scribes concerned corrected what they had heard in the process of writing it down, not to speak of variations introduced in subsequent manuscript transmission, it still remains the case that these records bring us (at least) incomparably *closer* to the spoken Greek of antiquity than is possible for any other period, and do so on a very extensive scale. As a very rough approximation, the verbatim transcriptions of proceedings listed in appendix B amount to some six thousand lines of spoken Greek. To offer an example, we will take a small extract from Ephesus I, and the first session held by Nestorius's opponents on June 22, 431.[51] After the reading of the Creed established at Nicaea in 325 and of a letter from Cyril of Alexandria to Nestorius, Cyril himself spoke, and was then followed, first, by a series of metropolitan bishops and then by a long list of others, no less than a hundred and twenty-six in all. All of the interventions expressed consensus, and many were very short—and were formal and repetitive in character. But they were not identical; each bishop used his own words. In some

51. The *Acta* of the first session of Ephesus I are printed in *ACO* I.1.2, paras. 33–62 (pp. 3–64). The extracts quoted, preserving the paragraph numbers, are to be found on pp. 24–25.

sections bishops from a single province follow each other in order. But in the extract which follows, the geographical sequence is random, and the text includes a translation of the words of one of the only two bishops from Theodosius's Empire who speaks in Latin (see figure X):

> (81) Promachios, bishop of Alinda, Caria, said: Acknowledging for my part that the letter of the most holy and beloved of God, our father and Archbishop Cyril, is concordant with the exposition of faith by the most holy and beloved-of-God bishops, our fathers, who gathered in Nicaea, I believe and think the same, and concur.

> (82) Saidas, bishop of Phaeno, Palaestina Salutaris, said: I assent to the doctrines laid down by the holy synod of the 318 (bishops) meeting in Nicaea; and to what was written by the most holy and beloved-of-God Cyril and the doctrines established by the most holy and beloved-of-God bishop of ours, Iouvenalios, being in agreement with the creed of the fathers, I cast my vote in accordance and assent.

> (83) Translation *(hermēneia)* of the deposition of bishop Senecio. Senecio, bishop of Scodra, said: According to the creed laid down by our holy fathers, the 318 filled with the Holy Spirit at Nicaea, and also according to the letter of the most holy and beloved-of-God father of ours Cyril, which has just been read out to us, I believe and assent.

> (84) Ioannes, bishop of Hephaistos, Augustamnica, said: Since the creed laid down by the holy synod constituted by the holy fathers in Nicaea and the letter written to the most pious Nestorius by the most pious and beloved-of-God father of ours and bishop, Cyril, contain a single meaning and a single faith, in different words, to these I too assent and am of the same doctrine, and pray to live by them by the grace of the Holy Trinity.

Later, we will cite some extracts from the crucial scene at Ephesus II in 449 when Dioscorus, the bishop of Alexandria, gets the Council to decree the deposition of Flavianus, the then bishop of Constantinople. That session also will illustrate the way in which, as a normal rule, the *Acta* record only in Greek translation those interventions which had actually been made in other languages.

This rule in fact holds without exception for languages other than Latin. But, as we have noted earlier, one manuscript of Ephesus I records both the original text (with a Greek translation) of an official letter in Latin, and also the subscriptions in Latin of the very few bishops or clergy present from the Adriatic coast, Italy, and Carthage.[52] As with the other languages which

---

52. See pp. 17–19 above.

we will consider shortly, it therefore seems that there must have been, for each session, an original document (codex?) with the handwritten subscriptions of each participant, in the language used. But the standard procedure when multiplying copies was to refer to these subscriptions in Greek, and to quote them in Greek translation. This too, therefore, is a very precise instance of the function of Greek as a "vehicular language," the language into which others were translated, to produce a uniform, universally intelligible text.

As regards "integration," subscriptions thus functioned both at this purely linguistic level, but also as a means of recording assent and consensus. Given, as we will see (chapter 4), that Ephesus I split from the beginning into two opposed factions which never held a joint session, it was a feature of all the recorded sessions from all three Councils that they never exhibited a divided vote. At the end of each session those who were present, and supported the conclusions arrived at, entered a brief written statement *(hypographē* or *subscriptio)* in their own hand stating their assent. If for any reason, such as ill health, they could not write in their own hand, they explained why, and who had written for them. Naturally enough, the texts of the subscriptions were often repetitive—but they were not systematically identical, and therefore did embody personal written statements. We would not in general doubt that bishops were literate, but nonetheless the written subscriptions, several thousand in all, do represent concrete evidence of literacy, at least at a basic level (clearly, if any of the originals had happened to survive, their importance would be incomparably greater).

Even the medieval copies which we have, however, thus provide another type of gazetteer, in no clearly discernible order, of the human, organizational, and geographical composition of the Greek Church, as well as being an explicit affirmation of consensus, and of integration across regional boundaries. So again it will be worth quoting two extracts from the list of a hundred and ninety-seven subscriptions given after the initial session of Ephesus I on June 22, 431. The bishops vary in how they allude to themselves or to their city, and whether they identify their province. One of them actually is illiterate:[53]

> (145) I, Bosporios, bishop of Gangra, the metropolis of the province
> of "Pamphylia" [an error for Paphlagonia], have subscribed
> declaring in accordance with the holy synod. I, Hypatios, a presbyter, entrusted by him, have subscribed because he is ill.

53. *ACO* I.1.2, para. 62 (pp. 61, 63).

(146) I, Arginos, bishop of Pompeiopolis of Paphlagonia, have subscribed, declaring in accordance with the holy synod. Synesios, a presbyter, subscribed on his behalf because he is ill.

(147) I, Helladios, bishop of the sacred church of God at Adramyttium, have subscribed, declaring in accordance with the holy synod . . .

(187) I, Thomas, bishop of Valentinianopolis, have subscribed, declaring in accordance with the holy synod.

(188) I, Libanios, bishop of the city of Palaiopolis, have subscribed, declaring in accordance with the holy synod.

(189) I, Euprepios, bishop of Bizye, have subscribed and declared in accordance with the holy synod.

(190) I, Theodosius, bishop of Gadara, have subscribed and declared my assent with the holy synod. I, Aitherios, *archidiakonos*, have subscribed, entrusted by him, as he is illiterate.

As will be obvious, there is ample scope both for complex questions as to errors which may have crept in, and as to the identification of cities, as well as a truly remarkable range of potential evidence for local history. What need concern us in this context, however, is the broad structural view of the integrative function of Councils in the life of the Church. In the event, Ephesus I was split from the beginning, and the decisions of Ephesus II were reversed two years later, while those of Chalcedon produced divisions, both between West and East and within the Greek Church, which were never healed. But this does not alter the fact that no barriers of distance or logistics or language stood in the way of the ideal—however unattainable—that the Church could assemble when and where the Emperors commanded, and could debate in a common language. The common language in question was Greek; but (as we will see in chapter 4) the entire hierarchy of the Church was structured by that of the "Roman" Empire, and it was the Emperor (or, formally, both Emperors), writing in Greek, who could summon an "oecumenical" council.

An "oecumenical" council, however, even if in principle it was conceived of as being " worldwide," was in fact, in all cases, including Ephesus I and II and Chalcedon, a Greek affair, in which nearly all the participants came from within the Greek-speaking Empire, and in which Greek was by far the predominant language. This was true, as we have seen repeatedly already, also in regard to Latin; and at Ephesus II in particular the priority of the Greek world was demonstrated also in the summary disregard for objections raised by the representatives of the Roman church.

Both the subordinate function of Latin and the brushing aside of objections from western participants are shown most clearly in the record of the crucial moment during Session I of Ephesus II, when Dioscorus of Alexandria declared the deposition of Flavianus of Constantinople. This verdict was introduced abruptly, following agreement to affirm the creed set out at the Council of Nicaea, and to allow no innovation. The relevant section of the *Acta* reads as follows:[54]

> Hilarus, deacon of the Church of the Romans, with Florentius, bishop of the Lydians, translating for him, said: As for that which has just been read out from the creed of those assembled in Nicaea, the same being confirmed in the holy council previously assembled in Ephesus, the apostolic throne teaches this and espouses it. I know, therefore, that this concords with the doctrines of the holy fathers, and the apostolic throne has incorporated it, holinesses, in letters addressed to you, which, if you were to order them to be read out, you would perceive as being in accordance with the truth.
>
> Basileios, bishop of Traianopolis, said: My insignificance also has been brought up in this same holy creed, and in it I pray to complete my life.
>
> Polychronios, bishop of Antipatris, said: We maintain among ourselves, by the grace of God, the divine and true definitions, and pray to be preserved in this same creed.
>
> The holy council said: We are all of the same opinion and faith.

Dioscurus then arose, repeated a similar affirmation at greater length, and then introduced the theme of the disturbance caused to the Church by Flavianus, "the former bishop of the church of the Constantinopolitans," and by Eusebius of Dorylaeum, proclaimed their deposition, and demanded the assent of the council:

> Wherefore we also, confirming their doctrines, have judged the aforesaid Flavianus and Eusebius as being deprived of all priestly and episcopal status. Let each most pious bishop here present declare his own opinion, and put it on record in the proceedings. All the measures taken today will be reported to our most pious and Christ-loving Emperors.
>
> Flavianus the bishop said: I repudiate you!
>
> Hilarus, deacon of the church of the Romans, said: *Contradicitur,* that is 'objection raised!'

The objection was ignored, and Flavianus's deposition was upheld, with ninety-five bishops in succession now expressing concurrence.

Latin apart, the only language, other than Greek, that played a significant part in any of the Councils, was Syriac. Later tradition asserts that Armen-

---

54. *ACO* II.1, paras. 958–64 (pp. 190–91).

ian was already an established Christian language in this period.[55] But there is no trace in the *Acta* of any of the Councils of anyone speaking or writing Armenian. This may however be a function of the fact, mentioned earlier, that the Councils were strictly Imperial meetings, summoned from the provinces of Theodosius's Empire. Bishops from "Armenia" did indeed attend—but "Armenia" in this context meant either of the two provinces in eastern Anatolia which were called Armenia I and II (see the maps in figures I and IX), not the area farther east, divided into two zones which were Roman and Sasanid protectorates. So the bishops in question used Greek.[56] Other evidence from the period illustrates how bishops from the two "Armenias" participated in the network of episcopal correspondence in Greek.[57] Indeed, it is equally in Greek that Theodoret writes to bishops of "Persian Armenia" *(Persikē Armenia)*.[58] There seems as yet to have been no wider awareness of Armenian as a language of public Christian discourse.

Rather more surprisingly, we may note that at the first session of the Council of Chalcedon in 451, the last of two hundred and fifty-two subscriptions runs, "I, Perses, have subscribed in Persian *(Persisti)*."[59] No such person is mentioned earlier in the record of the session, and there seems no explanation of who this was. Surprising in a different sense is the fact that, in the *Acta* of all three Councils taken together, there is only one reference to a bishop speaking Egyptian. Indeed, strictly speaking there is not even that. All there is is the record that at Ephesus II in 449 Kalosirios, bishop of Arsinoe, spoke twice, each time "with his deacon (Iulios or Helios) interpreting (for) him."[60] The use of the Egyptian language, or Coptic as we may call it in a Christian context, is thus implied, but no more. So far as the (extremely significant) evidence of the verbatim records of proceedings at the Church Councils goes, therefore, Coptic was accepted as a language in which one might speak, but had a very low profile. To say that is not, of course, to deny that Egyptian was and always had been a spoken and (in dif-

---

55. For a recent survey see R. W. Thomson, "Armenia in the fifth and sixth century," in *Cambridge Ancient History* XIV. *Late Antiquity: Empire and Successors AD 425–600*, ed. A. Cameron, B. Ward-Perkins, and M. Whitby (2000), 662 ff.

56. For the bishops from either province called "Armenia" attending the Councils, see, e.g., *ACO* I.1.2, para. 33 (Acacius of Melitene), who speaks at I.1.2, para. 44 (p. 13) and on several more occasions, and subscribes at para. 26 (p. 55); *ACO* II.1.1, para. 78[9] (Ioannes of Sebasteia), speaking at para. 884[12] (p. 183).

57. For instance the celebrated letter "to the Armenians" *(Tomus ad Armenios)* of Proclus, bishop of Constantinople 434–46, *Epp.* 2.

58. Theodoret, *Epp.* II.77–78.

59. *ACO* II.1.2, para. 98[252] (p. 41 [237]).

60. *ACO* II.1.1, para. 884 (p. 185); para. 1044 (p. 194).

ferent forms) written language, alongside Greek, or that Coptic already had an established place as a Christian literary language. But our subject in the context of this study is the public discourse of the Theodosian Empire, as regards either State or Church, or both. There seems to be no evidence of any of the Empire's subjects in Egypt, whether clerical or lay, addressing holders of public office in any language other than Greek. But it is significant, by contrast, that the Church, as an Empire-wide organization, did allow in principle for public spoken discourse in Coptic, duly translated on the spot.

A similar allowance might have been made, in the context of the Councils, for the bishops who represented another ethnic group, some of whose subgroups had already adopted Christianity: the "Arabs," "Saracens," or "Ishmaelites" of the desert, or steppe, on the fringes of Oriens. We have seen in chapter 2 how the preaching to them of Christianity played a part in the strategic competition for the services of the nomads between the pagan Sasanid Empire and the Christian Empire of the Theodosian dynasty. "Saracens," a word whose origin is unknown, had become the normal term for referring to them; "Ishmaelites," which was also commonly used, reflected the established belief that they could be understood collectively as the descendants of Abraham through his slave-girl Hagar and her son Ishmael. It hardly needs to be stressed that this example of ethnic, or genealogical, attribution—with no basis in biological descent, and unintelligible to anyone unfamiliar with Genesis—was to be of immense importance in the origins of Islam.[61] Here we may merely note that the conversion of Ishmaelites plays a prominent part in Theodoret's account of the life of Symeon Stylites,[62] and that the theme of their alleged descent from Abraham is explored most fully of all by Sozomenus.[63]

We may also note that from the sixth century, though not (so far) provably earlier, we find a small series of inscriptions in Arabic (both language and script), sometimes with accompanying texts in Greek (and on one occasion also Syriac), some put up by *phylarchoi*, and on occasion with explicitly Christian content,[64] and we can take it that the process by which

61. See F. Millar, "Hagar, Ishmael, Josephus and the Origins of Islam," *JJS* 44 (1993): 23 ff.; and "The Theodosian Empire (408–450) and the Arabs: Saracens or Ishmaelites?" in *Cultural Borrowings and Ethnic Appropriations in Antiquity*, ed. E. Gruen (2005), 297 ff.

62. Theodoret, *HR* XXVI.

63. See Sozomenus, *HE* VI.38.

64. See F. Millar, "Il ruolo delle lingue semitiche nel vicino oriente tardo-romano (V–VI secolo)," *Med. Ant.* 1 (1998): 71 ff., on pp. 86–88; see also Millar, "The Theodosian Empire and the Arabs" (n. 61).

some groups, or tribes, were converted to Christianity brought with it at least some level of exposure to Greek. As we saw earlier (chapter 2), one *phylarchos*, Aspebetus, transferred from Persian to Roman service, apparently during the conflict of 420/2, and converted to Christianity. Cyril of Scythopolis goes on to record that he was in fact ordained as a bishop with the Greek name "Petros."[65]

If his transfer to the Roman side did indeed take place in 420/2, as it seems, then it must be all the more striking that the same Petros, described as "bishop of the camps *(parembolai),*" not only attended Ephesus I in 431, but played a prominent part there. What is more, he both spoke and subscribed (in his own hand) in Greek. In the crucial opening session of the Cyrillian side, on June 22, he was one of the three emissaries to Nestorius who each reported orally in their own words the failure of their mission to urge him to attend. He later expressed orally his assent to the Council's decision, spoke again later, and finally subscribed in standard terms: "I, Petros, bishop of the camps, have subscribed, declaring my agreement with the holy synod." He also spoke at later sessions, and on one occasion is described as "bishop of the *parembolai* of Palestine."[66] This evidence of course tells us nothing about his normal language of daily life, nor in what language he preached to his flock. But it is very notable evidence for linguistic integration.

The evidence of the proceedings of Ephesus II and Chalcedon is even more explicit in simultaneously reflecting a recognition of the "federate Saracens" as a distinct ethnic group, and in revealing that their bishops, at these Councils too, functioned in Greek. At Ephesus II in 449 Auxilaos, "(bishop) of the federate Saracens" (*Sarakēnoi hupospondoi*), attended, gave his assent orally in Greek, and subscribed in Greek.[67] At Chalcedon, two years later, two different bishops "of the Saracens," or "of the people *(ethnos)* of the Saracens," Ioannes and Eustathios, attended. Eustathios spoke at the second session, apparently in Greek, and subscribed at session six, also in Greek.[68] In these *Acta* the use of languages other than Greek is carefully recorded; since it is not mentioned in these instances we must presume that these bishops spoke and wrote in Greek.

The evidence of contemporary observers, Jerome and Theodoret above all, makes quite clear that in their eyes "Saracens" were barbarian aliens,

---

65. P. 73 above.
66. *ACO* I.1.2, para. 38.3 (p. 9); para. 44 (p. 20); para. 25 (p. 34); para. 62[97] (p. 59).
67. *ACO* II.1.1, para. 78[88] (p. 80); para. 884[71] (p. 185); para. 1030 (p. 194).
68. *ACO* II.1.2, para. 96[144] (p. 33 [299]); para. 9[336] (p. 151 [347]).

even if their putative descent from Abraham gave them, as "Ishmaelites," a special claim to the inheritance of Biblical monotheism. Even when converted, and equipped with their own bishops, they could be categorized as a foreign "people" *(ethnos)*. As for language, there is absolutely no guarantee that every group whom a Graeco-Roman observer would designate as "Saracen" in fact spoke an early version of Arabic. But the pre-Islamic inscriptions in Arabic, few as they are, prove that at least some of them did, and that they might also have records of their actions inscribed in Greek. In the public life of the Church, however, no place was yet made for speech or writing in Arabic. The bishops of Saracen congregations symbolized their integration into Church and Empire by speaking and writing in Greek. But a quite different picture is revealed if we look at the only non-Classical language which already had an accepted place in the public life of the Church, Syriac.

4. THE PUBLIC ROLE AND STATUS OF SYRIAC IN THE FIFTH-CENTURY CHURCH

Given that Syriac did occupy a recognized place in the public life of the Church—if still, as we will see, in overall scope quite a modest one—a brief introduction is needed, firstly on the evolving role of the language, and secondly on the recognition of this role by Greek writers of the Theodosian period.

"Syriac" is the conventional modern name for that dialect and script of what contemporaries called "the Syrian language," and moderns call "Aramaic," but whose origins lay not in the area which the ancient world called "Syria," but in Osrhoene, east of the Euphrates (see the map of the Empire in figure I). In briefest summary, it is attested on pagan inscriptions of the first three centuries, including mosaic inscriptions, and on three third-century parchment documents from Osrhoene;[69] in the "subscriptions" of witnesses on a group of Greek documents, also of the third century, from the area along the Euphrates;[70] in important literary works perhaps beginning in the second, or possibly even in the first, century, notably *The Book*

---

69. For both the inscriptions and the third-century parchments see now H. J. W. Drijvers and J. F. Healey, *The Old Syriac Inscriptions of Edessa and Osrhoene* (1999), with the texts of the parchments in appendix A.

70. For the Syriac subscriptions on Greek documents of the third century see the archive designated as *P.Euphr.*, and published by D. Feissel and J. Gascou in *Journal des Savants* 1995, 1997 and 2000.

of the Laws of Countries, and in the fourth-century works of Aphraat and above all Ephraem.[71]

As we saw briefly earlier, it is also very significant that the language and script are represented in a magnificent series of Christian codices, of which the earliest known is still that written in Edessa early in Theodosius's reign, 411 (see figure II). The codex of several hundred leaves, elegantly written in three columns per page, must represent a mature scribal tradition. What is noteworthy is that the earliest Syriac manuscripts which indicate both place and date of writing were written east of the Euphrates, and it is not until 510/11 that we find one formally recorded as having been written west of the river in what we (like contemporaries) call "Syria."[72] A similar pattern can be observed in the slow spread of Syriac inscriptions, all from ecclesiastical contexts, in Syria in the fifth and sixth centuries, with one example from a church in Palestine from the first half of the fifth century.[73]

There is in fact an in-built ambiguity in the conceptions, and the vocabulary, applied both by contemporaries and by moderns to speakers and writers of "Syriac" or "the Syrian language." In an important and often-quoted passage Theodoret reports that "the Syrian language" was used by a variety of regional populations, whose names as he gives them are in fact derived from the official Roman names of provinces: the Osroēnoi, Suroi, Euphratēsioi, Palaistinoi, and Phoenikes. But he also indicates that, for what was in his view the same language, these different groups varied in their *dialexis* (just pronunciation, or also grammar or vocabulary?).[74] A valuable recent study shows that the grammar of simple sentences in local branches of the

71. See the surveys by Sebastian Brock: "Greek and Syriac in Late Antique Syria," in *Literacy and Power in the Ancient World,* ed. A. K. Bowman and G. Woolf (1994), 149 ff.; *A Brief Outline of Syriac Literature* (1997); "Syriac Culture, 337–425," in *Cambridge Ancient History* XIII: *The Late Empire,* AD 337–425, ed. A. Cameron and P. Garnsey (1998), 708 ff.

72. See M. Mundell Mango, "Patrons and Scribes Indicated in Syriac Manuscripts," *Jahrb. Öst. Byz. Ges.* 32.4 (1982): 3; "The Production of Syriac Manuscripts, 400–700 AD," in *Scritture, libri e testi nelle aree provinciali di Bisanzio,* ed. G. Cavallo, G. De Gregorio, and M. Maniaci (1990), 161 ff. For the MS of 510/11, see W. H. P. Hatch, *An Album of Dated Syriac Manuscripts* (1946), no. VIII.

73. See F. Millar, "Ethnic Identity in the Roman Near East, 325–450: Language, Religion and Culture," *Mediterranean Archaeology* 11 (1998): 159 ff., esp. p. 170. V. Tzaferis, "The Greek Inscriptions from the Early Christian Church at 'Evron," *Eretz Israel* 19 (1987): 36* ff., with A. Jacques, "A Palestinian-Syriac Inscription in the Mosaic Pavement at 'Evron," ibid. 54 ff.

74. Theodoret, *Qu. In Jud.* 19, PG LXXX, cols. 503–507.

"Syrian language" or Aramaic did in fact differ quite markedly.[75] So the spread of Syriac as a Christian language of culture outside Osrhoene and Mesopotamia should possibly be understood not as the acquisition of a public status by a long-suppressed "native language," but as the importation of an established Christian language from across the Euphrates. As regards the recognition of Christian Syriac literature by contemporary Greek writers, far the clearest expression relates to Ephraem, who had moved from Nisibis when it fell into Persian hands in 363, and died in Edessa in 373. His writings are celebrated in some detail both by Theodoret and by Sozomenus.[76] Equally, in a long letter addressed to monks in Constantinople, Theodoret speaks of Ephraem in glowing terms: "the lyre of the Spirit, daily bathing the *ethnos* of the Suroi in the waves of Grace."[77]

Were "Suroi," meaning speakers of "the Syrian language," in general conceived of as a distinct "people," and if so did this attribution of "ethnicity," based on language, apply anywhere in the Near Eastern provinces ("Oriens," in the narrowest of its contemporary uses)? Could those from west of the Euphrates in fact have read Ephraem's works in their original script, or the codex of 411 from Edessa, and did they do so?

What anecdotal evidence shows beyond doubt is that *speakers* of "the Syrian language" could be found in most (and in fact very probably in all) of the different provinces of Oriens; for instance they appear from time to time—but as an exception to the norm, which is the speaking of Greek—in Theodoret's *Philotheos Historia*, or "History of the Monks of Syria."[78] But it would represent a significantly different phase in the status of Syriac if the composition of Christian works in Syriac had now begun in the area west of the Euphrates. There are indeed indications, if few, that this was so: Balai (Balaeus) is associated with Beroea and Chalcis; and Rabboula, who became bishop of Edessa in 412, seems to have come from Chalcis, and could write in both Greek and Syriac.[79] It is very probable also that the long Syr-

75. D. Taylor, "Bilingualism and Diglossia in Late Antique Syria and Mesopotamia," in *Bilingualism in Ancient Society: Language Contact and the Written Word*, ed. J. N. Adams, M. Janse, and S. Swain (2002), 298 ff.

76. Theodoret, *HE* II.26; IV.26; *Haer. Fab. Comp.* I.22; Sozomenus, *HE* III.16.

77. Theodoret, *Epp.* II. 146.

78. See Theodoret, *HR* IV.13; V.5–6; XIII.2, 7; XIV.2; XVII.8.

79. There is a Syriac *Life* of Rabboula, preserved on a MS of the sixth century, and perhaps written in the fifth, which records his early education in a city which seems to be Chalcis. See most recently G. W. Bowersock, "The Syriac Life of Rabboula and Syrian Hellenism," in *Greek Biography and Panegyric in Late Antiquity*, ed. P. Rousseau and T. Hägg (2000), 255 ff.

iac *Life* of Symeon Stylites, whose earliest manuscript is dated very early indeed, namely 473, was written west of the Euphrates.[80]

So there need be no doubt that in the Theodosian period Syriac was emerging as a recognized language of Christian writing and theology. But precisely the contribution which the verbatim proceedings of the Councils can make is to provide concrete evidence for the function of the language in the specific context of the Councils, and of public proceedings reported at Councils. Was this an area in which the Church, if not the 'Greek Roman Empire' itself as a secular institution, conceded the possibility of *not* being wholly Greek, of allowing a place for diversity rather than uniformity?

The first thing to be said is that the evidence from the Councils shows categorically that there was no province, or even subregion, within Oriens where Greek was not (at least) an established language of the Church, and in fact everywhere the dominant language. Furthermore, as regards the nine provinces west of the Euphrates—the two Syrias and two Phoenicias, Euphratensis, Arabia, and the three Palestines (see the map in figure I)—there is not a single example of a bishop who speaks or subscribes in any language other than Greek.

What is more, even within the provinces of Osrhoene and Mesopotamia, we can find bishops who speak and subscribe in Greek. At Ephesus I in 431, in fact, bishops from these provinces played a very small part: but Asterios, the metropolitan of Amida in Mesopotamia, and Ausonios of Himeria in Osrhoene appear on the side of the "Oriental," or "two-nature," party, and seem to subscribe in Greek like the (not very numerous) others in the same group.[81]

By contrast, when we come to Ephesus II of 449, Himeria (whose exact location is not known, but which lay in Osrhoene) is the only bishopric associated with Syriac. We will take first the evidence from the first session, embedded within the proceedings of Chalcedon, and then that from the second session, derived from the Syriac MS of 535. At the first session we find a new bishop of Himeria, Ouranios, who is recorded as having had his spoken words translated by a presbyter from Edessa: "Ouranios, bishop of Himeria of the province of the Osrhoēnoi, Eulogios, a presbyter of Edessa translating (for) him." The same detail also appears twice more later.[82] It

---

80. See R. Doran, *The Lives of Symeon Stylites,* a translation with introduction (1992). The MS is no. V in Hatch, *Album of Dated Syriac Manuscripts* (n. 72), and is dated by the era of Antioch. The question of the date and place of writing of this MS is of course not identical with that of the composition of the work. But the two are likely to be very close.

81. *ACO* I.1.5, para. 16[13,24] (p. 123).

82. *ACO* II.1.1, para. 884[54] (p. 184); para. 945 (p. 190); para. 1006 (p. 193).

will be noted that once again, as with Kalosirios of Arsinoe, who by implication spoke in Coptic, the non-Greek language used is not actually named. Here too, a local presbyter is available to produce a translation into Greek.

In speaking in Syriac at Ephesus II Ouranios was joined by a much more famous and controversial figure, the archimandrite Barsaumas. Later in the same session as that at which Ouranios spoke, Barsaumas did also, through an interpreter, a monk named Eusebios: "Barsaumas, a presbyter and archimandrite, through an interpreter, Eusebios, a monk, said. . . . " In this case the record provides a translation of his one-sentence pronouncement in support of the archimandrite Eutyches, with a brief reference later.[83] Should we conclude that Barsaumas could neither speak nor read Greek? He attended as a result of a personal invitation sent by Theodosius, who wrote to him in Greek.[84] A translator may have been needed when the letter arrived.

In essence the same message is conveyed by the *Acta* of the second session of Ephesus II, originally recorded also in Greek, but preserved now only in Syriac translation. We may note also the reference, incorporated in the *Acta*, to an earlier allusion, made at a hearing before Chaereas, the governor of Osrhoene, to a letter of Ibas, the current bishop of Edessa, explicitly described as having been written in Syriac, and addressed to "Maris the Persian." That may also provide a further criterion for the public, or official, use of Syriac, namely its deployment in writing episcopal letters on matters of doctrine. But in fact this instance is the only known case offered by the *Acta*, or indeed by any of the evidence from Theodosius's reign, of any contemporary theological writing in any language other than Greek or Latin. A Syriac text then follows, but must very likely be a Syriac retranslation from a Greek translation of the original Syriac. In itself, the letter must rank as one of the most interesting and important contemporary accounts of the Nestorian controversy.[85]

In the actual proceedings as reported in the Syriac MS, Ouranios, bishop of Himeria, speaks twice, with someone whose name is apparently Libanios, deacon of Samosata, interpreting for him.[86] If the place name has been reported correctly, that is a relevant, if not surprising, indication that spoken Syriac (at least) was current also on the right bank of the Euphrates, in the province of Euphratesia.

83. *ACO* II.1.1, para. 884[112] (p. 186); para. 1006 (p. 194).
84. *ACO* II.1.1, para. 48 (p. 71).
85. *AGWG*, pp. 46–53; trans. Perry, pp. 111–20.
86. *AGWG*, pp. 68–69; trans. Perry, p. 159–60.

At a date which must fall in the early part of 449, there took place at Berytus a hearing by the bishops Photios of Tyre, Eustathios of Berytus, and the same Ouranios of Himeria of charges against Ibas of Edessa, Daniel of Carrhae, and Ioannes of Theodosiopolis (Rheshaina), all these being bishoprics in the province of Osrhoene. The record survives because it was quoted *in extenso* in the *Acta* of session XI at Chalcedon.[87] It is in fact this record which provides the fullest reflection (as always, entirely in Greek) of the public use of Syriac, and of the balance between the employment of Syriac and that of Greek. Representatives of the accusers, a group of nine clergy from Osrhoene, speak in Greek, but their main spokesman, Samouēlos, asks that the oral proceedings be translated for the benefit of Ouranios: "We request that what has been said should be said (again) in Syriac *(Suristi)* for the most holy bishop Ouranios."[88] Note that in this case the language concerned is explicitly named. Thereafter, the three episcopal judges collectively and Samouēlos all speak in Greek, as does Ibas himself (Daniel and Ioannes are not recorded as intervening). Similarly in Greek is the written *libellos* of accusation from Samouēlos and three other presbyters from Edessa, followed by the hand-written subscriptions of all four, written in Greek.[89] After further interventions, Photios and Eustathios give instructions that the interpreter assisting Ouranios should translate: " 'All that you have set forth, the person assisting the most pious bishop Ouranios will translate into his native language.' And it was translated."[90] Later in the proceedings there reappears in Greek translation *(hermēneia)* the same letter, referred to earlier, written by Ibas in Syriac to "Mares, a Persian"[91]—in fact, as mentioned above, a powerful and interesting account of the Nestorian controversy. Between them, therefore, the exchanges and the letter, as originally written in Syriac, prove that Ibas was bilingual.

The proceedings at Berytus, as quoted at Chalcedon, end abruptly with the introduction of a petition *(didaskalia* and *paraklēsis)* written in Greek, and addressed to Photios and Eustathios by a rival group of clergy at Edessa, who express support for Ibas.[92] Sixty-five clergy of various ranks add their subscriptions to the petition, all of them recorded in Greek. But in eighteen cases there follows the indication "and a Syriac subscription" *(hypographē Suriakē)*. What exactly is implied here needs a moment's examination. As

---

87. See appendix B, no. 20.
88. *ACO* II.1.3, para. 33 (p. 20 [370]); similarly para. 57 (p. 23 [382]).
89. *ACO* II.1.3, para. 56 (pp. 22–23 [381–82]).
90. *ACO* II.1.3, para. 58 (p. 23 [382]).
91. *ACO* II.1.3, para. 138 (p. 32–34 [391–93]).
92. *ACO* II.1.3, para. 141 (pp. 35–37 [394–96]).

always, a "subscription" in this sense is a (normally) one-sentence affirmation, written in the person's own hand, that they assent to a collective proposition, verdict, or written document. In this instance, the subscriptions include several actually written by another person on behalf of the individual, though none affirming explicitly that the person is illiterate, either in Greek or in Syriac. One example is: "I, Abibos, a deacon, have on request written (this) on behalf of the most pious deacon Valentinus because he is unable to." But both this and Abibos's own subscription are followed by "and a Syriac subscription." Does this mean that in reality the person wrote a single subscription in Syriac on the original document, which was then copied in Greek translation? Or did each of the eighteen persons who subscribed in Syriac do so by adding this to a subscription (in their own hand?) in Greek? There is no reason to suppose that literacy in both languages, at the modest level required, was unknown.

On the evidence both of the oral exchanges and of the documents laid before the hearing, both Greek and Syriac were established languages of public discourse in the churches of Osrhoene. But, if anything, given the very slight statistical basis for any such suggestion, the indications are that, even in Osrhoene, Greek remained the predominant language used within the Church in formal public contexts.

The hearing at Berytus was of course not a Church Council in itself, but earns its place here both because of the particular light which it throws on bilingualism in Osrhoene, and because we owe our knowledge of it to the *Acta* of Chalcedon. In the very extensive records of the proceedings of this Council there seems to be only one occasion on which anyone speaks in Syriac. We may note also that earlier in the session in question Nonnos, who is now bishop of Edessa, speaks in Greek.[93] The participant who does use Syriac is once again the famous archimandrite, Barsaumas: "Barsaumas, the most pious monk, with his own man translating as he spoke in Syriac, said . . . "[94] Once again the language is explicitly named. This remains, however, an isolated case. In Session X, of 26 October, Ibas, the former bishop of Edessa, appears, and speaks in Greek.[95] It should be noted that the *Acta* also show that bishops from Mesopotamia also might speak and subscribe in Greek, as Symeon of Amida did at Session IV at Chalcedon, while at Session VI he subscribed in Greek through a presbyter[96] (the 452 subscriptions

93. *ACO* II.1.2, para. 9^{116} (p. 103 [299]).
94. *ACO* II.1.2, para. 95 (p. 118 [314]).
95. *ACO* II.1.3, para. 4 (p. 13 [372]).
96. *ACO* II.1.2, para. 9^{16} (p. 95 [291]); Session VI, II.1.2, para. 9^{29} (p. 142 [338]).

at this session, at which the Emperor Marcian spoke, provide the fullest cross section of the Greek Church in the midcentury).

The pattern is, in one sense, quite clear. So far as bishops are concerned, only Ouranios of Himeria in Osrhoene is shown to be unable to follow spoken Greek. The same is perhaps true of Barsaumas, though the record merely shows him as invariably speaking in Syriac, rather than as being provably unable to understand Greek spoken by others. But that leaves a substantial problem. Do we know either where Barsaumas came from, or where the monastery of which he was archimandrite was located? We need to examine the evidence on these two points, since, as is obvious, it would be circular simply to assume that he came from Osrhoene.

The conciliar *Acta* themselves give no clue as to the location of Barsaumas's monastery, and if we have any evidence as to his origins and sphere of activity it can only come from later tradition, in particular from the Syriac *Life*, never fully published, which Ernst Honigmann considered largely legendary, and not written before the middle of the sixth century. For what it is worth, in this text his origin is ascribed to a village in the territory of Samosata, on the right bank of the Euphrates in Euphratesia, while tradition associated his name with a monastery in the mountainous area to the north, between Samosata and Melitene.[97]

The purpose of this survey has been to use a very specific and limited body of data, the *Acta* of the great Church Councils of the fifth century, to serve as a check on the role and status which Syriac had acquired in the public life of the Greek Church by the middle of the century. It should be stressed that no negative generalizations about wider speech patterns can be derived from this evidence. It cannot be used to show that spoken Syriac/Aramaic was not common in all the Near Eastern provinces, or that those bishops whom we encounter speaking in Greek at the Councils and in other formal contexts were not, to some degree or other, familiar with spoken Syriac/Aramaic. Clearly there are vast differences in the possible degrees of mastery which might have been achieved, from complete bilingualism, spoken and written, to a passive—partial or complete—comprehension of the spoken or written word, to the ability to identify a few common terms in the speech of peasants. To repeat, none of the material covered can serve as the basis for negative generalizations.

Nonetheless, it has to be stated emphatically that the evidence is clear

97. See E. Honigmann, *Le couvent de Barsauma et le patriarcat jacobite d'Antioche et de Syrie* (1954), ch. 2, "Le Barsaumā historique et la vie syriaque de Barsaumā."

and quite significant. No bishop from any of the provinces west of the Euphrates can be found to have expressed himself in Syriac/Aramaic at any of the three Councils concerned. As a language of public discourse in the Church, Syriac is still characteristic only of its original homeland as a language of culture, namely Osrhoene—and perhaps also of the region which lay to its north across the Euphrates, namely the eastern part of the province of Euphratesia, ancient Commagene. (The same well have been true of the other Roman province which lay east of the Euphrates, Mesopotamia, but no direct evidence is provided by these records).

Even in Osrhoene itself the linguistic pattern which is quite clearly attested is not the dominance of Syriac, but bilingualism as between Syriac and Greek. It is common for bishops from this area both to be able to express themselves publicly in Greek, and to choose to do so. Those major personalities who speak in public only in Syriac have available to them interpreters from the same region (plus one apparently from Samosata across the Euphrates, perhaps the area from which Barsaumas himself came) who can interpret for them, and reproduce their spoken interventions in Greek. In the case of the hearing at Berytus in early 449, the interpreter can also translate the Greek proceedings for the benefit of Ouranios.

If we think in terms of integration and diversity, and at the level of language, what must be stressed overall is linguistic integration, as revealed at the Councils, namely the ability of bishops from the whole area from the lower Danube to the upper and middle Euphrates and to Egypt to communicate in both written and spoken Greek. Statistically, the appearance of any other languages, even Syriac (and also even Latin), is a marginal phenomenon. Even so, the place occupied by Syriac is significantly different from that of any other non-Classical language, sufficient to give a faint hint of the immense importance which it would very soon come to occupy in the life of the Church in Oriens, and which it already occupied in the Christian communities within the Sasanid empire.[98] Christian writing in Syriac was already acknowledged within the Greek Christian culture of the Theodosian period, and one example of it, the letter to "Maris the Persian" written by Ibas of Edessa, was quoted both at Ephesus II and at the hearing at Berytus.

But at Edessa, as throughout Oriens, there were fundamental divisions between proponents of a "two-nature" Christology, like Ibas himself, and of a "one-nature" conception, like his predecessor Rabboula. The divisions were theological, and there is nothing to show that adherence to one con-

98. See now W. Baum and D. W. Winkler, *The Church of the East: A Concise History* (2003), ch. 1.

ception or the other corresponded either with monolingual speaking of Syriac or with what was quite clearly far more characteristic, among the clergy
at least, varying degrees of bilingualism in Greek and Syriac. Like the "Saracens," Syrians might be spoken of as an *ethnos;* but, as representing an alien
"nationality," the bishops who spoke for the Saracens had to speak Greek.
"Syrians" were not a nationality in that sense, but an element in society
defined by the use of a language diffused in varying degrees of density in a
world dominated still by Greek, and not marked out either by any sort of
"nationalism," or by belief. Unlike the Isaurians, who remained obstinately
alien and threatening, no one saw, or had any reason to see, "Syrians" as a
danger to the integrity of the State.

Nonetheless, the Christian Empire did most certainly see itself as confronting "others" within, but both were defined by belief rather than by
ethnicity: pagans and Jews.

5. THE EMPIRE, THE CHURCH, AND PAGANISM

At one moment of overconfidence, in sending a letter in 423 to the Praetorian Prefect of Oriens about heretics, pagans, and Jews, Theodosius committed himself in passing to the assertion regarding pagans that "We now
believe that there are none."[99] In a certain limited sense he was probably
correct. That is to say that it seems that public sacrifices, conducted by city
officials and financed by the communal funds of cities, no longer occupied
that central place which they had always had in the life of the Empire. A
negative generalization of this type can of course never be proved, and it
must remain possible that in some modest and obscure cities sacrifices continued. But in general the enormous change in communal life represented
by the cessation of public sacrifice had already taken place.[100] It was indeed
very recent. The major church historians writing under Theodosius all
recorded in detail the reassertion of paganism by Julian in 361–63, and his
measures against the Church, and Sozomenus noted the violent reactions
by mobs of pagans which had then been directed against bishops in Alexan-

---

99. *CTh* XVI.10.22, Apr. 9, 423.

100. For the fate of communal pagan observances, sacrifice above all, in this period
see, e.g., J. Geffcken, *The Last Days of Greco-Roman Paganism,* ed. and trans. S. Mac-
Cormack (1978); P. Chuvin, *A Chronicle of the Last Pagans* (1990); F. R. Trombley,
Hellenic Religion and Christianisation c. 370–529, 2 vols. (1993–94); K. Harl,
"Sacrifice and Pagan Belief in Byzantium," *Past and Present* 128 (1990): 7 ff.

dria and in various cities in Oriens.[101] But the categorical banning of pagan practice had been the work of the Emperor's grandfather, Theodosius I, especially in measures of the early 390s. Then too, there had taken place mass violence, backed by Imperial forces, which led to the destruction of the great temple of Serapis in Alexandria, also recounted in detail by the Church Historians,[102] followed, under the Emperor's father, Arcadius, by that of the temple of Marnas in Gaza. As the *Life* of bishop Porphyry, who died in 420, recorded, that too had been initiated locally by the bishop, but had been brought to fruition only by a mission to Constantinople to secure Imperial military backing. Arcadius had been reluctant, and success had only been achieved by presenting a petition to his infant son, the future Theodosius II, and proclaiming that he had assented to it.[103]

Traumatic, and symbolic, major episodes of a comparable sort are not attested for Theodosius's own reign. In terms of mass violence, initiated from either side, or of very prominent episodes involving the destruction of famous temples, the public trial of strength was, it seems, already over. But, as we have noted earlier,[104] that did not mean that paganism had disappeared as a form of devotion on the part of individuals or of small groups, or in contexts which were not too exposed to Christian observation and pressure. Pagan belief also continued to find literary expression, for instance in the revised version of Eunapius's *History*, or in Olympiodorus's *History*, in the *Life* by Marinus of the great Neoplatonist, Proclus, and later in Damascius's *Life* of Isidorus.[105] As the *Life* of Proclus illustrates, there were several possible phases in the disappearance of temples from their inherited role at the heart of communal life, even without destruction, or reconstruction as churches: the abandonment of public sacrifices and rituals; the locking of temples still with the cult statues inside, so that access was impossible, or possible only by individuals secretly, or at least privately; or the actual removal of the cult statues. Even after the public victory of Christianity, the temples could still represent a threat to Christians and a place of private devotion for pagans.

Moreover, even if very large-scale confrontations, as in Alexandria or

---

101. See Socrates, *HE* III; Sozomenus, *HE* V; Theodoret, *HE* III.

102. See Socrates V.16–17; Sozomenus VII.15; Theodoret V.22.

103. For the petition see Mark the Deacon, *Life* of Porphyry, 46–51. Cf. p. 26 above.

104. P. 26.

105. See Damascius, *The Philosophical History: Text with Translation and Notes*, ed. P. Athanassiadi (1999).

Gaza, are no longer recorded, action against the local observance of pagan rituals is still described in Christian texts. The Syriac *Life* of Symeon Stylites has him confronting pagans on Mt. Lebanon, and refusing to help them unless they abandoned pagan practices,[106] while Callinicus's *Life* of the monk Hypatius records how its hero attacked rural forms of pagan observance, evidently not dependent on temples, in Bithynia:

> He was filled with zeal for God, and calmed many places in Bithynia from (the influence of) idolatrous error. For whenever he heard that any people were worshipping a tree or something else of that sort, he repaired there at once, bringing with him monks who were his disciples, cut it down, and burned it with fire. Thus, step-by-step as time went on, they became Christians.

At occasional moments it could even be a matter of the overt reassertion of pagan observance, rather than passive maintenance. Thus a few chapters later Callinicus records how Hypatius heard that the Prefect Leontius (Prefect of Constantinople in 434–35) was attempting to reenact the Olympic festival in the theater at Chalcedon. Against the will of the local bishop, Hypatius determined to disrupt the ceremonial with a group of monks, drag the Prefect from his seat as president of the games, and if necessary court death. Leontius pretended illness, and went back to Constantinople.[107]

What distinguished the Christians was not only their capacity for personal zeal, but having not only local leaders (bishops) whose function was the exposition of true belief on the basis of a set of sacred texts, but provincial or regional, or on occasion Empire-wide, organizations of those leaders, who, even without meeting, could express either agreement or disagreement with each other through the medium of correspondence. They also could and, as this study shows throughout, did address a stream of demands and complaints—as well as expositions of what true doctrine consisted in—to the representatives of the State, including the Emperor in person.

From the pagan side there was no one to offer anything that resembled a systematic representation of ideology and belief of that type. So far as our evidence goes, no arguments in defense of paganism, such as Libanius had offered to Theodosius I in his Oration XXX *For the Temples*, were ever presented to Theodosius II. That did not mean that, at the level of private life, Christians were not confronted by pagan arguments. The massive surviving correspondence of Isidorus, a presbyter at Pelusium, reveals disputes

---

106. *Life* 62–63; R. Doran, *The Lives of Symeon Stylites* (1992), pp. 141–43.
107. Callinicus, *Vita* of Hypatius, 30.1; 33.1–11.

not only (as we will see below) with Jews, but with pagans. Thus one letter on the subject of divination is addressed to a pagan *scholasticus* named
Harpocras, who has been using Homer in defense of the validity of divination. Isidorus notes that he has dealt with the subject in his work *Against
the Hellenes* (in the sense of pagans).[108] A set of five further letters dis-
cusses pagan criticisms of Christian doctrine—the death of Jesus on the
Cross, the lack of education of the apostles, the modesty of Christ's sepul-
chre compared to the grandeur of temples. All of these served in fact, so
he claims, to show the opposite of what pagans claimed. Arguments in defense of pagan beliefs and against Christianity were thus advanced—but
not at the level of public discourse directed to high officials or the Emperor.[109] More significant perhaps is the way in which Christian correspondence of the time provides a precise parallel, and counterpart, to the
image of pagans, heretics, and Jews (and, notably, Samaritans) as a set of
hostile presences representing a systematic threat to Christianity, which
we find in Imperial letters. Yet, as we will see, though these three (or four)
very disparate groups may appear together in both the letters of bishops
and the pronouncements of Emperors, when it comes to actual decisions,
or Imperial "laws," the measures ordered are quite distinct. Pagan observance is forbidden, and liable to punishment; the observance of Judaism
by Jews is not. These two contrasting groups form the subject of the remainder of this chapter. Heresy, in its numerous different manifestations,
is also banned and penalized, and is the subject of incomparably greater
Imperial concern than the others. It will find its place in the next chapter,
on State and Church.

As regards episcopal correspondence, perhaps it will be sufficient to note
the two main letters of Theodoret in which, in the very troubled context of
448–49, he looks back over the quarter century of his tenure of the see of
Cyrrhus in Euphratesia; speaking in the one specifically about the local context, and in the other more generally about Oriens, he sees the life of the
Church as a constant battle against pagans, Jews, and heretics.[110] Such conceptions, however puzzling they may seem to us in the light of what may
appear as the conclusive victory of Christianity, are essential if we are to
understand the same widely shared conception of pagans as a hostile force
which appears in the rhetoric of the Emperor's own pronouncements.

There are indeed several such pronouncements in which, in highly

108. Isidorus, *Epp.* II. 228.
109. Isidorus, *Epp.* IV. 27–30.
110. Theodoret, *Epp.* II. 81; III. 113.

rhetorical style, the Emperor speaks of all three (or four, if we count Samaritans) of the dissident or divergent types of religious groupings with which the Christians felt themselves to be confronted. But, in the origin and framework of Imperial rhetoric, and in the content of the "laws" sent out to Praetorian Prefects, pagans play a very different role from that of either Jews or those Christians characterized as heretics. For a start, heresy was at all stages a major preoccupation of the State, even in the two decades before the first Council of Ephesus. At that point, of course, the claims on Imperial attention represented by the threat of heresy, and of disunity in the Church, rise far beyond anything which ever applied to either Jews or pagans. That was not least, as already indicated, because Christians were led by bishops who by the nature of their role were the bearers of doctrinal messages—and very frequently conflicting doctrinal messages. So, as has already been illustrated, even as regards military and frontier policy, the volume and intensity of persuasive discourse, in writing and in face-to-face speech, which was directed at the Emperor from within the Church had in effect no counterpart from either Jewish communities on the one hand, or from pagans. Indeed it is not clear who would have spoken for pagans, even if any had felt the confidence to address the Emperor directly. In the case of Jewish communities, by contrast, while there is only very slight evidence of persuasion directed to the Emperor or the authorities, there is some, as we will see, and there is also the fundamental distinction—which separated Jews both from pagans and from Christians belonging to groups currently regarded as heretical—that the practice of Judaism by Jews was not forbidden, indeed was positively protected.

Profound though these distinctions were, that did not prevent Theodosius from alluding to all of these different groups, Samaritans included, in issuing the longest and most fervent of his expressions of his duty to promote Christianity and repress deviance, in a letter sent on January 31, 438, to the Praetorian Prefect of Oriens. Equally expansive, detailed, and rhetorical letters may well have been sent by him before—but, as noted earlier, all the texts collected in the *Theodosian Code* are extracts. It is only when we reach the versions of the subsequent years, collected in his *Novellae*, that we can catch the full flavor of the Imperial rhetoric, self-justification, and denunciation of error. There is no clear indication in this case that the "law" was a response to any particular *suggestio*, or petition from private persons, and given the wide range (and incoherence) of its provisions it hardly could have so originated. The long paragraph towards the end represents as fully as any other text the depth both of the Emperor's hostility, and also (as seems clear) of his fear of the misfortunes felt to have arisen from continued observance of paganism:[111]

> Hence Our Clemency perceives that We must exercise watchfulness
> over the pagans also and their heathen enormities, since with their
> natural insanity and stubborn insolence they depart from the path
> of the true religion. They disdain in any way to practice the nefarious
> rites of their sacrifices and the false doctrines of their deadly supersti-
> tion in the hidden solitudes, unless their crimes are made public by
> the nature of their profession, to the outrage of the Supernal Majesty
> and to the contempt of Our times. A thousand terrors of the laws that
> have been promulgated, the penalty of exile that has been threatened,
> do not restrain them, whereby, if they cannot be reformed, at least they
> might learn to abstain from their mass of crimes and from the corrup-
> tion of their sacrifices. But straightway they sin with such audacious
> madness and Our patience is so assailed by the attempts of these
> impious persons that even if We desired to forget them, We could not
> disregard them. Therefore, although the love of religion can never be
> secure, although their pagan madness demands the harshness of all
> kinds of punishments, nevertheless We are mindful of the clemency
> that is innate in Us, and We decree by an unshakable order that if any
> person of polluted and contaminated mind should be apprehended in
> making a sacrifice in any place whatsoever, Our wrath shall rise up
> against his fortunes, against his blood. For we must give this better
> victim, and the altar of Christianity shall be kept inviolate. Shall we
> endure longer that the succession of the seasons be changed, and the
> temper of the heavens be stirred to anger, since the embittered perfidy
> of the pagans does not know how to preserve these balances of nature?
> For why has the spring renounced its accustomed charm? Why has
> the summer, barren of its harvest, deprived the laboring farmer of his
> hopes of a grain harvest? Why has the intemperate ferocity of winter
> with its piercing cold doomed the fertility of the lands with the disaster
> of sterility? Why all these things, unless nature has transgressed the
> decree of its own law to avenge such impiety? In order that we may
> not hereafter be compelled to sustain such circumstances, by a peaceful
> vengeance, as We have said, the venerable majesty of the Supernal
> Divinity must be appeased.

Just as in earlier centuries the dominant pagans had responded to natural disasters by demanding the punishment of Christians, now the Christian Emperor ascribes adverse climatic conditions to God's wrath. In high-flown and impressive language, he seems here to threaten the death penalty as a

111. *Nov. Th.* 3, para. 8; trans. Pharr.

punishment for pagan sacrifice, with persons executed being perceived as sacrificial victims in themselves.

Exactly what disabilities, and what punishments, represented the normal lot of persons convicted of carrying out pagan rites can hardly be determined from the scatter of "laws" on the subject issued by Theodosius from time to time. The principle that pagans should be banned from *militia* and the office of *iudex* (governor) is expressed in a brief extract from a law of 416,[112] but too little remains for any real interpretation. There are possible cases of known pagans who held high public office after this date,[113] so the scope of the application of the principle remains obscure.

Otherwise, the Imperial rhetoric does not concern itself very widely with the issue of paganism. A casual reflection of what had undoubtedly been a profound and traumatic change can, for instance, be found in a letter of May 13, 425, addressed to the Comes Rerum Privatarum on the rules governing the ownership of properties obtained by petition from among Imperial possessions; these rules did not apply to "patrimonial" properties or to those which had formerly belonged to temples.[114] A process of confiscation, or transfer, which has already taken place is simply taken for granted. But active measures could continue, and the Emperor's convictions could lead to positive commands, as we find in a letter addressed in 435 to Isidorus, the Praetorian Prefect of Oriens. In the brief extract which we have, typical of the texts as reproduced in the *Theodosian Code*, there is again no indication as to whether any particular local circumstance had given rise to it:[115]

> All persons of criminal pagan mind we interdict from accursed immolations of sacrificial victims and from damnable sacrifices and from all other practices prohibited by the authority of the more ancient ordinances, and we order that all their shrines, temples, sanctuaries, if any even now remain intact, should be destroyed by the magistrates' command and that these should be purified by the placing of the venerable Christian religion's sign [the Cross]—all persons knowing that if it shall have been established by suitable proofs before a competent judge that anyone has mocked this law, the said person must be punished with death.

The significance of the Imperial pronouncements relating to paganism in this period lies almost more in what is absent than what is explicitly present in them. A sense of anxiety may underlie the apparent expressions

---

113. See p. 30 above.

112. *CTh* XVI.10.21, Dec. 7, 416.
113. See p. 30 above.
114. *CTh* X.10.32.
115. *CTh* XVI.10.25, Nov. 14, 435; trans. Coleman-Norton, no. 424.

of dominance and triumphalism, but there is nothing in them to reflect either coherent public discourse, in any form, in defense of paganism, or local protests, or violence, on the part of communities or groups still attached to pagan observances and rituals. At all levels, doctrinal, communal, and (in a sense) political, Judaism and Samaritanism, both of which were officially tolerated, posed what was felt to be a more serious threat.

6. SAMARITANS AND JEWS

There were several senses in which either Samaritans or Jews might have been viewed as a diverse or anomalous element in an Empire which was strikingly homogeneous in various different ways: in its recruitment from a Greek-speaking population of public servants or office-holders, who then learned Latin, and used it for their internal communications; in the Church's use of Greek, sometimes in combination with other languages (Syriac), from one end of the Empire to the other; and above all, of course, in its adherence to Christianity. The first sense is that in which both Samaritans and Jews constituted a local population, or ethnic group, with their own distinctive customs, settled in their "homeland" in one corner of the Empire, namely Palestine. Given that major Jewish revolts, suppressed only with great difficulty, had broken out in the first and second centuries, it might have been the case that either Jews or Samaritans or both were seen as constituting an internal "enemy," with an internal "frontier," as the Isaurians actually did. In fact no such situation arose (though, as we will see below, the Samaritans could be perceived as a threat). Jerusalem had been transformed in the second century into the pagan *colonia* of Aelia Capitolina; the central area of Palestine, now the province of Palaestina Prima, was divided between Greek cities, and since Constantine's reign had been filled even more densely with monuments of Christian piety. Jerome's evocative *Letter* 108, written in the first year of Theodosius's sole reign, perfectly captures the Christianization of the Palestinian landscape. There was a concentration of Jewish settlement, but it was now grouped well to the north in Palaestina Secunda, namely in Galilee and the Golan.[116] Other Jews, like Samaritans, lived dispersed throughout Palestine, in a way which was not entirely different from that in which they lived in the Diaspora, as religious/ethnic com-

116. See the foldout map of "Synagogues and Jewish Centres," in *Tabula Imperii Romana: Iudaea/Palestina*, ed. Y. Tsafrir, L. Di Segni, and J. Green (1994). There is a scatter of synagogues in the coastal areas and the south (Idumaea), but the most clearly marked concentration is in northeastern Galilee and the Golan.

munities in cities dominated by Greek-speaking gentiles, many of whom
were now Christian.

There were distinctive, "diverse," features of these Palestinian Jewish communities, both in the area of concentrated settlement and elsewhere. By definition, they rejected Christianity. They used the Bible and the Mishnah, written in Hebrew; their religious experts could generate very lengthy and
abstruse texts in Aramaic; and they built, or were coming to build, elaborate
synagogues with mosaic floors. The recent argument by Seth Schwartz, that
these synagogues represent a reassertion of Jewish identity in Palestine, in
the face of Christianity, has real force.[117] But the inscriptions on these mosaic floors may be in Hebrew, Aramaic, Greek, or all three.[118] It is probable
that what we find in this area is a degree of bilingualism (or trilingualism)
comparable to that, in Greek and Syriac, which we found earlier in Osrhoene
and neighboring areas.[119] But, unlike the bishops and archimandrites of Osrhoene, whose voices were heard, in Greek and Syriac, on the wider stage of
the Greek Church, there is nothing in our evidence to suggest that the Jewish population of Palestine as such had a significant presence, or constituted
an object of attention, in the awareness of either the Church or the State. The
one probable exception to that generalization is that until the 420s they did
have a very prominent leader, or representative (with powers of jurisdiction,
though not as the ruler of any precise Jewish "territory"), the Patriarch.

How we should understand the relatively brief history of the Patriarchs,
who surface in Roman legal texts in the second half of the fourth century,
is too complex a problem to be dealt with here.[120] What we find, however,
in the (slight) relevant evidence from Theodosius's reign is very significant.
In 415, the current Patriarch, Gamaliel, had as it seems recently been elevated to the highest honorific rank in the Empire, with the title of Illustris,
and had in official eyes been led by that to misuse his powers (compare a
similar episode in Emesa, p. 93 above). The letter sent by Theodosius to Aurelianus, Praetorian Prefect of Oriens, incomplete as it clearly is, is certainly
a response to a complaint from the region: "Since Gamaliel has supposed
that he can offend with impunity, and all the more so since he was elevated

---

117. See Seth Schwartz, *Imperialism and Jewish Society, 200 BCE to 640 CE*
(2001).

118. See A. Ovadiah, *Hellenistic, Roman and Early Byzantine Mosaics in Israel* (1987), with Z. Weiss and E. Netzer, *Promise and Redemption: A Synagogue
Mosaic from Sepphoris* (1996). See now Z. Weiss, *The Sepphoris Synagogue* (2005).

119. Pp. 97–116.

120. See M. Jacob, *Die Institutionen des jüdischen Patriarchen: eine Quellen und
traditionskritische Studie zur Geschichte der Juden in der Spätantike* (1995).

to the highest of ranks, let Your Illustrious Authority be aware that Our Serenity has sent orders to the *vir illustris*, the Magister Officiorum, that the letters of appointment to an Honorary Prefecture have been stripped from him. . . . " He should not establish new synagogues, and should not judge between Jews and Christians. Non-Jewish slaves should not be circumcized, and Christian slaves (owned by Jews) handed over to the Church. We hear no more of the Patriarchs until Theodosius refers in 429 to their *excessus* (extinction?) and to some consequential arrangements.[121]

While no justice to this complex topic can be done here, it is clear that the Jewish community, or communities, settled in Palestine did not constitute a distinctive or problematic local *ethnos* like the Isaurians, or even (in a sense) the *Suroi*. What is striking by contrast is that there are hints, if no more, that even at this period the Samaritans of Palestine did. By "even at this time" is meant the fact that in 484 and again in 529 it was to be the Samaritans, and not the Jews, who generated major revolts against the Imperial power. But disturbances had broken out earlier than that. The *Life* of Daniel Stylites records his being warned in about 450 or 451 that it would be dangerous to pursue his plan of visiting Palestine, because the Samaritans there had risen against the Christians.[122] That might be dismissed as embellishment, perhaps derived from the revolt of 484. But in fact it is confirmed by a letter of the Emperor Marcian addressed in 453 to archimandrites and others in Aelia (Jerusalem) in response to petitions which they had sent to Pulcheria. The clergy had accused the Samaritans of outrageous actions, including murder and robbery, directed against the churches, and Marcian declares that he has given orders to a *comes* named Dorotheos to carry out a criminal investigation.[123]

We shall see shortly three comparable cases of insult or actual physical assault which were claimed to have been directed by Jews against Christians under Theodosius. But it is essential to stress that none of these is specifically related to Palestine. The very real problem of a hostile "other" which Christians, including the Emperor himself, felt to arise from the presence of Jews as a religious community was one which might arise anywhere.[124] In that

121. *CTh* XVI.8.22 (*CJ* I.9.15), Oct. 20, 415; Linder, no. 41; *CTh* XVI.8.29 (*CJ* I.9.17), May 30, 429; Linder, no. 53.

122. *Life* of Daniel, 10. See R. Lane Fox, "The *Life of Daniel*," in *Portraits: Biographical Representation in the Greek and Roman Literature of the Roman Empire*, ed. M. J. Edwards and S. Swain (1997), 175 ff.

123. *ACO* II.1.3, para. 26 (p. 127 [486]).

124. For what follows, see in much greater detail, F. Millar, "Christian Emperors, Christian Church and the Jews of the Diaspora in the Greek East, CE 379–450," *JJS* 55 (2004): 1 ff.

sense, the relation of the fervently Christian state to Jews was comparable
to its relation to pagans on the one hand, and to Christians who were labeled as heretical on the other. Thus there are various examples of Imperial rhetoric where pagans, Jews, and heretics are all grouped together.[125] At
the level of specific legislation, or administrative measures, however, there
was no "category error,"[126] for Jews were treated quite differently from
either pagans or heretics. To sum up the position briefly, the practice of Judaism by Jews was not forbidden, though the conversion of Christians (and
specifically of Christian slaves owned by Jews) was; existing synagogues
were (in principle) protected from attack or despoilment by their Christian
neighbors. In the later decades of the reign, however, the construction of
new synagogues was forbidden, and Jews and Samaritans were barred from
Imperial office. The very real tensions felt were religious. Documentary evidence from the late Empire, not precisely dated, shows that both gentile
"God-fearers" *(theosebeis)* and full proselytes might attach themselves to
synagogues; conversely, there was no bar to the acceptance of any Jew who
chose to convert to Christianity. Contemporary evidence shows a persist-
ent strain of anxiety about, and hostility to, Judaism on the part of Christians, as well as reports of disputes between Jews and Christians on matters
of doctrine and biblical interpretation.

Against that background, it will be sufficient to pick out a few instances
where issues involving Jews came, or might have come, to the Imperial attention. The earliest comes from the very beginning of Theodosius's sole
reign, in an extract from a letter of May 29, 408, to Anthemius, Praetorian
Prefect of Oriens. Nothing in the extract indicates explicitly that this is a
reply to a report about a specific incident, but it is evident that it must be.
The reference to "governors" makes clear, however, that its provisions are
intended to be general:[127]

> The governors of the provinces shall prohibit the Jews from setting fire
> to Aman in memory of his past punishment, in a certain ceremony of
> their festival, and from burning with sacrilegious intent a form made
> to resemble the saint cross in contempt of the Christian faith, lest they

125. See, e.g., *CTh* XVI.5.59 + 8.26 (*CJ* I.9.16) + 9.5 + 10.22, Apr. 9, 423, Linder,
no. 48; *CTh* XVI.5.60 + 8.27 + 10.23 + 10.24 (*CJ* I.11.6), June 8, 423, Linder, no. 49;
CTh XV.5.5 (*CJ* III.12.6), Feb. 1, 425, Linder, no. 50.

126. For the relevance of such a "category error" in a wider sense see A. Cameron, "Jews and Heretics—A Category Error?" in *The Ways that Never Parted: Jews
and Christians in Late Antiquity and the Early Middle Ages*, ed. A. H. Becker and
A. Y. Reed (2002), 345 ff.

127. *CTh* XVI.8.18 (*CJ* I.9.11), Linder, no. 36.

mingle the sign of our faith with their jests, and they shall restrain their rites from ridiculing the Christian Law, for they are bound to lose what had been permitted them till now unless they abstain from those matters which are forbidden.

"Aman" is of course "Haman," the villain of the pseudohistorical narrative in the book of Esther, and the festival will therefore be Purim. A much more overt conflict, indeed mass mutual violence, allegedly instigated by Jews, is recorded in a well-known passage of Socrates' *Ecclesiastical History,* referring to Alexandria in 415. We need not rehearse the details here, except to note that Socrates records that both the Praefectus Augustalis, Orestes, and the archbishop of Alexandria, Cyril, who took opposite sides in the conflict, sent reports to the Emperor, apparently without result.[128] This disputed local issue might thus have formed the subject matter of an Imperial "law" or "laws," as did the question of the *parabalani* in the employment of the archbishop.[129] But, so far as we know, it did not do so.

Similar local conflicts must lie behind the extract from a "law" of 420, addressed to the Praetorian Prefect of Illyricum, condemning oppression and violence directed against Jews or synagogues—but balancing that with a warning to Jews not to become overconfident, and hence take abusive action against Christian observances.[130] If we turn to Oriens (and, as it seems, specifically to Syria), a similar balancing act, in response to competing pressures, can be seen in three successive "laws" embodied in letters sent in the course of 423 to Asclepiodotus, the Praetorian Prefect, preventing the seizure or burning of synagogues (but banning the construction of new ones); responding to a "piteous petition" *(miserabiles preces)* from some Jews, not identified, and again banning the occupation or burning of synagogues—but punishing Jews who circumcize a Christian; and banning violence against peaceful Jews—and, in this occasion, also pagans.[131] The second of the three letters, that of April 9, 423, is notable as recording the only attested petition, evidently addressed to the Emperor, by any Jews. We can be certain that it will have been written in Greek, but are given no hint of the identity of the Jews concerned. The other side of the story, Christian pressure, is rep-

---

128. Socrates, *HE* VII.13; for the opposed reports, 13.18–19.

129. Contrast *CTh* XVI.2.42 (*CJ* I.3.17), Sept. 29, 416, addressed to the Praetorian Prefect of Oriens, and referring to an embassy from Alexandria, with *CTh* XVI.2.43 (*CJ* I.3.18), Feb. 3, 418, also to the Praetorian Prefect, and raising the limit on the number of *parabalani* set in the first announcement. See p. 141 below.

130. *CTh* XVI.8.21 (*CJ* I.9.14), Aug. 6, 420, Linder, no. 46.

131. For the "laws" of Feb. 15, 423, see *CTh* XV.3.6 (*CJ* I.2.7 + XI.75.4), Linder, no. 47. For those of Apr. 9 and June 8, see n. 125 above.

resented in vivid and novelistic fashion in the Syriac *Life* of Symeon Stylites. The dates and details are not quite secure, but the author represents the famous ascetic as responding to the perceived scandal of Imperial favor for the Jews by sending the Emperor an indignant letter, as a result of which the relevant measures were reversed, and the official in question (here called "Asclepiades") was dismissed. The letter as quoted runs:[132]

> Now that your heart is exalted and you have disregarded the Lord your God who gave you the glorious diadem and the royal throne, now that you have become a friend and companion and protector to unbelieving Jews, behold suddenly the righteous judgement of God will overtake you and all who are of the same mind as you in this matter. You will lift up your hands to heaven and say in your affliction, 'Truly this anger has come on me because I broke faith with the Lord God.'

While such a letter may seem a rhetorical fiction, caution is needed. As we noted earlier, the main manuscript of the Syriac *Life* was written in 473; and we will see shortly (chapter 4) at least one other example of a petition to the Emperor expressed in equally vigorous language. In short, this text, which must have been completed between 459 and 473, expresses contemporary attitudes, and perfectly illustrates the competing pressures, of legality on the one side and Christian conviction on the other, to which the Emperor was exposed.

Nevertheless, the principle was maintained that Judaism, as observed by Jews, though perceived as a system of offensive falsehood, was legal, and that synagogues were neither commanded, like temples, to be destroyed, nor even allowed to be so destroyed. The Emperor's attitude and language did however become steadily harder, and eventually came, for the first time in the East, to embody the principle that Jews and Samaritans were unworthy of public office. The principle appears in the same *Novella* of 438 of which part was quoted earlier:[133]

> Wherefore, although (?) according to the ancient maxim, no cure must be employed for hopeless diseases, in order that these deadly sects, oblivious of Our age, may not spread too wantonly into the life of Our people like an indistinguishable confusion, We finally sanction by this law destined to live until all ages, that no Jew, no Samaritan . . . shall enter upon any honors or dignities; to none of them shall the administration of a civil duty be available, nor shall they perform even the

132. Syriac *Life*, 121–23, trans. Doran.
133. *Nov. Th.* 3, quotation from para. 2, trans. Pharr, with adjustments; Linder, no. 54. See p. 121 above.

duties of a defender [of a city]. Indeed We believe that it is wrong that persons hostile to the Supernal Majesty and to the Roman laws should be considered the avengers of Our laws under the protection of a surreptitious jurisdiction; that they should be protected by the authority of a dignity thus acquired; that they should have the power to judge or to pronounce whatever sentence they may wish against the Christians and very often against the bishops themselves of the holy religion, as if they were insulting Our faith.

With an equally reasonable consideration also, We prohibit any synagogue to arise as a new building, but license is granted to strengthen the ancient synagogues which threaten immediately to fall in ruin.

As we have seen, there were various forms of diversity within the extraordinarily homogeneous—Greek and Christian—world of Theodosius's Empire. Contemporaries were aware of *Suroi* as speakers of a distinct regional language, and might know of the most famous of writers in Syriac, Ephraem. But no one seems to have perceived *Suroi* as likely to constitute an internal enemy like the Isaurians. The Arab or Saracen tribes of the frontier zone of Oriens, however, were seen as an unstable element and potential threat, who might carry out raids, or support either the Empire or its Sasanid rival. It is perhaps no accident that, in his directions to Nomus in 443 about the regulation of the army, Theodosius makes a particular point of laying down that there shall be no interference with provisions for the Saracen allies *(foederati).*[134] But, so far at least, none of these groups emerge as significant sources of conflict except those which embodied what was seen as religious deviance: pagan practice, effectively banished already from the public stage, and not (it seems) seen as representing any divergent regional culture; and Samaritanism and Judaism, of which the latter at least was of considerable importance—but as a religion not as a regional culture, or dangerous ethnic grouping. But, though non-Christian beliefs inspired impressive examples of Imperial rhetoric, and of the expression of the Emperor's piety, they were far outweighed as subjects of concern by forms of Christian belief which were felt to be deviant, and false.

134. *Nov. Th.* 24.1, para. 2. See pp. 44–45 above.

IV   State and Church

Civil Administration, Ecclesiastical Hierarchy, and Spiritual Power

Not seriously threatened by external military force until the last decade of the reign (and even then emerging with its boundaries intact), the Empire of Theodosius still felt itself to be in a position of potential danger on all sides. Internally, its administrative, cultural, linguistic, and religious homogeneity, viewed globally, was remarkable; such a level of coherence had never been achieved before over the same area, and would never be achieved again after the seventh century. Nonetheless, as regards religion, an intense awareness of deviance pervades both Christian writing of the period and the pronouncements of the Emperor. As regards paganism, crushing (and very sudden) as the effective abolition of public sacrifice had been, victory was still felt to be tenuous and incomplete. As for Judaism, while its practice by Jews was legal—and even, if somewhat halfheartedly, protected—it too was felt as a threat and a challenge. But such deviations from the ideal of an integrated, Greek-speaking, Christian state and society were a minor problem compared to the fact that uniformity of Christian belief and practice could not be attained. The hostile appellations given by outsiders to endless Christian subgroups alleged to be guilty of false belief haunt the pages of contemporary Christian writers, just as they do the pronouncements of the Emperor. As we will see in chapter 5, in 435 Theodosius was even to invent a new appellation for one of these groups, and to command that it alone should be used.

Theodosius's pronouncement of 435 represented a step in the evolution of the greatest of all the issues over doctrine, the Nestorian controversy, which gave rise to the first and second Councils of Ephesus, in 431 and 449, and to the Council of Chalcedon, called by the Emperor Marcian in 451. A brief outline of the successive phases of this conflict will occupy the latter part of this chapter, while from the uniquely detailed documentary evidence a few items will be picked out, to illustrate the interactions of Church and State, the rhetoric of persuasion, self-justification, and command, and the means available for the enforcement of the Imperial will. The following chapter (5) will also explore the fate of two of the key figures, Nestorius himself and his ally Irenaeus (an Imperial official with the rank of "Comes"), again with the aim of simultaneously illuminating the interaction of Church and State, and of Latin and Greek, as well as the workings of persuasion, command, reaction, and defiance.

But before we come to that story, covering the last two decades of the reign, and documented step-by-step in extraordinary detail, we need first to touch on a number of aspects of the complex interrelations of State and Church, as regards the regional and provincial structure of the Empire, the internal workings of provinces, the role of churches and bishoprics within the late antique city, and the Church as an organization functioning outside the urban context, in the territory of each city. As will quickly become apparent, almost every "rule" or generalization of which we can find evidence in our sources was marked by anomalies, exceptions, and disputed interpretations, giving rise once again to a rich rhetoric of persuasion. The same is true of the boundaries of clerical and lay status, and of the obligations and privileges of churches as organizations and owners of property. Equally, if we look from within the Church outwards to the cities within which bishops functioned, the bishops came, as is well known, both to play a large part in the management and physical development of cities, and to speak for them to officials in the Imperial service.

At all levels, therefore, from villages to the Imperial court in Constantinople, there were complex and frequently disputed interrelations between Church and State. But in the fourth and fifth centuries, there had arisen a new factor, whose origins go back, broadly speaking, to the period of the Tetrarchy and of Constantine, to complicate the discourse of conviction and persuasion still further: the ascetic movement.[1] The prominence, both in real life and in literature, of the ideal of abstinence, extreme physical self-denial, and devotion to piety, whether conducted individually, or in loose groups, or in tightly organized religious communities, could be thought to represent a revolution in the history of Christianity comparable to the conversion of Con-

---

1. For the broader conceptual background see P. Brown, *The Body and Society: Men, Women and Sexual Renunciation in Early Christianity* (1989), and also P. Rousseau, *Ascetics, Authority and the Church in the Age of Jerome and Cassian* (1978); D. Caner, *Wandering, Begging Monks: Spiritual Authority and the Promotion of Monasticism in Late Antiquity* (2002); and on monks who subsequently became bishops, A. Sterk, *Renouncing the World yet Leading the Church: The Monk-Bishop in Late Antiquity* (2004).

stantine itself. What needs to be stressed here, however, is the freedom from external regulation, by either Church or State, which ascetics possessed. Adopting an ascetic lifestyle was a choice which any Christian, of any social class, could make; no ordination was required, for a monk was not in orders. An individual, or a group, might establish a monastery if they had the will and the means; but not until the Council of Chalcedon did the Church lay down that the foundation of a monastery required the permission of the local bishop, and that monks should concentrate on prayer and fasting, and not disturb the peace.[2] Equally, a monastery might have its own internal rules; but no external authority determined the form of these. Furthermore, as had already become evident before Theodosius's reign, in areas like Egypt or Syria where there were large numbers of monks, they might represent a dangerous and turbulent concentration of manpower, capable of attacks on pagans or of mass physical intervention in doctrinal disputes within the Church. Similarly, on the evidence of a strongly worded letter addressed by Valens to the Praetorian Prefect of Oriens, subsequently posted up at Berytus in 370 or 373, the flight of *curiales* into the role of monks *(monazontes)* was already causing difficulties for the fulfillment of city obligations:[3]

> Certain devotees of idleness have deserted the compulsory services of the municipalities, have betaken themselves to solitudes and secret places, and under the pretext of religion have joined with bands of hermit monks. We command, therefore, by Our well considered precept, that such persons and others of this kind who have been apprehended within Egypt shall be routed out from their hiding places by the Count of the Orient and shall be recalled to the performance of the compulsory public services of their municipalities, or in accordance with the tenor or Our sanction, they shall forfeit the allurements of the family property, which We decree shall be vindicated by those persons who are going to undertake the performance of their compulsory public services.

No such hostile view of asceticism was likely to issue from the court of Theodosius, for contemporaries could conceive of the Imperial family, above all given the influence of his pious elder sister, Pulcheria, as being itself not unlike a monastic establishment.[4] They could also, as we saw earlier, envisage a famous ascetic like Symeon Stylites as sending the Emperor a fierce letter of rebuke for presuming to offer some protection to Jewish communities, and as allegedly getting the policy reversed.[5] Perhaps our most vivid

2. Canon 4 of Chalcedon, *ACO* II.1.2 (p. 159 [355]); Tanner, *Decrees*, 89.
3. *CTh* XII.1.63; trans. Pharr.
4. See esp. Sozomenus, *HE* IX.1.
5. P. 128 above.

representation, both of asceticism as a spontaneous spiritual vocation and of the presumption that it gave both the right and the real possibility of exerting influence even on the Emperor, comes from the collection of stories—*Plerophoriae,* or "Fulfillments"—later compiled by John Rufus. One example is the story of Basileios, who, after founding a monastery and a convent in Lycia, heard of the blasphemy of Nestorius (428–31) and went to Constantinople, where he denounced the Empress in church, approached the Emperor in person, and was arrested, flogged, and condemned to exile. But large-scale popular support gathered, the Emperor had a vision and repented, and the Council of Ephesus was called.[6]

The story might seem pure fiction but for the fact that, as we will see, we have the text of a petition from another monk called Basileios, addressed to Theodosius in terms even stronger than we might imagine from John Rufus's story,[7] as well as the text of the letter which the Emperor wrote to Symeon Stylites asking for his support in 432.[8] As will become clear, alongside the major episcopal actors, a very important role was played in the Nestorian controversy by monks—the two Basils just mentioned, Dalmatius, Eutyches, Barsaumas. Which is only to say both that the Church was closely integrated with, and dependent on, the State, and that the State, for all the sincere piety of the court and its commitment to unity of belief, could not control the infinite variousness of popular piety. Marcian, in calling the Council of Chalcedon, and directing its outcome far more firmly than Theodosius had at either Council of Ephesus, was to produce multiple divisions in the Church, between East and West, and within the East, which have not been resolved to this day. But, if the great crisis of 428 onwards dominates our surviving evidence, it is clear that many divisions and unresolved disputes had faced the young Emperor since the earliest days of his reign. State and Church existed in a permanent condition of mutual dependence, concern, conflict—and commitment to the unattainable ideal of unity and harmony.

2. STATE AND CHURCH: REGIONAL STRUCTURES OF HIERARCHY AND AUTHORITY

In a broad sense, allowing for many anomalies, the map of the civil administration of the Theodosian Empire (figure I) is also the map of the Church. Just as the Empire had always done, and still did, the Church rested on a

6. John Rufus, *Plerophoriae* 34.
7. See pp. 155–57 below.
8. *ACO* I.1.4, para. 121 (pp. 5–6).

network of cities, each with one bishop *(episkopos)*, whose responsibilities related also to parishes, which might be called *paroikiai*, scattered over the villages *(kōmai)* in the territory of the city. In a famous letter of 449 Theodoret, bishop from 423 onwards of the middle-ranking city of Cyrrhus in the province of Euphratensis, claimed that he had had to look after eight hundred churches—"for so many *paroikiai* does Cyrrhus contain."[9] In the previous year, defending his twenty-five-year record as bishop, he recorded that he had led back to orthodoxy eight villages *(kōmai)* of Marcionites, as well as other, apparently minor, villages lying near them, and also one village of Eunomians and another of Arians.[10] Yet both letters were written only because he himself was under attack as a follower of Nestorius.

In principle, therefore, the rule was one bishop for each city—which is why the lists of bishops attending, speaking, or subscribing at the Councils give so evocative an impression of the spread of cities across the Empire. Even here there could be exceptions: at Ephesus I a petition *(libellos)* was received from Euprepios, bishop of Bizye and Arcadiopolis, and Kyrillos, bishop of Koilai, which arose from the fact that in the province of Europa the established practice was that one bishop might preside over several cities. But Phritilas of Heraclea, a follower of Nestorius, was alleged to have ordained separate bishops for each.[11]

Overall, however, the number and distribution of bishoprics depended very closely on the number of places with the rank of city (the total must be well over a thousand). Hence, the number might change if the Emperor, as was still envisaged, gave the rank of city to a new place; exactly this was laid down at Chalcedon.[12]

Not all cities were of equal rank, however, and the level at which the hierarchy of the Church corresponded most closely to that of the State was within each province. For the chief city of each province, thus in principle only one per province, was the *metropolis*, or " mother city," and its bishop could be called a *mētropolitēs*, "Metropolitan," or occasionally *Archiepiskopos*. In fact all the different levels of bishop, up to those of Rome or Constantinople, were often referred to just as *episkopos*. But if the terminology of hierarchy was loose, the centrality of the bishop of each provincial metropolis is absolutely clear. Figure XI shows the northern provinces of Oriens, with the episcopal sees in each, and signals which was the metropolitan see

9. Theodoret, *Epp.* III. 113.
10. Theodoret, *Epp.* II. 81.
11. *ACO* I.1.7, para. 82 (pp. 122–23).
12. *ACO* II.1.2, Canon 17 (p. 161 [357]); Tanner, *Decrees,* 95.

in each case. The powers of a metropolitan bishop were considerable: he had to play at least a part in the consecration of any new bishop in his province; complaints against bishops were directed to him; he could call provincial synods; and when the Emperor called an oecumenical Council, the invitation might come through him. Thus Theodosius's letter of November 19, 430, summoning the first Council of Ephesus, was addressed, in the case of Egypt (where the metropolitan system did not apply), to the archbishop, Cyril, but simultaneously to the bishops of *metropoleis* in other regions.[13]

The concept of a city being a "metropolis," however, derived from the civil structure of the Empire, and went back well before the Christian period.[14] Although in the late Empire it normally implied the concept of being the capital of the province in question, and hence of being the only one, it was also, traditionally, an honorific title which could be bestowed by the Emperor at will. Hence, for instance, the centuries-long rivalry between the cities of Nicaea and Nicomedia in Bithynia had reached another phase under Valentinian and Valens, when Nicaea had been given the title "metropolis" in addition to Nicomedia.[15] Not surprisingly, conflict subsequently broke out between the two bishops, and Session XIV at Chalcedon was devoted to a detailed discussion of the case. The final ruling was that Nicaea should retain the title, but that alone, while Nicomedia enjoyed all the attendant privileges, and precedence over the other bishops, as in other provinces.[16] Similarly, at Chalcedon the Emperor Marcian had already in fact, at Session VI, announced a further variation: in commemoration of the Council, Chalcedon would also have the title "metropolis," but without loss to the rights of Nicomedia.[17]

Theodosius perhaps assumed that a similar convention, applicable also in the ecclesiastical sphere, would apply without controversy when near the end of his reign he wrote to Hormidas, the Praetorian Prefect of Oriens, to confer the title of "metropolis" on Berytus. The abbreviated text which survives is found only in the *Codex Justinianus*, and gives no explanation of

13. *ACO* I.1.1, para. 25.115–17 (pp. 114–16). For the Emperor's reference to parallel letters to metropolitans see para. 25.3 (p. 115).

14. See G. W. Bowersock, "Hadrian and Metropolis," *Bonner Historia-Augusta Colloquium* 17 (1985), 75 ff. = *Studies on the Eastern Roman Empire* (1994), 371 ff. For the question of provincial capitals see R. Haensch, *Capita Provinciarum: Statthaltersitze und Provinzialverwaltung in der römischen Kaiserzeit* (1997).

15. See L. Robert, "La titulature de Nicée et de Nicomédie: La gloire et la haine," *Harv. Stud. Class. Philol.* 81 (1977): 1 ff., referring to the early Empire.

16. *ACO* II.1.3 (pp. 56–62 [415–21]), quoting on p. 61 [420] a letter of Valentinian and Valens to Nicaea.

17. *ACO* II.1.2, *Actio* VI, para. 21 (p. 157 [353]).

the circumstances. Nonetheless it betrays an awareness that this rash step also represented an intervention in another local rivalry which had lasted for centuries:[18]

> For many just causes we decree that Berytus, which is already crowned by its own virtues, should be adorned by the metropolitan title and rank, so that this city also (hereby) possesses (that) rank. Tyre does not (thereby) lose any of her rights. May the former be mother of the province by the *beneficium* of our ancestors, and the latter by ours, and let each enjoy a similar dignity.

Nothing is said here about consequential ecclesiastical precedence, and it ought to have been presumed that nothing would change. Any such reasonable expectation was to be sorely disappointed. Session '19' (in the Greek text) of Chalcedon, dated to October 20, 451, was to hear a dispute between Photius of Tyre and Eustathius of Berytus, whose proceedings must rank as one of the most interesting treatments of constitutional and ecclesiastical law from antiquity, and would well deserve publication, translation, and commentary in their own right. The details cannot be followed here. Suffice to say that the petition (as ever, *deēsis* and *hikesia*), addressed formally to Valentinian III and Marcian by Photius of Tyre, alleged that Eustathius of Berytus had claimed on the basis of rescripts of Theodosius to have the right of supervising the consecration of bishops in several Phoenician cities: Byblus, Botrys, Tripolis, Orthosias, Arca, and Antaradus are mentioned later, and a glance at the map in figure XI will show how substantial a claim that was. Here too, it was in the end decided that Photius would retain his power of election throughout Phoenicia I, while (it seems clear) Eustathius, like his city, kept his new title.[19]

At the next level of precedence also, that of the two secular dioceses which formed the relatively restricted Prefecture of Illyricum, and the five (Thraciae, Asiana, Pontica, Oriens, and Aegyptus) which—confusingly—made up the Praetorian Prefecture of Oriens, the Church did, at least partially and in theory, follow the structure of the State. But various different factors combined to make the ecclesiastical structure at this level much more incoherent, anomalous, and disputed than at the intermediate and lower levels. One major factor was the place occupied by some cities in the early history of the Church. Both Alexandria and Antioch could claim such a place, and both were the seats of the civil governors of major dioceses, the Praefectus Augustalis and the Comes Orientis. So the bishops of these

18. *CJ* XI.22.1. Undated, but certainly 449/50; see *PLRE* II, Hormisdas.
19. *ACO* II.1.3 (pp. 101–14 [460–73]).

two cities each occupied a preeminent status, for which the title "archi-episkopos" or "Patriarchēs" was on occasion used, though not yet consistently. At Session II of Chalcedon the presiding officials spoke of "the most holy *Patriarchai* of each *dioikēsis.*"[20] But whether we can really see so consistent a system in action is unclear. As regards Illyricum, and the two civil dioceses of Dacia and Macedonia (see figure I), successive bishops (or archbishops or patriarchs) of Rome firmly maintained the primacy of the bishop of Thessalonica, as their "Vicarius."[21] As regards Asiana, the precedence should have gone to Ephesus, but its bishops never seem to emerge in that role. Nor do the bishops of any see in Pontica, or Thraciae. In short, a hierarchy at this third level, where a Patriarch held preeminence over the provinces grouped in each secular diocese, is clearly visible to us only in relation to two secular dioceses, Egypt and Oriens, and their chief cities, Alexandria and Antioch.

Even here, there might, as always, be conflicts and anomalies. It is evident that the archbishop or patriarch expected to exercise some authority as regards the election of bishops (or at least of metropolitan bishops) in the provinces under him. But though the province of Cyprus belonged to Oriens, its bishops claimed an independent ("autocephalous") status, allegedly going back to Apostolic times. The claim was controversial, as we see in a letter of Innocentius, bishop (or archbishop or patriarch) of Rome, to Alexander of Antioch, which must belong to 413–17, and refers to the presumptuousness of the Cypriot bishops in claiming complete independence in episcopal elections.[22] This is the issue which we have already seen as arising at Ephesus I, when the Cypriot bishops complained that they had received a letter from Flavius Dionysius, Magister Militum at Antioch, laying down the procedure for an election.[23] There is a puzzle here to which we will return: although it was the structure of the *civil* administration on which (in principle at least) the hierarchy of the Church was explicitly modeled, in a remarkable number of cases arising in Oriens it is not the Comes Orientis but the Magister Militum who appears as the representative of the State to whom the Church relates. In this instance, his intervention was attributed to machinations by the clergy of Antioch. At any rate, as we saw earlier, this intervention offers an absolutely precise example of the division of function between Greek and Latin. Dionysius wrote in Greek to the clergy of

20. *ACO* II.1.2, *Actio* "III" (in fact II, see appendix A), para. 6 (p. 78 [274]).
21. See p. 53 above.
22. Innocentius, *Epp.* 24.
23. Pp. 20–21 above.

Constantia, and in Latin, with almost exactly the same content, to the Consularis of Cyprus. His letter is of great importance, both as the best-preserved specimen of official Latin contemporary with the latest texts in the *Theodosian Code,* and also as a clear expression of the right of the State to enforce the rules laid down by the Church. For this reason, as an exception, the Latin text will be given here, and then translated:[24]

> Flavius Dionysius, vir clarissimus et magnificentissimus, Magi(ster) Utriusque Militiae, Theodoro, viro clarissimo, Consul(ari) Provinciae Cypri. Imperialis auctoritas multas ob causas et maxime ecclesiasticas reverentissimos antistites Efesum convenire divinis apicibus disposuit prorogatis. Quia itaque conperimus Constantiae civitatis antistitem a praesenti vita migrasse et diem sibi praefinitum complesse, necessariam hanc ad te auctoritatem esse censuimus emittendam, scilicet ut ne quis sine conscientia vel dispositione reverentissimi conventus audeat in defuncti locum aliquem nominare. Expectari namque convenit formam quam tot reverentissimorum episcoporum dabit adsensus. Sicut enim dictum est, harum gratia rerum memorati religiosissimi viri convenire praecepti sunt. Si itaque motum contumacibus debitum tam tua gravitas quam officium obtemperans sibi desiderat evitare, id modis omnibus prohibebit nec aliquem, quod dictum est, provehi patiatur ante auctoritatem horum quorum interesse reverentissimorum dicitur sacerdotum. Quodsi has auctoritates eius de quo agitur ordinatio praecessit antistitis, eum pro caelesti oraculo ad Efesum sicut alios facias pervenire. Nec enim ignorare debes quod si secus aliquid fuerit perptemptatum, tu quidem quinque libras auri, officium vero alias tot fisci viribus inferre cogimini. Ut autem haec quae pro postulatione religiosissimorum antistitum videntur esse disposita, maturum sortiantur effectum, Maturium et Adelfium iussimus ex officio specialiter destinari. Data duodecimo Calendas Iunias Antiochiae.

> Flavius Dionysius, *vir clarissimus* and *magnificentissimus,* Magister Utriusque Militiae, to Theodorus, *vir clarissimus,* Consularis of the province of Cyprus. For many reasons, especially ones affecting the Church, the Imperial Authority has laid down in letters which have been issued that the most reverend bishops should assemble at Ephesus. Since therefore we have learned that the bishop of Constantia has passed away from this present life and fulfilled his allotted span, we have determined that this necessary authority should be issued to you, to wit that no one should presume to nominate anyone in place of the deceased without the knowledge and approval of a most reverend synod. For it is appropriate to wait for the validation which the assent of so many most reverend men will confer. For, as has been stated, for

---

24. *ACO* I.7, para. 81 (pp. 119–20).

the conduct of these matters, the afore-mentioned most reverend men are instructed to convene.

So, if either Your Gravity or the staff subordinate to it wishes to avoid the steps taken against those guilty of contumacy, it will ensure by all means that no-one, as has been stated, should be permitted to be put forward before the authority of those most reverend priests who are said to (be entitled to) take part.

If however the election of the bishop concerned has forestalled these instructions, you are to see to it that, in accordance with the celestial proclamation (of the Emperor), he proceeds to Ephesus like the others.

Furthermore, you ought not to be unaware that, if any different steps are audaciously attempted, you are liable to pay a fine of five pounds of gold to the funds of the Fiscus, and the staff another of the same amount.

But in order that these measures, which seem to be laid down in accordance with the request of the most religious bishops, many reach a prompt conclusion, I have ordered Maturius and Adelfius from my staff to be assigned to this special duty.

Given on the twelfth day before the Calends of June, at Antioch. (May 21, 431)

Though this letter is the product of a high, but intermediate, level of government (as opposed to the texts in the *Codex*, all emanating from successive Emperors), it is absolutely compatible with them in the clumsiness and formality of its expression, in being the result of an episcopal request *(postulatio)*, and in twice threatening punishment for noncompliance—while also accepting that it might be too late anyway.

Thus the State, as known to us best through the Imperial "laws" in the *Codex* and *Novellae*, saw its duty as the enforcement of the internal rules of the Church, as well as the decisions of its Councils. Theodosius in 435, when formally banning the works of Nestorius (chapter 5), refers to "the decree of the most holy synod of bishops held at Ephesus." But the central role of the Emperor was itself to produce further anomalies. There was to be no place in the hierarchy of the Church for any equivalents of the Praetorian Prefects of Oriens (in the wider sense) and Illyricum, and a very anomalous and controversial place was occupied by the bishop (or archbishop, or patriarch) of Constantinople itself. The role and status of the occupant was controversial in several different ways: in relation to Rome; in relation to the Apostolic Sees of Alexandria and Antioch; in relation to the nearer provinces—what authority did the bishop have in relation, for instance, to the province of Asia? Or in relation to Illyricum, where, as we have seen, Theodosius's attempt to assert the authority of the bishop of Con-

stantinople was firmly rebuffed by Honorius?[25] By the time of the Theodosian dynasty at any rate it was clearly accepted *de facto* that the Emperor
could exercise a determining role, and could have prospective bishops of Constantinople (like John Chrysostom or Nestorius) summoned from distant
provinces and elected.

The Council of Constantinople of 381 had laid down that its bishop should
come in precedence immediately after that of Rome "because it (Constantinople) is a New Rome."[26] Chalcedon was to clarify some of the many
anomalies, but only at the cost of a permanent breach with Rome. Canon
28 of Chalcedon gave the bishop of Constantinople a patriarchal status, by
which he had the right to consecrate metropolitan bishops in the provinces
belonging to the dioceses of Pontica, Asiana, and Thraciae.[27] An (incomplete)
analogy to the Imperial power had thus produced rights comparable to those
apparently exercised by the "patriarchs" of Alexandria and Antioch. But Leo
of Rome would not accept that political structures could take precedence over
Apostolic origins, and thereby disturb the hierarchy of the Church.

These immensely complex and many-sided issues may be left aside here,
without being fully treated, above all because they are not explicitly at issue in the documentation from the reign of Theodosius himself (though profound issues of authority, as between Constantinople, Antioch, Alexandria,
and Rome, lie behind Ephesus I and II, and Chalcedon). Instead, we may take
some examples (out of many) in which complex issues arose at the boundaries where the functioning of the Church intersected with, or conflicted
with, the legal structure and practical needs of the State. In many instances
we can plainly see before us, and in others detect between the lines, the play-
ing out of conflicting claims and counterclaims, at a local or regional level,
or as involving the Emperor in person.

3. STATE AND CHURCH: CONTESTED BORDERS

Given the substantial scale of the manpower serving the Church, as well as
the possession of properties by individual churches, it is not surprising that
issues arose repeatedly concerning boundaries, obligations, and rules; some
of these issues would come to the attention of the Emperor, and his decision would be embodied in a "law"—which almost always meant, as we have

25. P. 54 above.
26. Council of Constantinople, Canon 3, see E. J. Jonkers, *Acta et Symbola Conciliorum quae saeculo quarto habita sunt* (1954), 108; Tanner, *Decrees,* 32.
27. Tanner, *Decrees,* 99–100.

seen repeatedly, a letter to a high official, most often the Praetorian Prefect. Thus, for example, a letter was addressed to Anthemius, Praetorian Prefect of Oriens, in 409 to lay down that any tenant who came to be ordained as a *clericus* must satisfy his tax obligations first.[28] Later in the same year Theodosius, or whoever was composing legislation in his name, wrote in August from Eudoxiopolis (as we have seen, a well-attested resort for the Emperor in the summer),[29] to lay down a limit on the number of *decani* in the service of the church in Constantinople. This number was large, nine hundred and fifty, but was not to be increased; equally, in a context which is not entirely clear, there were to be no more than five hundred and sixty-three *corporati*. The law was addressed to the Urban Prefect of Constantinople.[30] A similar impression of the sheer scale of the major churches as organized groups is gained from the two letters which concern the number of *parabalani*, or stretcher-bearers, in the service of the church at Alexandria. In the first, on September 29, 416, Theodosius wrote to Monaxius, the then Praetorian Prefect of Oriens, following an embassy *(legatio)* sent by the city. Their mission, or one of them, had evidently been to complain of interference in the secular affairs of the city by the *parabalani*. The number of these was to be restricted to five hundred, and their names were first to be approved by the Praefectus Augustalis and then to be referred to the Praetorian Prefect himself ("ad vestram magnitudinem"). The *parabalani* were barred from appearing at public spectacles in the city, or at the council chamber *(curia)*, and from violent interference with judicial cases.[31] The letter is unusual in the clarity with which it reveals serious local conflicts between a city and its church, and in its reflection of the hierarchical relations of the two Imperial officials. But even a great city like Alexandria could not necessarily hold out against ecclesiastical pressures. Within two years (February 3, 418), in another letter of Theodosius to Monaxius as Praetorian Prefect, the number of *parabalani* was raised to six hundred, with the right of choice falling once again to the bishop.[32] The reference to "the most reverend bishop of Alexandria" in the text makes quite clear that there must have been countervailing pressure, evidently from Cyril, the powerful current bishop. As we saw earlier, Jewish-Christian conflict in Alexandria had already brought the bishop and the Praefectus Augustalis into conflict.[33]

28. *CJ* I.3.16.
29. See p. 9 above.
30. *CJ* I.2.4 + ?IV.63.5, Aug. 21, 409.
31. *CTh* XVI.2.42 (*CJ* I.3.17).
32. *CTh* XVI.2.43 (*CJ* I.3.18).
33. P. 127 above.

Church and civil administration intersected, and came into potential conflict, in many different ways. But one of the most revealing issues which emerged under Theodosius was the question of the right of asylum in churches. As it happens, it also provides one of the most significant concentrations of evidence for the way in which legislation might be stimulated by particular episodes; for the generation and distribution of the text, or texts, embodying the legislation; for the interface between Latin and Greek within the Imperial system; and for the communication of the Imperial word in provincial localities, and its reception there. It is also one of three significant conjunctions of evidence where texts preserved in legal sources overlap with, and are complemented by, ones preserved in the *Acta* of the Councils.[34]

The legislation in question must have been prompted by an episode which Socrates reports in his *Ecclesiastical History,* and places just before the first Council of Ephesus.[35] Some armed barbarian slaves, escaping from a great household, invaded a church, apparently in Constantinople, clung to the altar, refusing to leave, killed one cleric and wounded another, and finally committed suicide. Theodosius's legislation on this topic was expressed, as was normal, in the form of a letter to Antiochus, the Praetorian Prefect of Oriens, issued from Constantinople on March 23, 431. The law affirms the right to take sanctuary in a church, while forbidding the carrying of arms into a church, or eating or sleeping there. Forceful removal of armed suppliants was permitted, but only after a formal invitation to surrender, and by permission of a bishop or governor, or of the Emperor himself.

The capacity thus conferred on churches to at least interrupt the normal course of jurisdiction was real, if strictly limited. The *Codex Theodosianus* preserves a Latin text of this quite lengthy and detailed piece of legislation.[36] Unusually, we also have a somewhat abbreviated version of the Latin letter, but in Greek, preserved by the sixth-century *Codex Justinianus.*[37] Does this mean that the Emperor in fact issued the law in Greek, or in both languages? This is possible, for we will see later an instance of a law which is explicitly stated to have been issued in Greek as well as Latin, in order that it should come to the notice of the public.[38]

Alternatively, the Greek translation will have been generated at a sec-

---

34. The other two cases both concern the fortunes of Nestorius and Irenaeus, discussed in chapter 5.

35. Socrates, *HE* VII.33.

36. *CTh* IX.45.4.

37. *CJ* I.12.3.

38. P. 187 below in chapter 5.

ondary stage, when it will (as many examples preserved in the *Novellae* show) have been the duty of Antiochus to publicize the law by having edicts posted up throughout the provinces. In fact, we know that this happened in this instance. For the *Acta* of Ephesus I include, without giving any context, a Greek text of the same law which is substantially longer than either of the two versions in the *Codices*.[39] No addressee is indicated, but there is a heading, "Royal Law about Those Taking Refuge in Church," at the beginning, and at the end "(The) Law was posted up in the fourteenth year of the indiction, Pharmouthi 12." The date indicated is April 7, remarkably soon after the initial issuing of the law. Pharmouthi is an Egyptian month, so what we are reading is the text posted up there.

This version, at some one hundred and fifty long lines as printed in *ACO*, is about twice the length of the Greek version in the *Codex* of Justinian, and constitutes a painful warning to students of Late Roman legislation. Every text to which we have access has been framed according to its intended function or to the interests of those who subsequently collected it, or both, and nearly all the texts are either somewhat abbreviated, or are no more than brief extracts from the originals.

In the case of this law the full text begins with some forty lines of reflections, entirely absent from either *Codex*, on the sanctity attributed to temples even in the period of pagan error, and contains a specific reference to the recent incident which had arisen "as a result of barbarian insanity." The quotation of the first half of these lengthy introductory reflections which follows is designed both to reinforce the warning as to how much most texts in the legal *Codices* omit, and to illustrate how close the rhetoric of an Emperor might come to that of a bishop. The theme of "Christianity and the rhetoric of empire" finds its perfect expression here:[40]

> A certain ancient custom from the times of error and a certain disposition of natural law, of a nature based on piety, have prevailed always to such an extent that divine ceremonies have been distinct in every period and people from public spheres of administration and human functions, and that these (ceremonies) have been arranged not only in the highest posture of affairs, but as if in a certain heaven on earth, and whither it is lawfully right for only pure and holy persons to approach. Hence the following, which naturally is implanted in all

39. *ACO* I.1.4, para. 137 (pp. 61–65).

40. The translation is taken, with emendations, from Coleman-Norton, no. 400, which provides the whole text, with references to *CTh* and *CJ*. Some extra punctuation has also been added, to assist the reader in following the pretty complex train of Imperial thought, which I am still not confident of having grasped.

persons' thoughts, also results: that in no way the things hallowed
to God can be polluted, and nor can men's insolence advance against
divine power. For how can that be defiled which is always necessarily
pure? Or how can that be befouled which, when once sanctified, ceases
not to be such?

Wherefore, although we have been persuaded by acts which lately
have been dared nefariously against the divine altar as a result of bar-
baric insanity, that neither the pure is defiled nor what is naturally holy
has been soiled, nevertheless, since that has happened which it had been
hoped in no way would happen, the audacity of abominable persons has
extended as far as piety, so that neither to unholy persons even may appear to be profane these things which are divine, nor in sanctified and
hallowed places may it be possible for these things to happen, which
not even in other places indiscriminately is it tolerable that these occur
irrationally, we, in respect to the preservation of pure religion and the
protection of piety, exclude every insolence, which arises from persons
acting either boldly or involuntarily, from Almighty God's Church.
And indeed, if the erroneous religion of heathen antiquity—God being
what was anyone's opinion—so practised the observance of its own
superstition that it entrusted altars not to all persons but to certain
priests, and it dedicated temples (just as if also elevated by the earth)
in the acropolises and the securer districts of cities, and it worshipped
idols, which were fabricated, and it regarded with very great and august
vanity fabricated idols, by how much more is it proper for us to guard
religion with all observance—us to whom God with true religion, not
deserting heaven, has descended, and (just as if by a certain exchange
made between God and men) man has received God upon earth and
God has raised man to heaven?

Then, apart from a number of passages in the body of the text which do not
appear in either *Codex,* the Greek version preserved in the *Acta* adds another ten lines or so at the end, concluding with instructions for public dissemination: "As for these things which . . . we have ordered, with what is
appropriate having been assigned both to the human and the divine, you
will see to it that, by posting-up edicts *(diatagmata),* they come to the knowledge of all, so that on the one hand those taking refuge may be reassured
by the benevolence of the provisions laid down, and on the other, without
precipitate action by anyone, the rules established for the honour of divine
worship may be preserved."

In its full form, preserved only in the *Acta,* Theodosius's law, addressed
to the Praetorian Prefect, and posted up by him throughout the provinces,
provides a very rich example both of elaborate Imperial self-justification
and of the effort to bring the content of the Imperial will, in remarkable

detail, before anyone who could read Greek. Not all reactions, however, were entirely favorable. For it must surely be the same law, duly posted up in the province of Augustamnica in northeast Egypt, about which Isidorus of Pelusium complains bitterly in a letter to Cyrenius, the governor of the province.[41] It had been posted in front of the church, and allegedly had the effect of barring altogether the taking of refuge in a church. Isidorus is relying on hearsay, but even so his comment, even from an exceptionally vocal observer, illustrates the difficulties of effective propaganda relating to complex issues. We shall see later how another edict, disseminated on Imperial orders, was to provoke hostile demonstrations in Antioch.[42]

Compared to the concentration of evidence relating to this law on asylum, only some imaginative reconstruction can provide a context for the letter which Theodosius issued on August 28, 436, addressed from Apamea to the Praetorian Prefect of Oriens.[43] Which city called Apamea is referred to? As we have seen, the Emperor, though he did travel, did not travel much, or very far from Constantinople; his journeys took him either along the coast through Thrace, or into Asia Minor. So it is very unlikely that this is Apamea in Syria. It might be Apamea in Bithynia—but there must be a good chance that the very concrete reference in the letter to Aphrodisias in Caria, which we know that he had already visited in August 443, means that the context is a journey through the area of the River Maeander, and as far as the Apamea which lay in the province of Pisidia. Even if that is not so, the text, which is known to be merely an extract from a longer law on taxation, gives a very clear impression of the interplay between general rule, the custom of granting exemptions in response to individual requests, the ambition to limit the effects of such favors—and the commitment to protecting a particular privilege all the same:

> Previous rescripts, however they were impetrated, shall remain in their own undisturbed force, since it is impious for the generosity of the Emperor to be revoked, but in the future—with the exception of Cyrus, the Most Reverend Bishop of the City of the Aphrodisienses, whose merits are so great that, even contrary to the provisions of a general sanction of this kind, he shall not be prohibited from the full enjoyment of a special grant of imperial favor—if any person, by permission granted him by Our annotation, should wish to pay his tribute in gold, an estimate shall be made by balancing the accounts for a five-year period, with the reckoning of barrenness and fruitfulness made in

41. Isidore, *Epp.* I. 174.
42. See pp. 188–89 below.
43. *CTh* XI.1.37 + XI.5.4 (*CJ* X.17.2); trans. Pharr.

accordance with the current market prices, and of such sum which is computed by carefully considering the fruits of the five-year period, they shall be compelled to pay a fifth part for each separate year.

The possibility that Cyrus had used his position to secure a special benefit while the Emperor was visiting his city, or traveling nearby, is attractive, but not strictly necessary. As is shown by the evidence of interventions, including episcopal ones, from frontier regions (chapter 2), requests and reports could be brought to the Emperor from a distance, even from considerable distances. Those same examples show also that the role which could be played by bishops was not confined to ecclesiastical matters, but could involve questions of crime and punishment, or military dispositions.

It is however in the person of Theodoret, bishop of Cyrrhus in Euphratesia, that we see most vividly how a bishop's exchanges with secular office-holders could involve his functioning as a representative of his city in matters lying outside the direct concerns of the Church. Although Theodoret personally was a well-known writer and controversial theologian, who was subject to repeated attack for his support for the "two-nature" understanding of Christ associated with the name of Nestorius, his city was a relatively modest one, which was not even the metropolis of Euphratesia (which was Hierapolis). Yet there are some sixty letters from Theodoret addressed to persons exercising power in the secular sphere—the Emperor, the Empresses (Pulcheria and Aelia Eudocia), and various office-holders and ex-office-holders. If there were to be a modern study taking into account all aspects of his very varied role, and his literary and polemical activity, these letters would deserve detailed analysis. As it is, a couple of examples will be offered, merely to illustrate his role in the defense of the interests of Cyrrhus.

This wider role which is visible in his letters was only the expression of a quite consciously assumed general mission, which embraced what he perceived as an unremitting struggle against pagans, Jews, and heretics on the one hand, and involved a responsibility for public works on the other. All this is seen most clearly in his famous letter of spring 448 addressed to Nomus, consul of 445 and one of the inner circle of Theodosius's regime.[44] We shall see at various points later how a number of apparent "outsiders," physically located far from the center of power in Constantinople, concurred in their view of where power lay, in which context the name of Nomus is prominent (chapter 6). In the letter in question, Theodoret complains of the Im-

44. Theodoret, *Epp.* II. 81.

perial order that he should be confined to Cyrrhus, and expostulates on his entitlement, in accordance with Roman tradition, not to suffer a penalty without a charge being heard in open court. He then complains that other cities are closed to him, but are open to the followers of Arius, Eunomius, Mani, Marcion, Valentinus, and Montanus, as well as to pagans and Jews. It had not been at his initiative, he says, that under successive bishops of Antioch he had been summoned there to participate in the affairs of the Church. During twenty-five years as bishop he had acted in the public interest without thought of personal gain:

> I erected public stoas out of the church revenues; I built two very large bridges, and saw to the public baths; finding that the city was not drawing water from the river which flows past it, I constructed the aqueduct, and filled the parched city with waters. Furthermore, to leave these things aside, I guided eight villages (subject to the influence) of Marcion, and those lying near them, gladly to the truth; I led to the light of the knowledge of God another village full of Eunomians and another of Arians . . .

The letter is valuable as indicating the ideological roots of the Imperial letters to which we will come, in which similar catalogues of heretical groups appear. But it also provides an insight into how and why it might be the bishop who felt obliged to intercede with the authorities when the tax burden on the city was felt to be too great. We may take as an example the series of letters which apparently belong to the mid to later 440s, and concern judicial issues as well as the taxation of Cyrrhus.[45] They are addressed to Dionysius, Comes Orientis; to Constantinus, a Praefectus (in fact Praetorian Prefect of Oriens); to Pulcheria, the Augusta, the Emperor's sister; to Senator, a *patricius,* and a major figure in Theodosius's regime; and to another very prominent *patricius,* Anatolius, who had just left office as Magister Militum in Oriens. All the letters, like all such communications to the holders of office or influence, were in Greek. The issues relating to types of land and their tax obligations were complex, and no attempt to spell them out will be made here. What is more significant is the clear indication, for instance in an extract from Theodoret's letter to Constantinus, that a long and detailed dialogue in letters, such as to deserve comparison to similar disputes on theological issues, had been conducted for years about the tax burden of the city:

---

45. Theodoret, *Epp.* XVII (Dionysius); II. 42 (Constantinus; see *PLRE* II, Constantinus 22); II. 43 (Pulcheria); II. 44 (Senator); II. 45 (Anatolius; see *PLRE* II, Anatolius 10).

Let your Wisdom observe the excess of injustice (in this case). For
if no part of the territory were uncultivated and if all of it lent itself
easily to cultivation by the workers, they would still have buckled
under the taxes, unable to bear the pressure of the assessment. There
is the clearest of proofs. For when under Isidorus of magnificent memory [Praetorian Prefect of Oriens in 435/6] 15,000 *zuga* (of land) were
liable for tax-payments in gold, unable to support the penalty (for non-
collection), the tax-collectors from the staff *(taxis)* of the Comes petitioned through memoranda *(anaphorai)* your lofty seat, asking to be
discharged (from the obligation to produce taxes) from two thousand
unproductive *zuga*.

Writing at about the same time to Pulcheria Augusta, Theodoret begins, as
one might expect, by stressing the piety which was the distinguishing mark
of her public role:

Since you adorn the kingship with piety, and illuminate the purple
with faith, we have confidence in this missive, and do not regard our
own insignificance; for you allot the appropriate respect to the sacerdotal office.

Common though this theme may be in the context of Theodosius's reign,
we should note again that not only to address a letter on issues of public policy to a woman, even an Augusta, but also for the text to be preserved and
made public, represents a new and distinctive phase in the structure of power
at the center, and in the image of it in the provinces.[46] After asking for the
Empress's support as regards current accusations, Theodoret turns again to
the question of tax, and the impoverishment of the territory of Cyrrhus:

As regards the territory, I say only this. That while the whole province
is benefiting from alleviations, it (Cyrrhus) has not yet enjoyed any
favour *(philanthrōpia)*, although having the heaviest burden pressing
upon it. Hence many of the estates have been deprived of their tenants,
and many have become altogether abandoned by their owners . . .

Enough has perhaps been said to at least illustrate the complex of ecclesiastical and secular issues which might confront a bishop in this period.
Far more could be said, even if there were to be a study which did no more
than fully explore the life and activity of Theodoret. But it is time to turn
back, first, to the expression of Imperial concern for perceived heresy within
the Church in the first two decades of the reign, and then to the great
conflict in which Theodoret himself was to be closely involved, the Nestorian controversy.

46. See further chapter 6.

4. THEODOSIUS AND HERESY, 408–430

In all respects, but particularly as regards the exchanges between State and Church, our evidence for the last two decades of the reign is incomparably more detailed and revealing than that for the first two. Even for the first thirty years, however, we have, thanks to the *Codex Theodosianus*, completed in 437, relatively full and illuminating evidence for the workings of the State. But it cannot be stressed too often that all the texts collected in the *Codex* are extracts, selected from what originally were much longer documents, and extracts which were designed to bring out the central legal or administrative point in each case. They thus tend to lack much of the original rhetorical self-justification, and often also allusions to the particular circumstances, or to the *suggestiones* from office-holders, which prompted them; and they almost always lack the instructions about dissemination which we find in the much fuller texts of 438 onwards collected as the *Novellae* of Theodosius. That distinction applies in all areas. But the other, and even more important, distinction between the first two decades and the last two is created by the enormous range of material found in the *Acta* of the Councils, where the earliest documents belong to 428 or 429. The law on asylum in churches of early 431 has already provided a precise example.

As a result, therefore, we can find in the *Codex* clear examples of positions taken up by Theodosius with regard to heretical groups on various occasions in the first two decades, but can rarely explore the wider context in any detail.[47] Nor do narratives by contemporaries add much, at least until we come (at the end of this section) to the early stages of the Nestorian controversy. But one anecdote in Socrates' *Ecclesiastical History*, relating to the early years of Theodosius's sole rule, is very revealing. A bishop of Synnada in Phrygia Pacatiana, named Theodosius, actively persecuted "Macedonian" heretics in his see, and went to Constantinople to petition the Praetorian Prefect (who must have been the great Anthemius) for further authority. But on return he found that the bishop of the Macedonian church there, Agapetus, had persuaded his whole flock to embrace the homoousian position, and take possession of the church. On his return, bishop Theodosius found himself excluded, and on appealing to Atticus, bishop of Constantinople, was advised to accept the position.[48]

The passage is a reminder, as is also much other evidence, that although

---

47. For the positions taken up by Theodosius see C. Luibhéid, "Theodosius II and Heresy," *JEH* 16 (1965): 13 ff.
48. Socrates, *HE* VII.3.

it is convenient to speak of "the Church," in fact there could be several different "Churches" ("Novatian," "Eunomian," "Arian," and so forth) in the same city, each of which might have their own bishop. Much of the legislation about "heretics" will unquestionably have arisen, even where the truncated surviving texts do not make this explicit, from local rivalries like those in Synnada. Secondly, Socrates, our best contemporary narrative source for the reign, while deeply committed to the unity of the Church, expresses reservations as to excessively violent or disruptive efforts to bring this about.[49] Nonetheless, anxiety about "heretics," as about pagans and Jews (chapter 2), pervades the Christian literature of the period, and everyone seems in principle to have supported attempts to produce a single, homogeneous Church.

All the known "laws" of Theodosius with regard to named heretical groups take the standard form of (extracts from) letters addressed to the Praetorian Prefect, and in these cases always the Prefect of Oriens. None gives any explicit evidence on the circumstances which gave rise to it; but they are on the other hand conspicuous for the level of reference to Imperial precedents, whether from East or West. Thus, for instance, the letter addressed to Anthemius on February 21, 410, refers back to laws issued by Honorius in 405 and 407, "in the western territories *(in occidentalibus partibus),*" banning Montanists, Priscillianists, and others from Imperial service. But such a ban should not serve as a convenient pretext for exemption from burdensome service on provincial office staffs *(cohortales)* or as town councilors.[50] Ten days later, another letter to Anthemius reaffirms the removal of various civil rights from Eunomians, as laid down by a "law of the sainted father of our Clemency *(lex divi patris clementiae nostrae)*"—in fact a law issued in 395 in Constantinople.[51] A similar reference back, to legislation by Theodosius I and Arcadius, appears in the extract from a letter of June 8, 423, addressed to Asclepiodotus, Praetorian Prefect of Oriens, which also referred to pagans and Jews:[52]

> We command to be enforced the provisions which were established by
> the sainted grandfather and father of Our Clemency *(divi avus et pater*

49. For this position as adopted by Socrates, note esp. T. Urbainczyk, *Socrates of Constantinople: Historian of Church and State* (1997), esp. ch. 8.

50. *CTh* XVI.5.48. The two western laws referred to are *CTh* XVI.6.4–5 (405), and XVI.5.40 (407).

51. *CTh* XVI.5.49, Mar. 1, 410. The law of 395 is *CTh* XVI.5.25, of Mar. 13, issued formally by Arcadius and Honorius.

52. *CTh* XVI.5.60 + 8.27 + 10.23 + 10.24 *(CJ* I.11.6); cf. p. 126 above in chapter 3. Trans. Pharr of XVI.5.60; Linder, no. 49.

nostrae clementiae) concerning all heretics whose name and false doctrine We execrate, namely, the Eunomians, the Arians, the Macedonians, and all of the others whose sects it disgusts Us to insert in Our most pious sanction, all of whom have different names but the same perfidy. All of them shall know that if they persist in the aforesaid madness, they shall be subject to the penalty which has been threatened.

The letter is typical in the emotionality of its tone, as in the clear implication that the identification of alleged heretical groups by name was primarily an exercise by hostile outsiders. In hardly any cases is it possible to be sure that any of these names had actually been adopted as a self-designation by the groups themselves. In the next chapter, indeed, we will encounter Theodosius quite explicitly following the precedent which Constantine had attempted to set in the case of the followers of Arius, and deliberately foisting on the followers of Nestorius an abusive designation borrowed from another context.

The rhetoric of abusive naming, or abusive recitation of derogatory names, reaches its height, however, in the long letter issued to Florentius, Praetorian Prefect of Oriens, on May 30, 428. The preamble is notable for its attribution to heretics of "madness" *(insania)*, which we can find also used of pagans or Jews, and also for reflecting a stage at which the words "orthodox" and "catholic" applied to the same Church. Equally, it reflects awareness that there were physical "churches" in use by heretical groups, as well as heretical clergy:[53]

> The madness of the heretics must be so suppressed that they shall know beyond doubt, before all else, that the churches which they have taken from the orthodox, wherever they are held, shall immediately be surrendered to the Catholic Church, since it cannot be tolerated that those who ought not to have churches of their own should continue to detain those possessed or founded by the orthodox and invaded by such rash lawlessness.
>
> Next, if they should join to themselves other clerics or priests *(sacerdotes)*, as they consider them, a fine of ten pounds of gold for each person shall be paid into Our treasury, both by him who created such a cleric and by him who allowed himself to be so created, or if they should pretend poverty, such fine shall be exacted from the common body of clerics of the aforesaid superstition or even from their offertories.

The rest concerns the differential communal and individual penalties, or civil disabilities, to be imposed on a long list of named groups, of whom some

---

53. *CTh* XVI.5.65 (*CJ* I.5.5 + 6.3); trans. Pharr, emended.

are given alternative names: "Novatiani or Sabbatiani," "Montanistae or Priscillianistae," "Eutychitae or Euthusiastae." As with Jews, particular attention is paid to the possibility of conversion from the orthodox or catholic Church to a heresy, and especially in the case of household slaves. In short, the Emperor provides between the lines a vivid picture of religious diversity, conflict, and rivalry within Christianity, not merely as concerned divergences of belief within a single "Church," but as involving actual organizations, whether or not any of them actually used of themselves one (or two) of the twenty or so different names which are listed.

It was paradoxical, therefore, that at this very moment the Emperor's piety, and desire for forceful leadership of the orthodox or catholic Church, had led him to take the initiative in identifying, bringing to Constantinople, and having elected as bishop a presbyter from Antioch, and former monk, from the small city of Germanicia, Nestorius. His preaching was to provoke contentions which would lead in the end to divisions both between the "Catholic" Church of the West and the "Orthodox" Churches of the East, and between the Greek, and eventually Syriac-speaking, Churches of the East themselves.

Nestorius had already been elected, on April 10, and we have encountered earlier his famous first sermon promulgating the idea that successful eradication of heresy would lead to military victory against Persia.[54] It is at this point in the history of Theodosius's reign that, at least as regards the involvement of the State with the Church, the volume of evidence, because of the *Acta* of the Church Councils as preserved on medieval manuscripts, increases out of all proportion. Between them, the two appendixes to this book attempt to lay out in detail some aspects of this material: a guide to the *Acta* as published; and a catalogue of those sections of the *Acta* which claim to contain verbatim records of spoken and written proceedings.

It is the combination of the *Acta* with the rich material in legal sources which makes this reign, at the level of public persuasive discourse, by far the most fully attested period of antiquity. Beyond that, in terms of records of *spoken* persuasive discourse, no earlier period can begin to compare with it. Full justice to all the documentation cannot be done here. Instead, in the remainder of this section, a few key items from the period of Nestorius's tenure of the see of Constantinople will be presented, up to Theodosius's summons of the Council of Ephesus. The remaining section of this chapter will give a broad account of the controversy from the first Council of Eph-

---

54. P. 39 above.

esus to Theodosius's death, again selecting a few key documents for fuller presentation. In the following chapter, a special place will be reserved for the truly remarkable documentation relating to the fate of both Nestorius and his ally, the Comes and later (briefly) bishop, Irenaeus. Apart from their intrinsic interest, these latter documents happen to represent some of the best evidence for the discourse of government, for the transmission and reception of Imperial commands, and for the functional relations of Latin and Greek within the Imperial system.

Returning to the impact of Nestorius, there were immediate reverberations both in Constantinople itself, and progressively throughout the Greek East, and very soon the Latin West as well, in response to his preaching of a "two-nature" understanding of the nature of Christ, in which the divine element was understood as not having wholly absorbed the human person of whom the Gospels recorded birth, childhood, and earthly experiences. It is not possible to deal here with the vigorous tripartite polemical correspondence between Cyril, bishop of Alexandria, his ally Caelestinus of Rome, and Nestorius himself.[55] But it is very noteworthy that, as a means of securing a hearing for his "one-nature" theology at the court in Constantinople, Cyril not only sent a long *Address (Logos Prosphōnētikos)* to Theodosius himself,[56] but also made the earliest recorded approaches to the notoriously devout women of the Imperial household: another long *Address (Logos Prosphōnētikos)* to "the most pious Empresses" (literally "Queens"), namely the two Augustae, Pulcheria and Eudocia; and a third to "the most pious Mistresses *(despoinai),*" namely the Emperor's younger sisters, Arcadia and Marina.[57] Such a step was certainly a novelty, and the public role of Imperial women, as actualized first in written approaches to them and then—and continuing into the reign of Marcian—of letters sent *by* them, is, as already noted, a very distinctive feature of the period. No replies are recorded at this stage, but this ploy by Cyril, or one very like it, certainly attracted the wrath of the Emperor. For soon after issuing his summons to the Council of Ephesus, sent out on November 19, 430, Theodosius wrote very indignantly to Cyril about what was perhaps a different, and later, approach to Pulcheria and Eudocia. For the Emperor's letter seems clearly to refer, not to a single *Address* to both, but to two different missives, with dif-

55. Note however the excellent recent study by Susan Wessel, *Cyril of Alexandria and the Nestorian Controversy* (2004), which the author was kind enough to show me before publication.

56. *ACO* I.1.1, para. 7 (pp. 42–72).

57. *ACO* I.1.5, para. 149 (pp. 26–61) and 150 (pp. 62–118).

ferent contents, sent to each. For what business, the Emperor asks, had Cyril had to write certain things to himself, and to his wife Eudocia, and other things to his sister Pulcheria? Was he trying to sow dissension?[58]

In the meantime a monk from Lycia, as we saw earlier, is recorded as having gone indignantly to Constantinople to confront the Emperor and complain of Nestorius's actions.[59] Similarly, Nestorius took steps against Arians and Novatians in Constantinople and Cyzicus. Socrates, who is the source for those actions, describes them in very hostile terms, and even reports that in Miletus and Sardis many deaths resulted from the conflicts which arose.[60] We would know no more about the effects of Nestorius's anti-heretical crusade, but for the report, contained in one medieval manuscript of the *Acta*, which records various steps taken by the anti-Nestorian side of the Council of Ephesus, meeting in July 431.[61] This report not only records the arrival of emissaries from Nestorius at Philadelphia in Lydia, and incorporates the text of the "distorted" creed to which some heretics there were caused to subscribe, but also quotes verbatim twenty-one declarations of renunciation of heresy, with (in principle) the written subscription of each penitent added to it. The various individuals had belonged, so they declare, either to the "Tessareskaidekatitai" (who believed that Easter should be celebrated following the Jewish calendar, on the fourteenth of Nisan) or to the "Nauatianoi" or "Katharoi," namely the purist sect of the Novatians. It will be sufficient to quote one of these declarations to catch the way in which the (very briefly) dominant forces in the Church could bring State and Church together in the form of the declarations somehow obtained in Philadelphia. The victims had been caught by pressure from the center at an unfortunate moment. For very soon Nestorius's own doctrines would be declared heretical, his enemies at Ephesus would agree to depose him—and after a few months the Emperor would finally side with them. The first of the attestations reads as follows:[62]

> I, Boudios son of Iounikos, Philadelphian, a *Tessareskaidekatitēs*, having acknowledged the true belief of orthodoxy, and having entreated the most holy bishop Theophanios, have approached the most holy and

58. *ACO* I.1.1, para. 8 (pp. 73–74). The letter carries no date, but seems to refer to the calling of the Council.

59. P. 133 above.

60. Socrates, *HE* VII.29, and also 31.

61. For what follows, see, in much fuller detail, F. Millar, "Repentant Heretics in Fifth-Century Lydia: Identity and Literacy," *Scripta Classica Israelica* 23 (2004): 111 ff.

62. *ACO* I.1.7, para. 76.12 (p. 100).

catholic church, and anathematise every heresy, and especially that
of the *Tessareskaidekatitai*, into which I formerly wandered in error,
and assent to the afore-written exposition of the orthodox faith, anathe-
matising also those who do not celebrate the holy day of Easter as
the holy catholic and apostolic church does, swearing by the holy and
consubstantial Trinity and by the piety and victory of the masters
of the *oikoumenē*, Flavius Theodosius and Flavius Valentinianus, the
eternal Augusti, that, if I ever contravene any of these I am subject to
the rigour of the laws. After the exposition has been read aloud to me,
I have subscribed through Hesychios, Philadelphian, city-councillor,
because I am illiterate.

The paradoxical nature of the changing circumstances under which this and
the other declarations of heresy had first been obtained, and then deployed
in the contentious context of the Council of Ephesus, cannot disguise their
immense significance for the interaction of State and Church. Whether or
not Boudios and his associates had previously used the designation *Tessareskaidekatitai* of themselves, they adopted it now, and did so in a form
which acknowledged jointly the authority of the "catholic" Church, of the
Emperors, and of the law.

As evidence for the conflicts unleashed by Nestorius's anti-heretical zeal,
the report to the Council of Ephesus on events in Philadelphia is surpassed
only by another document found in the *Acta*, the lengthy and powerful
petition addressed to Theodosius (and notionally to Valentinian III) by
Basileios, a deacon and archimandrite, Thalassios, an *anagnōstēs* and monk,
and other monks at some date before the definitive summoning of the
Council in November 430.[63] In a way comparable to the petition of bishop
Appion of Syene, preserved on papyrus,[64] the document describes itself as
a *deēsis* (petition) or *paraklēsis* (appeal), and then launches into an exposition of correct doctrine and a recitation of the names of the orthodox theologians who had preached it, including "Ephraem the Syrian" and Ambrose of Milan. The rest of the extensive text, occupying just over four pages
in the translation by Festugière (so far as is known, the only one in any
modern language), is devoted to a powerful exposition of both the theological errors of Nestorius and of the violence of which he had been guilty.
Popular protests had arisen, with the crowd in Constantinople shouting,
"We have an Emperor *(basileus)*, we do not have a bishop!" Then an episode
of private protest by an individual monk is recounted (possibly the same

63. *ACO* I.1.5, para. 143 (pp. 7–10). For a complete translation into French see
Festugière, pp. 523–27.
64. Pp. 22–23 and 63–64 above.

as the other Basileios, who had come from Lycia on his own initiative, as mentioned earlier):[65]

> One of the simpler of the monks felt compelled by his zeal to bar the herald of disorder (Nestorius) in the middle of the church from entering while the service was proceeding, on the grounds that he was a heretic. Having beaten him, he (Nestorius) handed him over to the most magnificent Prefects, and when he had been beaten and paraded publicly, with a herald crying before him, had him sent into exile.

The petition goes on to describe its authors' dialogue with Nestorius in the *episkopeion*, and the beating, imprisonment, and starvation which they too suffered. Church and State had collaborated again:

> Moreover, his madness was not content with that, but afterwards by some deception we were handed over to the Prefect of this renowned city, were led off in chains to the prison, and were then brought to the *praitōrion*, with our chains. And since no accuser appeared, we were escorted again to the *diakonikon*.

As their exposition continues, the petitioners make a formal appeal for the summoning of an oecumenical Council, and also resort to arguments from breaches of canon law by Nestorius:

> He has associated with himself not just, so to speak, his own clerics and officials, but also some from other sees, who are strictly forbidden according to the canons of the Church to move to another episcopal seat or another church, but are bound to (stay in) their own sees or cities, where they were elected, and to conduct themselves in peace, in order that, with the passage of time, as an effect of temporary dominance, disorder may not surreptitiously spread, and dishonour your Piety.

Their concluding appeal returns to the theme of order, and ends with another echo of Appion's petition, one which we will hear again below—that future prayer for the welfare of Empire and Emperor is conditional on a positive response:

> We have hereby appealed to you for an Oecumenical Council which will be able to establish and set right those things which have been shaken or even shattered. The gates of Hell, which are the mouths of the heretics, will be unable, through the grace and assistance of God

---

65. P. 133 above. D. Caner, in *Wandering, Begging Monks* (2003), 216, takes these two monks with the name "Basileios" to be the same person, which is certainly possible. But the one who is the main author of the petition seems to be settled in Constantinople, not a visitor.

in you, to damage it (the Council), so that having obtained this, we may be able, in a way which is pleasing (to God) and in accordance with right belief, to send up the accustomed prayers in harmony on behalf of the common safety and of your kingship.

In fact, all parties, including Nestorius himself, asked the Emperor to summon an Oecumenical Council, and, as we have already seen, he duly did so, sending out letters from Constantinople on November 19, 430.[66] State and Church were about to enter a phase in their mutual relations which would be of unprecedented complexity, would show the Emperor demonstrating an extraordinary level of reliance on persuasion rather than force or legal penalties, and which, over two decades, was to make this a more fully documented episode in the history of government than any other from the Graeco-Roman period up to this date.

5. THE NESTORIAN CONTROVERSY AND THE TWO COUNCILS OF EPHESUS, 431–450

A book far longer than this could easily be devoted to the interactions of State and Church in the last two decades of Theodosius's reign, and even to the evidence illustrating the two central themes of this book: the "rhetoric of empire" in the form both of persuasion directed to the holders of power, and of orders, proclamations, and expressions of self-justification issued by them; and the interaction between Greek, as the (almost) universal language of both people and Church, and Latin, as the inherited official language of government—but used only in its internal communications.

The procedure adopted will instead be to begin with the barest of summaries of the narrative, which will do no justice to the profundity of the theological issues at stake, or to the depth of commitment felt by individuals to different views of the nature of Christ.[67] To provide an observer's narrative is in no way to subscribe to the notion that what was at issue was simply a power struggle between Constantinople, Antioch, and Alexandria

---

66. *ACO* I.1.1, para. 25 (pp. 114–16).

67. A full bibliography of the Nestorian controversy would be an impossible task. But among works which have proved particularly helpful, note B. J. Kidd, *A History of the Church to AD 461 III: AD 408–461* (1922)—the best-documented step-by-step narrative known to me; see also W. H. C. Frend, *The Rise of the Monophysite Movement* (1972); P. Maraval, *Le Christianisme de Constantin à la conquête arabe* (1997), ch. 3; J.-M. Mayeur, C. and L. Pietri, A. Vauchez, and M. Venard, eds., *Histoire du Christianisme*, vol. 2, *Naissance d'une Chrétienté*, ed. C. and L. Pietri (1995), ch. 6; vol. 3, *Les églises d'Orient et d'Occident*, ed. L. Pietri (1998), ch. 1.

(or Rome). Power politics, including lavish use of bribery, did indeed play a significant part. But this was still in essence a deep division over belief, and was so on the part of the Emperor as well as of bishops, many hundreds of whom are found expressing their views, or of archimandrites or ordinary monks.

Against the background of a bare summary of events, this chapter will conclude by selecting a few examples of material from different stages which casts a particularly vivid light on the interaction of State and Church. The following chapter will be devoted to the exceptionally revealing documentation which relates to the personal fate of Nestorius and his ally, the Comes and later (briefly) bishop, Irenaeus. The final chapter will use material from this phase as well as from others, to ask what sort of political system the Theodosian empire was, and how decisions were made within it.

The controversy took its origin from widespread outrage, shared by both Cyril, the bishop of Alexandria, and Caelestinus of Rome, at Nestorius's proclamation of the doctrine that a distinction must be made between the divine and the human in the person of Christ: between the Son who shares the essence of the Father, and the human figure whose story is told in the Gospels, who was born, grew up, suffered human emotions, and was crucified. In consequence, it was legitimate to call Mary "Christotokos" ("Mother of Christ"), but not "Theotokos" ("Mother of God"). The opposite view, which commanded wider support in the Greek Church, and was supported, after initial hesitation, by Theodosius until his death by accident in July 450, was that the concept of salvation depended on the unambiguous divinity of Christ. Within this side, labeled in the modern world, but not by contemporaries, "monophysite" (or sometimes "miaphysite"), there developed complex gradations of opinion, the most extreme of which, associated with the name of the archimandrite Eutyches, was to be declared orthodox at Ephesus II in 449, but heretical at Chalcedon two years later.[68] The following treatment, sketching the succession of events, will where necessary use "one-nature" of the group led until his death in 444 by Cyril of Alexandria, and "two-nature" of that which followed Nestorius. Sebastian Brock has convincingly demonstrated that "Nestorian" is an improper label for the later Church of the East.[69] But that correct observation should not

68. All modern scholars, and in particular literal-minded historians, will be grateful for the brilliant schematic exposition of different shades of belief set out by Sebastian Brock in "The 'Nestorian Church': A Lamentable Misnomer," in *The Church of the East: Life and Thought*, ed. J. F. Coakley and K. Parry, Bull. John Rylands Library 78.3 (1996): 23 ff., on p. 27.

69. Brock, "The 'Nestorian Church'" (n. 68).

obscure the fact that in the fifth and sixth centuries "Nestorian" was used, exactly in the same way as with other designations of allegedly heretical groups, as a derogatory term deployed by others.[70]

To come to an outline of the sequence of events, the first Council of Ephesus, due to open on June 7, was marked by division, controversy, and mutual complaints of violence from beginning to end. The supporters of the "one-nature" theology, led by Cyril, waited some time for the main group of supporters of Nestorius, the "Anatolikoi," or bishops from Oriens, led by Ioannes of Antioch, to arrive. But then, against the vigorous public protests of the emissary sent by Theodosius to keep order (but not participate), Candidianus, the Comes Sacrorum Domesticorum, they met on June 22, examined Nestorius's doctrines, declared them heretical, and voted his deposition. When Ioannes and his associates arrived a few days later, they met separately, and duly voted the deposition both of Cyril and of Memnon, the bishop of Ephesus itself.

In July the delegates sent by Caelestinus of Rome arrived, and joined the Cyrillian side, and from then on until the autumn both groups remained in Ephesus without ever meeting, and conducted an immensely detailed correspondence of complaint, mutual accusation, and self-justification with the Emperor in Constantinople. For his part, Theodosius responded repeatedly and in detail: for instance, sending a letter brought by the Magistrianus, Palladius, to denounce the mutual proceedings; then sending an official, the Comes Sacrarum Largitionum, Ioannes, with a letter accepting all three depositions, after which Ioannes took all three bishops into custody. Then, it seems in September, both sides were allowed to send delegates to Chalcedon to make their case before the Emperor in person. As we will see later,[71] vivid narratives describe his personal reactions during the relevant dialogues. Eventually, but only at this stage, Theodosius, finally swinging to the Cyrillian side, allowed their delegates, but not those of the other side, to come to

70. "Nestorian" is therefore an attested item of contemporary late-Roman vocabulary, and is no more illegitimate in the context of the fifth- or sixth-century Empire than any of the innumerable terms for other "heretical" groups, most frequently (though not always) derived from the names of their alleged leaders or originators. For examples of the use of the term "Nestorian" taken from the fifth-century *Acta* see *ACO* I.1.4, para. 138 (p. 66)—Theodosius's law of 448, see p. 185 below in chapter 5; *ACO* II.1.4, para. 176 (p. 93)—Basil of Seleucia speaking at Chalcedon and quoting a slogan used at Ephesus II: ὁ λέγων δύο φύσεις Νεστοριανός ἐστιν. Cf. *ACO* II.1.3, para. 12 (p. 9 [368]); II.1.3, para. 73, clause 12 (p. 25 [384]). The term is regularly used in Liberatus, *Breviarium Causae Nestorianorum et Eutychianorum, ACO* II.5 (pp. 98–141).

71. See pp. 205–6 and 232 in chapter 6.

Constantinople, cancelled his previous confirmation of the deposition of Cyril and Memnon (but not of Nestorius), dismissed the Council, and had Nestorius sent back to his monastery in Syria—but did not commit himself to the view that his doctrines were heretical. In October 431 a new bishop of Constantinople, Maximianus, was elected.

Over the next four years Theodosius, while in essence backing the "one-nature" position, made repeated efforts to persuade the recalcitrant bishops, primarily those in Oriens led by Ioannes of Antioch, to find a basis for theological reconciliation with Cyril. A central role was played by another layman and Imperial official, Aristolaus, with the rank of Tribunus and Notarius, who by the winter of 432/3 had achieved a formula of reconciliation, as between Ioannes and Cyril, involving some compromise on Cyril's side.

But Ioannes' assent, under strong pressure from the Emperor, was itself taken as an act of treachery by a number of other bishops in Oriens. Through the documents preserved (if indirectly) in what remains of a priceless and neglected contemporary history, the *Tragoedia* of Irenaeus,[72] we can follow the bitter exchanges which culminated in (it seems) 435 with a second mission by Aristolaus, and the dispatch into exile of those who still resisted. Some key documents from this episode of regional ecclesiastical history will be highlighted below.

In this same year came the first systematic denunciation by Theodosius of Nestorius's doctrines as being heretical, and in the following year, 436, the order for both Nestorius and his loyal ally, the Comes Irenaeus, to go into exile. Thereafter, for some years, it seemed that victory for the "one-nature" position had been secured, even if in 436, prompted by the new bishop of Constantinople, Proclus, Theodosius wrote a warning letter to Ioannes of Antioch and a local synod, telling them to keep the peace; while perhaps in the same year Cyril wrote to the Emperor to advise him of the dangers posed by followers of the two, now deceased, theologians, Theodore of Mopsuestia and Diodorus of Tarsus, whose thought lay behind Nestorian doctrines.[73]

It was not, it seems, until the later 440s that overt conflict, involving the Emperor and the apparatus of the State, flared up again, and did so from two opposed directions. On the one hand we find Domnus, the new bishop of Antioch, writing to Theodosius in perhaps 447, openly defending the doctrines of Theodore and Diodorus, and attacking the extreme "one-nature"

---

72. For Irenaeus and his *Tragoedia* see more fully chapter 5 below.
73. *ACO* I.4, paras. 288 (pp. 210–11) and 310 (p. 241), both in the Latin translation offered by Rusticus's version of the *Tragoedia* of Irenaeus.

position now represented by Eutyches, archimandrite of a monastery in Constantinople.[74] In 448, on the other hand, came the promulgation of a strongly expressed law against the doctrines of Nestorius, himself still in exile. As we will see in chapter 5, every effort was made to disseminate this document, and vigorous opposition to its terms was expressed, at least in Antioch. At the same time the correspondence of Theodoret, who had retained his see in spite of his support at Ephesus for Nestorius, shows that an Imperial order had arrived commanding him not to leave Cyrrhus (and hence not to cause trouble in the Church at large). Simultaneously, accusations of heresy were being made against other bishops in Oriens, including Domnus of Antioch.

Thus, in the autumn of 448, we find the establishment of two separate ecclesiastical courts, one in Constantinople to examine charges of (extreme "one-nature") heresy against Eutyches, and one in Phoenicia, instructed by the Emperor to hear accusations of ("two-nature") heresy against Ibas of Edessa, Daniel of Carrhae, and John of Theodosiopolis. These complex procedures, dragging out over months, provide truly remarkable documentation on the working of relations between State and Church, particularly after Eutyches petitioned Theodosius about the alleged falsification of the records of the proceedings against him, and demanded an enquiry, which was duly held by secular officials.

Once again, however, in the context of mutual accusations, Theodosius emphatically supported the proponents of the "one-nature" position, and called the Second Council of Ephesus, to meet there in August 449, and to be presided over by Dioscorus, since 444 bishop of Alexandria. In the meantime he had also made clear his hostility to the current bishop of Constantinople, Flavianus, who had presided at the synod in autumn 448 which had declared Eutyches' doctrines heretical. In the event the Council was an unambiguous victory for the "one-nature" position, with Eutyches declared orthodox, and Flavianus, Ibas, and Theodoret (who had been forbidden to attend) deposed. Against a torrent of denunciation and protest, led by Leo the Great, the bishop of Rome, and supported by Valentinian and the Imperial family in Rome, Theodosius maintained to his death the proposition that the decisions of the Council were valid. That, it will be recalled, was the context of the unique letter from one "Augusta" to another, Galla Placidia to Pulcheria, written about the end of February 450.[75] When Theodosius's unexpected death occurred in July 450, everything would change.

74. Facundus, *Pro defensione trium capitulorum* VIII.5.1–5 (*CCL* XCA, 244–45).
75. Pp. 37–38 above, in chapter 1.

That, in the broadest of outlines, was the course of the Nestorian controversy, which in terms of Imperial intervention took place in two phases, from 430 to 436 and from 448 to 451. It shows an intense concern on the part of the Emperor with the (unattainable) goal of both correct doctrine and ecclesiastical unity, combined with a considerable degree of tact in encouraging the resolution of disputes by the Church itself. In the end, the Emperor's word was accepted as decisive. Only he could call an Oecumenical Council—but both of those which he called were presided over by bishops. Both Councils voted episcopal depositions, and the Imperial confirmation, though essential, followed on the Council's decision. Legal penalties, namely the enforcement of deposition by troops, or the exile of recalcitrant bishops, could in the end be imposed by the secular power, but only after complex processes of debate and decision within the Church. Even after such processes, as the cases of both Irenaeus and Nestorius will show (chapter 5), moral defiance might continue to be shown by even the most prominent alleged heretics. The same was true of Theodoret, as we see in the letter which he wrote to the *patricius* Anatolius, after the Second Council had deposed him.[76] At the Council, he says, he had been condemned unheard, in a way which would not be applied to common robbers, murderers, tomb breakers, or adulterers, who are condemned only after evidence has been given in their presence, and weighed by their judges. For justice he looks to the West, in effect to Leo of Rome (who himself was in fact currently denouncing the Council and demanding a new one in Italy):

> But so that none of those who do not know me will believe that the slanders uttered against me are true, or might be scandalised by thinking that I believe things contrary to the Gospel teaching, I beseech your Magnificence to beg thy favour of our victorious Head (Theodosius), that I should (be allowed to) journey to the most God-loving and holy bishops there.

We shall look later at the conceptions held, by Theodoret and others, of where and with whom influence with the Emperor lay (Theodoret would not in fact be restored until the reign of Marcian). But the sense of there being rights, and of there being a just cause based on doctrine or belief, which could be asserted even in the face of State power, pervades all of the dense literature, or rhetoric, of the relations of Church and State.

Theodosius, for his part, could and did give orders as to procedure, and could and did finally resort to rhetorical expostulation of a type which few

76. Theodoret, *Epp.* III. 119.

bishops could have surpassed, when it finally became necessary to impose criminal penalties. To illustrate the nature and the indirect and hesitant character of secular intervention in ecclesiastical affairs we will pick out just two phases: the later stages of the repression of resistance to the formula of reconciliation with Cyril, as conducted by regional officials in Syria, Euphratesia, and Cilicia; and the examination in spring 449 of the validity of the proceedings of the synod which had condemned Eutyches in the autumn of 448.

As already indicated, our knowledge of the aftermath in Oriens of the first Council of Ephesus comes almost entirely, but indirectly, from the *Tragoedia* written by Irenaeus. Indirectly, because we know it only in the version made in the sixth century in Latin, by the deacon Rusticus. Even though we have to deal with Latin translations of letters written originally in Greek, and indeed on occasion Latin retranslations of Irenaeus's Greek versions of letters between officials, originally written in Latin, few concentrations of material can equal this as evidence for the politics of Church and State.

The imperial will was, as always, influenced by local persuasion. In 434, as it seems, the Emperor had given orders, carried out by Dionysius, the Magister Utriusque Militiae, for the deposition of Meletius of Mospsuestia, and Ioannes of Antioch had then seen to the election of a new bishop. But Meletius had obstinately declined to leave the area. So Ioannes of Antioch addressed a petition to Theodosius (and notionally Valentinian), which the Latin translation calls a *postulatio et deprecatio* (in the original Greek certainly *deēsis* and *hikesia*). The bishop expounds the situation, and concludes in familiar style:[77]

> But the aforesaid Meletius, wishing to be superior to Your laws and the Roman peace, lurks in some part of that territory, inflicting disturbances and confusion on the holy churches of God, and usurping the episcopal office after deposition. We beg you that it is just that one who is alienated from the sacred discipline and the Church, should be alienated also from the whole province of the Cilicians, your pious *sanctio* being issued to the most magnificent and most glorious Magister Militiae of Your Oriens, so that he may be escorted from there, and conducted to wherever it pleases Your Piety. When this has been granted, we will send the accustomed prayer for the persistence and glory of the Empire.

The Emperor duly did as Ioannes requested, and Dionysius wrote to the governor of Cilicia to report the instructions received, and to tell him to

77. *ACO* I.4, para. 265 (p. 196).

arrange for Meletius to be exiled to Melitene in Armenia.[78] A similar process took place about the same time as regards Alexander, bishop of Hierapolis in Euphratesia, and the consequential public reaction was reported in a letter from the governor, this time addressed to the Comes Orientis.[79] According to Irenaeus, he also took care to record the (hostile) *acclamationes* directed by the crowd against himself, against the Comes Orientis, and against Ioannes of Antioch. His letter is a plea for allowance to be made for public opinion, and begins as follows:

> Hierapolis, in obedience to its loyalty and prompted by pious attachment, has yielded to the divine (Imperial) initiative and to the magnificent order, with groans. But now it asks for mercy for the longing which it pours out for him, for the aged Alexander, raising wails of grief in the streets, soaking the ground in tears . . . what is more I have examined petitions under oath made by all those who are thought respectable and who offer prayers on behalf of their father, and beg that they may be tended by him who brought them up from boyhood as the most gentle of teachers . . .

All this, however, was in vain. A couple of pages later Irenaeus lists the fate of all the recalcitrant bishops:[80] Alexander exiled to a mine or quarry in Egypt; Abbibus of Doliche replaced; Dorotheus of Marcianopolis, the metropolitan of Moesia, exiled to Cappadocia; Meletius of Mopsuestia, died in exile in Armenia—and so for a dozen others. The full details of this (predominantly) local history remain to be explored.

The story of the hearings conducted by a synod in Constantinople on accusations of heresy against Eutyches is known in even greater detail, since the relevant records were incorporated in the proceedings of Ephesus II, and again in those of Chalcedon, and were also the subject of a major article by Eduard Schwartz.[81] As regards these proceedings, the only direct intervention on the part of Theodosius took the form of a brief instruction, described as an *apokrisis*, addressed to the seventh session of the synod, held on November 22, 448, and read to it by an Imperial *silentiarius*, Magnus: in it the Emperor expressed (as ever) his commitment to orthodox Christian doctrine, and declared his wish that the *patricius* Florentius, a former Praefectus and consul, should participate in the synod.[82] Since this was a Church

---

78. *ACO* I.4, para. 268 (p. 198). Translated in Coleman-Norton, no. 417.

79. *ACO* I.4, para. 274 (p. 201).

80. *ACO* I.4, para. 279 (pp. 203–204).

81. See E. Schwartz, "Der Prozess des Eutyches," *SBAW*, Phil.-Hist. Abt., Heft 5 (1929).

82. *ACO* II.1.1, para. 468 (p. 138). Translated in Coleman-Norton, no. 448.

synod, it can be assumed that the Imperial message, recorded in Greek in the proceedings of Chalcedon, had in fact been sent in Greek.

Equally, when Eutyches subsequently decided to address a petition to the Emperor to complain that the record of these proceedings had been falsified, he too will of course have written in Greek. The date of the petition is uncertain, but must at any rate be before the beginning of April 449. It may be sufficient to quote the beginning and end of the text, which opens with the standard formal address to both Emperors, and concludes with the now familiar conditional anticipation of future prayers:[83]

> To our most pious and faithful, Christ-loving Emperors, Theodosius and Valentinianus, the eternal Augusti, from Eutyches, archimandrite. After God, it is Your piety which, of all things, has been the demonstration to me of salvation and truth, in that in no matter has it neglected issues concerned with faith, and makes enquiry into the accusations against me . . . [he then demands a hearing to examine the validity of the record] . . . And if I obtain this, offering the accustomed hymns, I will render constant thanks to Christ, the Lord and God of all things, and to Your piety.

The text of this petition was subsequently read out at the synod held on April 13, 449, presided over by Flavianus himself, and this was then followed by the reading of the brief note of assent, described as a *hyposēmeiōsis (adnotatio* or *subscriptio?)* issued by the Emperor:[84]

> Let it be placed before the most reverend bishops who recently assembled, and especially before the most reverend bishop Thalassios, so that before them, in the presence of all those of whom the petition speaks, the truth of the matter may be determined.

As a response to a petition in Greek, and giving approval to proceedings before a synod, this brief note too will surely have been issued in Greek. The long and heated discussion held on April 13 by the synod, whose verbatim record survives (appendix B, no. 25), left Eutyches still dissatisfied. So he presented a further petition to Theodosius, and nominally Valentinian, asking that evidence be taken from Magnus, an Imperial *silentiarius,* who had accompanied him at the seventh session of the synod of the previous autumn; and the Emperor again issued a brief *hyposēmeiōsis* of assent.[85]

However, the hearing on April 27, 449, at which both of these documents were read out, was of a quite different nature from those of the previous

83. *ACO* II.1.1, para. 572 (pp. 152–53).
84. *ACO* II.1.1, para. 575 (p. 153).
85. *ACO* II.1.1, paras. 834–36 (pp. 177–78).

few months, for with it we have crossed the border from ecclesiastical proceedings to governmental ones. Recorded in Greek among the proceedings of Chalcedon (and previously at Ephesus II), the text may look much the same as that of the others, with its formal record of those present, followed by the spoken interventions in succession. But we are in the context of high officialdom, not the Church, and the first thing that may strike the reader is the wholesale importation of transliterated Latin titles into a Greek text. The record expresses so vividly the linguistic symbiosis that encapsulated the nature of the Greek Roman Empire that in this case alone the opening section of the Greek text will be presented:[86]

Ὑπατείας Φλαυίου Πρωτογένους τοῦ λαμπροτάτου καὶ τοῦ δηλωθησομένου
[ὑπάτου] πρὸ πέντε Καλανδῶν Μαΐων, ἐν Κωνσταντινουπόλει, θείᾳ κε-
λεύσει διαγινώσκοντος Μαρτιαλίου τοῦ μεγαλοπρεστάτου κόμητος καὶ
μαγίστρου τῶν θείων ὀφφικίων, παρόντος Καρτερίου τοῦ περιβλέπτου
κόμητος καὶ προξίμου τοῦ θείου σκρινίου τῶν λιβέλλων καὶ τῶν θείων
κογνιτιόνων, εἰσελθόντων Μακεδονίου τοῦ περιβλέπτου τριβούνου νοταρίου
καὶ ῥεφερενδαρίου καὶ Μάγνου τοῦ καθωσιωμένου σιλεντιαρίου μετὰ
Κωνσταντίνου τοῦ εὐλαβεστάτου μοναχοῦ καὶ διακόνου,

Κωνσταντίνος ὁ εὐλαβέστατος εἶπεν· Δεήσεις ἐπιδέδωκεν Εὐτυχὴς
ὁ εὐλαβέστατος ἀρχιμανδρίτης τῷ εὐσεβεστάτῳ ἡμῶν δεσπότῃ φανερὰ
περιεχούσας καὶ ταύταις ἡ εὐσέβεια αὐτῶν ὑπεσημήνατο, ὑπεδέξατο δὲ
αὐτὰς ὁ περίβλεπτος τριβοῦνος καὶ ῥεφερενδάριος. ἀξιῶ ὥστε ταῦτα αὐτὰ
καταθέσθαι αὐτὸν καὶ τὰς δεήσεις ἀναγνῶναι καὶ τὰ δόξαντα τῇ εὐσεβείᾳ
αὐτῶν δῆλα γενέσθαι.

Φλαύιος Ἀρεοβίνδας Μαρτιάλιος ὁ μεγαλοπρεπέστατος κόμες καὶ
μάγιστρος τῶν θείων ὀφφικίων εἶπεν· Ἅτινα ὥρισεν ἡ φιλανθρωπία ἡ
βασιλική, διὰ τοῦ περιβλέπτου τριβούνου καὶ νοταρίου ταῖς ἡμετέραις
διανοίαις γνωρισθῶσιν.

There is no perfect way in which the latinized Greek record, full of transliterated official Latin, can be represented in translation. So it will be best to reproduce the transliterated terms in their Latin form, while attempting to preserve the extreme formality of the text, expressing perhaps more clearly than any other record the ponderous official procedures of the Theodosian court. The entire exchange, which in fact involves two further oral interventions, serves only to record formal agreement that the second petition of Eutyches may be read out.

In the consulship of Flavius Protogenes and of whoever will be declared, on the fifth day before the Kalends of May, in Constantinople,

86. *ACO* II.1.1, paras. 829–49 (pp. 177–79). The passage presented and translated is paras. 829–31 (p. 177).

when by divine (Imperial) command Flavius Martialius, the most magnificent Comes and Magister of the Sacra Officia, was holding an enquiry, there being present Carterius the distinguished Comes and Proximus of the Sacred Scrinium of the Libelli and the Sacred Cognitiones, (and) there entering Macedonius, the distinguished Tribunus, Notarius and Referendarius, and Magnus, the devoted Silentiarius, along with Constantinus, the most devout monk and deacon,

The most devout Constantinus said: Eutyches, the most devout archimandrite, has presented to our most pious master [Theodosius] a petition containing evidence, and this their [both Emperors'] piety has subscribed, and the distinguished Tribunus and Referendarius has received it. I request that he should place these same documents on the record, and should read out the petition, and that the decision of their piety be manifest.

Flavius Areobindas Martialius, the most magnificent Comes and Magister of the Sacra Officia, said: Whatever the royal (Imperial) benevolence determined, let it be made known to our minds by the distinguished Tribunus and Notarius.

Because these are in form legal proceedings before a lay official of the Imperial court, it is very likely that, unlike ecclesiastical proceedings, at least the third-person protocol had been recorded originally in Latin. That is the model which is provided by what seem to be the only two reports of proceedings on papyrus which survive from Theodosius's reign (appendix B, nos. 10–11). The initial paragraph is therefore a translation, deploying a high level of transliteration. But what of the spoken exchanges themselves? The same two papyri just referred to record that all the parties in court, including officials, spoke Greek, as was normal in either written or spoken contact with the public, whether lay people or clerics. Even though, in this case, the monk Constantinus was the only nonofficial present, it is probable, if not certain, that Greek was spoken. In this as in other respects the "Roman" government of Theodosius paid very close attention to the violently conflicting sensibilities and demands issuing from the Greek Church, and did its best to control them, and to keep disputes within bounds, but never achieved more than partial success. The same combination of elaborate rhetoric with the relatively tentative application of quite restricted official measures and legal penalties would be true, as we shall see in the next chapter, even of those whom it characterized as the most determined enemies of unity and true doctrine. For all the power of the Imperial rhetoric which was to be directed against Nestorius and his ally Irenaeus, both not only survived the measures taken against them, but were able to leave written records of their defiance.

V State Power and Moral Defiance

Nestorius and Irenaeus

1. INTRODUCTION: SOURCES AND PERSPECTIVES

From the mass of contemporary and later evidence for the interaction of State and Church in the last two decades of Theodosius's reign, it would be possible to isolate any number of revealing personal and local histories, showing the side effects of the Nestorian controversy, and the ways in which they affected different communities. But for a number of different reasons, two of the central figures in the conflicts of the time, Nestorius himself and his ally, the Comes Irenaeus, can claim a special place. Firstly, the penalties successfully inflicted on them illustrate both the intense concern of the Emperor with the doctrinal health and (hoped-for) unity of the Church, but also the tentative and—in comparison with other periods when secular power was wielded to secure doctrinal conformity—remarkably mild nature of the penalties imposed. In the entire course of the successive phases of the controversy it cannot be shown that any individual was killed as a direct consequence of Imperial orders. Secondly, that relative mildness in practice is obscured by the ferocity of rhetorical expression which marks some of the Imperial pronouncements inveighing against Nestorius, condemning his doctrines, and ordering the burning of copies of his works. Thirdly, however, it happens that the Imperial "laws" relating to Nestorius and Irenaeus have a special place in any study of how a "Roman" Empire, operating officially in Latin, functioned when it either needed to transmit instructions for action down through successive levels of the governmental hierarchy, or—as it did in this case—felt a particularly pressing need to see that its will, and the justification for it, was made known as clearly and widely as possible among its Greek-speaking subjects. Along with several documents already noted—the petition from bishop Appion of Syene, and the traces of

Theodosius's official letter in response, with his autograph subscription in Latin; the bilingual inscribed letters from Mylasa in Caria; and the measures of 431 concerning asylum in churches[1]—the Imperial "laws" or letters concerning Nestorius and Irenaeus, addressed to major Prefects, and the edicts which they in their turn then promulgated to the public, represent our best evidence for the coexistence, and mutual functions, of Latin and Greek in the Theodosian Empire.

That is not all, however. One of the most striking features of our evidence for the period is precisely the overlap, as already seen in the case of the law on asylum, between versions of the same law as transmitted through wholly distinct manuscript traditions: in the *Acta* of the Oecumenical Councils on the one hand, and the *Codex Theodosianus* and *Codex Justinianus,* on the other. It is indeed precisely this conjunction which allows us to see the relevant laws, unlike almost any others in the *Codices,* as disseminated step-by-step to their intended audiences in the provinces.

There are, however, further dimensions to the evidence available in these two cases for the diffusion and effects of the Imperial word. One is that from time to time we encounter powerful reactions, and expressions of their viewpoint, from each of the two main characters. More important still is the fact, which it would be difficult to glean from any modern account of the writing of history in late antiquity, that both wrote important and highly original accounts of contemporary events. The place that both of these works should occupy in our conception of Greek historiography, and of ecclesiastical history in Greek in particular, is obscured first by the fact that, though both were originally written in Greek, neither is preserved in Greek.[2]

It is also surely significant that of the two works concerned, that by Nestorius was certainly written in exile, since he remained in exile till his death, and Irenaeus's may have been. It was certainly written after his exile in 436, but there seems to be no clear indication of where it belongs in his adventurous (and in Theodosius's eyes scandalous) career after that. What is more, both of them, even Nestorius, isolated in the Great Oasis, were able to gain access to the texts of official letters and to the *Acta* of the Church Councils.

Nestorius's highly personal work is preserved only in a Syriac translation, apparently made in the sixth century, and known through a single me-

---

1. See pp. 20–23 and 142–45 above.
2. Note that in the generally excellent and illuminating volume edited by G. Marasco, *Greek and Roman Historiography in Late Antiquity, Fourth to Sixth Centuries* (2003), there is no systematic treatment of either work (indeed not even an allusion to Irenaeus's *Tragoedia*).

dieval manuscript. It is entitled *The Bazaar* (in Syriac TGWRT'), or *Book, of Heraclides* (why "Heraclides" was obscure even to the translator).[3] As a highly polemical exposition of his doctrines, and denunciation of those of his opponents, it is not as such a continuous narrative account.[4] But many sections of it are in fact extended narratives relating to particular episodes, both ones which had involved himself, and others which had not. In that sense it is a contemporary history, and one of the very few which derive from central actors in major episodes in the history of antiquity.[5]

Irenaeus, as we have already noted several times in passing, composed a history in Greek of the aftermath of the First Council of Ephesus up to 435 or 436. In effect, it too was a passionate polemic, directed to the betrayal of the "two-nature" position represented by the agreement to conform made by Ioannes of Antioch in 432/3, who then turned to active assistance in the repression, and ultimate deposition and exile, of the bishops who held to that doctrine. In the tradition of ecclesiastical history as established by Eusebius, the work was marked by regular quotation of documents. In the two hundred or so pages of Schwartz's *Acta* that it takes up in its present form, over two hundred contemporary documents are quoted—predominantly letters, but also reports of proceedings and texts of sermons.[6]

All this, as noted earlier, is known to us only as represented in the Latin version made in the sixth century by the deacon Rusticus, who both argues with the linking narrative and commentary which Irenaeus had supplied, and abbreviates it drastically. So it is not possible to be sure what proportion of the original was represented by the texts of the documents quoted. Furthermore, it is clear that Irenaeus had written in Greek, and had therefore translated into Greek any letters between officials (of which we saw some exam-

---

3. The Syriac text is provided by P. Bedjan, *Le Livre d'Héraclide de Damas* (1910). My discussion depends on the two major modern translations, F. Nau, *Nestorius, Le Livre d'Héraclide de Damas* (1910), and G. R. Driver and L. Hodgson, *Nestorius, the Bazaar of Heracleides* (1925). Page-references will be given to both, in the form "Nau" and "D/H." For the translator's puzzlement as to the identity of Heraclides see Praef. 4 (Nau, p. 3; D/H, pp. 4–5).

4. So far as I can find, there have been remarkably few major modern analyses either of this work of Nestorius or of his thought as such. Note however L. Abramowski, *Untersuchungen zum Liber Heraclides des Nestorius* (1963), and L. I. Scipioni, *Nestorio e il Concilio di Efeso: storia, dogma, critica* (1974).

5. For a very helpful tabulation, in chronological order, of the episodes of which accounts are given by Nestorius, and the relevant page-references to their translation, see D/H, pp. xvii–xxix.

6. The work, as translated, edited and (as regards the commentary linking the documents quoted) drastically abbreviated by Rusticus, occupies *ACO* I.4, paras. 49–294 (pp. 25–225).

ples earlier)[7] which had been written in Latin. Conversely, Rusticus reproduces everything in Latin translation, including (for example) a very important letter of Irenaeus himself written from Chalcedon to the followers of Nestorius at Ephesus during the Council; in this case the original Greek is preserved in the *Acta*.[8] It thus came about, as we will see, that Irenaeus quoted in Greek translation official instructions relating to the exile of himself, which Rusticus then preserves for us in a Latin retranslation.[9]

The entire story which Irenaeus told in his *Tragoedia* was an act of moral defiance, and of the assertion of the validity and consistency of his own position, as opposed to the treachery, conformism, and capacity for corrupt political manipulation of others, just as was Nestorius's even more overtly polemical reinterpretation of events. Just as there was explicit argument and self-justification on all sides, expressed in the innumerable letters exchanged, and in the verbal exchanges at sessions of the Councils and before the Emperor in person, so polemic was to be integral to the subsequent narratives of events. Indeed the two categories overlap, for many of the letters of contemporaries embody in themselves polemical retellings of events:[10] one example, to which we will come in the next chapter, is Theodoret's letter to Alexander of Hierapolis, in which he records his dialogue with Theodosius at Chalcedon, when sent there as a delegate from Nestorius's supporters at Ephesus in the early autumn of 431.[11]

2. EPISCOPAL PERSUASION AND THE IMPERIAL WILL

Theodoret had been with the "Orientals" *(Anatolikoi)* throughout the Council. So also had Irenaeus, a high-ranking Imperial official with the ti-

---

7. See, e.g., *ACO* I.4, para. 274, quoted on p. 164 in chapter 4.

8. See p. 173 below.

9. Pp. 179–80 below.

10. For a very selective list of examples of contemporary letters which themselves embody polemical narratives of events, either in the very immediate past or covering several years, see *ACO* I.1.3, para. 81 (pp. 3–5); *ACO* I.1.5, para. 146 (pp. 13–15); *ACO* I.1.5, para. 153 (pp. 124–25); para. 159 (p. 131)—all written during the First Council of Ephesus. Selected later examples: *ACO* I.1.7, para. 120 (pp. 157–58); *ACO* I.4, para. 271 (pp. 199–200). Given this multiplicity of conflicting contemporary sources, the idea that we can arrive at a justifiable modern narrative of events by following a single sixth-century source is untenable: see for an example J. A. McGuckin, "Nestorius and the Political Factions of Fifth-Century Byzantium: Factors in his Personal Downfall," in *The Church of the East*, ed. J. F. Coakley and K. Parry, *Bull. John Ryl. Lib.* 78 (1996): 7 ff.

11. *ACO* I.1.7, para. 69 (p. 79) = Theodoret, *Epp.* IV. 3a. See p. 206 in chapter 6.

tle Comes, of whose previous career nothing is known.[12] Theodosius had explicitly allowed him to accompany Nestorius to the Council as an act of friendship *(philia)*, but not to participate in the sessions themselves.[13] Each side in the event complained bitterly of violence instigated by the other, and Irenaeus, not surprisingly, is singled out in denunciations by the Cyrillian side.[14] More significant still, when Nestorius's supporters at Ephesus felt it necessary to back up their stream of letters of complaint to Theodosius in Constantinople with some personal representation of their position, it was Irenaeus who was commissioned to carry their letters, or memoranda (called in Greek *anaphorai*, like the *suggestiones* of officials), to the Emperor.[15] Thus the second of a pair of *anaphorai* apparently sent in early July is headed "Anaphora of the same (bishops) to the most pious Emperor which they gave with the afore-mentioned *anaphora* to the most magnificent Comes, Irenaeus." At the end of their communication they make his role explicit:

> For this reason we have been forced to commission the most magnificent Comes Irenaeus to approach Your piety, and expound the facts of the case. For he knows precisely what has happened, and has learned from us many means of healing by which it is possible to restore peace to the sacred churches of God. We beg Your beneficence to learn these means patiently from him, and to give effect quickly to the decision of Your piety, so that we may not be worn out here to no purpose.

After Irenaeus's departure, a further *anaphora* was sent to him, and it too is recorded as having been given by him to the Emperor: "which was sent to the Comes Irenaeus and was handed over by him."[16] At around the same time they wrote both to the "Empresses," Pulcheria and Eudocia, to an unnamed Praefectus and a Magister, and to the Praepositus of the Imperial bedchamber, (and to?) Scholasticius.[17] These letters are prime evidence for a

---

12. See *PLRE* II, Irenaeus 2. The fullest (relatively) modern account of Irenaeus appears to be that in *DTC* VII (1921), cols. 2533–36.

13. *ACO* I.1.1, para. 31 (pp. 120–21), Theodosius and (notionally) Valentinian to the Council of Ephesus.

14. *ACO* I.1.3, para. 84 (pp. 10–13), in section 5; *ACO* I.1.3, para. 101 (pp. 46–47), a letter from Memnon of Ephesus to the clergy of Constantinople.

15. *ACO* I.1.5, paras. 158–59 (pp. 129–31).

16. *ACO* I.1.5, para. 163 (pp. 133–35).

17. *ACO* I.1.5, paras. 160–62 (pp. 131–33). Para. 162 is headed "To the Praepositus and Scholasticius similarly," which implies two separate letters. Scholasticius is attested as a prominent Cubicularius at this time (*PLRE* II, Scholasticius 1), so it is uncertain whether the heading identifies two addressees or one.

theme which will be explored in the following chapter (6), namely the perception on the part of interested individuals and groups that power and influence were diffused, and that if success were to be achieved at the center of power, a variety of channels needed to be explored.

Step-by-step, however, as we have seen, it became clear that success would not be achieved by the followers of Nestorius. The process by which the Emperor finally came to accept the Cyrillian position took several months, and might have turned out otherwise. But it is very significant that at quite an early stage Irenaeus wrote back from Constantinople to the group of bishops supporting Nestorius at Ephesus to say that in spite of all his efforts the prospects of success were not good.[18] His letter must rank as one of the major documents of the period, and gives evidence of the testing political experience and the capacity for political narrative of which we can still detect traces in Rusticus's abbreviated Latin version of the *Tragoedia*.

The letter, which is undated, will have been written in summer 431, of course in Greek, as addressed to a group of bishops (but this will in any case have been Irenaeus's first language). It is the only piece of writing by him which survives in the original. His task had been difficult from the beginning, for the "Egyptians" (the emissaries of Cyril) had arrived in Constantinople three days before him, and had propagated the view that Nestorius's deposition had been in order. They had also persuaded the Cubicularius, Scholasticius, that Nestorius had not assented to the validity of the expression "Mother of God" *(Theotokos)*. Irenaeus, however, had presented his case to high officials ("the most magnificent *archontes*"), and had secured a hearing at which both he and the "Egyptians" would speak before the Emperor and his officials. All went well at first, and the earlier pronouncements and those of Candidianus at Ephesus were laid before the Imperial enquiry *(diagnōsis)*. But then another emissary from Cyril had arrived, and the climate changed, with some saying that all three depositions (those of Nestorius, and of Cyril and Memnon) should be confirmed, others that they should all be annulled, and that bishops should be summoned to Constantinople to clarify things, while others were campaigning to be sent to Ephesus with Imperial authorization, to settle the matter there. The friends of Nestorius's supporters were doing everything to prevent this, knowing what outcome was intended.

18. *ACO* I.1.5, para. 164 (pp. 135–36); Rusticus's Latin version is *ACO* I.4, para. 109 (pp. 60–61).

3. NESTORIUS: RETURN TO MONASTIC LIFE, CONDEMNATION AND EXILE, 431–436

As the only surviving letter of Irenaeus, this detailed report on the movement of opinion in the entourage of Theodosius would deserve fuller attention. For the moment, however, we hear no more of him; and Nestorius himself, for all the undoubted impetuosity of his character, seems to have fallen into a mood of resignation, and to have expressed a willingness to leave his see and retire to his monastery even before this was forced upon him. We know this, first, from the long letter to the Cubicularius, Scholasticius, which Irenaeus later quoted in his *Tragoedia*, and which Rusticus reproduces in Latin translation.[19] Even here, however, Nestorius vigorously criticizes Cyril, and defends his own theological position. He also seems to have written to the Praetorian Prefect, presumably of Oriens, expressing the same wish to return to the monastery from which he had been elevated to the see of Constantinople. At any rate a Syriac version of what may well be an authentic letter of Nestorius, addressed to a Praefectus (HYP′RK′—"Hyparchos") is quoted in the sixth-century *History of the Holy Fathers* by Barhadbešabba;[20] and when the current Praetorian Prefect of Oriens, Antiochus Chuzon, wrote to him, with great politeness, to say that arrangements for his return to Syria were being put into effect, he referred back to a letter, apparently addressed to himself, expressing this wish on Nestorius's part. The *Acta* preserve the original Greek of the Prefect's letter, but Irenaeus quoted it as well, so we possess also Rusticus's version in Latin.[21] As always, when an Imperial official addresses a bishop, he writes in Greek.

Nestorius assented readily to this instruction, and his letter is preserved in the same two forms. But, even in this context of obedience to the Imperial will, he introduces a strongly polemical note, in demanding official acknowledgement of the heretical nature of Cyril's position, and also deploys, or attempts to deploy, the stratagem of persuasion of highly-placed intermediaries which is so characteristic of the Theodosian empire. His letter runs as follows:[22]

> We have received the letter from your Magnificence, from which we
> have learned that our residence in the monastery has been commanded
> by the most pious and all-praiseworthy Emperor, and have greeted the

19. *ACO* I.4, para. 103 (pp. 51–53) = Loofs, no. IX (pp. 190–94).
20. Barhadbešabba, *History of the Holy Fathers*, 25 (*PO* IX, p. 553).
21. Greek original: *ACO* I.7, para. 55 (p. 71); Rusticus's version: *ACO* I.4, para. 113 (p. 64).
22. *ACO* I.1.7, para. 56 (p. 71); *ACO* I.4, para. 113 (p. 64); Loofs, no. X (pp. 195–96).

gift of this ordinance; for to us nothing is preferable to solitude for the sake of piety. But this I do beg of your Magnificence, that you should continually make representations to the Most Pious Emperor on the subject of religion, to the effect that, since the empty pretensions of Cyril have been condemned by His piety, He should through an Imperial letter publicise that condemnation to the churches of the orthodox everywhere, lest the fact that it might be said that Cyril's doctrines had been condemned by Him without a letter from the pious Emperor might provide a source of scandal to the more simple-minded, as being reported without a basis in truth. It would be appropriate to your spirit to contribute whatever you can to the advocacy of the truth. I need say no more to you, who are of good reputation in all matters entrusted to you.

It is not quite certain where this exchange belongs in the sequence of events in the autumn, by which the Emperor reversed his previous decision to confirm all three depositions, and allowed Nestorius's two main opponents, Cyril and Memnon, to resume their roles as bishops. Cyril, indeed, had already left Ephesus without permission, and had returned to Alexandria by the end of October. What is certain is that Theodosius now saw to the election of a successor to Nestorius, and that Maximianus assumed office in Constantinople on October 25.

That, for the moment, was all that the Imperial decision to take sides against Nestorius amounted to, so far as Nestorius himself was concerned. Theodosius, at this early stage, even affirmed that Nestorius's followers were not guilty of heresy,[23] and for his part, as we have seen in brief (chapter 4), made every effort to enforce reconciliation and compromise, with a considerable degree of success. But, as already noted, the vivid "local history," which Irenaeus's *Tragoedia* would be devoted to recounting and documenting, was one of continued resistance by a hard core of episcopal supporters of Nestorius primarily in the provinces of Euphratesia and Cilicia, culminating finally in the list of depositions and exilings which seems to belong to 435 or 436.[24] The historical study of these complex interchanges between State and Church, no more than hinted at here and in chapter 4, remains to be undertaken, as does the study of Irenaeus as a polemical historian of contemporary conflicts.

Though we have no direct evidence to connect the two, it must be very likely that it was this residual failure to achieve reconciliation and conformity which induced Theodosius to abandon his recent tone of (somewhat untypical) moderation, and return to the style of virulent expostulation and

---

23. *ACO* I.1.7, para. 97 (p. 142).
24. *ACO* I.4, para. 279 (pp. 203–204); see p. 164 above in chapter 4.

denunciation in declaring in 435 the wholesale condemnation of Nestorius's doctrines and works.

The "law" which Theodosius now issued, on August 3, 435, is known to us from three different sources: a Latin version, found in the *Codex Theodosianus*, which is in the form of a letter addressed to Leontius, Prefect of Constantinople; an (apparently) complete text in Greek, with no addressee or date or place of issue, and headed simply "Copy of an Imperial Law," known from the Greek *Acta*; and a brief note in Rusticus's version of the *Tragoedia*, summarizing the content of the law.[25] If, as it seems, Irenaeus had intended to tell his story in chronological sequence, there is a puzzle here, since it is placed after the law on the exile of Irenaeus himself and Photius, which might be supposed to have accompanied that of Nestorius, which apparently belongs in the next year, 436.[26]

The text of the law of 435, combining the fuller Greek and shorter Latin versions, deserves quotation in full, as one of the most vivid expressions of Imperial anti-heretical fervor; as an exemplification of the incomplete and abbreviated character of the texts in the *Codex*; and as containing an unusually explicit reference to the functional relations of Latin and Greek. It runs as follows:

COPY OF AN IMPERIAL LAW

The reverence which owed by us to the most pious religion urges that those who behave impiously toward the divinity should be punished with appropriate penalties and be addressed with names suitable to their baseness, so that, assailed with reproaches, they should endure an eternal punishment for their sins, and should not escape punishment while alive or dishonour after death. [[(*CTh* begins). The same (Emperors) to Leontius P(raefectus) U(rbi)]. Since Nestorius, the leader of a monstrous teaching, has been condemned, it remains to apply to those who share his opinions and participate in his impiety a condemnatory name, so that they may not, by abusing the appellation of Christians, be adorned by the name of those from whose doctrines they have impiously separated themselves. Therefore we decree that those everywhere who share in the unlawful doctrines of Nestorius are to be called 'Simonians.' For it is appropriate that those who, in turning away from the divine, imitate his impiety should inherit the same appellation as he, just as the Arians, by a law of the deceased Constantine, are called, because of the similarity of their impiety, 'Porphyrians' after Porphyry,

---

25. *CTh* XVI.5.66 (*CJ* I.5.6); *ACO* I.1.3, para. 111 (p. 68); *ACO* I.4, para. 280 (p. 204). Coleman-Norton, no. 422.

26. *ACO* I.4, paras. 277–78 (p. 203); see p. 179 below.

who, having attempted to battle against the true religion by the power of reason, left behind books, but not records of (true) learning.

(We also decree) that no one should dare to possess or read or copy the impious books of the said lawless and blasphemous Nestorius concerning the pure religion of the orthodox, and against the doctrines of the sacred synod of the bishops at Ephesus. These (books) it is required to seek out with every eagerness and burn publicly (for in this way, when every sort of impiety has been rooted out, the simple and easily-deceived populace will never find any seed of error); nor is it permitted to make any mention of these men who have thus been eradicated in the discourse of religion by any name other than that of Simon, or to provide, covertly or openly, a house or a field or villa or any other location for them to congregate. We lay down that such men are deprived of all right of assembly, it being clear to all that anyone who contravenes this law and imitates Nestorius will be punished by the confiscation of his goods (*CTh* ends).

Therefore your Greatest and Eminent Authority will see to it that this our constitution should come to the notice of all those dwelling in the provinces in the customary manner by means of edicts. We have issued this law in the language both of the Romans and the Greeks, so that it may be clear and understood by all.

(*CTh* only) Given on the third day before the Nones of August at Constantinople, in the consulship of our Lord Theodosius for the 15th time, and of whoever will be announced.

Unlike some other cases (see below), this Greek text is not specifically described as a translation of a Latin document, so it would be reasonable to conclude that the Greek version was issued from Constantinople in parallel with the Latin one. But it lacks, as already noted, both an indication of date and place (which will certainly have been present in the original) and any identification of who the official addressed in the last paragraph is. The answer to this question is however provided immediately by the long document in Greek which follows it in the *Acta*, and is headed "Flavius Anthemius Isidorus, Flavius Bassus, and Flavius Simplicius Reginus, the Praefecti, say." This is the normal verbal form for an *edictum* addressed to the public. The authors are three of the four Praetorian Prefects currently in office, in East and West, in 435: Flavius Anthemius Isidorus, very fully attested as in office in Oriens in 435–36; Flavius Simplicius Reginus in Illyricum; and (presumably as a purely nominal "author") Flavius Anicius Auchenius Bassus, evidently Praetorian Prefect in Italy.[27] The *Codex* naturally contains no parallel to this text, because it is entirely made up of the

27. *ACO* I.1.3, para. 112 (pp. 69–70). See *PLRE* II, Isidorus 9; Reginus 4; Bassus 8.

original Imperial "laws," issued in the form of letters to high officials. But the purpose that there should be consequential diffusion of the law to the public is quite explicit in the reference to the simultaneous issue of Latin and Greek versions which is preserved in the concluding paragraph of the longer, Greek, text, which will be the one issued by the Praetorian Prefects. It is likely, but not certain, that the same clause was found in the full original version of the letter sent simultaneously to the Prefect of the City.

In the text of their *edictum* (described in Greek as a *programma*) the Prefects, if anything, surpass the Emperor in richness of rhetorical expression, and their text can hardly have contributed much to its intended object, public awareness. In any case, as they make clear in their final paragraph, in any public display the Imperial law was to come first:

> So that you may recognise the severity and piety of what has been ordained, (and) the foresight which in all things they accord to their subjects, given that our most pious Emperors are alone able to give back to their Almighty, through their faith, a just return for the benefits conferred on them and on the whole inhabited world, we have ordered that, in accordance with custom the law filled with the divine (Imperial) light should shine forth before this our edict *(programma)*. By obeying this, you will render yourselves free of punishment, and for the future, having learned to act piously for the whole future course of the age, you will enjoy eternal benefactions, receiving such benefits as the Emperor by his legislation, and God, as the object of piety, by their nature grant.

However, thanks to the record made in Irenaeus's *Tragoedia*, we can trace the diffusion of this law in more specific terms in one province, Cilicia Prima. For Irenaeus quoted the letter which was now addressed to Theodosius and Valentinian by Helladius of Tarsus, the metropolitan, and four other bishops, declaring their assent, naming Xystus of Rome, Proclus, now bishop of Constantinople, and Ioannes of Antioch, and describing themselves as "co-anathematizing, along with Nestorius himself, also those who assert the same impious doctrines as he, that is the 'Simoniani,' as your order justly named them." It is perhaps a pity that Rusticus preserved no more of Irenaeus's commentary at this point than to describe him as "multiloque impetens" (delivering an extensive verbal attack?) The episcopal letter itself, however, records that in the case of Cilicia Prima, the Imperial letter *(sacra)* had been brought by Aristolaus, Tribunus et Notarius (the same emissary who had been involved at intervals since 432).[28]

These measures, in spite of their impassioned tone, in fact imposed no

---

28. *ACO* I.4, para. 281 (pp. 204–205).

specific penalty on Nestorius himself, who presumably continued to live peaceably in his monastery near Antioch. Measures against him were however not likely to be long delayed, and duly followed in (as it seems) the next year, 436; and it was now, as it also seems, that for understandable reasons, parallel measures were taken against Irenaeus (of whom we know nothing as regards the years since 431). Irenaeus was thus able subsequently to incorporate in his *Tragoedia* a version in Greek of the Imperial *sanctio* giving orders for the exile of himself, along with an order from the Praetorian Prefect of Oriens, and addressed to lower officials, about arrangements for his transport. Between the two closely parallel cases, therefore, we can follow quite closely the working of the Imperial will.

The Imperial *sanctio* ordering the exile of Nestorius himself appears in the *Acta* in Greek translation with the following heading: "Copy of the translation of the Imperial *sanctio (basilikon thespisma)* addressed to Isidorus, Praetorian Prefect and Consul, on the exile of Nestorius."[29] No place or date is given, but the consulship of Isidorus fell in 436, so the year seems secure (unless the consular title has been added later?). In Nestorius's case, as in that of Irenaeus, the original order was for confiscation of his goods, and for exile to Petra, now within Palaestina Tertia (Salutaris). As regards Nestorius at least, all the evidence shows that he actually passed the fifteen or so years of his exile in Egypt, in the Great Oasis. How or why the change came about is not attested.

At about the same time, or so we must presume (unless in fact it had been in the previous year),[30] Theodosius issued to "the Prefects," as Irenaeus has it, the order for the exile to Petra of Irenaeus himself and of Photius, a priest and ally of Nestorius. This letter, addressed in fact personally to Isidorus, was of course originally written in Latin, translated (as is explicitly stated) by Irenaeus, and is preserved as retranslated into Latin by Rusticus. It runs as follows:[31]

> The translation, so he [Irenaeus] says, of the *sacra* which was issued to the Most Magnificent and Most Glorious Praefecti concerning the exile to Petra of the Most Magnificent Comes Irenaeus.

---

29. *ACO* I.1.3, para. 110 (p. 67).

30. As indicated above (p. 176), the order in which Irenaeus places his documents in this section is: exile of Irenaeus and Photius (paras. 277–78); exile of a long list of bishops (279); law against Nestorius and name "Simoniani" (280)—which *CTh* dates to 435. On this hypothesis, entirely uncertain, the reference in para. 277 to the condemnation of Nestorius would be to the law of 435. Irenaeus does not report the exile of Nestorius.

31. *ACO* I.4, para. 277 (p. 203).

Since the leader of the most abominable form of worship, Nestorius, has been condemned, it is just that the participants in his impious worship should experience the severest penalty. For this reason, we have decreed that Irenaeus, who not only followed the accursed sect of Nestorius, but promoted it, and took steps along with him to subvert many provinces, to the extent that he himself was at the head of this heresy, having been stripped of all his ranks and also of his own property itself, along with Photius, implicated in the same impieties, also deprived of his property, which should go for the benefit of the public purse, should endure exile in Petra, so that they may be tormented by lifelong poverty and the solitude of the region, Isidorus, most honoured father.

Your glorious and magnificent Authority will therefore carry out appropriately this pragmatic decree of ours, having allocated sufficient resources, so that the aforesaid violators of our religion may be transported along the aforesaid route to exile.

The personal address to Isidorus, in the vocative, which concludes the main paragraph will serve to remind us that virtually all of the "laws" or specific orders issued by the Emperor took the form of letters directed to named high officials. In this case, there was no occasion for instructions to be given for the posting of edicts. Instead, Irenaeus's *Tragoedia* enables us to follow the chain of command one step further, in the form, once again, of a letter from Isidorus to an unnamed middle-ranking official whose post is not indicated (possibly the Comes Orientis), but who is addressed, in Rusticus's retranslation, as "your Magnificence." In the process of translation and retranslation the details have become obscure; but at any rate it is clear that detailed practical instructions are being issued for the escorting of Irenaeus and Photius through an area which at least included Syria.[32]

What subsequently happened to Irenaeus is not clear, except that, as we will see, within some years he had left his exile, apparently without explicit Imperial permission, and had embarked on a new (if fairly brief) career as a bishop. The *Tragoedia* seems not to have recounted any sequence of events beyond this point. What follows the instructions on the escorting of the author is first the long list of other bishops exiled (para. 279); then material on the condemnation of Nestorian doctrines (280), which, as noted earlier, seems to belong in the previous year, 435, followed by the letter of acquiescence from Cilicia (281); then a set of further ecclesiastical letters (282–92); and finally the two famous documents from Epiphanius, the *archdiaconus* and *syncellus* of Cyril of Alexandria, about the distribution of bribes to a

32. *ACO* I.4, para. 278 (p. 203).

wide range of persons at the Imperial court (293–94). Since the primary communication is addressed to Maximianus, elected to the see of Constantinople in October 431, and also refers to the *tribunus* Aristolaus, it seems clear that these at least date earlier, to around 432. So if, as it seems, Rusticus preserved the sequence of documents as they appeared in the *Tragoedia*, it is likely that it ended deliberately with these damning revelations of how the victory of the "one-nature" position had been achieved, which had been placed in this emphatic position by Irenaeus as a conclusive demonstration of just that. There will be more to say about the content of these documents in the next chapter. As for Irenaeus, as noted earlier, we cannot tell whether the *Tragoedia* was composed during his exile, or at some later stage in his varied life.

Nor do we know whether it was in fact in Petra that Irenaeus passed his period of exile. But as for Nestorius himself there is no doubt that in the event he spent the rest of his life in exile, not in Petra as originally ordered, but in the border regions of Egypt, and died there early in Marcian's reign, just as an Imperial emissary arrived with permission for his release.

There are two remarkable products of this fifteen-year exile. One is the extracts from the two letters mentioned earlier,[33] in which Nestorius gives a vivid account of the barbarian raids which briefly led to his liberation, and then to his being marched hither and thither around the Thebaid, following a series of contradictory orders. It is equally significant to note the vigorous terms in which, in the first of two letters, he addresses the Dux and Comes of the Thebaid:[34]

> Wherefore indeed we request your Greatness to consider our captivity
> in accordance with what is approved by the laws, and not to consign to
> the evil designs of men a captive who has been delivered into wickedness, lest for all subsequent generations there should be the tragic story
> that it is better to be a captive of barbarians than a suppliant of the
> Roman kingship.

In the second letter, equally, he maintained a polemical and argumentative tone, and referred obliquely to reports or petitions which had been sent both by the Comes and by himself, and had been formally addressed, as ever, to both Emperors:

> But be satisfied with what has been done, I beseech (you); and by
> the decreeing of so many banishments against a single body; and

33. See p. 65 in chapter 2.
34. Quotations contained in Evagrius, *HE* I.7, trans. M. Whitby, with slight emendation; Loofs, no. XIII (pp. 195–99).

in moderation desist, I beseech (you), from the investigation into
what was reported by your magnificence and by us, through whom it
was right that it be made known to our gloriously victorious emperors.
These exhortations from us are as from a father to a son. But should
you be vexed even now as before, do what you have decided, if indeed
no word is more powerful than your decision.

We know of these extracts only because they are reproduced in the *Ecclesiastical History* of Evagrius, who quotes them from a work by Nestorius which seems to have been entitled either *Apologia* or (once again) *Tragoedia*. Whatever its real title or character, it must, as is obvious, have been
written in exile. But the second, and truly remarkable, product of Nestorius's exile was the work of polemic, or autobiography or contemporary history, or contemporary exposition of true and false doctrine, written of course
in Greek, but preserved only in Syriac, the *Book*, or *Bazaar, of Heraclides*.
This unique work is significant in many ways, but not least for containing
stretches of very detailed narrative of events, not merely those at the First
Council of Ephesus and its aftermath, but those at the Second in 449. What
is more, Nestorius in exile was able to incorporate in passages of narrative
relating to this Council substantial verbatim quotations from the *Acta*,[35]
which had therefore reached him not long after the event, since he died only
two or three years later. In the work as preserved, however, though he refers
briefly to the banning of his works in 435,[36] he does not give any account
either of how he was exiled or of his experiences while there. This powerful work, which gives ample evidence of the contentiousness of his disposition, remains as testimony to his undimmed conviction of the rightness
of his theological views. Precisely because it does not fall into any recog-
nizable literary genre, it would deserve more attention from students of
Greek literature than it has so far received.

4. RENEWED CONTROVERSY, IMPERIAL CONDEMNATION AND POPULAR REACTION, 448–449

As we have seen, the later 440s saw the outbreak of renewed theological
disputes and accusations, from two diametrically opposed directions: accusations of holding extreme "one-nature" doctrines, directed against the
archimandrite Eutyches; and simultaneously accusations brought against

---

35. On his verbatim quotations from the *Acta* of Ephesus II see p. 190 below.
36. *Book of Heraclides* II. 1 (Nau, p. 327; D/H, p. 374).

Domnus, the bishop of Antioch since 441, and other bishops in Oriens, including Theodoret and Ibas, bishop of Edessa, of still supporting the "two-nature" doctrines associated with Nestorius, and before him with Theodore of Mopsuestia and Diodorus of Tarsus.

Moves against those thought still to be followers of Nestorius seem to have begun first. It seems at any rate to have been some time in the spring of 448 that Theodoret (who had retained the see of Cyrrhus when others were exiled), began, to his great indignation, to hear indirect reports of an Imperial order banning him from leaving Cyrrhus. It is perhaps at this point that we get the most vivid impression of the options which were open to a bishop who was admittedly well known as a theologian, but still spoke only from a minor city in a remote province. It is true that all the channels of influence which Theodoret sought to use proved ineffective, and the Imperial order stood. Nonetheless, it is striking that he could write directly to three of the major figures in the Theodosian regime. First, it seems, he wrote to the famous *patricius,* Anatolius, saying that he had been shown a *hypomnēstikon* (memorandum?), claimed to be in the Emperor's own hand, ordering his confinement to Cyrrhus, and asking him (Anatolius) to check its authenticity, and the reasons behind it.[37] Then, writing to Eutrechius, just appointed to a Prefecture in Constantinople, he quotes the text of the alleged autograph memorandum from the Emperor (why it is expressed without naming him is not clear):[38]

> Since x, the bishop of this city, is continually calling synods, and thus disturbs the orthodox, see to it with the appropriate care and consideration that he remains in Cyrrhus, and does not depart to any other city.

This document will of course have been in Latin, but is quoted by Theodoret in Greek. He continues by protesting against the breach of natural justice involved in his being subject to such an order without the opportunity to respond to his accusers. In the meantime, as it seems, Theodoret had received a letter from Anatolius about the accusations against himself, and replied to him about these, and those against Domnus of Antioch and Ibas of Edessa.[39] Finally, at this stage, he wrote to the most influential personality of all, Nomus, the consul of 445, complaining of his confinement, and defending at length his record as bishop.[40] Testimony put forward in the next year at the Second Council of Ephesus accused him of actively conspiring

---

37. Theodoret, *Epp.* II. 79.
38. Theodoret, *Epp.* II. 80.
39. Theodoret, *Epp.* III. 111.
40. Theodoret, *Epp.* III. 81.

with Domnus at Antioch, and it was presumably for this reason that the Emperor decided to restrict his activities.

In the meantime, however, a further cause for Imperial indignation had arisen. Irenaeus, now apparently either freed, or having simply escaped, from exile, had been elected as metropolitan bishop of Tyre, under the supervision of Domnus as bishop, or patriarch, of Antioch. The date is unclear, but must belong between 441 and 446, for we know from a letter of Theodoret to Domnus that at the time Proclus of Constantinople had expressed approval of the election.[41] Neither this letter nor any other evidence speaks of how it had come about that Irenaeus had been ordained as a priest, perhaps simultaneously with his election as bishop. The objections to him, about which some clergy in Constantinople had written to Domnus, were, first, that he had heretical views, and allegedly rejected the term "Theotokos;" and secondly that he had been twice married. Theodoret's letter does not refer to any Imperial action against Irenaeus, and on the contrary mentions letters from "the most magnificent *spatharius*" (who must surely be the influential Chrysaphius himself) and an ex-Magister, saying that the issue of bishop Irenaeus could be resolved. It was surely, therefore, written before any Imperial order was issued, and also serves to illustrate again the close and complex political ties which bound provincial society, and especially bishops, to the holders—or supposed holders—of influence at the center.

In this case, as in others, the confidence felt in a prospective peaceful resolution turned out to be misplaced. For reasons about which it would be futile to speculate in detail, Theodosius decided early in 448 that action was required against both Nestorius and Irenaeus. Once again, as in 435, he chose to drag in the name of Porphyry, following the precedent of the Emperor Constantine a century earlier. His letter, transmitted through two different channels, one considerably fuller than the other, but neither complete, again offers precious evidence on the generation and dissemination of Imperial "laws." Firstly, the *Codex Justinianus* preserves most of the main clause of the law, concerned with Porphyry and the followers of Nestorius, indicating the addressee, Hormisdas, the Praetorian Prefect, apparently of Illyricum, and at the end the date, February 17, 448. But it omits, as we will see, not only the first and last parts of this clause, but also all of the second clause, which refers to Irenaeus. Finally, it is almost unique among all the documents of the reign of Theodosius preserved in the legal *Codices*, in being

41. Theodoret, *Epp.* II. 110.

quoted in Greek, without any explanation.[42] There is no obvious explanation either of why a Latin version, if indeed there was one, was not included in the *Novellae* of Theodosius. But in fact there are many other such cases of laws of 438–50 not preserved among the *Novellae*, showing that the *Novellae*, though individually much fuller and more informative than the texts in the *Codices*, still represent only a selection of the laws of these years.[43]

The law of February 448, as preserved in the *Codex*, can in fact only be understood in the context of the fuller text, and the accompanying Prefectural edict, which are both provided by the *Acta*, which also supply a heading which we must take to be the work of the editors, and is certainly not part of the law itself. There are two puzzles here, however. The first is that this text is included, along with other documents, and immediately following the law on asylum in church of 431, among the material attached to, but not actually part of, the proceedings of the First Council of Ephesus.[44] So, as is obvious, it can only have been incorporated in this dossier at some later date. Secondly, the heading, but not the text of the law itself, uses the pejorative designation *Nestorianoi* of the followers of Nestorius. Moderns have raised objections to the use of the term "Nestorian," eventually as a label for one of the Orthodox Churches, the Church of the East; and like other such terms it was not used as a self-description, either in the middle of the fifth century or later. But, as such, the heading may well have been a contemporary addition; for, as we saw earlier, the *Acta* of Chalcedon show beyond doubt that, as a term used by their enemies, the label *Nestorianos* was already in use.[45] It is clear in any case, as will appear below, that the text in the *Acta*, and the Prefectural edict which accompanies it, both of them in Greek, had been acquired in Egypt, the main base of the supporters of "one-nature" theology.

It is time to present a translation of the composite text, following the version in the *Acta* wherever there are minor variations:

---

42. *CJ* I.1.3. The only other example of a law of Theodosius quoted in its Greek form in *CJ* is that of 431 on asylum in church, *CJ* I.12.3; see p. 142 above in chapter 4.

43. See, e.g., *CJ* I.2.9 + XI.18.1, Mar. 23, 439; I.52.1, May 30, 439; II.15.2, June 17, 439; II.7.7, Sept. 7, 439; VIII.11.20, Nov. 1, 439; IX.27.6, Nov. 26, 439; XII.50.21, 439/41; VIII.11.21, Jan. 22, 440; I.14.7, Apr. 5, 440; III.4.1 + VII.62.32 + VII.63.2, May 20, 440; II.7.8, Dec. 30, 440.

44. *ACO* I.1.4, para. 138 (p. 66). Also translated in Coleman-Norton, no. 445.

45. See p. 159 above.

[From *Acta* only] Copy of a divine ordinance of the most pious
Emperor Theodosius against Porphyry and the Nestorians and against
Irenaeus the bishop of Tyre.

[From *Cod. Just.* only] The Emperors Theodosius and Valentinianus
Augusti to Hormisdas, Praefectus Praetorio.

[From *Acta* only] We think it appropriate to our kingship to remind
our subjects about piety. For we think that thus it is the more possible
to gain the goodwill of our Lord and Saviour Jesus Christ when it is
the case both that we are zealous so far as is in our power to please him,
and we stimulate those subject to us to this end. [*Cod. Just.* begins]. We
therefore ordain that all those things that Porphyry, spurred on by his
madness, wrote against the Christian religion, in whomsoever's possession they are found, shall be given to the flames. For we wish that all
writings which rouse God to wrath, and wrong men's souls, shall not
even come to the hearing of men. We further ordain that those supporting the
impious beliefs of Nestorius, or following his unlawful teaching, if they
are bishops or clergy, shall be expelled from their churches; if they are
laymen, they are to be anathematised according to the legal provisions
already made by our Divinity, with any of the orthodox who follow our
pious prescriptions having the right, without fear or damage, to expose
and interrogate them. But since it has come to our pious ears that certain men have written and published teachings which are dubious and
not precisely in accord with the orthodox faith set out by the holy
synod of holy fathers who assembled at Nicaea and at Ephesus and by
Cyril, of pious memory, the former bishop of the great city of Alexandria, we order that any such writings, coming into existence either
formerly or even now, should be burned and committed to complete
annihilation, so as not even to come to (public?) reading, with any who
can bear to own or read such compositions in books being liable to the
extreme penalty. (We also order) that in future it is not permitted to
anyone to say or teach anything against the faith set out, as we have
said, at Nicaea and Ephesus [*Cod. Just.* ends], it being clearly established that those who contravene this our divine ordinance are subject
to the appropriate penalty under the law issued concerning the impious
beliefs of Nestorius.

In order that all may learn by experience that our Divinity rejects
the followers of the impious beliefs of Nestorius, we ordain that
Irenaeus, who was long since subjected to censure by us, and who
subsequently, we know not how, with two wives, as we have learned,
has become bishop of the city of the Tyrians against the apostolic
canons, should be ejected from the sacred church in Tyre, (and allowed)
to live peacefully only in his native city, stripped of the dignity and
name of priest.

These commands, therefore, your Magnificence, in accordance with
the purpose of our piety, will strive to observe and bring to completion.

[*Cod Just.* only]. Given on the 14th day before the Kalends of
March in Constantinople (February 17), in the consulship of Zeno
and Postumianus.

It is interesting to observe that, in order to reinforce some of the provisions of the law of 435 against the followers of Nestorius, the Emperor is
forced to break one of the provisions of his own law, and to refer to them
by the name of Nestorius. The provision relating to Irenaeus is of course
original to this law.

Neither the identity of the addressee, or addressees, of this version nor
the reason why it is in Greek, are made explicit in the text from the *Acta*,
and both are revealed only by the edict posted up by the Prefects, which follows the law in the *Acta*.[46] It too is preceded by a heading supplied by the
editors:

Edict posted up by the Prefects with the divine law against Porphyry
and Nestorius and Irenaeus.

    Having finely discerned that orthodox religion is the foundation
of laws and of the state itself, our most divine Emperor has through
his own ordinance destroyed every seed of impiety, healing through
appropriate chastisement those suffering from this disease, and showing
to all the path of well-being. What sort of provisions he laid down
against those books by Porphyrius which were written against the pure
doctrine of the Christians, and that no doctrine concerning faith is to be
valid unless it has been approved by the most pious bishops who met
long ago in Nicaea and subsequently, along with Cyril of pious memory, at the city of the Ephesians, and further concerning the deposition
of Irenaeus, the former bishop of the city of the Tyrians, you all will
know from the divine ordinance which shines forth before this, expressed in the Greek language, so that none may claim ignorance of
these things. It is fitting that all should observe these things with the
greatest precision, keeping before their eyes the punishment contained
in the divine missive.

    Read in the church of the monks in the desert region on the 23rd
of Pharmouthi, in year 1 of the 23rd indiction, year 164 of Diocletian
(April 18, 448).

Whether there ever was an original text of this law, written in Latin, must
remain uncertain. What is clear is that parallel texts in Greek, in the form
of an identical letter, will have been issued to each of the two Praetorian Prefects, Hormisdas, Prefect of Illyricum, and his unnamed counterpart in
Oriens. They then each issued an edict *(diatagma)* in Greek in their joint

46. *ACO* I.1.4, para. 139 (p. 67). Also translated in Coleman-Norton, no. 446.

names, and possibly naming one or both of the Praetorian Prefects in the West.[47] The law itself, attributed by the editors of the *Acta* to Theodosius alone, was in fact, as was universal, in the name of both Emperors—but, as it happens, even the Prefects followed the same convention. They did not need to explain why their own pronouncement was in Greek, since this was the rule. Their allusion to the fact that the Imperial law itself, posted up with their *diatagma* following it, had been deliberately composed in Greek to aid public understanding is interesting as regards the anomaly of original composition and issuance in Greek, but surprising as regards the public version. For we would assume that such a "law," or letter, was always disseminated publicly in Greek translation.

At any rate, what is clear is that dissemination, as with the law on asylum,[48] was quite rapid, the edict being read out to the monks in their church in the Egyptian desert (as the use of Egyptian dating shows) only two months later.

If these monks duly followed the "one-nature" theology of both the previous bishop of Alexandria, Cyril, and the present incumbent, Dioscorus, they will have heard the pronouncement with pleasure. In Antioch, it was not so. We know this from the priceless evidence of the proceedings at the Second Council of Ephesus, preserved in Syriac translation on by far the earliest manuscript with the *Acta* of any of the Councils, written less than a century later, in 535.[49] In these *Acta*, via the medium of reports of various proceedings directed against Ibas of Edessa earlier in 449 which are quoted verbatim,[50] we arrive at several different reports of the hostile reception of this Imperial law at Antioch, presumably around the same time as it was being read out in Egypt.

The various reports, as already mentioned, are quoted from subsequent proceedings, and each gives, in hostile terms, a description of what seems to be the same moment, or at least to record scenes which had taken place close together in time. In the first of these Eulogius, a presbyter from Edessa and one of the complainants against Ibas, describes being in the main church in Antioch when Domnus was taking the service, and Theodoret was seated near him. At this moment an Imperial letter *(sacra)* was published, evidently the law directed against Porphyry, Nestorius, and Irenaeus. It must have been read out, for there were hostile acclamations (or imprecations) from the con-

47. See the parallel offered by the law of 435 against Nestorianism, p. 177 above.
48. See p. 143 in chapter 4.
49. See the account in appendix A, p. 244.
50. See appendix B, no. 23.

gregation: "Cast out the edict! Nobody believes by an edict!"[51] Of itself, the description of this episode would not be sufficient to identify this moment as that of the publication of this particular Imperial letter (and Prefectural edict) as opposed to any other. Similarly, another deposition *(libellos)*, presented at the Second Council of Ephesus in August 449, from a presbyter named Kyriakos, confirms the hostile view of the cooperation of Domnus and Theodoret, and refers back to the Imperial order that Theodoret should be confined to Cyrrhus. Kyriakos goes on to say that Domnus had refused to ratify the deposition of Irenaeus, and had remained in communion with him. The *libellos* then concentrates on the heretical views of Theodoret—had any enemies of the Church, pagans, Jews, or heretics, ever been guilty of damaging it so profoundly?[52] We gain from this the most powerful impression of the theological divisions which currently marked the Church of Oriens, and a clear explanation of how Theodosius was induced to order the confinement of Theodoret; but, in this instance, we hear no further details on the reception of the Imperial letter. These are supplied by what seems to be a separate accusation laid before the Council by a presbyter named Ioannes. This does refer quite specifically to the posting-up at Antioch of the order from the Emperors against Nestorius and Irenaeus, who is said here to have had two wives, and to have been in no communication with the Church for twelve years (435–46, counted inclusively?) from the exile of Nestorius to his ordination by Domnus. It was indeed now, the report makes clear, that there were shouts of 'Cast out the edict!'[53]

Here at least, therefore, we can follow the dissemination of the Imperial order in two different regions, Egypt and Syria, and can understand that such a dissemination was not necessarily a formality, but could attract attention, and might be greeted with popular protest.

In the event, such protests were, at least for the remainder of the reign of Theodosius, unavailing. At the Second Council of Ephesus, while Eutyches was declared orthodox, Flavianus, the bishop of Constantinople, who had presided at his trial, was deposed, and died shortly afterwards, perhaps as a result of mistreatment. Domnus, Theodoret, and Ibas were all deposed, and the deposition of Irenaeus was confirmed. Moreover, extracts from the *Acta* at Ephesus, incorporated in those of Chalcedon two years later, show that in the eyes of their opponents the followers of Nestorius—whatever

51. *AGWG*, pp. 56–59; trans. Perry, p. 129.
52. *AGWG*, pp. 114–17; trans. Perry, pp. 288–94.
53. *AGWG*, pp. 117–19; trans. Perry, pp. 294–97. For uncertainties as to the date of Nestorius's exile (435 or 436?) see pp. 176–81 above.

the Emperor might have commanded in 435 about giving them the name "Simoniani"[54]—were now labelled as "Nestorianoi." A couple of examples will suffice. In the spring of 449 one of the charges laid before a hearing investigating Ibas, bishop of Edessa, was "that he is a Nestorianos, and declares the blessed bishop Cyril a heretic."[55] The term had thus entered the public vocabulary of the Church, and could also be deployed even more polemically at crucial moments. At Chalcedon Basil of Seleucia was to recall a moment of particular contention at Ephesus two years earlier: "Next all the Egyptians got up, and the monks who were followers of Barsaumas, and the whole mob, and began to say: 'Anyone who says two natures, cut him in two! Whoever says two natures is a Nestorianos!'"[56]

What became of Irenaeus after his deposition is not recorded. But it is surely striking that what is both one of the fullest and the most nearly contemporary accounts of the steps which led up to the Council itself and of the death of Flavianus should have been composed by the exiled Nestorius, apparently isolated, living the best part of two thousand kilometers away in the Great Oasis, and must have been completed within three years of the event.[57] Though it makes detailed use of the *Acta*, of which Nestorius had evidently received copies, an objective record is of course precisely what this narrative, like other stretches of narrative in the same work, is not. Taken as a whole, the work is an assertion that his theology represented orthodoxy, not heresy, so there could by definition be no question of his accepting "Nestorian" as a label for it. But it also, at different points in the argument, incorporates powerful and prejudicial sections of contemporary history. Moreover, it also represents, perhaps even more fully than Irenaeus's *Tragoedia* would, if his linking narrative had not almost disappeared, an expression of intellectual independence and moral defiance.

Yet, even as Nestorius will have been completing his work, everything was changing. He already knew of the death of Theodosius, and even refers, at the end of the work, to the deposition of Dioscorus at Chalcedon, but goes into no detail. A compromise formula, already expressed in the famous *Tome* of Leo, addressed to Flavianus in June 449, would provide the definition of faith adopted at Chalcedon, leading the previously victorious believers in a "one-nature" theology to see it as heresy, and as the adoption of Nestorian

---

54. P. 176 above.

55. *ACO* II.1.3, para. 73 (p. 25 [384]).

56. *ACO* II.1.1, para. 176 (p. 93). Cf. p. 159 above.

57. For the long section of the *Book of Heraclides* which narrates in great detail episodes from the Second Council of Ephesus, see II.1 (Nau, pp. 302–17; D/H, pp. 345–62).

doctrine. These issues go far beyond what can be discussed here. But we have already seen much evidence on the role of persuasive communications ultimately directed to the Emperor, matched, on the one hand, by the strength of Theodosius's convictions as to his Imperial duty, and on the other by the responsiveness and preparedness to adapt, or even change course radically, which mark the history of the reign, and not only in ecclesiastical affairs. So it remains to ask how far we can understand the workings of persuasion and communication, and how and by whom Imperial decisions were first formulated and then expressed to his subjects.

VI   Persuasion, Influence, and Power

1. STRUCTURES AND PERSONS

The third session of the Council of Chalcedon, meeting on October 13, 451, heard read out before it a long and moving petition *(libellos)* from Athanasius, a presbyter at Alexandria, the nephew of the great Cyril, bishop from 412 until his death in 444.[1] According to the petition, Dioscorus, upon succeeding Cyril on the episcopal throne, had oppressed and cheated the surviving members of Cyril's family, causing Athanasius and his brother to flee to Constantinople to seek protection. But Dioscorus had forestalled them by writing and sending gifts "to Chrysaphius of unholy memory, and moreover to the most magnificent and most glorious Nomus, who then had the affairs of the world in his hands." As a result, they were thrown into prison, had to borrow large sums to get themselves out, and then could not leave the city because their creditors brought actions to prevent them. Later he makes clear what had happened to the money raised:

> The money which was demanded from us, deriving partly from our own property and partly from loans made, as we said, at extortionate rates, amounts to just about 1,400 pounds of gold, which the most magnificent and most glorious Nomus took from us through the most devoted *magistrianus* Severus, the former *subadiuva* of the *schola* of the devoted *magistriani;* as for the barbarian Chrysaphius, we never even saw his face.

The two persons whom the unhappy Athanasius mentioned were Chrysaphius, the powerful eunuch *spatharius,* whose influence with Theodosius

---

1. *ACO* II.1.2, para. 57 (pp. 20–22 [216–18]). For the numbering and real sequence of the sessions see appendix A.

was notorious, and who had since been executed on Pulcheria's orders in the summer of 450, and Nomus, the Magister Officiorum of 443–46, consul of 445, and *patricius.*[2] Both names will reappear in what follows, and Nomus is also known as the addressee of a number of Imperial laws, or letters, of the period, above all the comprehensive provisions for control of the army dating to 443. Between them, they symbolize the two interacting spheres of influence and power which surrounded the Emperor: the household, or *cubiculum,* literally "bedroom," and the corps of high officials, both civilian, as Nomus was, and military, who, as individuals, occupied the most important posts and, as a group, made up both the Imperial council *(consistorium)* and the Senate. That much can be said for certain; but, as will be seen below, it is extremely difficult to discern precisely what the qualifications were for membership of either body, or indeed how they differed. Contrary to what might be supposed, however, contemporary evidence makes quite clear that both bodies were perceived as being potentially involved in decisions at the center.

Nomus is also inconveniently characteristic, in that our evidence for his career begins with his occupation of the very high office, close to the Emperor, of Magister Officiorum. Thus an illuminating new Greek inscription in his honor from Caesarea Maritima reflects his very high status, with the award of a gold statue, and his role in fulfilling the Emperor's commands— but says nothing of his earlier career: "Publicly, with a golden statue, the city honored Nomus, mindful of good order, the superintendent of the men who by the *cursus (publicus)* carry out the commands of the Emperors."[3] We know neither what his local origins were nor what the earlier stages of his career had been. It is in this respect, in trying to gain some conception of the social history of the occupants of Imperial posts, that the effective disappearance of the career inscription, so fundamental to our conceptions of the earlier Empire as a system, makes itself felt.[4] Holy men, bishops, or even a pagan philosopher like the great Proclus, might receive biographies

---

2. See *PLRE* II, Chrysaphius, and Nomus 1.

3. For the inscription see C. L. Lehmann and K. G. Holum, *The Greek and Latin Inscriptions of Caesarea Maritima* (2000), no. 25, adapting their translation in the light of R. Merkelbach, "Ehrenepigram auf (Flavius) Nomus aus Caesarea Maritima," *ZPE* 136 (2001): 298.

4. For the disappearance of the career inscription (except in the city of Rome) in late antiquity, see W. Eck, "Elite und Leitbilder in der römischen Kaiserzeit," in *Leitbilder der Spätantike—Eliten und Leitbilder,* ed. J. Dummer and M. Vielberg (1999), 31 ff. See also F. Millar, "Die Bedeutung der Cursusinschriften für das Studium der römischen Administration im Lichte des griechisch-römische Reiches von Theodosius II" in *Der Alltag des römischen Administration in der Kaizerzeit,* ed. J. Heinrichs and R. Haensch (in press.)

in this period; but as regards civil or military officials neither literary sources nor inscribed documents show any interest either in local origins, or in the process by which men entered the Imperial service, or by what ranks they progressed, or, consequently, what age they might have been when occupying high office. Passing references to origins are found of course, scattered in contemporary literature and some documents, and suggest that the Emperor's high officials, military and civilian, might come from anywhere in the Greek-speaking Empire, from Egypt to Cappadocia to Thrace. As noted earlier, it should be presumed, unless shown otherwise in particular cases, that the first language of one and all of them was Greek, and that command of Latin was acquired as an extra to the normal education, as a necessary qualification for the exercise of public office.[5]

At the Imperial court itself, in the immediate entourage of the Emperor, we can distinguish several different groups. Firstly, there were high civilian officials, whom we must assume (rather than can in most cases prove) to have risen through lower posts: the Magister Officiorum, the Quaestor Sacri Palatii, and the major financial officials, the Comes Sacrarum Largitionum and Comes Rei Privatae. Then, as noted, there were the officials of the Imperial *cubiculum,* who were normally eunuchs; whether they invariably were is not certain. Chrysaphius is unusual in having had the title *spatharius,* or "bodyguard." The more common title for the chief court official was Praepositus Sacri Cubiculi ("Superintendent of the Sacred Bedchamber"). Especially in the case of those who were eunuchs, we must conceive of their standing, and the source of their power, as being very different from that of Imperial officials. Nonetheless, there was a clear tendency for the Emperor to grant them equality of status. Thus in November 422 Theodosius wrote to the Prefect of Constantinople to say that past, present, and future holders of the post of Praepositus should rank with Praetorian or Urban Prefects and Magistri Militum.[6] Not only the Praepositus himself but the other Cubicularii could be perceived as exercising a significant level of influence. We have already encountered the eunuch Scholasticius in connection with the fate of Nestorius in 431,[7] and will see below further evidence on his role at that moment. Even earlier, in 422, what must be the same man is found with an honorific title and office, when Theodosius wrote to him as "Vir spectabilis, Comes and Castrensis Sacri Palatii."[8]

5. See pp. 86–91 above.
6. *CTh* VI.18.1.
7. Pp. 172–73 above, in chapter 5.
8. *CTh* VI.32.2. See *PLRE* II, Scholasticius 1.

As we have already noted, the power exercised both by the Emperor's elder sister, Pulcheria, and by his wife, Aelia Eudocia, was by no means just a matter of public perception, or rumor, but found concrete expression, in a way not paralleled for any earlier reign, in letters addressed to them for purposes of persuasion on major issues.[9] That being so, we find at crucial moments, such as after the first Council of Ephesus, that bribery and persuasion were directed also to their female "bedroom-assistants" *(cubiculariae)*. As will be seen, what can be observed is a complex interplay between the perceived (or hoped for, or feared) private influence of intermediaries who might or might not occupy any public position, on the one hand, and overt public persuasion, expressed either orally in person or at a distance by letter, on the other.

The Imperial entourage also included the Magistri of the various *scrinia*, or secretariats, of the Memoria, the (Latin) Epistulae, the Libelli, and the Greek Epistulae. The summary account of their functions provided in the *Notitia Dignitatum* for Oriens will give some impression of the range of their business, without illuminating either the interconnections between them, or whether their holders were mere functionaries, or exercised actual influence. The Magister Memoriae, on this account, dictated and sent out *adnotationes*, and replied to petitions *(preces)*; the Magister Epistularum (for letters in Latin), dealt with embassies from cities as well as *consultationes* (meaning letters from officials), and also handled *preces;* so did the Magister Libellorum, whose brief also covered Imperial judicial hearings *(cognitiones)*; while the Magister Epistolarum Graecarum either dictated letters in Greek or translated them from Latin.[10]

As individuals, the holders of these posts have very little prominence in our sources, except in the specific context of the two successive commissions set up to produce the *Codex Theodosianus:* in 429 there was an ex-Quaestor and Praefectus, the current Quaestor Sacri Palatii, a Comes and Magister Memoriae, two more Magistri Scriniorum, a former Comes "of our Sacrarium" (meaning uncertain), two more former Magistri Scriniorum, and a *scholasticus* named Apelles. In 435 the new commission of sixteen men included four current "Comites and Magistri Scriniorum" (apparently therefore the holders of all four posts).[11]

As the last title quoted suggests, our conception of relative status and (possibly) of influence tends to be complicated by the addition of extra hon-

9. P. 36 above.
10. *Notitia Dignitatum*, Oriens XIX.
11. *CTh* I.1.5 and 6.

orific titles, such as "Comes," which could be used in any branch of the Imperial service, whether in civil administration, finance, or the military. We also have to allow for the granting by the Emperor of the symbolic annual office of Consul, and of the purely honorific title of *patricius*.

Moreover, to complicate the picture further, it is clear that titles were retained and attached to individuals' names even after they had ceased to hold the office in question, and that ex-holders of important office could be perceived by contemporaries as still exercising a high level of influence even when not in occupation of any post. In short, contemporaries quite clearly envisaged influence as being exercised by an inner circle of either current or former holders of high office, and, in broad terms, were correct to do so. Whether in any particular circumstances the individual in question was either disposed to, or could, exercise the influence hoped for was another matter. The evidence shows clearly that Athanasius, the presbyter from Alexandria, and his brother had been right to imagine Chrysaphius and Nomus as the two major figures in Constantinople who were in a position to help them. It was just unfortunate that both yielded instead to the influence, and the cash, of the bishop Dioscorus, and that Nomus took money from them while giving no help.

In doing so, following Athanasius's account, Nomus had used the services of a named lower official, Severus, a *magistrianus* who was a former assistant in the *schola* of the *magistriani*. That detail points to a further very significant feature of the system as it actually worked, namely the quite prominent role often played by named officials whose titles might be read as suggesting a relatively modest role and status, but who in fact exercised some power, and might be commissioned to act with a considerable degree of independence and authority. One clear example is the Tribunus and Notarius, Aristolaus, who acted in 432/3 as the Imperial emissary commissioned to bring about reconciliation after the first Council of Ephesus.[12] Office-holders, major or relatively minor, might also combine what might seem to be different functions, or act in concert with each other in ways which we would not necessarily have expected. One example was quoted earlier, namely the hearing held in Constantinople in April 449 by Martialis, Comes and Magister Officiorum, "there being present" also Carterius, Comes and Proximus of the Libelli and the Cognitiones.[13] Precisely what roles an office-holder might be required to perform, and what degree of influence he might have on policy, cannot be safely deduced from the title and apparent standing of his current office.

12. See *PLRE* II, Aristolaus.
13. Pp. 166–67 above.

As noted in the case of Aristolaus, the same fluidity, or flexibility, of function is characteristic of those apparently middle-ranking officials who held the title of Tribunus and Notarius. Another conspicuous example is the Damascius who on October 26, 448, was the addressee of an Imperial *hypomnēstikon (adnotatio?)* instructing him to proceed to Oriens along with Ouranios, bishop of Himeria, and summon Ibas, bishop of Edessa, Daniel of Carrhae, and Ioannes of Theodosiopolis for examination at a hearing in Phoenicia.[14]

However, although the capacity to act as an independent agent with a degree of personal authority extended to a considerably wider range of office-holders than initial examination of the structure might suggest, it was still the case that there was, and was clearly perceived to be, an inner circle of high officials whose status was determined by the offices which they either currently held or had previously held, along with the two most prominent honorific titles, Consul and *patricius*. To gain a rather more concrete impression of what this amounted to, or how it seemed as demonstrated in public, we need to go one year beyond Theodosius's death, to the Council of Chalcedon, whose opening session was held on October 8, 451.

At both of the two Councils of Ephesus Theodosius had commissioned an Imperial emissary to keep order, but not to participate in the sessions, and not to intervene in actual debates: in 431 this was Candidianus, the Comes Sacrorum Domesticorum (of the household troops);[15] and in 449 he sent a *hypomnēstikon* to Helpidius, Comes Sacri Consistorii, and to Eulogius, again a Tribunus et Notarius Praetorianus, instructing them to perform the same function.[16] Marcian, on the other hand, clearly determined that a far more extensive and emphatic presence on the part of secular officials was required if Chalcedon was going to yield the results that he wanted. So a carefully selected group, or rather two separate groups, of Imperial office-holders were not only to be present at the sessions, but were to keep control of all questions of procedure. The *Acta* of the first session (as of the others) list them all with their offices, and in doing so provide a unique view of the inner circle of power as displayed in public. Given the short time that had passed since Theodosius's death, it is not likely that there will have been radical changes in the composition of this group. But in fact, as we will see, three independent sources of evidence which derive from, or relate to, the latter years of the reign, confirm that these were indeed, in broad terms, the

14. *ACO* II.1.3, para. 27 (p. 19 [378]), partially quoted on p. 229 below.
15. *ACO* I.1.1, para. 31 (p. 241). See *PLRE* II, Candidianus 6.
16. *ACO* II.1.1, para. 49 (p. 72).

persons who were currently perceived as wielding power at the center. The following translation of the opening section of the *Acta* of Session I at Chalcedon reproduces their official titles exactly as given, while adding in brackets the entry number in *PLRE* II, other offices attested (very few), and their region of origin if known. The results of three separate "tests" of perceived prominence, or influence, are also tabulated: letters to the individual from Theodoret; acclamation of the individual's name by crowds in Edessa in the spring of 449; and allusions to their role in Priscus's narrative of contacts with Attila in the last years of Theodosius's reign. It will be seen that nineteen men are listed, divided into two groups: seven "Archontes" (office-holders), and twelve members of the Senate. The latter are also designated in terms of offices held, but with one crucial difference, namely that they are all ex-holders of high office. In the elaborately formal style which characterizes reports of proceedings in this period, the text runs as follows:[17]

> Opening of the Synod of Chalcedon
> In the consulship of our lord Marcian the eternal Augustus and of whoever will be announced, on the eighth day before the Ides of October in Chalcedon.
> By order of the most divine and most pious lord of ours, Marcian the eternal Augustus, there gathering in the most holy church of the holy martyr Euphemia the most glorious office-holders, that is
> *the most magnificent and most glorious Stratēlates (Magister Militum) and ex-consul and patricius, Anatolius*
> [Fl. Anatolius 10: Magister Militum, Oriens, 434–c.446; Consul, 440; *patricius*, 446?; Magister Militum Praesentalis, before 449?. Theodoret, *Epp.* II. 45; 79; 92; III. 97; 111; 119; 121; 139; Edessa, 449, *AGWG*, pp. 16–17/Perry, pp. 46; 49; Priscus, Fr. 13.2; 15.3–5]
> *and the most magnificent and most glorious Prefect of the Sacred Praetorium, Palladius*
> [Palladius 9: Praetorian Prefect of Oriens, 450–55]
> *and the most magnificent and most glorious Prefect of the City, Tatianus*
> [Tatianus 1: *praeses* of Caria before 450?; Prefect of Constantinople, 450–52; later *patricius*, Consul, 466. From Lycia]
> *and the most magnificent and most glorious Magister Sacrorum Officiorum, Vincomalus*

---

17. *ACO* II.1.1, paras. 1–2 (pp. 55–56). For all the issues concerning office, status, and precedence in the lists of office-holders and members of the Senate attending successive sessions at Chalcedon, not just the first, as here, see the masterly treatment by R. Delmaire, "Les dignitaires laïcs au Concile de Chalcédoine: Notes sur la hiérarchie et les préséances au milieu du Ve siècle," *Byzantion* 54 (1984): 141 ff. Some of the details given here embody corrections by Delmaire of the entries in *PLRE* II.

[Ioannes Vincomalus: Magister Officiorum, 450?–52; Consul, 453.
Theodoret, *Epp.* III. 141]

and the most magnificent Magister, Martialis

[Fl. Areobindus Martialis: Magister Officiorum, 449. Edessa, 449,
AGWG, pp. 16–17; Priscus, Fr. 11.1–2]

*and the most magnificent Comes Sacrorum Domesticorum,
Sporacius*

[Fl. Sporacius 3: Comes, 448; Comes Domesticorum Peditum,
448?–51; Consul, 452. Theodoret, *Epp.* III. 97]

and the most magnificent Comes Sacrarum Privatarum, Genethlius

[Genethlius 2: Comes Rerum Privatarum, 450–51]

and the glorious Senate, that is

*the most magnificent and most glorious ex-Prefect and ex-Consul
and patricius, Florentius*

[Fl. Florentius 7: Prefect of Constantinople, 422; Praetorian Prefect
of Oriens, 428–29 and 438–39; Consul, 429; *patricius*, 446/8. From
Syria. Theodoret, *Epp.* V and II. 89]

*the most magnificent and most glorious ex-Consul and patricius,
Senator*

[Senator 4: Consul, 436; *patricius*. Theodoret, *Epp.* II. 44; III. 98;
AGWG, pp. 16–17; 24–25/Perry, pp. 49; 67; Priscus, Fr. 9.2; 13–14.2]

*and the most magnificent and most glorious ex-Magister and ex-
Consul and patricius, Nomus*

[Nomus 1: Magister Officiorum, 443–46; Consul, 445; *patricius*.
Theodoret, *Epp.* II. 58 = XVI; II. 81; III. 96; *AGWG*, pp. 16–17,
24–25/Perry, pp. 49; 67; Priscus, Fr. 13.2; 15.3–5]

*and the most magnificent and most glorious ex-Praefectus and ex-
Consul and patricius, Protogenes*

[Fl. Flor(entius?) Romanus Protogenes: Praetorian Prefect of Oriens
earlier, and again 448/9; Consul, 449; *patricius*. Theodoret, *Epp.* II. 94;
AGWG, pp. 16–17/Perry, p. 49]

The list continues with eight further members of the Senate: Zoilus, Theodorus, Apollodorus, Romanus, another Theodorus, Constantius, Artaxes, and
Eulogius. All are identified as ex-holders of one office each (including two,
Romanus and Artaxes, who are former Praepositi Sacri Cubiculi). None was
either an ex-Consul or *patricius*, and only one, Constantinus, was the recipient of a letter from Theodoret *(Epp.* XIX). It is striking that of this group
it was Constantinus, from Laodicea in Phrygia, who was to hold important
offices later in the 450s.[18]

Other senators presented themselves at later sessions of Chalcedon, and
especially (and unsurprisingly) at Session VI, when the Emperor Marcian

18. *PLRE* II, Fl. Constantinus 22.

attended and spoke. On that occasion a total of twenty-eight senators attended, and again all those on whom details survive were former holders of high office. Of those who had not been present at Session I, only one, Antiochus, a former Praetorian Prefect (of Oriens in 448) and a *patricius,* had earlier been the recipient of a letter from Theodoret (*Epp.* II. 95, of 448).

Therefore, as regards a possible inner group composed of those holders of high office who were perceived by their contemporaries as exercising personal power and influence, a very clear and coherent pattern emerges. The evidence of the two-part list, of "Archontes" on the one hand and of "the Senate" on the other, is matched to a very striking degree by the addressees of Theodoret's letter writing of the later 440s on matters of communal or theological concern, by the names which were shouted by the crowd in Edessa in spring 449, and by those which were recorded in Priscus's detailed narrative of negotiations with Attila. In particular, of the group made up of seven current office-holders, and of those four members of the Senate who are listed first, and who clearly stand out from the others, no less than seven had received letters from Theodoret. He was of course a well known and controversial figure, confined to Cyrrhus by a personal order from Theodosius in 448, deposed by the Council of Ephesus in the next year, and due to be restored—against vigorous protests—at Chalcedon itself. But it remained the case that he was bishop of a middle-ranking city which was not even the metropolis of Euphratesia. So the fact that he knew very clearly where to direct his letters is of real significance, as is his assumption that he was entitled to justice, and had a claim to be heard.

In a different way, the (hostile) acclamations uttered on the streets of Edessa tell the same story. In Edessa, as in Alexandria, the power of Nomus was known, and his name was joined with those of Anatolius, Senator, and Protogenes. Priscus's narrative produces a closely similar list—Anatolius, Martialis, Senator, and Nomus. Moreover, both Priscus and the acclamations at Edessa add the same two further names: Chrysaphius, the powerful eunuch *spatharius,* and Zeno, the Isaurian Magister Militum of 447–51, and Consul of 448.[19]

Edessa was at least the metropolis of its province, Osrhoene, and the scene of profound theological divisions within the Church, accompanied by accusations of malpractice. But as a province, Osrhoene, in the partially Syriac-speaking region east of the Euphrates, was one step more remote from the political center at Constantinople even than Euphratesia across the river to

19. Priscus, Fr. [3].1; 11.1–2; 15.2–3; 5 (Chrysaphius); Fr. 14; 15.2; 16 (Zeno). *AGWG,* pp. 16–17/Perry, p. 46; 24–25/Perry, p. 49.

the west. So even if some indoctrination had been deployed to put the appropriate names into the mouths of the people, the scenes there in the spring of 449 still show an extraordinarily vivid perception of where power lay in the distant Imperial capital.

The question of where, how, and by whom power was exercised—and hence to whom persuasion or bribery should be directed—could mean three different things. Firstly, what were the relevant posts whose holders had a place in the chain of transmission of requests and proposals addressed to the Emperor, and of orders coming down from him? Secondly, which individuals, whether currently holding office or not, enjoyed a personal influence? As we have seen, these might include the "Empresses"—the Emperor's sister and wife—and their *cubiculariae*. Thirdly, what collective bodies, if any, played a role in the formation of policy and in the discussion of decisions? Two such bodies certainly existed: the Senate itself and the Imperial council, or Consistorium. But it remains to be seen whether their influence or policy was more than nominal.

These questions, which go along with the wider issue of who, from outside the ranks of officialdom, had the authority to direct effective persuasion at the Emperor, will be discussed below. Added to them at the end will be the issue of the Emperor's individual role. In this long reign in particular, which began when Theodosius was only seven, part of the answer, for the initial years at least, must be that a collectivity ruled in his name. But what collectivity, and how were decisions reached? Progressively, however, the Emperor will have been of an age, and potentially of the authority, to decide for himself as between contrasting advice and conflicting pressures. But did such an evolution into effective personal monarchy in fact take place?

All these topics will be explored below, but on the basis that what is being attempted is not to decide "what really happened," or whose influence had been the dominating factor at a particular moment (about which even the best-informed contemporaries will have disagreed), but to explore what presumptions about the location and exercise of power governed the actions of contemporaries. Before we explore the evidence, however, we need to take account of the only systematic contemporary representation of the principles of decision making at the center which we possess. As will be seen in a moment, this representation, though it comes from very late in the reign, proclaims a strongly collectivist ideal of decision making, involving both the Senate and the Imperial Consistorium.[20]

20. For valuable discussions of the law quoted below see J. Harries, "The Roman Imperial Quaestor from Constantine to Theodosius II," *JRS* 71 (1988): 148 ff., on

The document in question is in the form of a letter to the Senate, sent by Theodosius and Valentinian on October 17, 446.[21] It comes from the *Codex Justinianus,* and did not find a place in the collection of *Novellae* of either Emperor. As preserved in the *Codex,* it is almost certainly no more than an extract, shorn of any allusion to the circumstances which had given rise to it. Worse still, the normal indication of the place of issue has dropped out, so that we have no formal proof of whether it in fact emanated from Theodosius or Valentinian. But, given the generality and significance of the principles laid down, Theodosius was most probably the originator; and in any case it is unlikely that the public representation of collective decision making will have followed different lines in East and West. In view of its significance, it deserves quotation both in the original and in translation:

> Idem A.A. ad senatum. Humanum esse probamus, si quid de cetero in publica vel in privata causa emerserit necessarium, quod formam generalem et antiquis legibus non insertam exposcat, id ab omnibus antea tam proceribus nostri palatii quam gloriosissimo coetu vestro, patres conscripti, tractari et, si universis tam iudicibus quam vobis placuerit, tunc allegata dictari et sic ea denuo collectis omnibus recenseri et, cum omnes consenserint, tunc demum in sacro nostri numinis consistorio recitari, ut universorum consensus nostrae serenitatis auctoritate firmetur. Scitote igitur, patres conscripti, non aliter in posterum legem a nostra clementia promulgandam, nisi supra dicta forma fuerit observata. Bene enim cognoscimus, quod cum vestro consilio fuerit ordinatum, id ad beatitudinem nostri imperii et ad nostram gloriam redundare.
>
> D. XVI k. Nov. Aetio III et Symmacho conss.

The same Emperors (Theodosius and Valentinian) to the Senate
> We judge it to be appropriate that, if any question arises in the future, in either a public or a private case, of a nature such that it requires a general ruling, and is not already incorporated in ancient laws, it should be considered in advance both by all the chief officials of our palace and by your most glorious assembly, Patres Conscripti, and, if it is approved both by all the office-holders and by yourselves, then the proposed matters should be dictated, and finally checked in the presence of all, and, when all have consented, then at last it should be read out in the sacred Consistorium of our Majesty, so that the consensus of all may be validated by the authority of our Serenity. Be aware, therefore, Patres Conscripti, that for the future no law is to be promulgated by

---

pp. 164–65; C. F. Wetzler, *Rechtsstaat und Absolutismus: Überlegungen zur Verfassung des spätantiken Kaiserreichs anhand von CJ I.14.8* (1997), esp. pp. 120–21.
  21. *CJ* I.14.8.

our Clemency, unless the above-mentioned procedure has been followed. For we are fully cognizant of the fact that whatever has been ordained with your advice redounds to the blessedness of our empire and to our glory.

Given on the 16th day before the Kalends of November in the consulship of Aetius for the third time and of Symmachus (446).

We shall see below many indications that the broad principle that decisions at the Imperial court were the work of a collectivity is amply borne out in the evidence. It will also be clear that contemporaries were aware that the Senate of Constantinople and the Imperial Consistorium were distinct bodies, either or both of which might be involved in decisions. Beyond that, however, we are remarkably short of concrete evidence as to working and procedures, especially in the case of the Senate. The *Notitia* of Constantinople, composed in Latin under Theodosius, reveals that there were two Senate houses in the city, one near the Imperial palace and one on the Forum of Constantine, near his Column.[22] But while fourth- and fifth-century laws devote considerable attention to the rights, privileges, exemptions, and obligations associated with "senatorial" status,[23] none of this information deals concretely with the issue of who was actually entitled to attend meetings. Indeed there is no better contemporary evidence than the lists of members of the Senate who attended successive sessions at Chalcedon. On this evidence, meetings of the Senate were the preserve of former holders of high office, namely Praefecti, Magistri, and Praepositi, some being also ex-Consuls or *patricii*. It would be reasonable to presume that, as with the Senate in Rome, the Praefectus of the City presided. But there seems not to be, from the Theodosian period, any narrative account of an actual session.

Nonetheless, it is significant that the initial proposal for a program of legal codification which led to the composition of the *Codex Theodosianus* was addressed to the Senate of Constantinople in 429, and the same was surely true of the revised proposal of 435, even though the address "Ad Senatum" is missing.[24] That was a formality, or a gesture intended to gather support, and apart from that there is only one further example from Theodosius's reign of an Imperial letter embodying legislation that is directed to the Senate. This is the letter sent on September 12, 439, and formally addressed "Ad

22. *Notitia Urbis Constantinopolitanae*, in *Notitia Dignitatum*, ed. O. Seeck, pp. 231, 234.

23. See, e.g., Jones, *LRE*, ch. XI and XV; G. Dagron, *Naissance d' une capitale: Constantinople et ses institutions de 330 à 451* (1974), 191 ff.

24. *CTh* I.1.5 (repeated in *Gesta Senatus* 4, of 438), Mar. 26, 429; I.1.6, Dec. 20, 435.

Senatum Urbis Constantinopolitanae." That it is so addressed is clearly explained by the fact that it concerns the complex rules under which town councilors *(curiales)* might rise to senatorial status. Very typically, the issue arose from a *suggestio* by the Praetorian Prefect of Oriens, Florentius, and with remarkable delicacy the Emperor manages to imply both that the Senate has an overall responsibility for the Empire, and that it is not normally expected to have a heavy workload:[25]

> You are accustomed to provide especially for the municipal councils *(curiae)*, since, indeed, by Our decision the state *(res publica)* is customarily entrusted to you for guidance. For even though at certain times We allow you to enjoy leisure, in order that you may not appear to be harassed by continuous labor, nevertheless the responsibility for the best guidance of the State does not forsake you.

Given what seem to have been the relatively restricted responsibilities of the Senate as a body, it is striking that amid the flurry of self-justification and mutual denunciation as between the followers of Cyril and of Ioannes of Antioch at the Council of Ephesus in 431, which led to a constant stream of letters between Ephesus and Constantinople, Ioannes and his supporters remembered to address a letter to the Senate in Constantinople, describing the misdeeds and heretical views of Cyril and his party.[26] No reply is recorded.

That letter, too, could be seen essentially as a gesture to gather support in official circles (and certainly not as implying that the Senate might have intervened independently of the Emperor). All the evidence shows both that quite a wide range of intermediaries, high office-holders and palace officials, as well as, on occasion, the Emperor's sister and wife, needed to be canvassed when a major decision was at stake, and that in the end it was the Emperor's personal decision which would prevail. Nonetheless, it is precisely some of these letters from 431 and just after which show awareness that the Emperor acted with a Consistorium whose attitude might be important. As it happens, no contemporary source reveals how the members were selected, or how many would normally be present. But it is safe to assume that the participants were drawn from the same corps of high officials as the Senate itself.

Interested parties, indeed, while aware that the Emperor did not act entirely alone, were apparently not always clear as to whether the body with whom he deliberated was the Consistorium or the Senate. Writing from Ancyra on his way back to Antioch in the winter of 431/2, Ioannes asked an

---

25. *Nov. Th.* 15.1, trans. Pharr.
26. *ACO* I.1.5, para. 156 (pp. 551–56).

unidentified Praefectus (almost certainly the Praetorian Prefect of Oriens) to ensure that his letter was read not only to the Emperor and "the most magnificent and most glorious Praepositus (of the Cubiculum)," but also to the Consistorium or Senate "so that all may take heed of the fact that until now we have not been subject to any charge, but have done everything in order and propriety and in accordance with the rules."[27] A similar slight ambiguity is shown in the petition addressed to Theodosius by the representatives of Nestorius's side who were sent to Chalcedon in the late summer of 431 to argue their case before the Emperor. They say that since arriving they have not ceased to do so "either before your Piety or before the illustrious Consistorium"—almost as if the latter body might have met (like the Senate) in the absence of the Emperor.[28] A similar impression might well be gained from the message of instructions sent by the "Orientals" (the followers of Nestorius, kept at Ephesus until the Emperor gave them permission to leave) to their representatives who had gone to Chalcedon. In principle, indeed, the representatives had been supposed to continue to Constantinople itself, to argue their case there. But in the event they were told to stay at Chalcedon, and were never allowed to enter the capital. For the moment, however, it was still envisaged that they would be allowed to speak. Several different contexts were imagined: "either before the most pious Emperor or in the Consistorium or before the sacred Senate or in a synod of fathers (bishops)."[29] We could reasonably deduce from this that it was supposed that the Emperor might give the bishops a personal hearing, without the members of his Consistorium being summoned, or that he could do so at a formal session with the Consistorium in attendance, or leave the hearing to the Senate.

In the event, the representatives of the Nestorian side at Chalcedon were able to report back to their colleagues at Ephesus that there had been a formal hearing before the Emperor (in fact, in the event, several). Their description represents an optimistic view of a prospective Imperial decision, which in the end turned against them. The concurrence of belief, reason, and power is rarely exhibited so clearly as here. The Emperor's (temporarily favorable) reaction is what counts most—but so also does that of the Consistorium which attended him:[30]

27. *ACO* I.4, para. 127 (p. 234). Originally written in Greek, but preserved in Latin in Rusticus's version of Irenaeus's *Tragoedia*.

28. *ACO* I.1.7, para. 62 (pp. 72–73).

29. *ACO* I.1.3, para. 96 (p. 36).

30. *ACO* I.1.7, para. 66 (p. 77).

Through the prayers of your holiness, we gained an audience with
our most pious Emperor, and receiving divine assistance we have so
far overcome those who take the opposite view in the contests, that all
our propositions have been acceptable to our Christ-loving Emperor,
while their propositions have appeared unacceptable and illogical. While
they referred again and again to Cyril and begged that he should be
summoned and offer his defence on his own behalf, until now they
have not been persuasive, but have been informed that the issue on the
table was one of piety, and that the faith of the blessed fathers had been
confirmed. We have also refuted Acacius, who had laid down in his doctrinal works that the Deity is capable of suffering—and our pious Emperor was so enraged that he shook his purple robe and took a step back
because of the enormity of the blasphemy. Moreover we perceived that
the whole Consistorium was strongly of a mind to accept us as fighting
on the side of piety.

Two decades later Nestorius's *Book of Heraclides* was to recall this same
scene, with its dramatic exhibition of the Emperor's (then) partiality.[31] But
their confidence was soon to be dashed. One of the representatives of the
Nestorian side was Theodoret himself, and in a long letter to Alexander of
Hierapolis (who, as we have seen, would four years later be driven out of
his see by Theodosius's order),[32] he describes how every effort had been
made before the Emperor and the Consistorium to defend their cause, but
without gaining a secure advantage.[33] Later he speaks of the references they
had made to Nestorius "either before the Emperor or before the famous Consistorium," once more implying that there were two separate contexts. But
again, they had felt opinion hardening against them: bribery had had its effect, and the "judges" (the members of the Consistorium) supported the "one
nature" doctrine. In the meantime they had tried with some success to rouse
mass popular support, leading to a pitched battle (described as a "clash"—
symbolē), with injuries on both sides. After that, the Emperor had granted
an audience "to us alone" (meaning without their opponents, or without
the Consistorium in attendance?), and had engaged in a remarkably frank
dialogue with Theodoret on how order should be kept.

The centrality of the Emperor in this very delicate process of reaching a
decision between the major competing factions is clear, but so is the significance of movements of opinion among the wider circle of high officials, or
former officials, whether in the context of the Senate or of the Consisto-

---

31. *Book of Heraclides* II.1 (Nau, p. 252; D-H, pp. 284–85).
32. P. 164 above in chapter 4.
33. Theodoret, *Epp.* IV. 3a = *ACO* I.1.7, para. 69 (pp. 79–80).

rium, or neither. Thus a little later, as it seems, the "Orientals" at Chalcedon reported to their colleagues at Ephesus that they had repeatedly begged "the most pious Emperor and the most significant office-holders *(archontes)*" to allow both them and those still assembled at Ephesus to return home. The Emperor had indeed given this order, but with the proviso that "the Egyptian" (Cyril) and Memnon of Ephesus should retain their sees; so bribery had prevailed.[34]

So far as can be determined, our evidence for Theodosius's reign provides no other examples of reports by contemporaries relating to so intensive a competition to win over the Emperor's opinion as in the later months of 431. So it is only here that we get some impression of the significance of the two collective bodies which evidently did, or could, exercise a real influence. As regards the great mass of Imperial decision making, or lawgiving, what we can perceive is on the one hand the influence which contemporaries attributed to a wide range of individuals of very ranging statuses, and on the other the very clearly established pattern by which office-holders (primarily, but not solely, the Praetorian Prefects) presented to the Emperor written submissions *(suggestiones* in Latin, or *anaphorai* in Greek) which very often went beyond reporting on problems which had arisen, and made positive proposals for action or legislation.

2. THE ROUTINE OF PUBLIC PERSUASION: THE *SUGGESTIO*

We have already encountered, in the context of frontier dispositions, the letter of Synesius, as bishop of Ptolemais, in which he puts some detailed issues to the local military commander (Dux), and asks him to prepare either one *anaphora* or two separate ones for dispatch to the Emperor.[35] Equally, we have noted the group of inscriptions from Mylasa in Caria, with the remains of a Latin original of the Emperor's reply to a *suggestio* from the Comes Sacrarum Largitionum, and a Greek translation of the same letter.[36] The place of such *suggestiones* is thus, at one level, already established, and it is worth repeating that both of these instances concern very minor local matters—a small unit of soldiers in a distant province in the one case, and the taxation of a single village on the other. But it remains to explore the working of the system somewhat further, to get an impression of the

34. *ACO* I.1.7, para. 70 (p. 81).
35. Pp. 60–62 in chapter 2 above.
36. Pp. 21–22 in chapter 1 above.

relative importance of such *suggestiones* in the generation of Imperial legislation, and to ask how influence exerted through official *suggestiones* was
conceived of, or spoken of, by contemporaries. As in all aspects of the workings of influence and power, our evidence is incomparably fuller and more
revealing from 428, and the inception of the Nestorian controversy, onwards,
and fuller still in the period after the completion of the *Codex Theodosianus*
in 437, when we have available the much more complete texts collected in
the *Novellae*. But this pattern necessarily leaves relatively obscure the workings of influence in the early years, and especially in the decade after the
assumption of sole power by the seven-year-old Emperor in 408. In that
period it is evident that some wider group of persons, whether constituted
as a body such as the Consistorium, or exercising an influence based on the
occupation of office, or some more personal influence, must have determined
policy. But we are relatively short, for those years, even of representations,
either by interested contemporaries or by later writers, of where power lay.

The role of the *suggestio* must be significant at all periods, even though
not all proposals contained in them will have received a positive response, or
any response at all. By the nature of our evidence, almost entirely provided
by those Imperial letters to high officials which enunciated "laws," we are
not going to hear about those *suggestiones* which arrived at the Imperial court
but were not acted upon. But the fact that the procedure of making positive
proposals in the form of *suggestiones* was an established aspect of the system, and that not only could they give rise to "laws" issued by the Emperor,
but they could be given explicit credit in those "laws," meant that contemporaries knew that persuasion addressed to the Emperor might be effective.

It can be taken as certain that the very high frequency of references to
suggestiones in the laws of 438 onwards preserved in the *Novellae* is a function of the fact that these are relatively complete texts, not the drastic abbreviations, or rather extracts, found in the *Codex Theodosianus*, and even
more so in the *Codex Justinianus*. To be precise, twenty-three out of the
thirty-five laws preserved in the *Novellae* refer to a previous *suggestio* by
an official. It can therefore be assumed that many more of the laws of the
period up to 436 preserved in the *Codex* would be known to derive equally
from *suggestiones*, if we had fuller texts.

A few of the laws of the first three decades of the reign preserved in the
Codex do contain reflections of the submission of *suggestiones*. Thus, for
instance, a ruling of 415 on the redisposition of appointments to minor offices
as between the office of the Magister Militiae and the Scrinium Memoriae
derived from a *suggestio* by Eustathius, the Quaestor (Sacri Palatii). The decision was issued in letters to one Magister, Florentius, to the other Magister

Militiae, Sapricius, to Helio, Magister Officiorum, and to Eustathius himself.[37] The rules relating to access to official positions, and to the privileges which the occupants were to enjoy, were a subject of perpetual dispute, further complicated by the granting of posts to individuals as a personal favor. Thus Florentius, Praetorian Prefect of Oriens, named various individuals in a *suggestio* which led the Emperor in 428 to issue a law banning them and any other former *primipilares* from official posts "even if they seem to have obtained them by a special *adnotatio* of our indulgence."[38]

From 438 onwards, as mentioned above, references to *suggestiones* become common, and it will not be necessary to refer to all of them. But a few of these texts do deserve extensive quotation, in that they exhibit so fully various essential features of Imperial decision making: firstly, the reliance on *suggestiones*, either from the addressee himself or from another official; the personal greeting which marked Imperial letters to officials; the elaborate rhetoric of moralizing self-justification which these "laws" share with Imperial letters on ecclesiastical or doctrinal matters; and, in nearly all cases, the provision for the diffusion of the provisions laid down, by the posting of *edicta*. A further feature which appears in some laws and deserves note, and which is also directly relevant to the public ideology of collective responsibility for decision making, is the tone of studied respect for the contribution either of the addressee himself or of another office-holder who had raised the issue in question.

Three examples will suffice, the first being a law, or letter, addressed to Florentius, Praetorian Prefect of Oriens, in 439, on the subject of preventing the exemption of ships from the obligation of transporting official supplies. The law ends as follows:[39]

> But in order that any contempt of the present law may not appear to go unpunished, if anything should be attempted in any manner whatsoever to the fraud of this law, We punish such attempt by confiscation of the ship which is so exempted, O Florentius, dearest and most beloved Father
>
> Therefore Your Illustrious and Magnificent Authority by posting edicts shall command to be brought to the knowledge of all Our law which shall be valid forever.

In December of the same year, 439, Florentius was the subject of elaborate praise in an Imperial letter addressed to Cyrus, who had evidently just

37. *CTh* I.8.1, Oct. 15, 415.
38. *CTh* VIII.4.29, Jul. 10, 428; trans. Pharr.
39. *Nov. Th.* 8 (*CJ* I.2.10 + XI.4.2), Apr. 7, 439; trans. Pharr.

succeeded him as Praetorian Prefect. The subject matter, namely procurers (*lenones*), is admirably suited to the Emperor's moralizing tendency:[40]

> The history of the past shall obtain verification from the examples of
> the present, and henceforth antiquity, which has indicated to Us that
> the highest men have preferred the State to their own wealth, shall be
> freed from all doubt, since We observe that the Illustrious Florentius,
> who is exalted by the administration of the praetorian prefecture, no
> longer vies with the glory of his ancestors but with his own great
> merits toward the State, with the emulous virtue of his noble spirit.
> Thus not only by his counsel and foresight but also by his devotion and
> generosity he has freed the reputation of the State from the stigma and
> ignominy of disgraceful turpitude. For when he saw that the negligence
> of the ancients was being circumvented by the damnable cleverness of
> procurers, so that under the pretext of a certain lustral tax payment
> they were permitted to practice the business of corrupting innocence,
> and that the State (*res publica*) itself somehow in its ignorance was
> not repressing this injury to itself, with his devoted purpose toward
> the honour of all persons, he reported (*suggessit*) to Our Clemency,
> because of his love for honor and chastity, that such practice pertains
> to the injury of Our times, if procurers should be permitted to engage
> in business in this City or if the treasury should appear to be increased
> by their most shameful profits.

In the next year Theodosius wrote again to Cyrus on a very different topic, on the status of landed properties whose shape and extent was affected by either rivers changing their course or by swamps drying up. The law issued arises from a report or reports (*suggestiones*) from Cyrus, evidently relating to Egypt; but the occasion is explicitly taken to generalize the principles to cover all provinces. Three extracts will be sufficient to catch the tone of this letter:[41]

> By the reports of Your Eminence the material is always afforded to
> Us for conferring some great advantage upon the State; something is
> always presented to Us for correction. It is therefore undoubtedly made
> manifest through these reports also how great is the solicitude of Your
> Magnitude for the provincials.
> The nature of alluvial lands, which customarily arise in the case of
> the landed estates that are bounded by the banks of certain rivers, is
> such that possession of such lands is always uncertain, and the owner-
> ship is uncertain of the land which accrues to a landholder through
> alluvion . . .

---

40. *Nov. Th.* 18, Dec. 6, 439; trans. Pharr.
41. *Nov. Th.* 20, Sept. 21, 440; trans. Pharr.

Therefore We accept the report of Your Eminence, and We are not speaking of Egypt alone or only about the alluvial lands of the Nile, but what We promulgate is salutary for the world and for all the provinces. We sanction by this law which shall be valid forever that those lands that are acquired by landholders through alluvion shall neither be sold by the treasury nor petitioned for by any person whatever, and they shall not be separately assessed nor shall compulsory public services be exacted of them. Thus We shall not appear to disregard the disadvantages of the alluvial lands nor to impose a regulation that is hurtful to the landholders . . . .

We decree that rash violators of this law shall be punished by a fine of fifty pounds of gold. Among these must be considered the office staff also of your exalted office if they should suggest that anything of the kind should be arranged or if they should draw up the requests of a petitioner, O Cyrus, dearest and most beloved Father.

Therefore Your Illustrious and Magnificent Authority by posting edicts shall command this law to be brought to the knowledge of all, since because of the report of Your Eminence this regulation was not only admitted but was also lauded.

For reasons which are quite obscure, the laws collected, out of chronological order, in the *Novellae* of Theodosius nearly all fall in the years 438 to 441, with a heavy concentration in 439, with one from 442, three from 443 and three from 444, and a solitary one from 447 (the apology to Valentinian with which this study begins). None are later than that. Of all of them, it is perhaps the latest of the three dating to 444 which most fully illuminates the complex process of decision making, and the carefully advertised sharing of responsibility, and of public credit, within it.[42] The law is addressed to Hermocrates, the current Praetorian Prefect of Oriens, with the usual personal address ("Hermocrates, dearest and most beloved parent"), with a copy going to Theodorus, Praetorian Prefect of Illyricum, and ends with the normal instruction for the posting of edicts. The subject matter is a complex set of regulations concerning taxation on land, and exemptions and remissions which had been obtained in the past, and might (contrary to the Emperor's purpose) be sought in the future. In this case the regulation is not explicitly stated to be a response to proposals by Hermocrates, though the Emperor does refer to current procedures, about which he can hardly have learned otherwise. But its distinctive feature is that it refers back first to the *dispositio* "of Antiochus of most honored memory," and then to innovations which may have occurred since his *administratio*. This seems clearly to be a refer-

42. *Nov. Th.* 26, Nov. 29, 444; trans. Pharr.

ence to the law on taxation and tax relief addressed on December 31, 430, to Antiochus, the then Praetorian Prefect of Oriens.[43] This extremely detailed document does not refer explicitly to any *suggestio* by Antiochus, though it is difficult to believe that its complex provisions were not in fact a response to proposals submitted. It is notable for its reference to regulations which had been in effect "from the beginning of the rule of my father Arcadius of divine memory" and those "under my grandfather of celebrated memory," Theodosius I. (As always, therefore, the inclusion of Valentinian in the heading is a pure formality.) The effect is that the rules promulgated by Theodosius in 444 relate to a sequence of administrative provisions stretching back, over three separate stages, for at least half a century. But there is also a more immediate process of response. No *suggestio* by Hermocrates himself is mentioned, but considerable attention is paid by the Emperor, in setting out his lengthy and detailed law, to the content of a *suggestio* submitted by the "*vir illustris* and *consularis,* Florentius," the same man whom we have already encountered, both at the Council of Chalcedon and as Praetorian Prefect. He had been Praetorian Prefect of Oriens in both 428–29 and 438–39, and his *suggestio* might have been presented during either tenure, though more probably the more recent one.[44] Taken as whole, the law illustrates the complexity of different statuses of land, the variety of forms in which tax liability could potentially be discharged, the way in which a sort of dialogue stretching over decades between successive Prefects and the Emperor might shape the relevant rules—and the extra complexity added by exemptions granted by the Emperor as a favor. On the one hand it was only just that an exemption, *if* properly obtained, should retain its validity (or, as here, that necessity should be pleaded if it could not be). On the other, we frequently find the Emperor, as here, trying to limit in advance the effect of favors apparently granted by himself, and often in fact secured from officials without his knowledge or approval. If the theological issues in which the Emperor became embroiled seem complex, they were no less so than those of liability and exemption in the civil sphere (or of rights and status among Imperial military or civilian employees), over both of which he conducted a continuing dialogue with his senior officials. It will be sufficient to quote some extracts from Theodosius's "law," or letter, of 444:

> Liberality is complete and full whereby previous munificence is
> strengthened, and then each person has confidence that he holds in

43. *CTh* XI.20.6.
44. *PLRE* II, Florentius 7.

the greatest security what he has obtained, if that which was specially
granted to each person is confirmed by a general provision. We call
to mind that the landholdings of many persons have been relieved of
the burden of tribute to some extent, by Our special grant of imperial
favor, and that afterwards a certain part of the amount that had been
granted was assessed upon them for taxes, because necessity demanded
it. Therefore, in order that what was derogated from Our liberality may
not seem to have been an indication of repentance rather than a sign
of the times, We are content with the collection of the sum that had
already been paid in accordance with the tax assessment and We free
them all in the future from the disquietude of such exaction. Thus the
exaction of delinquent taxes for past time is remitted for the landed
estates that have been relieved, and in the future no such tax assessment shall be feared . . .

However, this liberality of Ours diminishes nothing from the regulation of Antiochus, of Most August memory, whereby he levied a certain amount, in the name of the regular tax on the landholdings that
had been previously relieved. For that which has already become the
regular tax and must be paid in an annual payment We do not permit
to be remitted for the future or for the past. The opportunity shall be
left to no person hereafter to request tax inspectors for himself only,
unless, according to Our sanction which was issued in reply to the
report *(suggestio)* of the Illustrious Consular, Florentius, such inspectors should be requested by the common desire of the city or the
province . . .

But just as We have provided with great liberality for those persons
who freed their landholdings before the issuance of the law, in accordance with the report of the Illustrious Florentius, it is Our will that
they shall be freed from all fear forever, and thus those persons who
attempted to relieve their landholdings after the tenor of the aforesaid
constitution shall not gain any advantage. Wherefore, if any persons
should have obtained such benefit after the issuance of this constitution, they shall know that it is fruitless, and that no persons hereafter
shall be permitted, contrary to the divine imperial statutes, to relieve
their landholdings of tax payments or to demand commutation into
money or transfer of their tax payments. If they should impetrate such
request by surreptitious prayer to the Emperor, We sanction that such
a special grant of imperial favor shall not be valid . . .

It would indeed be instructive to analyze the very frequent references in
the legislation of Theodosius, as of other Emperors, to benefits, exemptions,
or favors obtained by individuals (the normal word for this activity is *im-
petrare*), often by approaching lower officials for a document in the Em-

peror's name.[45] But instead we will turn to the evidence—once again overwhelmingly from the last two decades of the reign—which illustrates how the Emperor's subjects, whether situated in distant provinces or addressing the center of power from close range, attributed to individual intermediaries the capacity to exercise decisive influence. It should be stressed again that the purpose is not to construct yet another narrative about who "really" was powerful at court. Opinion at court could change, as we have seen happening in the autumn of 431. Petitioners in distress, like the presbyter from Alexandria, Athanasius, and his brother, could identify correctly the two men who were best placed to help them, but still get no help. Or there could be rival and competing conceptions of where power lay. The purpose of the analysis is not that, but to use the perceptions and expectations of contemporaries as a way of casting some partial light on the nature of the Theodosian Empire as a political system.

3. IDENTIFYING POWERFUL INTERMEDIARIES

The examples discussed below, of how interested parties set about identifying and approaching intermediaries whom they believed to have influence, will fall into several distinct groups: from very early in the reign, and from a remote province, Synesius's efforts to exert influence in Constantinople; the remarkable series of letters in which Isidorus, a presbyter at Pelusium, sought to prevent the current *corrector* of the province, Augustamnica, from gaining further office; some material from the aftermath of Ephesus I, including the notorious provisions made by the church of Alexandria for offering inducements to personalities at court; Theodoret's attempts to exert influence, on behalf both of his city and of himself, in the late 440s; and finally the barrage of letters sent, or instigated, by Leo, as bishop of Rome, in the attempt to reverse the decisions of Ephesus II. The common feature of all of these is that they are directed to decisions which would be made in Constantinople, in most cases by the Emperor himself, or at least by high officials close to him. But in none of these cases does the interested party approach the Emperor directly (or if he—or in the last case also she—does so, approaches are also made to others). Such direct approaches, by individuals or communities or organizations, above all by sections of the Church,

---

45. For this important theme, not explored here, see now R. W. Mathisen, *"Adnotatio* and *Petitio:* The Emperor's Favor and Special Exceptions in the Early Byzantine Empire," in *La pétition à Byzance,* ed. D. Feissel and J. Gascou (2004), 23 ff.

were possible, and will be considered in the final section. But what is significant is firstly, as we have already seen, that people in quite remote areas believed themselves to know who were the individuals in Constantinople who exercised real power; and secondly the varied efforts which they made to put this belief to good effect.

The evidence of Synesius, as bishop of Ptolemais in Libya at the beginning of the second decade of the century, is distinctive as being effectively the only "voice" which we hear from that region, and as being the only surviving conceptualization of power at the center which belongs to the period when the Emperor was still a child, of no more than eleven. Whether we can grasp how decision making worked in this context remains to be seen. But it is noteworthy that nowhere in the relevant considerations offered by Synesius is there any reference to the Emperor's extreme youth (any more than could the reader of the "laws" in the *Codex Theodosianus* from these years detect anything distinctive). One factor which is confirmed by all the evidence is that at all periods decisions depended on the interplay of influences, and on arrival at something like consensus, among a quite large and loosely defined group at the center.

Synesius's conceptions of where power lay were centered, not unnaturally, on the long-serving Praetorian Prefect of Oriens of these years, Anthemius, known also as the builder of the still-standing walls of the capital, and in office, as a long series of "laws" in the *Codex* attest, from 405 to 414.[46] It is perhaps the address, described as a *katastasis*, which Synesius delivered in 410/11, under the governorship of Gennadius, and while Innocentius was Dux of the two Libyas, which most clearly catches the sense of a distant Imperial government in which Anthemius was the key element. The address urges someone to write to Constantinople, though who is not clear. The context is the sufferings of the province under barbarian raids:[47]

> But since God is aware of those who weep, it is essential that those also who hold the Roman sceptres should know. You therefore write who are in a position to bring word before the Emperor's council *(synedrion)* . . . Those of them are aware who take care for the public good in attesting to affairs, of whom I hear, and believe, that the great Anthemius has the first place. For he knows under what great difficulties, and above all in times of tyranny, we have been unhesitatingly loyal to the Emperor.

46. *PLRE* II, Anthemius 2.
47. *Katastasis*, ed. Terzaghi, pp. 285–86. For the military context, see pp. 59–62 above in chapter 2.

The reflections of the power of Anthemius in Synesius's letters are by their nature more precise and focused: for instance those addressed to a poet, Theotimus, first asking him to invoke the influence of a sophist, Troilus, with Anthemius, to secure a favorable outcome in a case, and then suggesting that the prospect of immortality through Theotimus's own poetry may influence Anthemius.[48] On another occasion he writes to Troilus himself, emphasizing his influence with Anthemius, and asking him to use it to complain of the appointment of a man from Berenice as governor of his home province, against the normal rule.[49] The unnamed person concerned is evidently the Andronicus about whom Synesius also wrote a long and indignant letter to someone called Anastasius, who is not known otherwise, but who was evidently influential in Constantinople. Synesius hopes for his help against Andronicus, and implies that Andronicus was claiming Anthemius's support for the condemnation of two men from the province.[50] Appointments to provincial governorships were made formally through *codicilli* issued by the Emperor. So, in seeking to expedite a change of governor, Synesius was working through a chain of connections (or hoped-for connections) which stretched through Theotimus, Troilus, and the Praetorian Prefect, Anthemius, to the Emperor himself. Moreover, in writing to Troilus, Synesius imagines his correspondent addressing Anthemius in person: "Were you not responsible for the sending out of that law which, following earlier precedents, laid many and harsh penalties on anyone who took on the governorship of their native province?"[51] He also goes on to imply that the actual responsibility for making acceptable appointments rested with Anthemius. As we have seen earlier, it was very common for "laws" issued in the form of a letter addressed to a particular high office-holder in fact to derive their content from a *suggestio* submitted by him. It may well be that appointments to posts such as governorships also depended on a wider consensus.

That at least is certainly the implication of the series of seven letters sent by Isidorus of Pelusium, and designed to thwart the alleged ambitions of the current governor of his native province, Augustamnica in northeast Egypt, a man from Cappadocia called Gigantius, whom Isidorus supposed to be seeking further promotion. Given the very abbreviated forms in which many of the very numerous letters of Isidorus are preserved, we cannot securely date these approaches, nor identify all of the recipients, each of whom appears sim-

48. Synesius, *Epp.* 47; 49.
49. *Epp.* 73.
50. *Epp.* 79.
51. *Epp.* 73.

ply with his single name, and no title. But it is possible that these letters date to 431/2, and several of the recipients are identifiable as major figures of that time: the man addressed as "Synesius" was perhaps a former Comes Sacrarum Largitionum; "Seleucus" was perhaps Fl. Taurus Seleucus Cyrus, in other words the famous Cyrus who was later Praetorian Prefect and Prefect of Constantinople simultaneously; "Florentius" was surely the very prominent Fl. Florentius who was twice Praetorian Prefect of Oriens; and "Rufinus" was perhaps the Praetorian Prefect of Oriens in 431/2.[52]

Given the uncertain state both of the texts of the letters themselves and of the identifications of the addressees, we need not follow in detail the abusive rhetoric which Isidorus deploys to argue against any further preferment for Gigantius, displaying a strong regional prejudice of a sort which appears relatively rarely in the highly integrated Theodosian empire. But, unless no genuine letters lie behind the brief versions which we have, they are clear testimony to a belief that provincial appointments made by the Emperor could be swayed by currents of favor or disfavor among high officials.

It is of course with the Nestorian controversy that we find ourselves for the first time confronted with a dense array both of persuasive communications directed to, as well as emanating from, the Emperor, and of considerations by interested parties as to how the results which they sought were to be achieved. Once again, though all would in the end rest on the Imperial will, persuasion spread more widely than that. In a letter to Juvenalius of Jerusalem, which dates from before the calling of the Council of Ephesus, and which also refers to his correspondence both with Nestorius himself and with Caelestinus of Rome, Cyril says that if persuasion of Nestorius fails, it will be necessary to write not only to "the Christ-loving and most pious Emperor" but also to "all those in authority" to advise them that consideration for a person must not be preferred to the demands of piety.[53] The reference is surely to letters addressed individually to holders of high office.

In the period of intensive communication between the initial meetings of the rival factions at Ephesus and the Emperor's ultimate decision to send Nestorius back to his original monastery near Antioch, and have a successor elected, we find innumerable letters to and from the Emperor, who corresponded both with the episcopal factions and with the officials sent suc-

---

52. In Migne's edition the letters are Isidorus, *Epp.* I. 483, to Synesius (*PLRE* II, Synesius 2); 484, to Seleucus (? Cyrus 7); 485, to Isidorus (? Fl. Anthemius Isidorus 9); 486, to Florentius (Florentius 7); 487, to Archontius (no post known); 489, to Rufinus (Rufinus 8); 490, to Catilianus (no post known).

53. *ACO* I.1.1, para. 15 (pp. 66–69).

cessively, if vainly, to bring things under control.[54] But we also find letters seeking support going, as we have seen, both to the "Empresses" (Pulcheria and Eudocia) and to the Senate in Constantinople.[55] Alternatively, the "Orientals" (Nestorius's supporters) wrote for support to high officials. For instance they addressed a despairing letter, complaining of the violence committed by Cyril's supporters, to "the Prefect" (either the Praetorian Prefect of Oriens or the Prefect of Constantinople) and "the Magister" (either the Magister Sacri Palatii or the Magister Officiorum). They beg to be allowed to escape from Ephesus and come to Constantinople to present their case (before the Emperor, though this is not explicitly stated).[56] They also wrote, about the same time, a letter which is headed (by the original compiler, or some editor) "to the Praepositus and to Scholasticius similarly."[57] Scholasticius was a *cubicularius* at the time, and evidently one who exercised some individual influence; for, as we saw earlier, it was to him that Nestorius addressed a long letter setting out his own doctrinal position, and expressing his willingness to retire again into monastic life.[58] In their letter the "Orientals" complain of the violence of "the Egyptians," and urgently request that their letter should be read out to the Emperor—a reminder that even letters which were addressed to the Emperor in person had to be handled by intermediaries. Indeed, as a rule, the Emperor, in a literal sense, neither read nor wrote letters. Both incoming letters and those drafted and ready to be sent out were read aloud to him, and outgoing ones were (always?) given a *subscriptio*—a personal greeting—in his own hand.[59] There is therefore only a difference of degree between letters directly to the Emperor and those sent to persons believed to have influence with him.

---

54. See for example the reference in *ACO* I.1.3, para. 83 (pp. 9–10), addressed to the Council, and referring to a report from Candidianus, Comes Sacrorum Domesticorum, on the irregularity of the proceedings; *ACO* I.1.7, para. 45 (pp. 67–68), Ioannes, Comes Sacrorum Largitionum, to Emperors.

55. See pp. 36 and 204 above.

56. *ACO* I.1.5, para. 161 (pp. 132–33).

57. *ACO* I.1.5, para. 162 (p. 133). The (apparently) two persons named may be one and the same. See p. 172.

58. See p. 174 above in chapter 5.

59. The formal characteristics (or "diplomatics") of Imperial letters in this period would require further study, not attempted here. But note, as examples of elements explicitly stated to have been added in the Emperor's own hand, various cases attested in the *Collectio Avellana* (*CSEL* XXXV): no. 3 (Valentinian II, Theodosius I, Arcadius, 386): "ET ALIA MANU PRINCIPIS 'Divinitus te servet per multos annos, parens karissime atque amantissime;'" no. 11 (Valentinian I, Valens, Gratian): "ET MANU IMPERATORIS 'Vale Ampeli karissime atque amantissime,'" and other examples.

In the period after the Council of Ephesus, and even after the deposition of Nestorius and the election of Maximianus as his successor, Theodosius continued to make very determined efforts to achieve reconciliation. Of many accounts of the steps taken in 432, perhaps the most vivid is a letter from Cyril to Acacius of Melitene. As Cyril records, the Emperor had summoned Maximianus and other bishops to consult with him, had accepted their view that there could not be peace in the Church without agreement on doctrine, and had send the Tribunus and Notarius, Aristolaus, to bring this about.[60] This same letter was one of a series of doctrinal writings which Cyril subsequently requested Eulogius, a priest from Alexandria currently in Constantinople, to give to the Praepositus Sacri Cubiculi:[61]

> Present to the most magnificent Praepositus the two books sent by
> me, one against the blasphemies of Nestorius, the other containing
> the proceedings at the Council taken against Nestorius and those who
> follow his views, and the replies made by me to those writing against
> the Kephalaia . . .

That was the intellectually serious, doctrinally committed side to the dispute, and it would be absolutely misleading to see this as a mere cover for an ecclesiastical power struggle. We may recall the copy of Ambrose's *De Incarnatione* which Martin of Milan sent to Theodosius,[62] or Cyril's later reference to his exposition of Nicene doctrines, which was taken, bound in leather, to Constantinople by Maximinus, a presbyter from Antioch, and presented to the Emperor and to "the most pious mistresses" (Pulcheria and Eudocia).[63]

But, as the "Orientals" complained repeatedly, other less elevated factors were certainly at work, and, as so often, we owe our knowledge of them to the *Tragoedia* of Irenaeus.[64] It will presumably have been for rhetorical effect that at the end of his narrative, stretching to 436, Irenaeus seems to have turned back to lay before his readers two uniquely detailed documents revealing the scandalous means by which Cyril, early in 432 as it seems, had exercised influence at court. The first is a letter from Epiphanius, an Archidiaconus and Syncellus at Alexandria, to Maximianus of Constantinople, urging him to greater efforts, and detailing the steps being taken

---

60. Cyril, *Epp.* 40 (35) = *ACO* I.1.4, para. 128 (pp. 20–31). For the Emperor's intervention, sections 2–3 (p. 21).
61. Cyril, *Epp.* 44 (37) = *ACO* I.1.4, para. 132 (pp. 35–37).
62. P. 36 above.
63. Cyril, *Epp.* 70 (53).
64. See pp. 170–71 above, in chapter 5.

currently by Cyril. The second is the list of gifts sent to individuals. It will
be sufficient to quote two paragraphs from Epiphanius's letter; originally
in Greek, and quoted by Irenaeus in Greek, but reproduced by Rusticus in
Latin translation:[65]

> Now, therefore, my most holy lord, direct all your zeal to this cause.
> For a letter has been written by my lord, your brother, both to the most
> reverend servant of God, the lady Pulcheria, to Paul the Praepositus,
> to Romanus the Cubicularius, to lady Marcella the Cubicularia, and to
> lady Droseria, and worthy blessings *(benedictiones,* or gifts) have been
> dispatched to them. And to him who is against the church, to Chryseros,
> the Praepositus, the most magnificent Aristolaus has been prepared to
> write about some things which your messenger ought to obtain; and
> to him himself worthy blessings indeed have been sent. Moreover, my
> lord, your most holy brother, also wrote to lord Scholasticius and to the
> most magnificent Artabas, so that they should meet with and persuade
> Chryseros to desist at last from his assault on the church; and to them
> truly worthy blessings have been dispatched.
>
> Hasten, therefore, you also, most holy one, to beg the servant of
> God, lady Pulcheria Augusta, so that she pay heed to Christ our Lord,
> for I think that now there is not sufficient care of your most holy
> brother Cyril, and so that you ask all who are in the palace and (furnish)
> whatever is lacking to their avarice, although there are not lacking dif-
> ferent blessings for them also, so that they write to Ioannes (of Antioch)
> chidingly in order that not even the memory of that impious one may
> exist; and indeed let a letter be written to the most magnificent Aristo-
> laus so that he may swiftly urge him on. And ask lady Olympias that
> she also should help us and that she also ask Marcella and Droseria,
> because they heed her patiently enough. For there is eagerness among
> some of the "Easterners" to receive Nestorius.

The attached schedule of gifts in kind can not be explored here in detail.[66]
It will be sufficient to list the names and functions of those for whom gifts
had been prepared, with some examples of the roles envisaged for them:
Marcella, the Cubicularia, "so that she may persuade the Augusta by be-
seeching her;" Droseria, another Cubicularia, to help Marcella; Chryseros,
Praepositus, to dissuade him from opposition; Claudianus, function unknown, and his *domesticus,* Solomon; Heleniana, wife of the Praetorian Prefect, so that she might persuade her husband to be helpful; and his (her?)
assessor Florentius; then a series of Cubicularii—Romanus, Domninus (the

65. *ACO* I.4, para. 293 (pp. 222–24); trans. J. I. MacEnerney in *St. Cyril of Alexandria, Letters 51–110* (1987), pp. 188 ff., on pp. 190–91, with corrections.
    66. *ACO* I.4, para. 294 (pp. 224–25).

man mentioned in the case about taxation at Mylasa five years earlier),[67] Scholasticius, mentioned several times already, and his *domesticus* Theodorus. Finally, there came three high officials: "the most magnificent Artabas," whose post is not indicated; an unnamed Magister (Officiorum?); and the Quaestor (Sacri Palatii) and his *domesticus* Ablabius.

Both documents are rightly seen as scandalous, and were quite certainly deployed by Irenaeus precisely for that reason. But, as so many other contemporary documents also do, they illustrate how complex, indirect, and widespread were the channels of influence at court. The Court, and the central group of officials and advisers, whether constituted as a formal Consistorium or not, formed policy and took decisions in the context of a wider climate of opinion, unpredictably vulnerable to pressures from outside.

Much the same is true even of the process, first, of obtaining, and then of securing the actual issuing of, an Imperial letter *(sacra)*. As noted earlier, persuasion and Imperial pressure did lead Ioannes of Antioch, over the years 432/3, to accept a formula of reconciliation with Cyril. That left those bishops in Oriens who were still loyal to Nestorius's teaching acutely exposed, and under pressure to follow him. The politics of that situation, and the beliefs of local bishops about machinations and countermachinations at court, are nowhere better revealed than in the letter which Meletius, bishop of Mopsuestia, sent to Maximinus of Anazarbus, the metropolis of Cilicia II. Once again, we owe it, in Rusticus's Latin translation, to Irenaeus.[68] He reports that an agent of Ioannes at Constantinople had deployed bribery to secure a *sacra* ordering that dissident bishops must be in communion with Ioannes or leave. However, Dometianus, the current Quaestor (Sacri Palatii), had written to bishop Helladius (of Tarsus, the metropolis of Cilicia I) to say that he was holding back the *sacra* to allow time for reconciliation. But all this was a charade *(scaenica simulatio)* in consideration of Ioannes' bribes. However, an evidently new governor *(iudex)* had arrived from Constantinople, and had confirmed that a *sacra* with this content had been prepared, but that Taurus, the Praefectus (Praetorian Prefect of Oriens), had prevented it being issued, going in to see the Emperor, and expostulating that there would be uproar in the cities if the *sacra* were put into effect, and that Cilicia would join Thrace in ceasing to provide tribute. Meanwhile, Dometianus had written to Helladius, claiming for himself the credit for holding back the *sacra*. . . . We need not follow the details further. There were many different actors, of different statuses and functions, who might intervene either

67. Pp. 21–22 above.
68. *ACO* I.4, para. 212 (p. 155).

in the formation of the Imperial will or in its being put into effect. No contemporary, and no modern scholar, could be in a position to grasp which intermediary was really exercising effective influence at any one moment.

That did not prevent contemporaries, when urgent necessity arose, from trying all the channels of influence which they could. The clearest case of such an attempt, or rather repeated attempts, is provided by Theodoret, sending off a whole series of letters from his modest provincial see of Cyrrhus in 448–49. They were all, in the short term, in vain. He was first, in 448, ordered not to leave Cyrrhus, then was not allowed to attend the Second Council of Ephesus in 449, and was then deposed by the Council as a follower of Nestorius. It was only in Marcian's reign—and at the price of finally anathematizing Nestorius—that he would be restored, against considerable opposition at Chalcedon.

The letters of 448 still represent extraordinary testimony to the perceived openness of the ruling elite in Constantinople, and to the conviction that it was possible to bring about change through the medium of the persuasion of individuals who belonged to that elite. As noted earlier, we should not take for granted the mere fact that Theodoret could identify so many potentially influential individuals in the capital.[69]

We will leave out of account in this context Theodoret's letters of 446/7 about the tax liability of Cyrrhus, and about accusations brought by a bishop, Athanasius of Perrha, while noting that the addressees include Constantinus, the Praetorian Prefect of Oriens, Pulcheria, and two *patricii*, Senator and Anatolius.[70] But his most intensive correspondence with the perceived holders of powers and influence begins in the spring of 448, with the news, which first reaches him indirectly, that the Emperor has issued an order *(hypomnēstikon)*, reputedly in his own hand, ordering Theodoret not to leave Cyrrhus.

In the letter which he now addressed once again to Anatolius, currently *patricius,* Theodoret refers to an earlier letter of his to Anatolius, in which he recorded that the staff of the Comes, Rufus, had shown him a copy of the Imperial order. Subsequently, Rufus had sent an official to him to obtain his written acknowledgement of the order.[71] In the current letter he complains bitterly about the injustice, as he does also in writing to a Praefectus in Con-

69. Pp. 198–200 above.

70. Theodoret, *Epp.* XVII, to Dionysius, Comes Orientalis (*PLRE* II, Dionysius 6); II. 47, to Proclus, bishop of Constantinople; II. 42 to Constantinus, *eparchos* = Praefectus (Constantinus 22); II. 43, to Pulcheria Augusta; II. 44, to Senator, *patricius* (Fl. Senator 4); II. 45, to Anatolius, *patricius* (Fl. Anatolius 10).

71. Theodoret, *Epp.* II. 79.

stantinople, Eutrechius (probably Prefect of the City), and again to Anatolius, to Nomus (the Magister Officiorum of 443–46, and consul in 445), to Taurus and Florentius, both *patricii*, and to Lupicinus, Magister (Officiorum).[72]

It seems to have been later in 448, in the autumn, that Domnus of Antioch sent a delegation of bishops to the capital to defend Theodoret. This step is recorded in a further letter of Theodoret's to Anatolius,[73] and this was accompanied by another to Senator, others to two Prefects of Oriens, namely Antiochus, who had just retired, and Protogenes, and another to Nomus.[74] It is surely significant that this last letter complains of the lack of reply to two or three previous letters. From a Comes named Sporacius, however, he did receive a letter, which indicated that there was support for him in Constantinople.[75] Several other letters to office-holders were sent at about the same time.[76] Not all the details need be pursued, for the pattern is clear. Once again, what is perceived as important is status, or official rank, rather than current occupation of office. Once again too, a quite wide range of individuals is conceived of as exercising influence. But if they did lend Theodoret the support for which he asked, it was in vain. There was no change in the order confining him to Cyrrhus, and the Emperor's disapproval of him continued.

Indeed, in the following year Theodosius's partisanship became even more evident. Flavianus, the bishop of Constantinople, was forced to send the Emperor a handwritten statement of his doctrines, with anathema on Nestorius,[77] and, when the Second Council of Ephesus was called, Dioscorus of Alexandria was given the presidency, and Theodoret was specifically forbidden to attend, unless the Council, once assembled, voted that he should.[78] It not only did not do so, but voted his deposition, along with that of other bishops. That decision gave rise to the latest recorded letters of Theodoret to high officials; once again the first went to the *patricius*, Anatolius. As we saw earlier, he complains of the affront to the basic legal principle that the accused should be present, and able to reply to charges against him. Hence the procedure had been unjust: "For, with the Imperial law confining me at

72. Theodoret, *Epp.* II. 80, to Eutrechius (*PLRE* II, Eutrechius); 111, to Anatolius (see n. 70); 81, to Nomus (Nomus 1); 88, to Taurus (Fl. Taurus 4); 89, to Florentius (Fl. Florentius 7); 81, to Lupicinus (Lupicinus 2).

73. *Epp.* II. 92.

74. *Epp.* II. 93, to Senator (see n. 70); 94, to Protogenes; II. 95, to Antiochus (Antiochus 10); III. 96, to Nomus (n. 72).

75. *Epp.* III. 97 (Fl. Sporacius 3).

76. *Epp.* III. 98–99, 103.

77. *ACO* II.1.1, Epist. H, 1 (pp. 35–36).

78. *ACO* II.1.1, para. 24 (pp. 68–69). Trans. in Coleman-Norton, no. 449.

home, and preventing me from crossing the borders of the city of which I am the shepherd, they set up the Council against me, and condemned some-one who was thirty-five stages distant."[79]

Theodoret's first objective was to secure permission to be heard by a Council called in the West by Leo of Rome, and two letters to Roman clergy (one of whom, unknown to him, had died) carried that plea, as did the let-ter to Anatolius himself. Failing that, he sought permission, like Nestorius, to retire to a monastery. Later, he continued, in another letter to Anatolius, to defend his own orthodoxy, and to recommend that of Leo.

As we will see, Leo himself, in 449 and 450, was directing a stream of persuasion from Rome to Constantinople. But, though he deployed very powerful intermediaries, including the members of the western Imperial family, he did not concern himself with the possible influence of high officials in Constantinople, but pressed his case, and had it pressed by others, directly to Pulcheria and above all to Theodosius in person. Though he was no more successful than Theodoret, in spite of his much greater standing, it is time finally to turn to persuasion aimed at the Emperor in person. As will be seen, there is every reason to think that policy did depend ultimately on his at-titudes and beliefs.[80]

4. APPROACHING THE EMPEROR

When, on November 19, 430, Theodosius took the momentous step of sum-moning the first Council of Ephesus, which led to a secure dominance of a "one-nature" Christology in his own reign, and to multiple doctrinal divi-sions ever after, he was still only twenty-nine, and had already reigned as sole Augustus in the Greek East for over twenty-two years. So when in Jan-uary of 438 he prefaced a long series of measures against Jews, Samaritans, pagans, and various groups of heretics with a reference both to the religious duties of his office and to the length of his own life, we may well under-stand that, looking back, his role did indeed already seem both heavy and prolonged:[81]

> Among the other anxieties which Our love for the State has imposed
> upon Us for Our ever watchful consideration, We perceive that an

79. Theodoret, *Epp.* III. 119. See p. 162 above.
80. It would have been much to my benefit if I had read earlier Susan Wessel's invaluable paper, "The Ecclesiastical Policy of Theodosius II," *Annuarium Historiae Conciliorum* 33 (2001): 285 ff. Our two approaches are however entirely compatible.
81. *Nov. Th.* 3, trans. Pharr; cf. pp. 120–21 above.

especial responsibility of Our Imperial Majesty is the pursuit of the true religion. If We shall be able to hold fast to the worship of this true religion, We shall open the way to prosperity in human undertakings. This We have learned by the experience of Our long life, and by the decision of Our pious mind We decree that the ceremonies of sanctity shall be established by a law of perpetual duration, even to posterity.

As to the burdens, or occasions for decision, which fell to Theodosius personally in the two decades which would remain of his life after the summoning of the Council, we are uniquely well informed, and in far more detail, in many respects at least, than for any previous Emperor. If nothing else, the commitment to the establishment of correct Christian belief which he shared with the profoundly divided bishops and monks of his Empire, and the responsibility which he felt as Emperor for the enforcement of correct belief, generated, as between himself and the Church, an unprecedented traffic of written and oral persuasion, and of self-justification and command, preserved for us above all by the *Acta* of the Councils. We have seen already many specimens of the rhetoric of persuasive communication in which the Emperor was involved, in secular contexts as well as ecclesiastical ones, and will encounter a few final examples before the conclusion of this study.

But before returning to the richly documented last two decades of the reign, some consideration needs to be given to the first two, and above all to the initial decade, after his father's early death left him, at age seven, as sole Augustus in Constantinople. For this period, a few broad generalizations will be all that is necessary, or possible, as regards the analysis of how the Imperial government worked at the center. Firstly, the functional separation of Latin West and Greek East is already present, and on occasion is explicitly acknowledged.[82] Whatever it is that we are analyzing, it is a system established in Constantinople. Secondly, the series of Imperial "laws," issued almost invariably in the form of letters addressed to high officials, the Praetorian Prefects above all, continues with no apparent break. Nothing would betray to the reader who surveyed, for example, the laws of 408–17 that the nominal author was aged between seven and sixteen. More significant still, when Synesius supplies the Dux Libyarum with material for two *anaphorai (suggestiones)* to be sent to the Emperor, there is no hint of their intended addressee's age.[83] Whether or not the *anaphorai* requested were ever sent, or answered, Synesius could assume that at Constantinople there was a system for receiving them.

---

82. See *CTh* VII.16.2, of Apr. 24, 410, quoted on pp. 52–53 above.
83. See pp. 60–62 above.

Thirdly, though, as we have seen above, the direct evidence for *suggestiones* submitted by officials is (Synesius's reference apart) very sparse for the early years, there is no reason to assume that it was not functioning.[84] That is extremely relevant, for it is quite clear from the much better-attested later period that a significant proportion of the content of Imperial legislation was derived from that of the *suggestiones* submitted. Part, therefore, of the central legislative function consisted in the digestion and reformulation of proposals put forward by individual officials.

Fourthly, the abundant evidence from the last two decades makes quite clear that decisions both were, as a matter of observable fact, arrived at by consensus, or competitive influence, among a quite extensive group of officials, and could even be advertised publicly as doing so. If a formal public statement as to the role of the Praepositus Sacri Cubiculi, or the lower-ranking *cubicularii* (or *cubiculariae*), was hardly to be expected, their influence was in reality known to all.

Fifthly, the testimony of Synesius, writing in Cyrene at the beginning of the reign, is highly significant also in stressing the known fact of the importance and influence of Anthemius, the Praetorian Prefect of Oriens for the crucial period of transition, 405–14, who was also responsible for constructing the walls of Constantinople, destined to play a vital role for another thousand years. Looking back from later in the reign, the Church historian Socrates, our most important contemporary narrative source, confirms the fact of Anthemius's overall influence, his role in the construction of the walls, and his preparedness to take advice, in particular from the rhetor or sophist Troilus, whom Synesius mentions also.[85]

Given what is said above about *suggestiones* it is only an apparent paradox that the vast bulk of our evidence for Anthemius's role comes not from orders issued *by* him, but from Imperial laws addressed *to* him—to be precise forty in the period 408–414. For, firstly, many of these may well have been prompted and shaped by *suggestiones* from himself, and secondly it would not be misleading to allow for his influence on the formulation of laws whether they were to be addressed to himself or not.

Finally, all—or nearly all—our sources, whether contemporary or not, agree on the influence exerted by Theodosius's elder sister, Pulcheria, known for her rigid piety and resolute virginity (at least until her acceptance of Marcian, as husband and Emperor, in 450, and very possibly after

---

84. Pp. 207–9 above.
85. Socrates, *HE* VII.1; for Synesius's reference, p. 216 above.

that also).[86] The partial exception is Theodoret, who manages to bring his *Ecclesiastical History* to its conclusion in 428 without ever mentioning her by name, though he does stress the piety both of Theodosius and of his sisters.[87] But in reality he was of course well aware of her importance, since he was one of the group of "Orientals" at Ephesus in 431, and must at least have been aware of the appeal which they sent to the "Empresses" from there.[88] Much later, in 446/7, he was to write to Pulcheria from Cyrrhus to ask for her help over local problems: "Since you adorn the kingship *(basileia)* with piety, and illuminate the purple with faith, we have confidence in this missive, and do not regard our own insignificance; for you allot the appropriate respect to the sacerdotal office."[89] But that letter, in its open recognition of Pulcheria's public status, precisely underlines the contrast between the first two decades and the last two. Allowing for the fact that Pulcheria herself had been only nine when Arcadius died, we can accept that, both as an adolescent and later, she exerted a powerful influence on the conspicuous piety which marked the Court. But we can add no detail,[90] and encounter her (in the contemporary documents) first, obliquely, in Cyril of Alexandria's *Prosphōnētikos Logos* of 430, and Theodosius's sharp reproof to Cyril for sending such a thing to his sister and his wife, and thereby stirring up doctrinal divisions.[91]

In short, therefore, the overall pattern of the evidence makes it perfectly possible to envisage, at least in broad terms, how a collective system involving provincial civil and military officials, high officials at Court, the Praetorian Prefects above all, and household staff, could have "carried" a juvenile Emperor as symbolic ruler until such time as he attained a degree of adult authority, and might decide for himself between competing influences and pressures.

That is not to say that Theodosius's rule ever developed into an individual autocracy. All that is said above about the diffusion of power, influence, and responsibility (and of the appropriate recipients of persuasion, and bribes) still applied in the period from 430 until the Emperor's death—and indeed

86. For the theme of Pulcheria's influence, as reflected in contemporary sources, see, e.g., Philostorgius, *HE* XI.6, XII.7; Sozomenus, *HE* IX.1.1–12, 2.7–18, 3.1–3.

87. Theodoret, *HE* V.36.

88. *ACO* I.1.5, para. 160 (pp. 131–32).

89. Theodoret, *Epp.* II. 43. Also quoted on p. 148 above.

90. I omit to analyze here stories in later sources relating to a breach between Theodosius and Pulcheria towards the end of his reign, excellently treated in Holum, *Theodosian Empresses*, 191–92.

91. See p. 153 above.

almost all the evidence for it derives from these years. Equally, in both the first and the second halves of the reign, official reports, episcopal letters, and petitions from individuals were all directed formally to the Emperor as individual ruler (and, even more formally, to both current Emperors, West and East). Even with such written communications, as we have seen, it could not be taken for granted that there would not be intervention from among the members of the court, or that every document addressed to him would come to be read before him.

Since even Synesius, in the earliest years of the reign, writes as if a *suggestio* directed to the Emperor would really receive his attention, there is no way of tracing the steps by which, with the passage of time, Theodosius came to be able to exert an independent power of decision. But this stage has surely been reached when we read the letter of Atticus, bishop of Constantinople, who died in 425, to Cyril of Alexandria, setting out the multiple popular and ecclesiastical pressures on him to restore the name of John Chrysostom to the church diptychs. Such a step was acutely controversial (and Cyril in reply firmly upbraids him for it), but Atticus feared major popular disorders. So, as he reports, he had approached "the most pious Emperor," and laid before him the question of peace and public order; the Emperor had replied that there would be no harm if for the sake of tranquility the name were restored.[92]

From the later 420s onwards, as a mass of evidence illustrates, a constant stream of issues, both secular and ecclesiastical, was directed to Theodosius. Certain very specific reports, to which we will come finally, show the Emperor in dialogue with interested parties. But even with written exchanges, attested with particular intensity and frequency before, during, and after the two Councils of Ephesus, there is no good reason to deny that the Imperial response represented his personal will. For instance, a whole series of contested "local histories," in which aggrieved or interested parties brought matters to the Emperor's attention, are revealed by the *Acta* of the Councils, and other contemporary sources: the attempt to declare Theodore of Mopsuestia, who had died in 428, anathematized;[93] the disputed election of Bassianus as bishop of Ephesus in the 440s;[94] the case of Sophronius, whose wife was taken from him by Macarius, a leading citizen *(politeuomenos)* of Alexandria.[95] In these and other cases Imperial intervention was sought, and in the latter two obtained.

92. Cyril, *Epp.* 75, 76; trans. McEnerney.
93. Cyril, *Epp.* 77; trans. McEnerney.
94. *ACO* II.1.3, *Actio* XII (pp. 407–12).
95. *ACO* II.1.2, para. 64 (pp. 23–24 [219–20]).

We need not accumulate instances, though all of these would deserve study. But we may select a few, of particular centrality, beginning with the petition sent to Theodosius (and in principle Valentinian) by Ioannes of Antioch in about 435. Like so much of our evidence for the concrete workings, and the rhetoric, of Church-State relations, it is preserved for us, through Rusticus's Latin translation, in the *Tragoedia* of Irenaeus:[96]

> To our most pious and Christ-loving Emperors, Flavius Theodosius
> and Flavius Valentinianus, the triumphators, victors, Augusti, a request
> and petition from Ioannes, bishop of the church of God at Antioch.
> Faith in God has raised the empire of the house of your piety and led
> it forward to the present glory, faith by which you wish that the most
> holy and catholic Church should continually be increased, and are eager
> that all those tares which arise in it should be cut off.

Ioannes goes on to recall that various bishops, including Meletius of Mopsuestia, had been deposed, and that he, Ioannes, had seen to the election of a new bishop in his place. He then continues, as we saw earlier, to complain that Meletius, though deposed, has refused to leave the territory of his see, and he asks for orders to be given to the Magister Militiae to see to Meletius's forcible removal.

Meletius was among those finally exiled, probably in 436; he was duly dispatched to Melitene in the province of Armenia, and died there.[97]

As a counterpart to this Latin version of an effective episcopal petition originally written in Greek (and concluding with the same emphasis on the conditionality of future prayers as in other petitions), we may take the Greek translation of an Imperial *hypomnēstikon*, originally written in Latin, by which Theodosius in October 448 ordered Damascius, a Tribunus and Notarius Praetorianus, to arrange for the hearing of charges against Ibas of Edessa, Ioannes of Theodosiopolis, and Daniel of Carrhae.[98]

> Being aware of the disposition of your excellence, and knowing how
> great is your eagerness to serve God and Our piety, we have deter-
> mined that you should depart along with Uranius, the most pious
> bishop of the city of the Himerians, to the regions of Oriens, and with
> the assistance of the officials in the locality should make ready Ibas, the
> most pious bishop of the city of the Edessenes, and Daniel, the most
> pious bishop <of the city of the Carrheni, and Ioannes the most pious
> bishop> of Theodosiopolis to depart to the province of the Phoenicians,
> and that there there should be examined the matters raised . . .

96. *ACO* I.4, para. 265 (p. 196).
97. See pp. 163–64 above in chapter 4.
98. *ACO* II.1.3, para. 27 (p. 19 [378]).

As regards the Emperor's personal responsibility for such an order, Theodoret believed that the *hypomnēstikon* ordering his confinement to Cyrrhus, issued earlier in the same year, had been written in Theodosius's own hand.[99] That is not impossible, though it is more likely that, like other Imperial communications, it did carry a subscription, or final greeting-formula, written by Theodosius in person.

What these examples of the written mechanics of the evocation and activation of Imperial action show is that there were procedures, both indirect and direct, and that it was possible—if entirely unpredictable in each case—for persuasion directed to the Emperor to secure effective responses. Yet equally, the most apparently powerful of actors, bringing continued pressure, might be entirely unsuccessful. Thus, in the most conspicuous case of all, Leo of Rome, using, through letters, every rhetorical and political weapon at his disposal, had—for the time being—no effect at all on the setting-up, conduct, or aftermath of the Second Council of Ephesus in 449.

His correspondence with Flavianus of Constantinople and the archimandrite Eutyches had begun in the summer of 448. His first recorded letter to Theodosius was sent on February 18, 449, in reply to one from the Emperor, and referring to *libelli* sent to him (Leo) both by Eutyches and by his accuser, Eusebius of Dorylaeum.[100] On June 13, 449, he sent to Flavianus the "Tome" expressing the doctrines which two years later would provide the basis for the statement of faith adopted at Chalcedon, and simultaneously dispatched a letter to Theodosius appointing representatives to the Council. But he too, like everyone involved, also acted indirectly, in his case by writing on the same day to Pulcheria.[101] Writing to Theodosius, more than once, after the Council, he condemned the violence which had occurred, and demanded that a new Council be held in Italy.[102] But meanwhile both he and the deacon Hilarus, who had attended the Council, also wrote to Pulcheria.[103]

Perhaps the most striking demonstration of the combined deployment of persuasion, addressed, whether directly or through others, to the Emperor, and also simultaneously to Pulcheria, comes from the stratagem adopted by

---

99. Theodoret, *Epp.* II. 79: ὑπομνηστικὸν τῇ βασιλικῇ γεγραμμένον χειρί.

100. Leo, *Epp.* 24 = *ACO* II.4, para. 2 (pp. 3–4).

101. Leo, *Epp.* 28 = *ACO* II.2.1, para. 5 (pp. 24–33), the "Tome" addressed to Flavianus; *Epp.* 29 = para. 7 (pp. 9–10), to Theodosius; *Epp.* 30 = para. 8 (pp. 10–11), to Pulcheria.

102. Leo, *Epp.* 44 = *ACO* II.4, para. 18 (pp. 19–21); *Epp.* 54 = para. 9 (p. 11).

103. Leo, *Epp.* 45 = para. 23 (pp. 23–25), Leo to Pulcheria, Oct. 13, 449; *Epp.* 46 = para. 26 (pp. 27–28), Hilarus to Pulcheria.

Leo in late February 450. When the western Imperial family entered Rome on February 22, they were petitioned by Leo and other bishops in St. Peter's, for the holding of a Council in Italy. The support of the western Imperial Court was granted. As a result, there was a dense exchange of letters between Rome and Constantinople, which can be set out as a list:[104]

a. Valentinian to Theodosius

b. Galla Placidia to Theodosius

c. Licinia Eudoxia to Theodosius

d. Gallia Placidia to Pulcheria

e. Theodosius to Valentinian

f. Theodosius to Galla Placidia

g. Theodosius to Licinia Eudoxia

Galla Placidia's letter to Pulcheria, referred to much earlier, and partially quoted,[105] retains its significance as the only example from Classical antiquity of a letter from a woman to a woman on a major matter of public policy. That in this case alone no reply is recorded is understandable; for a further letter of Leo's to her, sent in March 450, implies that he knew from other letters of hers (not preserved) that their views were in agreement.[106] She could, however, hardly have said that in any letter to her fellow Empress. But she no longer had the influence over Theodosius with which contemporaries had earlier credited her. When Leo wrote again, to both Theodosius and Pulcheria, on July 16,[107] it would be, in one sense, too late. For the Emperor's fatal accident took place on July 28, when the letters will still have been en route. A new phase in ecclesiastical and doctrinal history could now begin. For, no matter how many, or how forceful, the competing streams of rhetorical persuasion, sometimes accompanied by concrete inducements, directed to the high officialdom, or to *cubicularii*, or to the Emperor's sister (or, earlier, to his wife, Eudocia, now settled in Jerusalem), in the end the Imperial system was a monarchy, and the Emperor, at least when once arrived at adulthood, could decide.

That was how it proved to be, as is shown above all by the evidence from the time of the First Council of Ephesus. Theodosius's plan had been to have

---

104. (a) Leo, *Epp.* 55; (b) 56; (c) 57; (d) 58; (e) 62; (f) 63; (g) 64.

105. Pp. 37–38 above.

106. Leo, *Epp.* 60 = *ACO* II.4, para. 28 (p. 29), Mar. 17, 450.

107. Leo, *Epp.* 69 = *ACO* II.4, para. 30 (pp. 30–31), to Theodosius; *Epp.* 70 = para. 29 (pp. 20–30), to Pulcheria.

the bishops decide the doctrinal issues at stake, with an Imperial emissary present to keep order, but not intervening. As such, the plan was a complete failure, and Isidore of Pelusium was surely right (if the brief letter preserved really is genuine) to tell the Emperor that he should be present in person.[108] In the end, as we have seen, selected emissaries from each side were summoned to Chalcedon, and there repeatedly argued their case (apparently, at least on some occasions, face to face).[109] We have also seen earlier how the "Orientals," in a phase of optimism, reported that the Emperor had shaken his purple robe, and taken a step back in shock, at the blasphemies attributed to the opposing side.[110] In another letter they claim that, at five separate meetings with the two sides, Theodosius had ordered Cyril's followers to renounce their doctrines.[111] In the end, of course, they were disappointed, and, as we also saw earlier, the "Orientals," Theodoret among them, felt a hostile movement of opinion among the Emperor's entourage, and suspected that bribery was at work (as it certainly was some months later).[112] Nonetheless, the crucial role was still played by the rhetoric of persuasion on the one side, and by the Emperor's personal commitment to Christian piety on the other. We see this best in the important episode which evidently took place not long after the deposition of Nestorius at Ephesus on June 22, 431, namely the interview between Theodosius and the famous archimandrite of a monastery in Constantinople, Dalmatius. The meeting is recorded in brief in a contemporary memorandum *(hypomnēstikon)* composed by some anti-Nestorian bishops in the capital, who claim that followers of Nestorius in Constantinople had been preventing news of events in Ephesus from getting through[113] (the claim, if true at all, cannot apply to official communications, for Theodosius had received a report from Candidianus by June 29, and then wrote in stern terms to the Cyrillian side refusing assent to their proceedings).[114] But at any rate the anti-Nestorian memorandum records that Dalmatius made the momentous gesture of emerging from his monastery for the first time in forty-eight years (thus, since the early years of Theodosius I), parading through the streets, accompanied by a large crowd, and being received by Theodosius in the palace. Afterwards, Dalmatius appeared before the crowd, and reported that he had agreed with the Emperor the terms of a new letter.

108. Isidore, *Epp.* I. 311.
109. Pp. 205–6 above.
110. P. 206 above.
111. *ACO* I.1.3, para. 97 (pp. 39–42).
112. Pp. 219–21 above.
113. *ACO* I.1.2, para. 66 (pp. 65–66).
114. *ACO* I.1.3, para. 83 (pp. 9–10).

Exactly which letter this was (if any of those attested), and whether it was actually sent, is not clear. What is important, first, is that this audience can be taken as representing the initial stage in Theodosius's step-by-step move away from outright condemnation of the actions of Cyril's followers to eventual deposition of Nestorius. But second, and most important, the fullest account—or dramatized reconstruction—of the exchanges between Emperor and monk is provided by Nestorius himself, writing his *Book of Heraclides* in exile two decades later. His recreation of the beginning of the audience is quoted in the archaic and biblical style of the translation by Driver and Hodgson:[115]

> And they took for them[selves] as organizer and chief, in order to overwhelm the Emperor with amazement, Dalmatius the archimandrite, who for many years had not gone forth from his monastery; and a multitude of monks surrounded him in the midst of the city, chanting the offices, in order that all the city might be assembled with them and proceed before the Emperor to be able to hinder his purpose. For they had prepared all these things in advance in order that there might not be any hindrance and they went in with [the chanting of] the office even to the Emperor.
>
> But when the Emperor saw Dalmatius, he shook his head and put up his hand as one who is in astonishment at the sight of a person; and he said: 'What is the cause which has constrained thee to break thine own pact? For we were coming unto thee, but now why has thou come unto us? And especially in the midst of the city! Thou, one that not even in thy monastery hast been seen outside thy cell nor usest to let thyself be seen of all men, has now made thyself as it were a spectacle both unto men and unto women. For why should there not have been many constraining causes which would have needed thy coming forth? . . . '
>
> Dalmatius says: 'Yea, Emperor, it was by no constraint such as this among these things that there was need of my coming forth. For this reason indeed God has not made me to know [aught of these difficulties], for he has settled them otherwise. But now God has commanded me, [even] me, to counsel thy Majesty, and I have been commanded to bear thee witness that thou transgressest against thyself in transgressing against the Council and perverting its judgement. Thou hast assembled the Council for judgement and it has judged; it knows how it has judged; it is responsible unto God.'

We need not believe that Nestorius, who at that time had been at Ephesus, could ever have known what his adversary had actually said. That is not important. What is important is that it was a representative of that element of

---

115. Nestorius, *Book of Heraclides* (D/H, pp. 272–73; Nau, p. 241).

Christian piety which was least under the control of either Church or State, the monks, who both did in fact confront the Emperor in person, and could be imagined later as having spoken to him as the emissary of God. Of course this encounter, recorded for us in a sixth-century Syriac translation, took place in Greek. His own officials still wrote, and spoke, to the Emperor in Latin. But it was in Greek that the mass of his subjects, and the Church, addressed their Roman Emperor, and pressed upon him conflicting interpretations of where his sense of his Imperial mission should lead him; and it was in Greek that his word was proclaimed to them.

The Acta of the Fifth-Century Councils: A Brief Guide for Historians

I. INTRODUCTION

No historian who approaches the reign of Theodosius II will take long to appreciate the enormous importance, first, of the three great Church Councils themselves. In theological terms, the two Councils of Ephesus represent the emphatic victory of the "one-nature" view, led by two successive bishops of Alexandria, Cyril and Dioscorus, over the "two-nature" view of Nestorius, briefly bishop of Constantinople (428–31) before his deposition. Chalcedon, summoned by Marcian a year after Theodosius's death, was to adopt a compromise formula, already proposed by Leo of Rome in his *Tome* (*Ep.* 28), addressed to Flavianus, bishop of Constantinople, in June 449—a compromise which was widely seen in the Greek East as a betrayal, and as an expression of heresy in itself.

To the historian, these Councils, at which, as a maximum, several hundred bishops met and expressed their views, almost all in Greek, represent vital evidence for social and religious history. But it is the availability, in manuscripts of various periods, from the sixth century to the High Middle Ages, written in Greek, Latin, Coptic, and Syriac, of *Acta* relating to these Councils which both provides exceptionally important material and poses very real practical and intellectual problems. If there already is in print a succinct guide to this material, the author has not found it. (Note now, however, the publication of *The Acts of the Council of Chalcedon*, translated with an introduction and notes by Richard Price and Michael Gaddis, *TTH* XLIV, Liverpool University Press, 2005.) So the intention of this appendix is to provide such a thing, glossing over immense complications in the interests of brevity and clarity. The discussion relates primarily to a peerless—but to the historian extremely difficult—work of scholarship, Eduard Schwartz's

Acta Conciliorum Oecumenicorum I–II, dealing with *Acta* in Greek and Latin; and secondly to the Syriac *Acta* of Ephesus II, edited by Johannes Flemming. A number of key points may be set out summarily:

1. All three Councils were conducted in Greek, with occasional contributions in Latin or Syriac (and at one point Coptic, and at another Persian) being translated into Greek.

2. What we designate by the term *Acta* includes long stretches of verbatim transcription of words spoken at sessions of the relevant Council, or of written attestations ("subscriptions") by each bishop in his own words and (in principle) in his own hand, of assent to agreed conclusions.

3. These records of proceedings are apparently verbatim; but the available texts do not incorporate, and are not accompanied by, any systematic information as to what systems of recording or stenography were employed. The proceedings at Chalcedon, however, provide evidence of heated debate as to how the recording of the proceedings at Ephesus II had been conducted. This evidence is discussed in appendix B. Overall, there is no reason not to see these records as the best evidence, however imperfect, which we have for the spoken Greek of (to varying degrees) educated men in the fifth century (and hence by far the best evidence, in both volume and character, for the spoken Greek of any period of antiquity).

4. In very many cases these formal, apparently verbatim, records include the citation before the relevant Council of earlier documents, some of which are themselves records of oral proceedings (thus for example the proceedings relating to the views of the archimandrite Eutyches in autumn 448 and spring 449 were read out at Ephesus II later in 449, and again at Chalcedon, and were then incorporated in the written *Acta* of both).

5. The documents read out at Councils and then incorporated in their written *Acta* were not, however, confined to records of previous proceedings. A considerable number of letters from and to Emperors and high-ranking officials, mainly in correspondence with bishops, and of letters between bishops, were also read out and incorporated. So also were substantial extracts from earlier theological writings.

6. It is thus a straightforward, if laborious, matter to extract from the texts which moderns label "the Acts of the Councils" those

elements which actually constitute what survives of the formal record of each Council, namely the written record of what was said at each session, with any documents (earlier proceedings, or letters, or extracts) which had been read out and then incorporated in the written record. These verbatim reports of proceedings are summarily surveyed separately, in appendix B.

7. There is no systematic evidence, in the case of any of these Councils, as to who was responsible for preserving and then disseminating copies of the proceedings. It is, however, clear from the evidence for the contemporary historiography of the Nestorian controversy that such records were widely available, even (for instance) to Nestorius in exile in Egypt (see chapter 5).

8. The manuscript texts which moderns call the "the Acts of the Councils," however, are not confined to such records of proceedings. Even those manuscripts which do include conciliar proceedings also include selections of other relevant contemporary documents, primarily letters and homilies of bishops, and letters from Emperors and officials. Some manuscripts contain only such selected Imperial and episcopal communications.

9. It seems evident from the character of these various manuscript assemblages of material that some at least go back to contemporary collections made for partisan purposes, and thus for use in current debates. With two exceptions, however (see below), there is no explicit evidence, either in the manuscript texts themselves or from external testimony, as to who the authors of these contemporary assemblages of material were, or precisely when they were made.

10. As stated earlier, the language of all three Councils was Greek, and spoken interventions in Latin, Coptic, or Syriac, or documents which were cited and written into the record but which were in Latin or Syriac, were translated into Greek, and recorded in Greek, usually described explicitly as a translation *(hermēneia)*, without the Latin or Syriac original being included (for one very significant exception, an official letter in Latin, see p. 138 above). One indignant verbal intervention by a papal delegate at Ephesus II is recorded in Latin, but in Greek transliteration *(ACO* II.1, para. 964, p. 191, see p. 103 above).

11. The primary body of evidence which the *Acta* offer is therefore contemporary texts in Greek of extremely important material,

the vast majority of which had originally been in Greek, but of which a minority represents contemporary Greek translations of material originally written or spoken in Latin.

12. Not surprisingly, the Councils, and the impassioned debates and exchanges which accompanied them, attracted immediate attention in the Latin West, and Latin translations appeared, both of the verbatim records of proceedings, and of documents included within them, and of associated documents. It should be noted that, as a result of the production of Latin versions of bodies of material which were also circulating in Greek, our information may (and does) include Latin versions—either contemporary or later (sixth-century)—of texts written originally in Latin, but which are themselves retranslations from Greek versions.

13. Once again, in most cases, our evidence for this process of contemporary translation into Latin, and of subsequent dissemination, is solely what is implicit in the Latin manuscripts themselves.

14. The one exception is the extremely important work, or works, by Marius Mercator (*ACO* I.5.1, pp. 5–215), written in the 430s to explicate and denounce contemporary heresies, and incorporating in Latin translation letters and treatises of Cyril, Nestorius, and others, and also including, for instance, a Latin translation of the sermons given in Constantinople by Nestorius on December 6–7, 430 (pp. 39–46), and of the proceedings of the "one-nature" side of the Council of Ephesus on July 22, 431 (pp. 85–116). This major Latin commentary on, and record of, contemporary theological disputes, in both West and East, occupies over two hundred pages in Schwartz's edition, of which much of the first, narrative, part, and all of the longer second part, consists of Latin translations of Greek theological texts. Whether the text as preserved derives from a single work, or from extracts from a series of related works, is not clear.

15. Equally, within the Greek world, the only named contemporary author who emerges, if indirectly, from the manuscripts of the *Acta* as edited is Irenaeus, who was present at Ephesus I on Nestorius's side, was exiled probably at the same time as he in 435/6, somehow subsequently evaded exile, and by 448 had been ordained bishop of Tyre, but was then deposed by order of Theodo-

sius. It was apparently after that (but possibly earlier) that he wrote his own history, under the title *Tragoedia*, of events from Ephesus I to 435 or 436, defending the Nestorian position and incorporating a large number of documents (see especially chapter 5). The *Tragoedia* is known essentially from the work called *Synodicum*, composed in Latin in Constantinople by the deacon Rusticus, in about A.D. 565. Rusticus produces very brief notes summarizing Irenaeus's narrative ("inquit"), but provides complete versions in Latin of a large number of letters which Irenaeus had quoted, of which the great majority will have been written originally in Greek (*ACO* I.4, pp. 25–245). Some of Irenaeus's material, however, consisted of letters between officials, which will originally have been in Latin. It is clear that the *Tragoedia* was written in Greek, and had quoted the letters, of both types, in Greek.

16. With these exceptions, the origins of the different manuscript collections, which overlap with each other, thereby producing on occasion alternative Greek texts of the same document, and sometimes variant Latin translations of documents written originally in Greek (themselves sometimes preserved and sometimes not), can only be deduced from their internal character and structure. No other contemporary "author" (or compiler) is identified within the texts, and no explicit dates or places for the relevant compilations are given. When there was an original contemporary compilation, it always remains possible that elements have subsequently been subtracted from or added to it.

17. The collections thus offer priceless evidence for fifth-century Greek, both written and spoken, and for the interplay between Greek and Latin, in both the fifth and the sixth centuries, in providing (a few) Greek translations of Latin texts, and a vast range of Latin translations of Greek texts, including retranslations into Latin of documents available in Greek, but originally written in Latin.

18. The essential point, for the historian approaching this material, is that Schwartz's work (whose various elements are tabulated below) is an edition of the separate manuscripts in the form in which they have come down to us. Where, as in *ACO* I.1.7, documents from minor collections repeat those in the primary MS, namely the Vaticana (*ACO* I.1.1–6), the redundant texts are

listed, but not printed. Cross-references are given, as also for Latin versions of Greek documents, but to manuscript and number, not to *ACO* volume and number. The volumes are equipped with immensely long and discursive introductions in what is often (it must be confessed) quite difficult Latin. In spite of many excellent and detailed indexes for Ephesus I in *ACO* I.1.8, and a chronological table (in the same volume, pp. 6–14), it should be clear that what the *Acta* offer is a vast range of raw material for the historian, which each has to reassemble and digest for him- or herself.

19. The *Acta* of Ephesus I therefore consist of several different elements. The primary element is represented by the contents of the Vatican MS (*ACO* I.1.1–6), all in Greek, comprising proceedings of Ephesus I, and associated documents, presumed to have been assembled by a contemporary, from both before the Council (from about 428 onwards) and after, up to 435, and in one case 448. *ACO* I.1.7 comprises other Greek MSS, mainly containing texts already represented in the Vatican MS, but one, Atheniensis, with an independent collection of documents (some of them also in the Vatican MS, but many not) and some records of proceedings. It is here alone that an official letter written in Latin is reproduced in the original Latin, with a Greek translation (*ACO* I.1.7, para. 81, pp. 119–20; for the text see p. 138 above).

20. All the remainder of the *Acta* of Ephesus I (*ACO* I. 2–5) consists of MS collections of material in Latin, of which the most significant elements have been described above: Rusticus's abbreviated version in Latin of Irenaeus's *Tragoedia* (I.4), and Marius Mercator's contemporary commentary and collection of material (I.5). This material is important in two different ways: (1) as representing Latin translations, made in the fifth or sixth centuries, of documents and records of proceedings which are also transmitted in Greek; and (2) as providing fifth- or sixth-century Latin versions of documents or records which are not preserved in Greek.

21. For Ephesus I we also possess two quite extensive MSS recounting events of the Council in Coptic, including translations of documents found in the Greek *Acta*. The narratives contain what seem clearly to be unhistorical elements, but may also contribute to the history of events. Probably composed already in the fifth

century, these texts are, at the least, further testimony to the diffusion of the Greek *Acta*, and to their translation into other languages (most obviously Latin and Syriac, see below) and their redeployment in their translated form. See W. Krantz, *Koptische Akten zum Ephesinischen Konzil von Jahre 431: Übersetzung und Untersuchungen, TU* XXVI (1904). No use has been made of these texts in this book, which is in no way to presume that they might not make a valid contribution to historical reconstruction.

22. The *Acta* for Ephesus II have a very different character, and derive from two quite distinct sources:

 (a) The MS written in A.D. 535 which preserves, in Syriac translation, a very similar collection of material to that in the Greek and Latin *Acta* relating to Ephesus I: Imperial letters, some known also in their original Greek, some not; the proceedings of the second and last session of Ephesus II, all concerned with the deposition of bishops deemed to have heretical views; and, quoted within these proceedings, three reports of proceedings conducted earlier in 449 in Edessa and directed against its bishop, Ibas.

 (b) From within the proceedings of Chalcedon in 451 (see below), verbatim records, both in the original Greek and in Latin translation, of the first session of Ephesus II. These records themselves incorporate earlier documents, written into the record, including both Theodosius's letter summoning the council, and the record of the successive stages, between autumn 448 and spring 449, of proceedings against Eutyches. The record of the first session of Chalcedon thus comprises α) words spoken at Chalcedon; β) words spoken at Ephesus II, two years earlier; γ) documents and records of proceedings belonging to 448–49 read out at Ephesus II and incorporated in its *Acta,* then to be reincorporated in those of Chalcedon.

23. The *Acta* of Chalcedon are of exceptional detail and historical interest, but, as records of proceedings, they are directly relevant for the reign of Theodosius II only insofar as these proceedings incorporated documents and reports of proceedings from before July 450 (e.g., quoted in sessions X and XI, the *Acta* of proceedings against Ibas in 449). As regards the Council itself, held between October 8 and 20, 451, the sequence of the successive sessions is tabulated below. But, as with the two earlier Councils,

the manuscript collections of material edited in the modern era consist not only of proceedings, but of assemblages of related letters of Emperors and bishops, including many dating back to the reign of Theodosius, even where these were not quoted in formal proceedings. The *Acta* (in this wider sense) of Chalcedon, as of Ephesus I, were also edited by Schwartz manuscript by manuscript, beginning with the primary Greek texts, and continuing to the Latin versions. Given their more indirect significance for the events of Theodosius's reign, the contents of these volumes will be tabulated relatively summarily below.

A complete list of those texts which represent (apparently) verbatim reports of proceedings from the reign of Theodosius, including both Ephesus I and II and the cases of Ibas and Eutyches, is set out separately in appendix B.

Given the complexity of the material, and the need for as much clarity as possible at each point, I have not sought to avoid redundancy, or overlap, as between the various discussions and tabulations appearing in these two appendixes, or in the main text.

II. ANALYTICAL LIST OF *ACTA*, AS IN SCHWARTZ, *ACO*

Note that it is essential to observe the correct numbering, with I indicating, in Schwartz's usage, the whole *Tomus* of eight *Volumina* containing the *Acta* (in the wider sense) of Ephesus I, and *Pars* indicating a numbered subdivision of a *Volumen*. Not all the *Volumina* have such subdivisions. So, for example, *ACO* I.1.1, para. 8, is a letter of Theodosius in Greek to Cyril of Alexandria, while I.2, para. 8, is a letter in Latin from Caelestinus of Rome to Theodosius. A similar precision is required as regards the separate *Volumina* of *Tomus* II, on Chalcedon.

A. First Council of Ephesus, A.D. 431

1. Manuscripts in Greek

I *(Tomus)*. 1 *(Volumen)*

Partes 1–6. Greek. *Collectio Vaticana* (MS of 13th century). Evidently from contemporary private collections by interested parties, on the side of Cyril of Alexandria.

1. *(Pars)* Paras. 1–32

2. 33–80

3. 81–119

4. 120–139

5. 140–164

6. 165–172

Note especially a) Collection of Letters, from Emperors (Theodosius II and Valentinianus III), Cyril of Alexandria, Nestorius of Constantinople, Caelestinus of Rome, et al. (paras. 1–32). The letters cover both Ephesus itself and events before it, and its aftermath up to A.D. 435, and in one case 448 (paras. 138–39, see pp. 184–89 in chapter 5). b) List of bishops at Ephesus I, as on 22 June, 431 (para. 33), and record of proceedings on that day (paras. 34–62).

It should be noted that the collection of associated documents is not in chronological order, and that the reports of proceedings incorporated in this MS do not cover all the known sessions (cf. appendix B).

7. *(Pars)* Greek. *Collectio Seguierana* (MS of 12th century), *Collectio Atheniensis* (late 12th), *Collectiones Minores.* Most, but not all, are alternative versions of Greek documents from *Vaticana,* paras. 1–172, above. *Collectio Atheniensis* (note new numerical sequence, paras. 1–130) is an independent series of Greek texts including many already represented in *Collectio Vaticana,* and therefore listed, but not printed, by Schwartz; but also some fifty documents which are not in the *Vaticana;* note especially paras. 73–79, the proceedings of July 22, 431, with (para. 79) some subscriptions recorded in Latin. Reports of proceedings in this MS are also incomplete and episodic. Note especially para. 81, dated to August 31, 431, but perhaps belonging to July, and significant as quoting in Latin a letter of Flavius Dionysius, Magister Utriusque Militiae, to Theodorus, Consularis of Cyprus, on rules for conduct of election of bishop of Constantia, Cyprus (the only text quoted in its original Latin in the entire Greek *Acta* of Ephesus I and Chalcedon). See p. 138 above, in chapter 4. This collection is particularly important for its inclusion of many documents relating to the aftermath of Ephesus I in the second half of 431 and in 432.

8. *(Pars).* Indices

2. Manuscripts in Latin

I *(Tomus).* 2 *(Volumen). Collectio Veronensis.* MS of 10th century. Paras. 1–31, Letters and *Acta,* relating to Ephesus I, particularly from Caelestinus of Rome. Some reproducing texts found in Greek in *ACO* I, 1.1–6 (paras. 1–172), most preserved only in Latin. Apparently from contemporary collection? Note that most of the letters are precisely dated, between August 430 and September 433, for example para. 1, not dated in Greek (*ACO* I.1.1, para. 9), from Caelestinus to Cyril, written on August 10, 430.

I *(Tomus)*. 3 *(Volumen)*. *Collectio Casinensis*. MSS *(Vaticanus* and *Casinensis)* of 13th century. a) Paras. 1–176. Latin versions of letters of Emperors and of Cyril of Alexandria, Nestorius, Iohannes of Antioch; b) *Acta* of Ephesus I (for example para. 24, Jun. 22, 431). All also preserved in Greek; collection put together, along with the content of I.4, by Rusticus, a deacon of the Roman church, working in Constantinople about A.D. 565.

I *(Tomus)*. 4 *(Volumen)*. *Collectio Casinensis*, continued. Paras. 81–294 (pp. 25–225) represent the *Synodicum* written by Rusticus, using the *Tragoedia* composed in Greek by the Comes, and later bishop of Tyre, Irenaeus, a supporter of Nestorius, either after his exile in 436, or after his deposition in 448. Texts not given dates. See especially chapter 5 above.

I *(Tomus)*. 5 *(Volumen)*. *Pars 1*. *Collectio Palatina*. Largely from work of Marius Mercator (contemporary and associate of Augustine) on heresies (see above). MS of Carolingian period. Latin. (Plus Greek extracts from writings of Cyril at end).

Pars 2. a) *Collectio Sichardiana* (16th-century printed collection), including Latin translations by Dionysius Exiguus of Synodical Letter of Cyril, and letters of Theodoret and Cyril. b) *Collectio Quesneliana* (16th-century printed collection). Theological letters and documents relevant to Ephesus I in Latin translation (from compilation made c. A.D. 600). Most, but not all, also extant in Greek. c) *Collectio Winteriana* (16th-century printed collection). Theological documents in (contemporary?) Latin translation.

B. "Robber" Council of Ephesus, A.D. 449

(1) Manuscripts in Greek (from proceedings of Chalcedon, see below)

(a) Proceedings of first session of Chalcedon, Oct. 8, 451 (*ACO* II.1, paras. 1–1072, pp. 55–196), with repeated quotations of proceedings of first session of Ephesus II, and, within these, of proceedings relating to Eutyches, autumn 448–spring 449. See below and appendix B.

(b) Numerous letters from period before and after Ephesus II in *Epistularum Collectiones* M and H (*ACO* II.1.1, pp. 3–52), and B (*ACO* II.1.2, pp. 45–65). See further tabulation below.

(2) Manuscript in Syriac

BM Add. 14530, ed. J. Flemming, *AGWG*, N.F. XV (1917), pp. 6–151 (Syriac text with facing German translation). Documents relating to Ephesus II, and

Acta of second session, Aug. 22, 449. English trans. By S. G. F. Perry, *The Second Synod of Ephesus* (1881).

C. Council of Chalcedon, A.D. 451

II *(Tomus).* 1 *(Volumen).*

Pars 1. Greek. Codex Venetus 555 (= M), 11th century; Codex Vindobonensis hist. gr. 27, 12th century.

(a) *Epistularum Collectio* M, paras. 1–17, pp. 1–32 (letters of Leo of Rome, Theodosius II, Valentinian III, and Marcian, also Licinia Eudoxia and Pulcheria, in Greek translation).

(b) *Epistularum Collectio* H, paras. 1–16, pp. 35–52 (letters of Flavianus of Constantinople, Leo, Galla Placidia).

(c) *Proceedings of First Session (Actio* I) (Chalcedon, October 8, 451), paras. 1–1072 (pp. 55–196). Proceedings, with repeated verbatim quotation of earlier letters and proceedings, including many from Ephesus II, 449, going back to 448.

II *(Tomus).* 1 *(Volumen).*

Pars 2. Greek. MSS as above, plus Codex Vaticanus 831.

(a) Pp. 3–42 [199–238]. Proceedings of *Actio* 'II' (in fact III), October 13, 451. (Correctly ordered and dated in Latin version, *ACO* II.3.2, pp. 3–101 [261–360], see below).

(b) *Epistularum Collectio* B (pp. 45–56 [241–61]): letters of Theodoret, Anatolius of Constantinople, Leo of Rome, Valentinian III, Marcian, and others, in Greek.

(c) Pp. 69–84 [265–80].   *Actio* 'III' (in fact II)   October 10, 451

84–121 [280–317]	IV	October 17, 451
121–130 [317–26]	V	October 22, 451
130–158 [326–54]	VI	October 25, 451
158–163 [354–59]	VII	Canons 1–27. (No date given. Differently ordered in Latin version, see below).

II *(Tomus)*. 1 *(Volumen)*.
Pars 3. Greek. MSS as above.

Pp. 3–7 [362–66.]	*Actio* VIII	October 26, 451 (= *Actio* VII in Latin version, *ACO*) II.3.3, p. 3 [442])
7–11 [366–70]	IX	October 26, 451 (VIII in Latin)
11–16 [370–75]	X	October 26, 451 (IX)
16–42 [375–401]	XI	October 27, 451 (X)
42–53 [401–12]	XII	October 29, 451 (XI)
53–56 [412–15]	XIII	October 30, 451 (XII)
56–62 [415–21]	XIV	October 30, 451 (XIII)
63–83 [422–42]	XV	October 31, 451 (XIV) (= *Actio* XV, Latin, *Canons*, *ACO* II.3.3, pp. 92–98 [531–37])
83–85 [442–44]	XVI	October 31, 451 (Not in Latin)
86–99 [445–58]	XVII	?October "28," 451 (XVI in Latin)
99–101 [458–60]	'18'	?October "20," 451 (Not in Latin)
101–10 [460–69]	'19'	?October "20," 451 (Not in Latin)

There is clearly confusion in the dating and/or numbering of the later sessions, apart from the anomaly created by the position and numbering of the Canons. Sessions '18' and '19' have no numbers in the Greek text.

II *(Tomus)*. 2–5 *(Volumina)*. Latin documents, letters (original, or translated Greek), Latin translations of *Acta* of Chalcedon (with incorporated records of earlier proceedings, and associated documents, as above).

In brief:

2. *(Volumen) Pars 1. Collectio Novariensis de re Eutychis.* Documents in Latin translation relating to case of Eutyches, including in para. 10 (pp. 43–77) contemporary Latin version of *Acta* of Ephesus II, compiled on the instructions of Leo of Rome before the death of Flavianus of Constantinople (April/May, 450).

2. 2. *Rerum Chalcedonensium Collectio Vaticana. Canones et symbolum.*

3. 1. a) *Epistularum ante Gesta Collectio;* b) proceedings of *Actio* I.

3. 2. Proceedings of *Actiones* II–VI.

3. 3. Proceedings of *Actiones* VII–XVI (in Latin numbering, see above).

4. Letters of Leo, bishop of Rome (selection concerning Chalcedon and after, in chronological order).

5. *Collectio Sangermanensis:* a) *Epistulae,* of Marcian, Leo (the Emperor), Pulcheria, bishops, et al., paras. 1–48 (pp. 3–98); b) *Breviarium causae Nestorianorum et Eutychianorum collectum a sancto Liberato* (pp. 98–141): sixth-century Latin narrative by Liberatus, archdeacon at Carthage, with allusions to documents and literary texts, and quotations from them in Latin (pp. 98–141). Note (pp. 119–23) his detailed summary of the successive sessions at Chalcedon.

6. *Indices*

Verbatim Reports of Proceedings from the Reign of Theodosius II

I. INTRODUCTION

Reports of proceedings, usually hearings in court, are preserved on a number of papyri from the Imperial period,[1] and a few examples can also be found on inscriptions.[2] But it is with the Late Empire, and primarily in the context of the Church, that really extensive records, representing themselves as verbatim transcriptions of meetings, sessions, or hearings, become available to us, almost all from manuscript sources.[3]

The importance—though also the problematic nature—of this evidence should be obvious. If it is the case that we have access to the actual words spoken or written (in the form of brief personal statements of assent to agreed conclusions, called "subscriptions") in Greek (and Greek translations

---

1. See esp. R. A. Coles, *Reports of Proceedings in Papyri* (1966); see also the list given by J. Rea in *P.Oxy.* LI, no. 3619. Note also the extensive report from A.D. 375, *P.Oxy.* LXIII, no. 4381, and see now the discussion of bilingual transcripts of proceedings in J. N. Adams, *Bilingualism and the Latin Language* (2003), 383–84.

2. For example, the inscription from Dumeir, Syria, recording exchanges during a trial relating to the temple there, held by the emperor "Caracalla" (M. Aurelius Antoninus) at Antioch during his visit to Syria in 216, *SEG* XVII, no. 759. Note that, as in various cases listed below, the protocol is in Latin, but all the parties, including the Emperor, speak in Greek.

3. The law codes contain several examples of brief extracts from verbatim reports of proceedings: *CTh* VII.20.2 (repeated in *CJ* XII.46.1), a dialogue between Constantine and a group of veterans; *CJ* X.48.2, an exchange between *principales* of Antioch, whose representative speaks in Greek, and Diocletian, who speaks in Latin (the protocol is also in Latin, "Pars actorum . . ."); *CTh* XI.39.5, of 362, protocol in Latin, while the Emperor (Julian) speaks in Greek; XI.39.8 (*CJ* I.3.7), of 381 ("Pars actorum habitorum in consistorio . . ."); *CTh* IV.20.3 (*CJ* VII.71.6), of 386.

of such words spoken or written in other languages of culture, Latin, Syriac, and Coptic), by a large number of individuals—several hundred in some cases—coming from different areas, we gain, first, a level of access, even if indirect, to the spoken Greek of the period which is unparalleled for antiquity; secondly, on major issues, such as the two major Church Councils at Ephesus in 431 and 449, we can appreciate the positions adopted publicly by many individuals (normally bishops) from far outside the circle of the main actors, such as Nestorius himself, or Cyril and Dioscorus of Alexandria. Thirdly, we see the actual processes of decision making, at least as operated in public sessions, both within the Church, by Church and State in uneasy collaboration, and in one case by the State itself, examining the conduct of a synod by the Church (no. 25 below). Fourthly, we see the interaction between Greek and Latin: who, in the Theodosian empire, speaks in public in Latin (since it is beyond question that the actual first language of nearly all was Greek); how far a Latin vocabulary has penetrated into the Greek normally used in official or ecclesiastical circles; how far spoken utterances or written texts in Latin were intelligible to educated Greeks, such as bishops (the short answer is not at all—at Church Councils all oral or written material in Latin had to be translated).

In a word, the surviving reports of proceedings from Theodosius's reign, all but three (nos. 10, 11, 28, from papyri) of which are dependent on later manuscripts, of the sixth century onwards, and which are preserved in Greek, Latin, and Syriac, represent a priceless source for historians. The present appendix aims simply to list the available texts of reports of proceedings, given in the chronological order of the relevant sessions. Almost all of the material comes from the original Greek version of the Acts of the Councils, of which appendix A has given an equally elementary account for historians.[4] So it should be noted that some grasp of what the various so-called Acts of the Councils, as preserved in manuscripts, actually consist of is taken for granted here. In particular, verbatim recording is a significant feature of the Acts of Ephesus II in 449, which in their turn quote various proceedings from earlier in 449, and they in their turn from proceedings in 448. In the context of this appendix, therefore, which is devoted to the material from the reign of Theodosius, no attention is paid as such to the priceless and ex-

---

4. The *Acta* of the Church Councils of the fourth century also contain some examples, though none which compare in extent and detail with those of the fifth century: see E. J. Jonkers, *Acta et Symbola Conciliorum quae Saeculo Quarto habita sunt* (1954), pp. 61 ff. (Serdica, A.D. 343); pp. 74 ff. (Carthage, 345); pp. 111 ff. (Carthage, 390); pp. 120 ff. (Carthage, 397).

ceptionally interesting Acts of Chalcedon, from the reign of Marcian (451–57)—as it happens, a reign which provides remarkable and neglected evidence for the working of the Late Roman state.

It should be noted, however, that both the most famous and most detailed reports of proceedings in the first half of the fifth century come from the Latin West. By far the best known example is the so-called *Gesta Senatus*, namely the text, preserved in a single eleventh-century manuscript, of the proceedings in the Senate of Rome in 438, when the *Codex Theodosianus* was formally presented to it.[5] But the most detailed text of proceedings, and the one which has been most fully edited and commented on in the modern world, is the *Acta* of the Council of Carthage in 411. Derived from a single manuscript of the ninth century, this very full and detailed text, amounting to several hundred pages of Latin in the excellent *Sources Chrétiennes* edition, is an important point of comparison for the reports from the Theodosian empire.[6] For it is an incomparably fuller and more formal record, for instance listing the *exceptores, notarii,* and *scribae* responsible for taking down and supervising the record of the proceedings; describing the procedures by which an agreed record of each day's session was produced by representatives of the two ecclesiastical factions involved, the Catholics and the Donatists; and incorporating, after the text of each oral intervention by an individual bishop, a note "in another hand" *(alia manu)* to confirm that the speaker has checked the text attributed to him.[7]

That in itself of course must raise the suspicion that the text as recorded may have been purged of grammatical errors or repetitions of the sort characteristic of spoken language, and a similar problem must arise over all of the Theodosian reports.[8] Nonetheless, the *Acta* of Carthage are extremely important as confirming that in principle both the technical capacity to note down spoken interventions and a procedure for producing an agreed record

---

5. For the Latin text see Th. Mommsen and P. M. Meyer, eds., *Theodosiani Libri XVI cum Constitutionibus Sirmondianis* I (1905), 1–4, with English translation by C. Pharr, *The Theodosian Code* (1952), 3–7. See the invaluable discussion by J. F. Matthews, *Laying Down the Law: A Study of the Theodosian Code* (2000), ch. 3, "Senatus Amplissimi Gesta."

6. S. Lancel, ed., *Actes de la Conférence de Carthage en 411*, 3 vols. SC, vols. 194, 195, 224 (1972–75).

7. See Lancel, *Conférence de Carthage* I, 342 ff.

8. On this subject note the valuable study by H. C. Teitler, *Notarii and Exceptores: An Inquiry into the Role and Significance of Shorthand Writers in the Imperial and Ecclesiastical Bureaucracy of the Roman Empire (from the early Principate to c. 450 AD)* (1985).

were available within contemporary culture.[9] That said, it has to be stressed that none of the records of proceedings from the Theodosian empire are equipped as they stand with the level of self-reference as to recording and authenticating procedures which is characteristic of the *Acta* of Carthage. But the Greek Acts do reveal—precisely in cases where there was subsequently dispute as to what had actually been said—that there had in fact been identifiable recording procedures, organized separately by different participants, but without the same arrangements for reconciliation of the record.

We find therefore, for example, that after the archimandrite Eutyches had had his allegedly heterodox views examined in a series of sessions of a synod in Constantinople in November 448, held first in his absence and then, finally, in his presence (nos. 14–20 below), he afterwards challenged the record, and a further series of sessions in spring 449 (nos. 23 and 25–26 below) was devoted to very detailed disputes as to the record. More specifically, as regards the record of the second Council of Ephesus in 449, disputes arose at the Council of Chalcedon in 451 as to what had been said, and who had recorded it (*ACO* II.1, paras. 121–39, pp. 87–88). The details of this dispute, which is of course itself a prime example of verbatim recording, deserve to be set out here, in what is (to the best of the author's knowledge) only the second English translation.[10] The passage comes just after the point (para. 120) in the (alleged) record of Ephesus II where the Council was recorded as having called out collectively: "If anyone reverses [a doctrine], let him be anathema! If anyone overelaborates, let him be anathema! Let us preserve the faith of the Fathers!"

The response to hearing this read out was immediate (paras. 121–30, pp. 87–8):

> While this was being read out, the *Anatolikoi* (Easterners) and the most pious bishops with them shouted out "We did not say these things! Who said these things?"

9. Note that Augustine received and commented on the Greek *Acta* of a council at Lydda (Diospolis) in 415; see Augustine, *Ep.* 179, 7–10, and *De gestis Pelagii*, in *Bibliothèque Augustinienne* 21 (1966): 415 ff. This is significant for the availability and diffusion of conciliar *Acta*, but not enough of the proceedings is quoted in coherent form to be worth their being pursued here.

10. Note however that a translation will be published in the brilliant paper by G. E. M. de Ste Croix, "The Council of Chalcedon," included in a posthumous collection of his Late Roman papers, edited by Michael Whitby, to be published by Oxford University Press under the title *Christian Persecution, Martyrdom and Orthodoxy;* and that another is already available in *The Acts of the Council of Chalcedon*, translated with introduction and notes by R. Price and M. Gaddis, *TTH* XLIV (2005), vol. I, 152–53.

Theodorus, the most pious bishop of Claudiopolis, said, "Bring his (Dioscorus's) *notarii*. For, throwing out the *notarii* of everyone else, he had his own *notarii* write. Let the *notarii* come forward and say if these things were written or if they were read out in our presence or if anyone checked or subscribed (them)."

The most distinguished (civil) officials and the most magnificent Senate said: "By whose hand are the records written?"

Dioscorus, the most pious bishop of the church of the Alexandrians, said: "Each wrote through his own *notarii*, mine taking my record, those of the most reverend bishop Iuvenalius his, those of the most reverend bishop Thalassius his; there were also many *notarii* of the other most pious bishops taking things down. So the record is not that of my *notarii*; each has his own."

Iuvenalius, the most pious bishop of Jerusalem, said: "My *notarius* was one along with the other *notarii* taking notes."

Dioscorus, the most pious bishop of Alexandria, said: "See, the *notarius* of bishop Iuvenalius was taking notes and the *notarius* of bishop Thalassius, and that of (the bishop) of Corinth, and not mine alone!"

Eusebius, the most pious bishop of Dorylaeum, said: "I ask that the most God-loving bishop Stephanus of the (church of) the Ephesians should be asked whether his *notarii* did not take down the records of the sacred synod, and what they suffered at the hands of the most God-loving bishop of the (church of the) Alexandrians, Dioscorus."

The most distinguished officials and the most magnificent Senate said: "What does the most pious bishop Stephanus say in reply to this?"

Stephanus, the most pious bishop of Ephesus, said: "My *notarii*, Iulianus, the present bishop of Lebedus, and Crispinus, deacon, were taking a record, and there came the *notarii* of the most pious bishop Dioscorus and wiped out their tablets and all but broke their fingers in their desire to take their pens. Neither did they take copies of the records, nor do I know what happened. But on the very day on which the scrutiny took place we placed our subscriptions on a sheet, and those bishops who had not (then) subscribed did so on the next day under my guarantee."

There is no need to prolong the quotation, though it transpires immediately that the sheet on which the subscriptions had been placed had been blank. Enough has been presented to illustrate the extreme formality of style of such verbatim records, combined (in the instance referred to) with their vulnerability to violence and fraud. Such immediately disturbing factors will only have compounded the intense difficulty, in the absence of any technology for sound recording, of taking a written record of spoken speech by hand, in shorthand *(tachygraphia)*, and then having it written out and authenticated. But, in spite of these problems, the hundreds of pages of text in the Acts of the Councils represent by far the best evidence which we have—and far better evidence than we could reasonably expect—for the thought, and for the spoken and, in subscriptions, the written language of (again) several hundred different educated Christians of the fifth century. Spoken and written pronouncements in Latin were almost always, but not quite universally, reproduced only in Greek translation (for one MS with proceedings at Ephesus in 431, in which a number of subscriptions are reproduced in Latin, see no. 8 in the catalogue below). So also were spoken contributions in Coptic (for example, Kalosirios of Arsinoe, *ACO* II.1, para. 884[90], p. 185) or Syriac (for example, the archimandrite Barsaumas, *ACO* II.1, para. 1065, p. 194), and one written subscription at Chalcedon in Persian (*ACO* II.1.2, para. 97[252], p. 41 [237]). See pp. 103–16 in chapter 3 above.

II. CATALOGUE

1. June 22, 431. *ACO* I.1.2, paras. 33–62 (pp. 3–64). Council of Ephesus (Cyrillian side). Date, and names of 155 participants (para. 33). *Acta*, with quotation of successive summonses sent to Nestorius (paras. 34–44). Statement of subscription to doctrines of Nicaea by 126 participants in succession (45). Reading of letter of Nestorius (46). Condemnation of doctrines of Nestorius by 35 participants in succession (47). Joint exsecration of Nestorius (48). Reading of translation of letter of Caelestinus of Rome (49). Reading of letter of Cyril to Nestorius, and attestation of its (non-)reception by Nestorius (50–53). Extracts from orthodox texts (54–60). Reading of translation of letter from Capreolus of Carthage (61). Anathema on Nestorius, and subscriptions by 197 participants (62).

2. June 26, 43. *ACO* I.1.5, para. 151 (pp. 119–24). Council of Ephesus (Ioannes' side, "Anatolikoi"). Address by the Comes, Candidianus, reply by Ioannes, on misconduct of Cyrillians. Further dialogue, departure of Candidianus, decision on deposition of Cyril and Memnon of Ephesus. Names of 43 who subscribed.

3. June–July, 431. *ACO* I.4, para. 95 (pp. 43–46). Council of Ephesus (Ioannes' side). After June 26 ("secunda commenta"). Latin version (no Greek text). Dialogue between Ioannes and Candidianus. Pronouncements of *synodus* on irregularity of Cyrillians' conduct. Quotation of letter of *synodus* to congregation of Hierapolis, Eufratensis. Names of 53 who subscribed.

4. July 10, 431. *ACO* I.1.3, para. 106.1–24 (pp. 53–59). Council of Ephesus (Cyrillian side). Proceedings devoted to statements by newly arrived delegates from Roman see, all given in translation *(hermēneia)*, as also letter from Caelestinus of Rome (106.12–18). Acclamations (106.19).

5. July 11, 431. *ACO* I.1.3, para. 106.25–39 (pp. 59–63). Council of Ephesus (Cyrillian side). Further statements by Roman delegates, in Greek translation. Reading of anathema on Nestorius of June 22, 431. Confirmation of record. Translation of *subscriptiones* of the three Roman delegates.

6. July 16, 431. *ACO* I.1.3, paras. 87–89.12 (pp. 15–21). Council of Ephesus (Cyrillian side), with representatives of Roman see. Proposal to read *libellos* from Cyril and Memnon of Ephesus (87–88.1). Text of *libellos*, on conflicts with Ioannes of Antioch (88). Opinions by 11 participants, and declaration of excommunication of Ioannes (89).

7. July 17, 431. *ACO* I.1.3, para. 89.13–90 (pp. 21–26). Council of Ephesus (Cyrillian side). Discussion of abortive contacts with Ioannes. Excommunication of Ioannes and 33 named associates, and decision on report to Emperors. Subscriptions (reference only); translation of subscriptions of Roman delegates.

8. July 22, 431. *ACO* I.1.7, paras. 73–79 (pp. 84–117). Council of Ephesus (Cyrillian side). Date, and list of 157 participants (73). Beginning (74.1–75.2) of verbatim record. Reading of Nicene creed and of examples of correct doctrine (74–75). Record, but without verbatim report of proceedings, of report on heresy of Tessareskaidekatitai at Philadelphia, Lydia, and presentation of *libelloi* of abjuration from 25 Philadelphians, of whom 10 have subscribed with their own hands (76). Affirmation of orthodoxy (77), quotations from works of Nestorius (78). One-sentence verbatim quotation of *Acta* (78.26). Subscriptions of 197 participants (79), of which six are given in Latin (for example, 79[49] [p. 113]: "Senecion episcopus Scodrinae civitatis subscribsi"). A record of this session is preserved in the Latin translation of Session I of Chalcedon (as recited there originally in Greek, but not preserved in the Greek *Acta*). For the Latin text see *ACO* II.3.1, paras. 911–45 (pp. 196–235). This version shows the same absence of verbatim quotation of interventions as the Greek.

9. Aug. 31, 431 (?).[11] *ACO* I.1.7, para. 81 (pp. 118–22). Council of Ephesus (Cyrillian side). Reginus, bishop of Constantia, Cyprus, requests permission to present *libellos* on rules governing episcopal elections on Cyprus, and on (improper) claims of Antiochene church. Agreed. Text of *libellos* (influence of Antiochene clergy on Dionysius, Magister Militum). Quotation of letter of Dionysius to Consularis of Cyprus in Latin, with Greek

11. The same date is given in the Latin translation (*ACO* I.5, *Collectio Winteriana*, para. 6, p. 357), but must be uncertain, as being more than a month later than any other recorded proceedings of the Council. On the other hand, it was not until the autumn that Theodosius formally permitted the participants to leave.

translation, and of that to the clergy of Constantia (in Greek). Explications by Zenon of Kourion and Euagnus of Soloi. Decision that episcopal elections in each province should be free of outside influence. No subscriptions recorded.

10. 434, no precise date. *P.Oxy.* XVI, no. 1879 = *CPL*, p. 434, no. 11 (Latin only). Report of proceedings for debt before Fl. Anthemius Isidorus Theofilus, *praeses* of the province of Arcadia, Egypt (*PLRE* II, Theophilus 7). Protocol of proceedings recorded in Latin, but the governor speaks in Greek, and the *libellus* presented to him is quoted in Greek.

11. 434? C. Wessely, *CPR* XIV (1914), p. 4, no. xii. Fragmentary report of proceedings before the same *praeses*, again with protocol in Latin, but record of spoken words in Greek.

12. No date indicated (444–49, possibly 445). *ACO* II.1.3, paras. 15–147 (pp. 69–81 [428–40]). Proceedings at Antioch under Domnus (441/9) on *libelloi* of complaint against Athanasius, bishop of Perrha, Euphratensis, quoted in *Acta* of Chalcedon, *Actio* XV. Verbatim record of interventions, reading of documents. Deposition of Athanasius. Subscriptions referred to, not quoted.

13. Nov. 8, 448. *ACO* II.1.1, paras. 223–25; 229–35 (pp. 100–102). Synod at Constantinople presided over by Patriarch, Flavianus, to hear accusations against archimandrite Eutyches by Eusebius of Dorylaeum; first session.

14. Nov. 12, 448. *ACO* II.1.1, paras. 238–46; 270–71; 301–302; 307–308; 330–31; 339–40; 342–46; 348–53 (pp. 103–23). Hearing about Eutyches, second session. Proceedings, with extensive quotation of earlier documents.

15. Nov. 15, 448. *ACO* II.1.1, paras. 354–404 (pp. 123–29). Hearing about Eutyches, third session.

16. Nov. 16, 448. *ACO* II.1.1, paras. 405–19 (pp. 129–31). Fourth Session.

17. Nov. 17, 448. *ACO* II.1.1, paras. 420–44 (pp. 131–34). Fifth Session.

18. Nov. 20, 448. *ACO* II.1.1, paras. 445–57 (pp. 135–37). Sixth session. Further proceedings relating to nonappearance, and alleged doctrines, of Eutyches. Depositions *(katatheseis)* entered in minutes *(hypomnēmata)*.

19. Nov. 22, 448. *ACO* II.1.1, paras. 458–90; 498–503; 511–27; 534–45; 549–52 (pp. 137–47). Seventh session. Appearance of Eutyches, with soldiers, monks, and *silentiarius* Magnus. Reading of letter from Emperor requesting participation of *patricius* Florentius (468). Acclamations. Record of previous proceedings read (472). Cross-examination of Eutyches. Eutyches excommunicated. 53 subscriptions.

20. No date indicated. *ACO* II.1.3, paras. 47–51, 54 (pp. 21–22 [380–81]). Proceedings against Ibas before Domnus at Antioch, briefly quoted at Berytus (see no. 21 below).

21. Jan.–Feb., 449, exact date uncertain.[12] *ACO* II.1.3, paras. 28–141 (pp. 19–37 [378–96]). From *Acta* of Chalcedon, *Actio* XI. Quotation (para. 27) of Imperial *hypomnēstikon* addressed to Damascius, *tribunus et notarius*, with instructions for an episcopal hearing of charges against Ibas of Edessa, Daniel of Carrhae, and Ioannes of Theodosiopolis, dated Oct. 26, 448. Proceedings at Berytus, held by bishops Photius, Eustathius, and Uranius. Extensive spoken dialogue (in Greek, with provision for translation into Syriac, for the benefit of Uranius), with quotation of previous exchanges at Antioch (47–51, 54, no. 20 above), of a *libellos* from presbyters at Edessa (56), of eighteen specific charges (73), of a translation of Ibas's letter in Syriac to the "Persian" Maris (138), and of the address and petition *(didaskalia* and *paraklēsis)* addressed to Photius and Eustathius in defense of Ibas by the clergy of Edessa, with 65 subscriptions, of which 18 are recorded (in Greek) as having been in Syriac (141).

22. Apr. 8, 449. *ACO* II.1.1, paras. 558–59 (pp. 150–51). Fragmentary report, read at session of Apr. 13 (no. 24 below), of session at Constantinople presided over by Thalassius of Caesarea on complaint of Eutyches about falsification of record. Macedonius, *tribunus* and *referendarius*, reports on complaint.

23. (a) Apr. 12 and 14, 449. *AGWG*, pp. 14–20; Perry, pp. 44–54. Syriac trans. of Greek original. Proceedings (no details) against Ibas in Edessa before Chaereas, Comes and Praeses of Osrhoene. Acclamations (Apr. 12). Further proceedings (no details), acclamations (Apr. 14).

(b) Apr. 12, 449. *AGWG*, pp. 20–32; Perry, pp. 55–83. From report *(anaphora)* of Chaereas to Praetorian Prefects, undated. The report must have been in Latin; Syriac text is translation from Greek version. Record of first session of proceedings against Ibas in Edessa. Petition from presbyter Micallus, read out. Record of subscriptions. Record of acclamations. Proceedings. Verbal affirmations by 49 clergy and monks. Response by Chaereas.

(c) Apr. 14, 449. *AGWG*, pp. 32–54; Perry, pp. 84–123. From report *(anaphora)* of Chaereas to Flavius Martialis, Comes and Magister Officiorum, undated. Syriac trans. from Greek trans. of Latin original. Proceedings at second session (Apr. 14). Presentation to Chaereas of petition by Comes Theodosius, representing Edessa, demanding submission of formal charges against Ibas. Record presented by Samuel, presbyter, of previous actions

---

12. In the MSS these proceedings are dated to September of 449, but, as noted by E. Schwartz, "Der Prozess des Eutyches," *SBAW*, Phil.-hist. Kl. (1929), on p. 63, this must simply be an error. The report which the bishops made on their hearing is dated to February 25, 449; see *ACO* II.1.3, para. 7 (pp. 14–16 [373–75]).

against Ibas. Further depositions. Quotation of Syriac letter of Ibas to Maris. Further depositions. Statement by Chaereas that he will report to higher authority.

24. Apr. 13, 449. *ACO* II.1.1, paras. 555–828 (pp. 148–76). Synod of Constantinople presided over by Flavianus, with Florentius, ex-Praefectus, ex-consul, and *patricius*, on authenticity of acts of previous synod over Eutyches. Names of 34 other bishops and of Mamas, Comes and Proximus of the *scrinium* of the *libelli* and the *divinae cognitiones*. Reading of *Acta* of Apr. 8, 449 (558–58) = no. 22. Proceedings. Petition of Eutyches (572). Written attestations, and extensive verbal exchanges.

25. Apr. 27, 449. *ACO* II.1.1, paras. 829–49 (pp. 177–79). Hearing presided over by Martialis, Comes and Magister Sacrorum Officiorum, on second petition by Eutyches (834), asking that Magnus, *silentiarius*, give evidence. Imperial *hyposēmeiōsis* giving assent (835–36). See pp. 166–67 above, in chapter 4.

26. Aug. 8, 449. *ACO* II.1.1 (covering pp. 77–195, with extensive quotation of earlier proceedings and documents). Second Council of Ephesus, first session. (Excerpts from record of proceedings, read out at Council of Chalcedon, *Actio* I, Oct. 8, 451). Date, place, and names of 137 participants (paras. 68; 70; 78). Initial proceedings, statements by bishop Iulius and deacon Hilarus, representing Leo of Rome, interpreted by Florentius, bishop of Sardis. Letter of Leo read (this disputed at Chalcedon) (79–86). Further initial proceedings (108–20). [Note esp. the dispute at Chalcedon over the validity of record of Ephesus II, and over whose *notarii* had recorded it, 121–35, see pp. 252–53 above]. Further initial proceedings (136–37; 141–48). The case against Eutyches, archimandrite, and reading of records of previous proceedings (151–57; 164; 185–86; 197–235; 238–46; 261; 270–71; 301–22; 330–31; 339–40; 342–46; 348–495; 498–529; 534–850; 864 (reversion to verbal record of Ephesus)–964: restoration of Eutyches, affirmations of 113 participants (884; 884$^{7-113}$ is abbreviated, with a full text available in the Latin version, *ACO* II.3.1, pp. 173–92); *libellos* from monks of Eutyches' monastery (887–88), and agreement on their restoration; reading of *Acta* from Ephesus I. Agreement on doctrine, Florentius, bishop of Sardis, translating. Dioscorus proposes deposition of Flavianus and Eusebius (962). Objection by Hilarus (κοντραδικιτουρ, 964). Votes for condemnation by 95 participants (966–1065). Subscriptions (1067).

27. (a) Aug. 22, 449. *AGWG*, pp. 6–12; trans. Perry, pp. 13–27. Syriac trans. of Greek original. Council of Ephesus, second session. Names of 113 participants. Discussion on absence of delegates from Leo, bishop of Rome, and of Domnus of Antioch.

(b) Aug. 22?, 449. *AGWG*, pp. 12–150; Perry, pp. 38–363. (After lacuna in MS). Syriac trans. of Greek original. Council of Ephesus, second session. Proceedings, in many cases with extensive quotation of earlier documents and proceedings, against Ibas of Edessa, Daniel of Carrhae, Irenaeus of Tyre, Aquilinus of Byblus, Sophronius of Tella, Theodoret of Cyrrhus, and Domnus of Antioch.

28. Mid-fifth century, date uncertain. J. Gascou, "Décision de Caesarius, gouverneur militaire de Thébaïde," *Mélanges Gilbert Dagron, TM* 14 (2002), 269 ff. Papyrus record of proceedings before Flavius Aspar Nomus Candidianus Caesarius, Comes of the Thebaid. Protocol in Latin, (fragmentary) written and spoken material in Greek.

FIGURE IA. THE THEODOSIAN EMPIRE: CIVIL GOVERNMENT, NORTHERN HALF

This map shows the two Praetorian Prefectures, of
Illyricum A and Oriens B; the seven civil dioceses,
mainly under Vicarii; and the individual provinces

A. Prefecture of Illyricum: Dioceses of Dacia (1) and Macedonia (2),
under Vicarii;
B. Prefecture of Oriens: Dioceses of Thracia (3), Asiana (4),
andPontica (5), all under Vicarii; Oriens (6), under Comes
Orientis; and Aegyptus (7), under Praefectus Augustalis

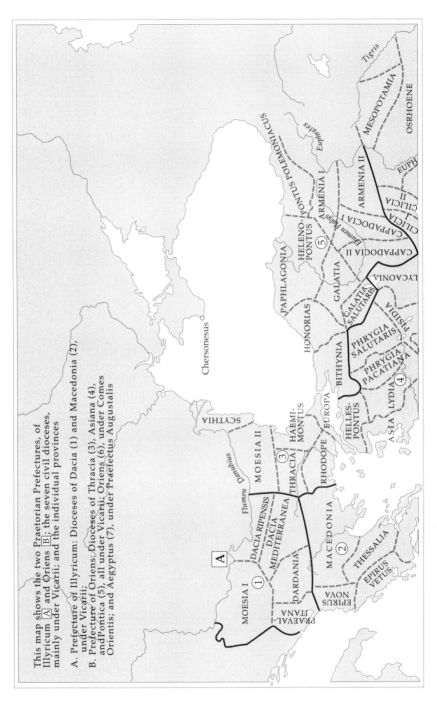

Drawn by Paul Simmons from the map in A. H. M. Jones, *The Later Roman Empire.*

FIGURE 1B. THE THEODOSIAN EMPIRE: CIVIL GOVERNMENT, SOUTHERN HALF

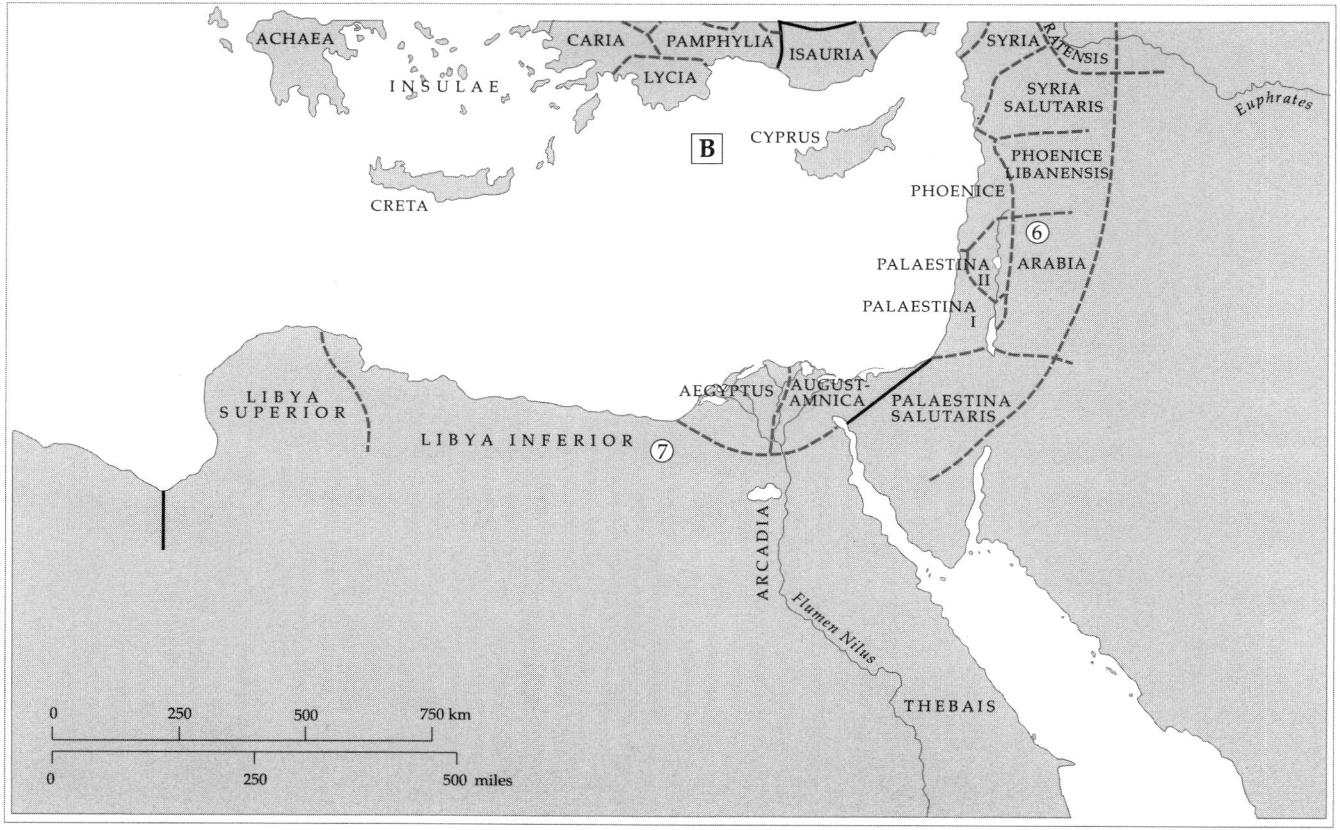

Drawn by Paul Simmons from the map in A. H. M. Jones, *The Later Roman Empire.*

FIGURE II. THE SYRIAC CODEX OF 411, WRITTEN IN EDESSA

A page from the earliest known Syriac codex, written in Edessa in Osrhoene in November 411. The codex of 255 leaves, each with three columns, contains Syriac translations of six Christian texts written in Greek, of which the last (of which one extract is shown here) is a catalogue of martyrs. At the end of the text, not reproduced here, we find the following words: "this volume was finished in the second month Tishri, year 723 [of the Seleucid era] at Orhay (Edessa), a city of Beth-Nahrin (Mesopotamia)." The status of Syriac in the fifth-century Church is discussed in chapter 3. Reproduced by kind permission of the British Library.

FIGURE III. AUTOGRAPH GREETING BY THEODOSIUS ON A LETTER TO AN OFFICIAL

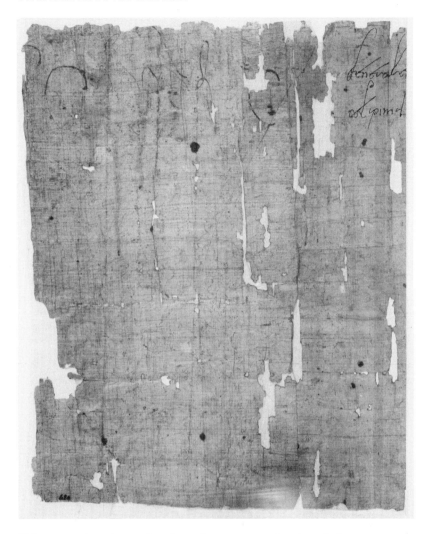

This apparently uninteresting sheet of papyrus contains the only known example of the handwriting of a Roman Emperor. Between 425 and 450, Appion, the bishop of Syene on the southern border of Egypt, wrote a petition in Greek to the Emperor to ask him to order the Dux and Comes of the Thebaid to provide military protection. The petition is preserved, in a copy made at court, headed by "Exemplum Precum" ("Copy of the Petition") in Latin. This sheet preserves traces of a letter, also in Latin, almost certainly to the Dux (see chapters 1 and 2), with the normal personal greeting, in what must be the Emperor's own hand, at the end (top right-hand corner): "Bene valere te cupimus" ("We wish that you [singular] are well.") By kind permission of the Rijksmuseum van Oudheden, Leiden.

FIGURE IV. CHURCH BUILT AT DAR QITA, SYRIA, IN 418

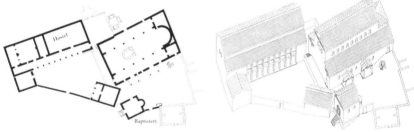

The Church of SS Paul and Moses at Dar Qita, in the Limestone Massif of northern Syria, is a prime example of the parallel expansion of both settlement and the construction of churches in this region. An inscription (*IGLS* II, no. 535) records that the church was built in 418. It was followed by a hostel in 431, and a baptistery built in the sixth century. The photograph and plans are taken, by kind permission of Ediciones Encuentro, Madrid, from I. Peña, *The Christian Art of Byzantine Syria*, p. 87.

FIGURE V. STATUE OF THE GOVERNOR
OECUMENIUS FROM APHRODISIAS

Aphrodisias Museum. Copyright Society for the Promotion of Roman Studies.

FIGURE VI. RECONSTRUCTION OF THE STATUE OF THE GOVERNOR OECUMENIUS FROM APHRODISIAS WITH ITS INSCRIBED BASE

The statue of the current governor (Praeses) of Caria was voted by the city council *(boulē)* of Aphrodisias, and erected in the street which ran along the front of the council chamber *(bouleutērion)*; it is a rare case where the complete statue can be reunited with its base, and its precise original location identified. Both the statue and the inscription (see chapter 1) emphasize Oecumenius's intellectual and moral qualities. Drawn by K. Görkay; reproduction by kind permission of the Society for the Promotion of Roman Studies.

FIGURE VII. THE STRUCTURE OF
THE ARMY OF THEODOSIUS'S EMPIRE

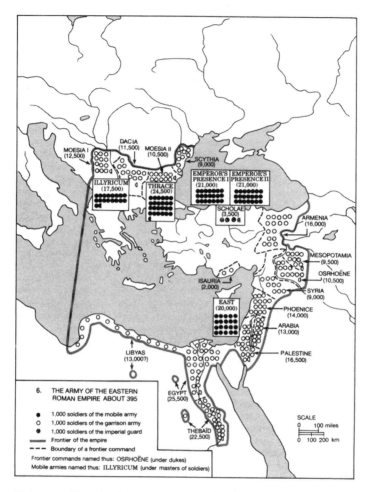

This map reflects the dispositions reported in the *Notitia Dignitatum* of c. 401. The rectangles with black dots represent the forces under the two Magistri Militum *in praesenti,* and the one each in Illyricum, Thraciae, and Oriens. There is no indication even of the provinces where they were stationed, let alone precise locations. The *Notitia* does generally indicate precise stations for units under regional military commanders (Comites or Duces), and the distribution of those units which were legions is shown in Figures VIII (Danube) and IX (East). The above map indicates the scale of forces in each province, but not precise locations. Reproduced, by kind permission of Stanford University Press, from W. Treadgold, *Byzantium and Its Army, 284–1081.*

FIGURE VIII. LEGIONARY DISPOSITIONS ON THE DANUBE FRONTIER

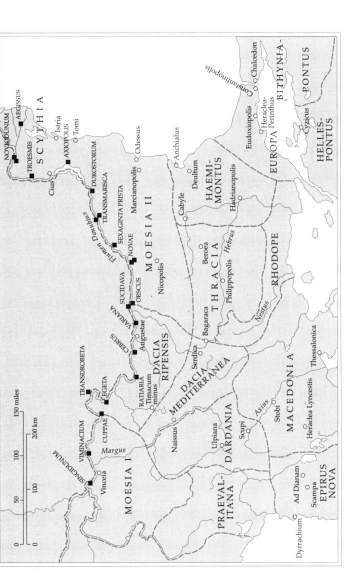

This map is intended to give an impression of the frontier forces under the command of middle-ranking officers (Duces), as set out in the *Notitia Dignitatum*, by picking out the stations given for those units described as legions. From west to east, they are those under the Dux of Moesia I, the Dux of Dacia Ripensis, the Dux of Moesia II, and that of Scythia. Twenty-five legions are listed in the *Notitia*, divided among these four commands, all of them, it seems, stationed along the frontier defined by the River Danube. The border between Moesia II and Scythia is uncertain. The stations of two legions in Dacia Ripensis and two in Scythia cannot be identified. Drawn by Paul Simmons from the map in D. Hoffmann, *Das spätrömische Bewegungsheer.*

FIGURE IX. LEGIONARY DISPOSITIONS
ON THE EASTERN FRONTIER

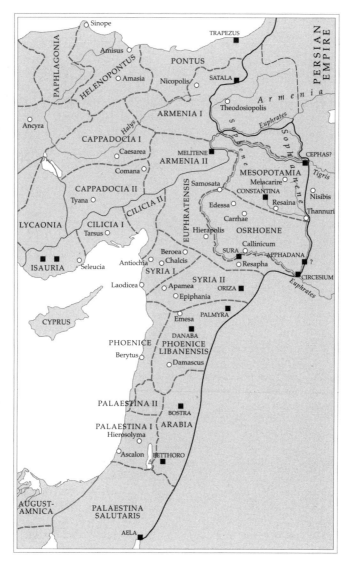

The Dux of Armenia disposed of three legions, stationed in the provinces of Pontus and Armenia I and II. The Duces of Mesopotamia and Osrhoene each had two; the Duces of Syria and Euphratensis (a combined command), of Phoenice (Libanensis), and of Arabia had two each; and the Dux of Palaestina had one, stationed at Aela in Palaestina III, at the head of the Gulf of Aqaba. All the legions were stationed on or near the frontier. The higher rank of Comes rei militaris was reserved for the commander of the "internal frontier" of Isauria, with two legions, whose precise station is not known. All will have been under the command of the Magister Militum per Orientem, stationed in Antioch. Drawn by Paul Simmons from the map in D. Hoffmann, *Das spätrömische Bewegungsheer*.

FIGURE X. CITIES IN THE BALKAN AND DANUBIAN REGION WHOSE BISHOPS ATTENDED ONE OR MORE OF THE FIFTH-CENTURY CHURCH COUNCILS

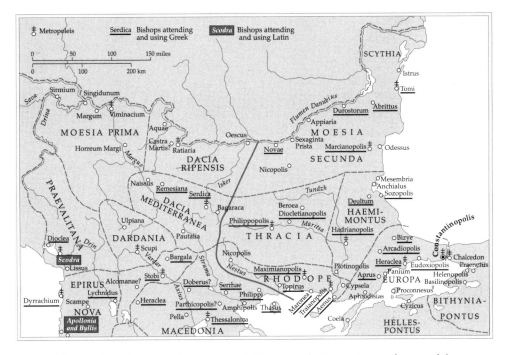

The provinces in this region were divided between the Praetorian Prefecture of Illyricum (the western part) and the northern extension of Oriens in the eastern part, marked by a shaded line. The names of provinces are relevant also for ecclesiastical organization, because one city was the metropolis of each (the border between Moesia Secunda and Scythia is not clear). The map is further intended to give a visual impression, firstly, of participation in the Church Councils (Ephesus I, 431, and II, 449, and Chalcedon, 451); and secondly of the use of either Greek (the vast majority) or Latin by bishops attending these Councils. There is no evidence of participation by bishops from Dardania, Moesia Prima, and Dacia Ripensis. Drawn by Paul Simmons from the map in *Atlas zur Kirchengeschichte.*

FIGURE XI. THE ECCLESIASTICAL HIERARCHY IN THE NORTHERN PART OF THE SECULAR DIOCESE OF ORIENS

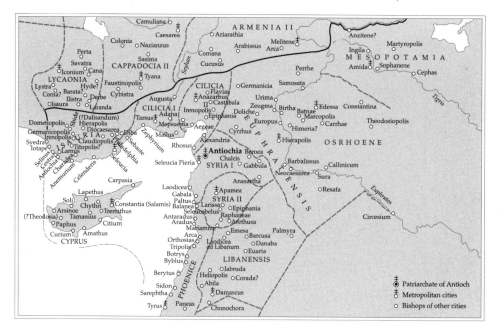

The map shows the northern section of the Diocese of Oriens, governed by the Comes Orientis, who, like the Magister Militum per Orientem (and the Consularis of Syria I), presumably had his seat at Antioch. It is in fact only in Oriens that the three-level model of the Church hierarchy can be seen clearly in operation: the bishop (or Archbishop, or Patriarch) of Antioch; the metropolitan bishop of the chief city ("metropolis") of each province; and the bishops of other cities. The province of Cyprus was part of Oriens, but claimed "autocephalous" status, meaning independence from Antioch in electing the metropolitan of Constantia (see chapter 4). Drawn by Paul Simmons from the map in *Atlas zur Kirchengeschichte.*

Indexes

The Indexes which follow, prepared by Priscilla Lange, are designed deliberately to be selective, indicating major themes and subjects, without including items which are alluded to in passing, and listing only those items of literary, legal, manuscript (meaning the *Acta* of the Church Councils), or documentary evidence which are either quoted or discussed. The material in the two Appendixes, both relating to the contents of the *Acta*, has not been included.

INDEX OF LITERARY, LEGAL, AND MANUSCRIPT SOURCES

See Abbreviations, pp. xix–xxi.

Text: 10/13 Aldus
Display: Aldus
Compositor: Integrated Composition Systems
Printer and binder: Thomson-Shore